SPANISH FEMALE WRITERS AND THE FREETHINKING PRESS, 1879–1926

Spanish Female Writers and the Freethinking Press, 1879–1926

CHRISTINE ARKINSTALL

UNIVERSITY OF TORONTO PRESS
Toronto Buffalo London

Toronto Buffalo London
www.utppublishing.com

ISBN 978-1-4426-4765-7

Library and Archives Canada Cataloguing in Publication

Arkinstall, Christine, author
Spanish female writers and the freethinking press,
1879–1926 / Christine Arkinstall.

(Toronto Iberic)
Includes bibliographical references and index.
ISBN 978-1-4426-4765-7 (bound)

1. Domingo Soler, Amalia, 1835–1909. 2. López de Ayala, Ángles. 3. Sárraga, Belén de. 4. Women and journalism – Spain – History. 5. Feminism – Spain – History. 6. Women – Political activity – Spain – History. 7. Spanish literature – Women authors – History and criticism. 8. Women intellectuals – Spain – Biography. 9. Feminists – Spain – Biography. I. Title. II. Series: Toronto Iberic

PN5317.W58A75 2014 070.4'4930540946 C2013-906520-2

University of Toronto Press acknowledges the financial assistance to its publishing program of the Canada Council for the Arts and the Ontario Arts Council.

University of Toronto Press acknowledges the financial support of the Government of Canada through the Canada Book Fund for its publishing activities.

For Amalia, Ángeles, and Belén,
and all our sisters in ideas, past and present

Table of Contents

Acknowledgments

Researching and writing this book has been an enthralling voyage of discovery and a painstaking labour of sleuthing. It has been possible only because of the superb professionalism, expert knowledge, and dedicated support, at times well beyond the call of duty, of librarians and archivists in Spain. The personnel at Barcelona's Arxiu Històric de la Ciutat warrant special thanks for facilitating microfilmed materials that have been indispensable for the elaboration of the project; in particular, I am indebted to Albert Gil Lecha, Alicia Torres Déniz, and Manel Alfaro López. Similarly, I value enormously the contributions of Manel Aisa, director of Barcelona's Ateneu Enciclopèdic Popular (Centre de Documentació Històrica i Social), who ensures that what my writers stood for is never forgotten. On various occasions I benefited from the expertise of the wonderful archivists at Salamanca's Centro Documental de la Memoria Histórica, especially Manuel and Jesús, who set me on the right path time and again, while recently Ana Quiroga Gil and Susana Romero Martín have been of great assistance. I also deeply appreciate the librarians at Spain's National Library in Madrid and at Barcelona's Biblioteca de Catalunya for their incredible patience in transporting from their shelves to my desk the many other primary and secondary texts that have nourished the study. Other invaluable institutions have been the Hemeroteca Municipal in Madrid, Seville, and Zaragoza, and Barcelona's Centre Espírita de Amalia Domingo Soler.

I thank the University of Auckland for the material support and sabbatical leaves that have advanced the manuscript, and I am especially grateful to my colleagues, academic and professional, for their generous encouragement in myriad ways. Melanie Johnson and Mark Hangartner helped me resolve potential copyright issues, while William Hamill (microtexts assistant) and especially the incomparable Tim Page (digital media support specialist) have been vital for the majority of the excellent reproductions. I owe a special debt to Siobhan McMenemy, editor at the University of Toronto Press, whose enthusiasm for and belief in the project have been unflagging. It has been a rare privilege to work with her and the splendid production and marketing team at UTP, particularly Frances Mundy and Ian MacKenzie.

At different stages the manuscript has gained from the insightful critique of my contemporary "sisters in ideas," who have given unstintingly of their time and specialized knowledge: Maryellen Bieder, Roberta Johnson, and, as always, Mercedes Maroto-Camino, not to mention the many other intellectuals, female and male, whose scholarship enhances the study. I also thank the anonymous second reader of the manuscript for a highly constructive evaluation. I acknowledge the input of Jose Manuel Bolado García, whose inspirational work on Rosario de Acuña propelled me into the freethinking world and who has regularly assisted with detective work. My sincere thanks go to Amelina Correa Ramón, who furnished me with two images relevant to Amalia Domingo Soler from her personal archives at the eleventh hour, and to Julia Antivilo Peña, for clarifying details regarding Belén Sárraga. Grounding and sustaining me physically and emotionally has been the love of family and friends, while in Spain my work would not have been possible without the enduring friendship and deep affection of my Asturian "family," above all Marilis, and the invaluable support and companionship of Antonio, Jayne, Alfredo, and Félix in Salamanca.

Earlier versions of material from the book first appeared as follows: "Making Freethinking Spain: The Sociopolitical Poetics of Belén Sárraga (c.1873–c.1950)," *Revista de Estudios Hispánicos* 44, no. 1 (March 2010): 81–106, and reprinted by permission of the editors and Washington University in St Louis; "Domestic Politics, National Agendas: Reforming Don Juan and the Liberal Subject in Ángeles López de Ayala's *De tal siembra, tal cosecha*," *Modern Language Notes, Hispanic Issue* 125, no. 2 (March 2010): 326–47, and reprinted by copyright permission of the Johns Hopkins University Press; and "The Novellas of Republican Intellectual Ángeles López de Ayala (1856–1926)," *Bulletin of Spanish Studies* 88, no. 5 (2011): 667–90, ISSN 1475-3820, and reprinted by permission of the editors. I am very grateful to all the journals for permission to reprint here.

SPANISH FEMALE WRITERS AND THE FREETHINKING PRESS, 1879–1926

Introduction

In late nineteenth- and early twentieth-century Spain, recent memories of the First Republic (1873–4) and aspirations to bring back a second republic were the galvanizing forces that held together an often divided minority group of writers, intellectuals, and political figures critical of Restoration governments. They perceived the restoration in 1875 of a constitutional monarchy, in alliance with the two main political parties, as achieving little to shift established socioeconomic structures and grant the lower classes greater agency. The reforms initiated under the Glorious Revolution (1868) and the short-lived First Republic had only intimated the democratic society that was the ideal for these intellectuals.

Within these Republican groups, there thrived in fin-de-siècle Spain a sisterhood of female intellectuals and writers, highly influential in their day, who coalesced around the intertwined movements of freethinking, feminism, republicanism, and freemasonry. Unrecognized in most literary and political histories but contemporaries of the male writers customarily included in the so-called Generation of 1898, they were comparably engaged in seeking solutions to Spain's sociopolitical problems, always in accordance with the advancement of women. Cultural and political associations, press publications, and their literary production were the means by which they advanced causes essential for a freethinking Spain, which would enable women and the working classes to effectively enter the public sphere as sociopolitical subjects. For these writers, freethinking and feminist societies, secular schools, freemasonry lodges, and the fourth estate formed the warp and woof of their daily lives.

When the dominant paradigm of femininity for women, regardless of class, was encapsulated in the bourgeois symbol of the Angel in the House,[1] figures such as Rosario de Acuña, Concepción Arenal, Carmen de Burgos, Amalia Carvia, Amalia Domingo Soler, Ángeles López de Ayala, and Belén Sárraga constitute but the tip of an iceberg of politicized female writers who participated successfully in spheres culturally proscribed to women during the last decade of the nineteenth century and the first three decades of the twentieth; indeed, Kirsty Hooper highlights the fact that "more than 250 women were active in Spanish cultural and intellectual circles in the two decades around the turn of the twentieth century" (2008, 10).

The intense activity of freethinking women in political and cultural associations and the numerous testimonies in freethinking periodicals to their interaction, mutual support, and mentoring disprove the belief, such as that voiced by Amparo Hurtado, that female writers during the late nineteenth century and early years of the twentieth did not know one another personally nor participate in the type of association that contributed to forging democracy in Spain (1998, 139, 143).[2] Their lives and works also call into question established notions of female intellectuals in fin-de-siècle Spain, like that articulated by Maria Aurèlia Capmany: "In Catalonia the search is fruitless; we will not encounter female intellectuals who are clearly conscious of the public role of intellectual life" (1973, 27). This alleged absence of fin-de-siècle female intellectuals from sociopolitical processes in modern Spain has been vigorously contested by scholars such as Maryellen Bieder (1992), Alda Blanco (1989), Lou Charnon-Deutsch (2003), and Roberta Johnson (2003). It is true that, with few exceptions, their histories of activism and prolific literary production, well known in their day, have now all but disappeared. Nevertheless, this situation simply underlines the point, as Pere Sànchez i Ferré remarks, that liberal historiography, like its Marxist counterpart, has been written according to androcentric models of progress (1990, 147). For her part, Mary Nash underlines that the role played by women in the struggle between liberal forces and the Old Regime has yet to be examined in depth (1999, 64).

My study, both historical and literary, seeks to foreground the exceptional contributions made by female freethinking writers in the late nineteenth and early twentieth centuries to the beginnings of democracy and feminism in Spain. In particular, it focuses on three intellectuals, Amalia Domingo Soler, Ángeles López de Ayala, and Belén Sárraga, whose enthralling histories of activism are inseparable from their constant presence in contemporary freethinking associations and periodicals. All three founded and edited periodicals of a radical bent and distinct feminist orientation, constituting a committed press granted little attention in histories of the Spanish press. While there are a few historical studies on these writers, no scholarship has been forthcoming on their substantial output in the form of newspaper contributions and literary works. This project, then, aims to fill a gap in histories of the Spanish press, early Spanish republicanism, and the development of Spanish feminisms, and feed into the literary recovery of the female equivalent of the Generation of 1898 signalled by Hurtado (1998). It also wishes to contribute to the burgeoning field of studies on fin-de-siècle Spanish literature – an area that the scholarship of Bieder, Charnon-Deutsch, Hooper,

Catherine Jagoe, Johnson, Jo Labanyi, Susan McKenna, and Akiko Tsuchiya has enriched immeasurably, especially over the past decade. How my study can add value, I suggest, is in its focus on writers who do not form part of an established canon, even though they were prominent contemporaries of canonical authors whose works have enjoyed vital critical re-readings.[3]

Building on work by historians such as María Dolores Ramos, Sànchez i Ferré, Luz Sanfeliu, Luis Vitale, and Julia Antivilo Peña, I illuminate the role that the three writers played through the substantial body of material that my archival research on female freethinkers and periodicals has unearthed. In order to do so, I piece together scattered references to these women to bear witness to the rich tapestry of their intersecting lives and undertake an analysis of the periodicals that they edited and the literary works that they published. While I place their endeavours within the broader frameworks of freethinking, feminism, and republicanism to which they were all committed, I do not set out to deliver an exhaustive account of these liberal movements. Nonetheless, I do seek to provide not just a study of three writers but also of the multiple strands of the democratically oriented associations that they inhabited and shaped. I thus situate my project within what Elizabeth Fay terms a "methodology of identity," which she defines as "a recuperative strategy attempting to understand who the woman being studied was despite large gaps in material information ... but that might include texts a woman wrote but did not publish, snatches of information on texts now lost to us, information on how women lived their lives during this period, and details of the particular woman's life experience" (1998, 24).

Some of the questions that my study seeks to clarify are: What do their lives tell us about the presence and participation in sociopolitical life that left-wing educated women in fin-de-siècle Spain were demanding and enjoying? Why have their lives disappeared from histories of republicanism and their works from literary histories? How does an examination of their feminist concerns and political activities modify and enrich current studies of the development of democracy and feminisms in Spain? What might their experiences and production offer to feminist projects in the early twenty-first century?

In this introduction, I will first outline issues in the intersected movements of republicanism and freethinking that are crucial to the aspirations revealed in the lives and writings of Domingo Soler, López de Ayala, and Sárraga. Second, I will touch on the importance of associationism as the indispensable vehicle for fostering freethinking activities and democratic thought, and address the spaces in which associationism thrived. Third, I will explore the implications of the press as a public associative space conducive to the greater participation of women in left-wing politics in Spain and the use of this space to forge and consolidate what they defined as a sisterhood. Fourth, I will provide an overview of the chapters dedicated to the three writers respectively. The issues debated in each chapter overlap with one another, given that the lives and literary activities of all three writers are, to a large extent, intertwined. Nevertheless, despite their commonalities, I will argue that Domingo Soler, López de Ayala, and Sárraga bring distinct perspectives to bear on the freethinking enterprise that are informed by their historical moment and the sociopolitical movements with which they identified.

In the late nineteenth century, Republican premises were closely aligned with freethinking. Yet freethinking was a much broader, heterogeneous movement than a political orientation, constituting, as Buenaventura Delgado stresses, "all dissidents: Masons, anarchists, socialists, Republicans, etc." (1979, 42).[4] At the 1902 International Conference for Freethinkers in Geneva, which Sárraga attended, freethinking was defined as "the right to freedom of conscience ... may no one attempt to impose their truth on others in the name of an authority other than and superior to that of reason" (quoted in Mateo Avilés 1986, 155). This precept, Mary Dietz observes, is essential to liberalism, since it conceives of "the individual as the 'bearer of formal rights' designed to protect him from the ... interference of others and to guarantee him the same opportunities or 'equal access' as others" (1998, 380). Nevertheless, Dietz continues, the desire to protect individual rights was instrumental in the creation of a private sphere separate from the feared interference of the public realm. This private/public division, gendered as feminine/masculine, would prove highly detrimental to the full citizenship of women (380–1). The considerable limitations placed on women's participation in the public sphere were sanctioned through the previously mentioned cultural model of Woman as Angel in the House, obedient wife, and self-sacrificing mother, a paradigm with which my writers engage, negotiate, and, where possible, contest.[5] It is precisely the recasting of the domestic/public division to argue for women's necessary participation in the public sphere that constitutes a primary concern of the writers in my study and their feminist programs for women's sociocultural and political emancipation.

For freethinkers and their quest for democracy, secular education was paramount, as Nash elucidates, for creating in Kantian terms subjects empowered through the cultivation of their reason to act without requiring the tutelage of others and thus participate in civic society and assume historical agency (2000, 4–5). Secular education, informed by the philosophy of Karl Krause (1781–1832) and the ideals of the Institución Libre de Enseñanza (Free Institute of Education), founded in 1876, would counter the Catholic Church's monopoly over family and society, foster the scientific progress vital for a modern Spain, and enable the emergence of sovereign subjects. The stress by liberal thought on the capacity for reason innate to all human beings, irrespective of their sex, and that affirmed their theoretical equality, made secular education essential for feminist aims. Yet, as

Pilar Ballarín notes, in late nineteenth-century and early twentieth-century Spain, the education available to most women, not to mention men, was woefully lacking and, in the case of women, was dedicated more to forming women's hearts than their minds (1993, 600–1).[6] Thus the concepts of progress and modernity, Nash affirms, were rendered incompatible with Woman, who was identified with progress only within the domestic economy and the administration of the home (2000, 8). The 1870 Penal Code, the 1885 Commerce Code, and the 1889 Civil Code ensured women's subservience in the private home and placed them firmly under the tutelage of men, who officially acted for them in the public sphere (Scanlon 1986, 123–37).

Hence secular education was an important step towards the transformations in the private sphere necessary for female citizenship, since, as María José Lacalzada de Mateo indicates, it removed women from the influence of the Catholic Church and the confessional. A major contribution to this debate was the publication of Arenal's *La mujer del porvenir* in 1869, which had been delivered in the Sunday lectures that year on women's education, organized by Krausist Fernando de Castro (Lacalzada de Mateo 1999, 243–5).[7] A more contentious matter, Lacalzada de Mateo elaborates, was the nature of women's participation in the public sphere, always circumscribed by concepts pertaining to maternal care (247). As I will develop in individual chapters, secular education is paramount for all three of my writers, who demonstrate their commitment to this endeavour in their acts and literary works. They argue for women's equal education and presence in political life by pushing at the boundaries of their culturally sanctioned role as mother and insisting that political reform begins with domestic revolution.

The development of alternative networks of sociocultural power that might cross class divisions and establish common sources of identification depended on strong urban centres and the left-wing political movements that they facilitated. The places with which Sárraga's activities within Spain were most linked were Valencia and Málaga, cities with marked Republican identities. For Domingo Soler and López de Ayala, Barcelona, the most industrialized and progressive city in Spain at the time, and an epicentre for workers' movements, trade unions, and regional nationalism, was the crucible for their freethinking undertakings. Vital for creating these networks and communities were associations, entered into through free consent and shared beliefs and ideals, all of which were directed at not only freethinking upper and middle classes but also women and workers. Associationism, briefly legalized during the years 1868–74, strengthened workers' economic rights and fostered sociopolitical equality (Castro Alfín 1987, 207). Thus associations worked to create a common sense of purpose among economically disparate social actors, with the potential to generate powerful inter-class alliances dedicated to establishing a republic and a freethinking society. Unsurprisingly, the restoration of the Bourbon monarchy in 1875 saw strong measures taken against associations that vindicated working-class concerns, and associationism was not again officially sanctioned until 1887 (Bahamonde Magro and Toro Mérida 1978, 155–6).[8]

Among the available networks for freethinkers and Republicans, the Masonic lodges occupied a powerful position. As Pedro Álvarez Lázaro notes, freethinkers and freemasons provided one another with mutual support in their anticlerical goals. Nevertheless, it was precisely the anti-religious fanaticism of certain freethinkers that created divergences from freemasonry, which, governed by an ethos of tolerance, proclaimed itself "above political parties and all church doctrines" (Álvarez Lázaro 1985, 169, 252). As for Republicans and freemasons, Rosa Ana Gutiérrez Lloret stresses their common aspirations, such as the defence of freedom of thought and liberal beliefs, the critique of the Catholic Church and religious intransigence, the desire for reform and progress in Spanish society, the insistence on the education of the people as a means of moral and social elevation, and the search for social harmony. These similarities had a comparable origin and evolution, since both republicanism and freemasonry were able to enjoy a public presence after 1868, thanks to the rights granted in the 1869 Constitution. With the Restoration, however, their public presence became officially limited (Gutiérrez Lloret 1990, 620–2).

Although freemasonry was not a political organization, many Republican leaders were well-known freemasons, and the relationship of freemasonry with politics was real, particularly among federal Republicans and Progressive Republicans (Sànchez i Ferré 1990, 177); not coincidentally, Sárraga embraced this first modality, while López de Ayala leaned towards the more revolutionary stance of the second. Furthermore, the symbolic names of many freemasons commemorated leaders of Spanish or European republicanism, such as Emilio Castelar, Manuel Ruiz Zorrilla, Francesc Pi y Margall, Estanislao Figueras, and Víctor Hugo (Gutiérrez Lloret 1990, 626–7). As far as the political right was concerned, republic and freemasonry were synonymous terms (Álvarez Rey 1990, 246–7).[9]

As in France, in Spain women were allowed access to so-called lodges of adoption under the tutelage of male masons, so as to foster their education and promote a secular society through the mother's influence over her family.[10] What was even more unusual in the development of Spanish freemasonry was the fact that some lodges were mixed, admitting women along with men. In some cases, Lacalzada de Mateo points out, women in practice ran their own lodges (2006, 157).[11] From 1872 onward, following the 1868 Revolution and the temporary consolidation of progressive liberalism, a significant number of female liberals were affiliated with freemasonry through lodges of adoption, including Rosario de Acuña, López de Ayala, and Sárraga, while female freemasons in the later context of the Second Republic (1931–9) were Carmen de Burgos, Clara Campoamor, and Victoria Kent (Ortiz Albear 2005, 118–20, 129–30). The transnational impetus of freemasonry kept these women in close contact with what was occurring in other nations through international conferences and the press, and facilitated their formulation of common objectives.

Hence freethinking associations contributed to the ideal of a cosmopolitan society envisaged as transcending gender, class, ethnic, political, and national boundaries. Cosmopolitanism, as an ethos and practice, is built on a sense of belonging to broader, more universal communities that extend beyond individual, regional, and national concerns. Vivienne Boon and Gerard Delanty explain how the idea of being a citizen of the world and having a responsibility to humanity in general was rooted in the thought of the Cynics and Stoics. Later developed by Immanuel Kant (1724–1804) and, more recently, Jürgen Habermas in particular, cosmopolitanism has important implications for ethics, political governance, and sociocultural practice (2007, 20–30).[12] The rise of cosmopolitanism and its challenge to established cultural and sociopolitical borders, as Margaret Jacob (2006) elucidates in the context of early modern Europe, depended on the emergence of vibrant urban centres and a rich civil society facilitated through associations that coalesced around freethinking, republicanism, freemasonry, and scientific inquiry, all of which operated on local as well as transnational levels.[13] Belonging to these more open and more horizontal networks brought men and women into contact with different ways of being in and perceiving the world, and engendered, as Jacob puts it, "previously unimagined political and personal transformations" within a revolutionary spirit (122).

That cosmopolitanism seeks to remove all forms of discrimination is central to Robert Fine's argument that cosmopolitanism demands "the emergence of new forms of right in the sphere of inter-societal relations … international laws, international organizations …, international courts, global forms of governance, the idea of human rights, declarations and conventions on human rights, and mechanisms for securing peace between nations" (2007, xi). Consequently, Fine affirms, "cosmopolitan social theory is at its most powerful in addressing the needs of those who are outside or on the margins of the nation" (x). Important for my own study is the fact that a key premise of cosmopolitanism, as Michael Scrivener emphasizes, is gender equality: "It is impossible to conceive of a cosmopolitan political culture that does not make sexual equality an indispensable principle as a central part of its ideology because the violence of the hierarchical exclusions based on gender always becomes expressed in other violent forms as well" (2007, 96).

The attraction of cosmopolitan movements for minority political groups such as the late nineteenth-century Spanish Republicans, and for disadvantaged social groups such as women and the working classes, cannot be underestimated. In the case of all three of my writers, cosmopolitan values inform their lives and writings and underpin their enterprises on behalf of feminist causes, the rights of the socially disadvantaged, and international peace. However, the figure who most fully embraces a cosmopolitan ethos is Sárraga, whose engagement with international organizations and movements is a corollary of her commitment to the cause of federal republicanism. Also important for the period encompassed by my study is Fine's observation that, although logically "cosmopolitan right presupposes a complex network of already existing social forms of right ... [i]n some circumstances the order of historical sequence might be reversed and cosmopolitan rights might precede other forms of right" (2007, xi–xii).[14] As I will develop in this book, such a vindication of rights prior to their materialization in social, economic, and political systems characterizes the contexts in which my writers fought their battles for rights for women and the working classes in national and transnational arenas.

A crucial terrain in which the battle for rights was played out in Restoration Spain was in the Republican press. Throughout most of the nineteenth century, politics was intimately connected with periodicals, which were essentially mouthpieces for contesting parties in their struggle for political power (Seoane 1996a, 15). Such a scenario was particularly pertinent in the case of the Republican press after the Restoration. According to Isidro Sánchez Sánchez, the failure of the Republican-led period (1868–74) resulted in an increase in divisions among Republican groups, which was reflected in their press.[15] The first great Republican newspaper of the Restoration period was the daily *El Progreso* (1881–7), substituted by *El País* (1887–1921). Among federal Republican periodicals were *El Solfeo*, *La Unión*, *El Mundo Moderno*, *La Vanguardia*, and the longest-lasting, *La República* (1884–91). Another publication, also entitled *El Progreso* and founded by Alejandro Lerroux and most contributors of *El País*, was published in Madrid from 1897 until 1898, before going to Barcelona. Also important were Barcelona's *El Motín* and Madrid's *Las Dominicales del Libre Pensamiento*, directed by Fernando Lozano Montes (alias Demófilo) and Ramón Chíes (Sánchez Sánchez 2001, 184, 195–6).[16] This last periodical, the leading freethinking weekly of the Restoration period, was also deeply involved with the freemasonry world. Both its editors were prominent freemasons, as were many of its contributors, including Odón de Buen y del Cos, professor of mineralogy and botany at the University of Barcelona from 1889 until 1911.[17] As my study will highlight, Domingo Soler, López de Ayala, and Sárraga knew these figures very well and would publish regularly in *Las Dominicales del Libre Pensamiento*.

Joan B. Culla and Àngel Duarte remark that, from 1875 onward, periodicals constituted practically the only means for Republicans to maintain a critical public presence within a Restoration climate of apparent liberalism but real obstruction of the participation of subaltern classes in political life. Despite the official recognition of political rights such as the freedom to organize political parties (1879), freedom of association (1880), freedom of the press (1883), freedom of workers' associations (1887), and universal male suffrage (1890), the majority of these democratic victories were neutralized by the frequent suspension of constitutional rights, states of emergency, and electoral corruption (Culla and Duarte 1990, 15).

Within this context and of particular relevance was the ongoing censorship of the press, from which the periodicals of Domingo Soler, López de Ayala, and Sárraga frequently suffered. The Press Law, passed on 26 July 1883, guaranteed freedom of expression only in principle; in practice, Article 17 of the Constitution allowed the suspension of constitutional rights to protect state security. This proviso resulted in twenty-three suspensions of the press between 1898 and 1923; more commonly still, certain newspapers were forbidden to publish on specific matters (Seoane 1996b, 65). As Culla and Duarte note, especially affected were newspapers in Barcelona, the city with which both Domingo Soler's and López de Ayala's lives were inextricably linked. There, between 1902 and 1923, the press enjoyed full freedom of expression only in 1904, 1914, and 1915 (Culla and Duarte 1990, 46).[18]

In fin-de-siècle Catalonia, radical republicanism, Duarte explains, took a strong interest in workers' struggles, as a result of the Republicans' need to oppose Antonio Cánovas de Castillo's Restoration government and strengthen their cause by attracting potential supporters from, or closely involved with, the working classes (1987, 82).[19] Since the failure of the period from 1868 to 1874, which had seen the working classes emerge into political life through the so-called Glorious Revolution of 1868 and the First Republic, socialism and particularly anarchism were proving formidable magnets in drawing workers away from radical bourgeois parties (Seoane 1996a, 263).[20] Hence, in an effort to increase Republican numbers, from the late nineteenth century until Miguel Primo de Rivera's dictatorship in 1923 the Republican press also supplemented workers' periodicals, the existence of which was precarious, by reporting on strikes, societies of resistance, and local federations, and inviting theoretical debate on social matters from key players in anarchism and socialism (Culla and Duarte 1990, 28–9). In fact, according to Sánchez Sánchez, the majority of Republican publications frequently defended the disadvantaged with greater radicalism than the workers' publications (2001, 196).

The extent of Republican involvement in working-class issues can be partially gauged, Duarte argues, by the strong presence of Republicans from 1898 onward in the Montjuich campaign. Comparable in its significance to the Dreyfus Affair in France, the campaign sought amnesty for anarchists, working-class leaders, and Republicans convicted of alleged conspiracy in the 1896 bombing of the

Barcelona Opera House and of inciting popular protest against sending working-class soldiers to the Spanish-American war in Cuba (Duarte 1987, 82–3). As this study will explain, López de Ayala played a prominent role in the Montjuich campaign, serving as its secretary (Sànchez i Ferré 1990, 220). In turn, Republican opposition to the colonial conflict is not only present in López de Ayala's writings but also surfaces with a vengeance in Sárraga's essays and poems.

Undeniably, identification by Republican intellectuals with the working classes occurred from an outsider's position, with the artificiality of that situation reflected in their discourse (Castro Alfín 1987, 200). In contrast, with regard to my three writers, I suggest that their positioning in support of working-class issues acquires greater legitimacy than that of contemporary male intellectuals in that they represent a social group that, by virtue of their sex, was even more lacking in civil rights than those males granted universal suffrage in 1890. Spanish women were not granted the vote until the Second Republic came to power in 1931. As for women's legal rights, at the turn of the twentieth century they were determined by the aforementioned 1889 Civil Code, in great part based on the 1803–4 French Civil Code known as the Napoleonic Code, which gave all legal, economic, and cultural power to the male.[21]

In histories of the Spanish press, the periodicals edited by Domingo Soler, López de Ayala, and Sárraga, well known in their day, are afforded scant space.[22] Indeed, Adolfo Perinat and María Isabel Marrades's study on the women's press in Spain from 1800 to 1939 barely touches on the radical press edited in the late nineteenth and early twentieth centuries. They contend that no feminist, communist, or socialist periodical was published prior to 1936, despite the vitality of utopian socialist ideas and anarchism in the period in question (1980, 330). Furthermore, they go so far as to declare that "participating in public life will certainly not be the goal of women who write for nineteenth-century women's magazines" (377). This statement clearly contradicts the affirmations and attitudes evident in the prolific press contributions of my three writers and their female intellectual contemporaries.

Despite its lacunae, Perinat and Marrades's research is an indispensable point of departure for tracing the development of Spanish women's press. In order to underline the fact that the periodicals edited by Domingo Soler, López de Ayala, and Sárraga did not appear in a vacuum, it is worth highlighting the milestones in this evolution. Perinat and Marrades observe that among the most important early women's periodicals was *La Moda* from Cádiz. Appearing in 1841 and published until 1927, it changed its name in 1861 to *La Moda Elegante Ilustrada* and in 1870 was published in Madrid. Among its contributors were María del Pilar Sinués de Marco, Robustiana Armiño de Cuestas, and Gertrudis Gómez de Avellaneda. Another women's periodical of a conservative bent was *El Defensor del*

Bello Sexo, edited by José de Souza and dedicated exclusively to women (Perinat and Marrades 1980, 18–19). For two months in 1851 there appeared the Madrid feminist periodical, *Ellas, Órgano Oficial del Sexo Femenino*, edited by Alicia Pérez de Gascuna and with contributions by Carolina Coronado (24–5). Subsequently it became a periodical similar to others dealing with literature and fashion, changing its name to the *Gaceta del Bello Sexo* in 1851 and in 1852, to *El Correo de la Moda y Álbum de Señoritas*. During its last reincarnation it was edited by Ángela Grassi from 1874 until 1883 (24–7).[23] The majority of these female writers and editors, as Jagoe indicates, "compensated for the transgressive combination of being women in the public sphere by making advertisement of the feminine ideal their ostensible theme" (1994, 32).

Of greater import for the orientation of the periodicals edited by the three writers featured in this book was the emergence from 1846 onward of publications influenced by the utopian socialist ideas of Charles Fourier (1772–1837),[24] such as the Barcelona *Pensil del Bello Sexo* edited by Víctor Balaguer, and *El Pensil Gaditano* (from 1857 renamed *El Pensil de Iberia*) and *La Buena Nueva*, both of which were edited by Margarita de Celis, María José Zapata, and José Bartorelo (Perinat and Marrades 1980, 20–3). During the last third of the nineteenth century some twenty serious periodicals edited by and for women were published. Among the most significant were *La Voz de la Caridad*, founded by Arenal and published bimonthly for fourteen years, the Barcelona periodical *La Mujer* (1882–87), which became after a few months *El Álbum del Bello Sexo*, and *La Ilustración de la Mujer* (1883–7). Edited by Gómez de Avellaneda, Josefa Pujol de Collado, and Dolores Monsedá de Maciá, this last publication constituted a noteworthy attempt to spread a women's movement throughout Spain and saw a new vocabulary appear, founded on the defence of and struggle for women's rights rather than feminine sacrifice, abnegation, modesty, and virtue (29–33). Another periodical of note that appeared between 1891 and 1893 was Emilia Pardo Bazán's *Nuevo Teatro Crítico*, which carried, McKenna comments, "some of her most critical condemnations of the state of women's affairs in Spain" (2009, 34). Nonetheless, Perinat and Marrades stress that a women's press with a working-class orientation does not emerge until the twentieth century (1980, 76) – an evaluation that belies the marked earlier engagement by Domingo Soler, López de Ayala, and Sárraga with the working classes in their periodicals and writings.

Other excellent books on fin-de-siècle periodicals that have informed my own project are Charnon-Deutsch's research on illustrated magazines and newspapers in *Hold That Pose* (2008) and Isabel Segura and Marta Selva's *Revistes de Dones 1846–1935* (1984), which addresses the Barcelona women's press directed primarily at women. Hardly any study, however, examines the women's press of a more politicized, anticlerical nature and directed at readers of both sexes during the late nineteenth century and early twentieth century, such as López de Ayala's and Sárraga's periodicals. In contrast, anarchist women's periodicals, and especially *Mujeres Libres*, have enjoyed considerable attention.[25] Hence my book further extends the understanding of fin-de-siècle women's participation in the fourth estate from a more radical positioning that embraces not only feminism but also Republican agendas in their most progressive form.

What factors were conducive to the participation of freethinking women like Domingo Soler, López de Ayala, and Sárraga in the radical press? One reason, as already noted, was the minority status of the multi-factioned Republican movement and its need to garner support and participation from as broad a social base as possible and represent those viewpoints in its press. A second, equally important reason was the liberal principle of equality for all, irrespective of sex or class, which demanded that women be granted equal access to the public sphere. However, with regard to women's status, this premise was regularly disregarded by liberals in practice, as seen in the discrimination levelled against women who participated more fully in the public sphere, as was the case with López de Ayala and Acuña.[26] A third reason, I posit, pertains to the composition of the public sphere itself, which, for Habermas, as Scrivener explains, consists of "literary and political spheres that mediate between private individuals and the state" (2007, 33).[27] The periodicals that Domingo Soler, López de Ayala, and Sárraga edited and those to which they contributed were both political and literary spaces, in that all their creative works published there promoted freethinking values and pursued political objectives. Judged against strictly aesthetic criteria, their literary outputs were clearly propagandistic. Set within a Marxist framework, however, theirs was an engaged literature, advocating the marriage of art with politics.

This blurring of political and literary aspirations in the freethinking periodical is particularly pertinent for women's relationship with and entry into the public sphere. As Scrivener has remarked, "The tension between the literary and the political public sphere" requires more careful examination, given that "women were prominent in the former and marginalized in the latter" (2007, 43). The space of the freethinking periodical, I argue, afforded women the opportunity to cross the culturally constructed, gendered divide between a feminized literary realm and a masculine political sphere, and articulate their political opinions not just through more literary vehicles such as poems and fables but more directly through their political essays. The press gave them a virtual presence that, by not requiring a face-to-face engagement with a public sphere, was not as culturally problematic as their physical presence in the public arena. Moreover, the last decades of the nineteenth century and the first decade of the twentieth – the years in which my writers were most active in the freethinking press – is a temporal space prior to the emergence of national newspapers of wide circulation, which, Seoane affirms, were founded less on promoting specific political viewpoints than on providing an ostensibly more objective reporting of news (Seoane 1996b, 23). The context of the press in which these women wrote was one that privileged diversity precisely because it was concerned with the promotion of particular political agendas that depended on alliances between the upper-middle, middle, and working classes, irrespective of gender.

Hence, when considering the press in which Domingo Soler, López de Ayala, and Sárraga wrote, an additional point made by Scrivener also warrants attention: the need to distinguish more carefully "between the bourgeois public sphere and the plebeian public sphere, ... not as a fully autonomous counterpublic defining itself wholly against the bourgeois sphere, but as a sphere connected with but different from the bourgeois sphere" (2007, 43). The intersections between the bourgeois and so-called plebeian public spheres are apparent in the periodicals of all three writers and increasingly so in the works of the two younger women, López de Ayala and Sárraga.

In scrutinizing the relationship between the private and public spheres, it is also necessary to consider my writers' negotiation of inherited Romantic paradigms. "Romanticism," Marlon Ross contends, "is historically a masculine phenomenon." Drawing on seminal texts such as Harold Bloom's *The Anxiety of Influence*, Ross notes that the male Romantic writer's quest for self-possession and domination over all rivals maps out a paradigm that is practically impossible in cultural terms for his female contemporaries to follow (1988, 29). Nevertheless, such an understanding of the Romantic tradition and its exclusion of female writers have been challenged by feminist scholars such as Mary Favret, Fay, Kari Lokke, and Anne Mellor, who have sought to extend Romanticism's conceptual and chronological parameters in the British and European contexts. Equally, Susan Kirkpatrick's work *Las Románticas* (1991) has been pivotal for repositioning female Romantic writers in Spain.

Sections of my study aim to contribute to a better understanding of just how Romanticism's recent legacy constitutes both a hindrance and source of empowerment for the later, more politicized generations of female writers that feature in this project. Romanticism's stress on revolution, as a result of the influence of the emotions, indirectly provided women, identified with the emotions, with a conceptual framework through which to argue for their more direct involvement in transformative politics. According to Fay, two of the features that female writers deployed for political purposes were the letter and the figure of the mother, which I will examine in relation to works by Domingo Soler and Sárraga respectively. In comparison, Mellor draws attention to the stress that many female Romantic writers placed on rationalism and gender equality (1993, 2) – a model that is most defended by López de Ayala and her contemporary, Acuña.

Undeniably, the periodicals that Domingo Soler, López de Ayala, and Sárraga headed provided women with a safe forum in which they could articulate their views and receive encouragement and mentoring from fellow female writers. These newspapers frequently featured their proclamations of friendship and mutual support and testify to the numerous sociopolitical activities that brought them together and honed their relationships. This striking sense of solidarity continued a tradition of literary sisterhood that had taken root among female Romantic writers during the 1840s, who used it, as Kirkpatrick explains, to improve the condition of their sex while apparently conforming to the qualities of the normative Angel in the House (1991, 87). Their main focus, Kirkpatrick continues, had been vindicating women's access to intellectual activity and literary expression (90). As I will discuss, these strands continue to be present in the letters, essays, and poems exchanged in friendship among the writers of my study. At the same time, while their writings acknowledge similarities in their positions, they also reveal their differences on such themes as the place of emotion in reason, the role of women in society, and the virtues of social revolution versus gradual transformation. Hence their sisterhood, I argue, moves from being founded on their common sex, as was more the case with the previous literary generation, to being rooted in shared but contested ideological debates. They are truly, as López de Ayala calls them, "hermanas en ideas" (sisters in ideas).[28]

Feminist ideals were at the forefront of the sociopolitical activities and writings of all three of the intellectuals featured in this study and gained momentum in the case of López de Ayala and Sárraga. That Domingo Soler, López de Ayala, and Sárraga were acutely aware of their role in agitating for women's extended rights within and beyond the home is evident in their creation of feminist organizations and periodicals that carried feminist content, their unceasing involvement in projects to improve the situation of women nationally, and their participation in international conferences that lobbied for women's presence in the public sphere.

In the 1890s in Spain the term *feminism*, as Concha Fagoaga signals, was "widely used" and commonly employed in the press (1985, 79). For those of a conservative bent, regardless of their sex, feminism was a negatively charged term, representative of a sea change that threatened traditional hierarchical privileges of not only gender but also class. For popular movements such as anarchism, socialism, and communism, feminist aspirations were seen as bourgeois and damaging to the unity between the sexes considered necessary to bring about the major sociopolitical changes that would empower economically disadvantaged actors. Nevertheless, as María Ángeles García-Maroto traces, while anarchist opposition was due largely to feminists' demands for suffrage, anarchists and feminists found common cause in the principle of equality that both groups embraced (1996, 57–73). It is relevant that all three of my writers were associated with key anarchist figures, such as Teresa Claramunt and Anselmo Lorenzo, and participated in events and causes common to Republicans, anarchists, and socialists.

In historiographical terms, Domingo Soler, López de Ayala, and Sárraga belong to the first wave of Spanish feminism, officially concerned more with women's social rights than their political demands. This particular orientation, as Sànchez i Ferré rightly maintains, differentiates this generation of Spanish feminists from their Anglo-Saxon and French counterparts, who, living in more secular societies, did not have to shake off the heavy shackles of the Catholic Church (1990, 170). Nevertheless, the connections among the three writers and their radical female contemporaries, their participation in freethinking press, and their feminist associations bear comparison with the nucleus of French feminism anchored by Marie Deraismes (1828–94), Clèmence Royer (1830–1902), and Marguerite Durand (1864–1936), whose periodical *La Fronde* (1897–1903) was also, like my writers' periodicals, dedicated to feminist, political, and cultural matters.[29] Moreover, the feminist activities and thought particular to López de Ayala and Sárraga anticipate the second wave of Spanish feminists who sought to go beyond civic rights for women to secure them the vote. Both are formidable forerunners of the women who, in the context of the Second Republic, lobbied for and obtained female suffrage on the grounds that Republican ideals demanded that women be given rights equal to men's.

I now turn to outline the fundamental ideas that sustained the literary production of my three writers and the content of the chapters dedicated to each. Domingo Soler (1835–1909), the subject of chapter 1, is today allegedly considered the greatest female figure in Hispanic spiritism (Correa Ramón 2002, 21). Spiritism can be seen as but one manifestation of the cultural and political revolution that arose out of the Enlightenment ideal of rational subjectivity and its challenge to established religions. As Elias de Mateo Avilés explains, spiritism aims to demonstrate the existence of the spirit and eternal life through experimental contact with those who have passed from this world. It believes in one inclusive God, the constant progress of the spirit through successive reincarnations, and solidarity with all humankind (Mateo Avilés 1986, 192–3). Such features reveal spiritism's freethinking and cosmopolitan thrust, as do also its advocacy of secular education, theoretical gender equality, a society built on cooperative principles, and the rejection of militarism and slavery (Horta 2001, 196–8).

Domingo Soler's intense association with spiritism is the reason why, of my three writers, her voluminous production is the best preserved and most readily available in print; between 1990 and 2000, many of her works, invisible in literary histories, were successively republished by minority spiritist presses. In 1879 Domingo Soler founded *La Luz del Porvenir*, a spiritist weekly dedicated to freethinking women. For some fifteen years she would remain as editor of and major writer in this periodical, which mostly published contributions from women and served as an important platform from which authors like Acuña, Sárraga, and López de Ayala would launch their literary careers and gain a public profile. As I will illustrate, *La Luz del Porvenir* provides insights into the diverse positions adopted by Spanish feminists to argue for women's education and emancipation. It also reveals the keen political thrust of spiritism, its acknowledged purpose of fostering personal and collective sovereign subjects, and its defence of the social underdog.

All of Domingo Soler's works are dedicated to spreading freethinking principles through spiritist thought. In my examination of her substantial production, I give special emphasis to her autobiography, *Memorias de una mujer*: a personal memoir, a spiritist text, and the chronicle of what it meant to be a female writer in late nineteenth-century Spain. Through this text I take up her deployment of *testimonio* as a means to vindicate the rights of subaltern classes, including women. I also explore the diverse nuances that informed the sociocultural and political positions of Domingo Soler's literary sisterhood in her collected writings, *Sus más hermosos escritos* (1903).

The second figure, the focus of chapters 2 and 3, is Ángeles López de Ayala (1856–1926), freethinker, freemason, and feminist, whose indefatigable presence in the radical press over the course of thirty-five years contributed to keeping alive the Republican flame. Like her fellow writers, by embracing republicanism López de Ayala took up a position at odds with mainstream Restoration politics, which saw conservative and liberal ministries alternately share power in prearranged turns of office known as the *turno pacífico*, so as to absorb and neutralize the opposing forces of Republicans and Carlists on the left and extreme right, respectively (Carr 1982, 347, 366). López de Ayala's republicanism, however, was independent of any specific political party, as she was fiercely critical of the divisions that undermined the Republican cause.

Between 1896 and 1920 López de Ayala founded and headed four major Barcelona Republican periodicals: *El Progreso*, *El Gladiador: Órgano de la "Sociedad Progresiva Femenina," El Libertador: Periódico Defensor de la Mujer y Órgano Nacional del Libre-Pensamiento*, and *El Gladiador del Librepensamiento: Órgano de la Federación Librepensadora de Barcelona y otros Pueblos Adheridos*. These publications debated the major issues of the day, with López de Ayala regularly providing the always politically oriented lead article. Perhaps the most high-profile political activity in which López de Ayala engaged was the campaign for a review of the Montjuich trial, as noted above. Described by Sànchez i Ferré as the key figure in the struggle for women's rights in fin-de-siècle Spain (1990, 169), López de Ayala founded, together with Domingo Soler and Claramunt, the Sociedad Autónoma de Mujeres (Independent Women's Society), which later became the Sociedad Progresiva Femenina (Progressive Women's Society). From 1889 until at least 1919, these women's organizations maintained strong links with international feminist associations and worked tirelessly to advance the situation of the so-called second sex and the working classes.

In chapter 2 I offer a composite picture of these primary facets of López de Ayala's life, examining her outstanding career as an editor, writer, and feminist activist. I interface this discussion with analyses of her political and feminist poetry and essays published in freethinking press. Chapter 3 deepens this profile by addressing López de Ayala's engagement with the premises of civic society and the position of women and the lower classes therein through my discussion of three extant works. These are a play, *De tal siembra, tal cosecha* (1889) and two novellas until now considered lost: *El abismo* ([1896] 1907) and *Primitivo* (1906–7).

As for Belén Sárraga (ca. 1873–1950), the subject of chapter 4, her life and literary production are intimately connected with the aspirations of federal republicanism, which had played a vital role in overturning the monarchy in the Glorious Revolution of 1868. Fundamental to federal republicanism, Victoria López-Cordón notes, were the premises of unity married with diversity and equal rights and obligations for all, which demanded that alliances between individuals, communities, and nations arise from consensual pacts. At a local level, such alliances were promoted through associations, which created networks founded on common affinities and dreams, and with the power to transcend socioeconomic divisions. At a national level, the adoption of a federative model would ideally protect national unity while guaranteeing regional rights. As the monarchy was seen as incompatible with individual rights, federal Republicans fiercely opposed the Restoration state, which, from 1875 onward, rested on the alliance between liberal governments and the Crown. On a transnational dimension, it was hoped that the free association of nations in a progressively greater federation – from a federation of Iberian and Latin nations to a European and transatlantic one – would produce liberty, equality, and fraternity within a universal *patria* and the abjuration of relationships based on dominance and war (López-Cordón 1975, 346–64).

Federal republicanism is attractive to feminist aspirations to equality within a framework of positive difference, because it promises to reshape hierarchical, centralized models of power, and privileges qualities such as cooperation and interdependence, traditionally associated with the feminine (Arkinstall 2009, 82). As I will develop, Sárraga's writings furnish a window on the shortcomings of liberalism and imagine a nation inclusive of all its constituencies. In this sense my analysis attempts to respond to the need that Johnson signals to examine in greater depth the implications of discourses on gender for formations of the Spanish nation between 1868 and 1939 (2003, 13).

Unlike contemporaries such as Domingo Soler and Acuña, who left a substantial corpus,[30] Sárraga's extant production is relatively slim. It consists of surviving issues of her weekly, *La Conciencia Libre*, published intermittently from 1896 to 1907, uncollected articles and poems dispersed in freethinking periodicals of the day, a compilation of poetry, *Minucias*, published in 1901, and a 163-page volume of nine essays with Responses entitled *Conferencias* (1913), which consists of Sárraga's public lectures from an eighteen-month tour throughout Latin America.[31] These works provide a fascinating lens through which to examine how left-wing female writers like Sárraga, as Ramos's pioneering studies attest, conceived of literary publication as but one arm of a multi-pronged attack to further the objectives of freethinking, federal republicanism, feminism, and popular movements within Spain and abroad.[32] In addition, Sárraga also published in Lisbon in 1914 a 336-page study, *El clericalismo en América: A través de un continente* (Vitale and Antivilo Peña 2000, 23).

Sárraga's dedication to feminist causes is evident in the flavour of *La Conciencia Libre*, her creation in Valencia of a major women's association, the Asociación General Femenina (General Association for Women), and her role in establishing feminist organizations in Portugal and Latin America. Her close association with the anarchist movement is palpable in the Federación Malagueña de Sociedades de Resistencia (Málaga Federation of Societies of Resistance) that she founded in Málaga and her connection with leading anarchists. Furthermore, she was prominent in the Valencian political movement known as *blasquismo*, led by Vicente Blasco Ibáñez between 1895 and 1910, as Sanfeliu's valuable research explores. Always committed to federal republicanism, Sárraga promoted the freethinking cause in the Latin American republics, as Vitale's and Antivilo Peña's study illuminates, and stood for the Federal Republican Party in the Second Spanish Republic's 1933 elections. In chapter 4 I expand these spatial and temporal coordinates to engage with Sárraga's life as a whole, interwoven with analyses of Sárraga's essays and speeches published in the contemporary freethinking press and her poems in *Minucias*. What stands out is the pronounced cosmopolitan thrust of Sárraga's political activism, together with her assiduous participation in international forums and debates.

The import of the intellectual legacies of these three writers, representative of a much larger cohort that awaits further research, is the crux of my Final

Reflections, which will return to their omission from liberal histories and literary canons. Their works envisaged a comprehensive revolution in politics, culture, and society that has only partially been forthcoming and remains still pending in our contemporary society. It is to their denouncement of social inequalities, their transnational aspirations, and their feminist concerns that this study is dedicated.

1.1 Portrait of Amalia Domingo Soler, by kind permission of the Centre Espírita de Amalia Domingo Soler, Barcelona, and donated by Amelina Correa Ramón, University of Granada

1 Transcribing the Past, Writing the Future: Spiritism, Feminism, and an Aesthetics of Emancipation in the Writings of Amalia Domingo Soler (1835–1909)

Mujeres que me escucháis,
mis palabras no olvidéis,
comprended lo que valéis
y haceos cargo cómo estáis.
Estudiar necesitáis,
porque vivís sin vivir.
...
no más sueño, despertad,
y decid: la libertad
¡es el sol del porvenir!

(Domingo Soler, "A las mujeres," 371)[1]

(You women who listen to me, / don't forget my words, / comprehend your worth, / and take stock of how you are. / You need to study / because you live without living. / ... / don't continue to sleep, awaken, / and say: freedom / is the sun of the future!)

Amalia Domingo Soler, recognized in international bibliographies on spiritism as the most significant female figure in that movement,[2] played an extremely active part in freethinking circles and anticlerical thought from the end of the 1870s until her death from pneumonia on 29 April 1909. According to María del Carmen Simón Palmer, Domingo Soler began publishing as early as February 1858 in the Sevillan periodical *El Museo Literario*. She also contributed to Madrid's *Álbum de las Familias* (May–July 1866), Madrid's *Amigo de las Damas* (1873), and Barcelona's *Revista de Estudios Psicológicos* (1876). From 1894 she was editor-in-chief of the spiritist journal, *Luz y Unión*, the official mouthpiece for the Unión

Espiritista Kardeciana de Cataluña (Spiritist Union of Allan Kardec in Catalonia) (Simón Palmer 1991, 240, 242; 1993, 738).

A great proportion of Domingo Soler's writings appeared in the spiritist weekly that she founded and edited, *La Luz del Porvenir*. In addition, they have been preserved in volumes of poetry, essays, short stories, and spiritist texts, among which features her autobiography, *Memorias de una mujer*.[3] Most of what is known about Domingo Soler's life comes to us through these prolific writings, which warrant a book-length study on their own. In this chapter I will examine the positioning of Domingo Soler's remarkable periodical, *La Luz del Porvenir*, within its sociocultural and political contexts, address her deployment of the genre that we now term *testimonio* in her *Memorias*, and analyse the debates that her volume *Sus más hermosos escritos* (1903b) records among freethinking women on aesthetics, female emancipation, and the right of women to write in fin-de-siècle Spain. With respect to this last work, I will argue that Domingo Soler's literary output engages with core tenets of Romantic thought that are the traditional province of male writers to carve out a culturally valid space for female creativity.

Domingo Soler's *La Luz del Porvenir*, a Spiritist Crucible for Feminism

The most important element in the birth of Domingo Soler's long-lived, influential periodical *La Luz del Porvenir* was the dissident, heterodox movement known as spiritism, already outlined in my introduction. The belief that the living could enter into direct contact with departed spirits responded to what John Warne Monroe explains as a perceived "*crisis of factuality* in religious life," which could be resolved through "inventing new 'sciences of God,' approaches to the beyond capable of turning faith into fact by providing empirical evidence for metaphysical propositions" (Monroe 2008, 3). Nevertheless, as Lynn Sharp highlights, spiritism "offered a secular form of spirituality popular with those who may have wanted to reject Catholicism in favor of science but definitely wanted to retain a deep-seated religious outlook on the world," granting the possibility for traditional religious beliefs to be restructured and redirected to further aspirations of democracy and solidarity (2006, xii–xiii).

Spiritism, Monroe elucidates, arose out of modern American spiritualism, which first appeared in New York State in 1848 and by the early 1850s had spread to Britain and Europe. Spiritualism's development into spiritist philosophy was confirmed in 1857 with the publication of *Le Livre des Esprits* by Hippolyte Revail (1804–69), better known as Allan Kardec (Monroe 2008, 15–16, 96). Although spiritism was, as Monroe indicates, indebted to Romantic socialism and positivism, particularly drawing on Fourier's belief in reincarnation, Kardec undercut the revolutionary potential of those foundations by promoting the acceptance of social

AÑO XIII — NÚM. 1

La Luz del Porvenir

Gracia 21 de Mayo de 1891.

PRECIOS DE SUSCRICION. Barcelona un trimestre adelantado una peseta, fuera de Barcelona un año id. 4 pesetas. Estranjero y Ultramar un año id. 8 pesetas.

REDACCION Y ADMINISTRACION Plaza del Sol, 5, bajos, y calle del Cañón, 9, principal. SE PUBLICA LOS JUEVES

PUNTOS DE SUSCRICION En Lérida, Cármen 16, 3. En Madrid, Ballesta 4, principal derecha. En Alicante, San Francisco, 28, imprenta.

SUMARIO.—La mujer.

¡LA MUJER!

I.

Siguiendo mi antígua costumbre, al dar comienzo al año XIII de LA LUZ quiero atraer sobre mi trabajo la protección divina; y no encuentro mejor oración que referir á mis lectores la historia de una mujer, que aun se halla en la Tierra, tiene *noventa y cuatro años y cinco meses*, y en tan largo tiempo ha sido un modelo de virtudes, digno de estudio y de profunda admiración.

La Providencia la puso en mi camino, y agradeciendo tan inmenso favor, no quiero privar á mis lectores de narración tan interesante, refiriendo (aunque sea á grandes rasgos) una historia que pasaría completamente desapercibida, si yo no me hubiese convertido en cronista de los pobres por consejo especial de los espíritus, que en sus comunicaciones me han dicho muchas veces:

"Pregunta, inquiere, indaga, no en las Crónicas que se escriben bajo la presión de tal ó cual ideal político-religioso, no en la historia de los guerreros y de los reyes; porque en esos libros no encontrarás mas que relaciones y hechos de los afortunados, de los que se creen elegidos de Dios, los unos por su fuerza, valor y arrojo para matar, y los otros por su omnímodo poder para tiranizar á los pueblos y dominar las conciencias. Desciende de esas alturas creadas por las ambiciones y el desconocimiento absoluto de la ley de Dios, entra en los tugurios de los pobres, pregunta á los ancianos que han hecho en su penosa existencia, y algunos de ellos te contarán verdaderas heroicidades; tiempo es ya que los pobres tengan un cronista. Escribe, que su historia vale tanto como la del conquistador mas esforzado; si un Gran Capitan sometió muchas naciones bajo su férreo yugo, el plebeyo ignorado dominó con la enérgica fuerza de su voluntad las indómitas pasiones de su alma, y fué más grande en su pobreza que el señor feudal disponiendo de la vida y hacienda de sus siervos."

No me podian encomendar trabajo mas agradable, porque siempre he estudiado lo infinitamente pequeño: cuando he visto grupos de mendigos, he procurado con insistencia hablar con alguno de ellos, para estudiar y aprender en el lastimoso relato de sus vicisitudes.

1.2 *La Luz del Porvenir* 1, Year XIII (1891): 1. By kind permission of Spain's Ministerio de Educación, Cultura y Deporte, Centro Documental de la Memoria Histórica (M30)

1.3 Image of the cover of the first edition of Amalia Domingo Soler's *Cuentos espiritistas*, donated by Amelina Correa Ramón, University of Granada

inequality as a necessary atonement for previous lives (97, 106–7).[4] This tension between what Monroe describes as "egalitarianism and acceptance of inequality" (107) permeates Domingo Soler's works and would constitute the source of her greatest discrepancies with López de Ayala's more radical stance.

Especially significant in France and England, spiritism came under fire not only from official religions but also from positivists, who denied the existence of the soul (Mateo Avilés 1986, 193). Therefore, the claim by many spiritists that spiritism was a positivist religion was a contested one,[5] as Domingo Soler herself reveals in her *Memorias*: "A nosotros nos obliga un deber sagrado a deshacer ese error por todos los medios imaginable diciendo muy alto que no se confunda el Espiritismo con el Empirismo" ([1912] 1990, 140; We are bound by a sacred duty to right that error by all conceivable means by loudly proclaiming that spiritism must not be confused with empiricism). Spiritism, she claims, is "únicamente la práctica del Evangelio" (purely the Gospel in practice) and "la primitiva enseñanza de Cristo" (139; the original teachings of Christ), or what she terms a Christian rationalism (209).

Referring to Marcelino Menéndez Pelayo's *Historia de los heterodoxos españoles*, Mateo Avilés affirms that spiritism entered Spain as early as 1850 through an Englishman, M. Home, and in 1865 the Spanish Spiritist Society was established in Madrid, later to merge in 1871 with the Sociedad Progreso Espiritista (Spiritist Society for Progress). Other spiritist centres, predominantly urban, were set up throughout Spain under the General Centre for Spiritism in Spain. Its members were drawn mainly from the military, liberal professions, and aristocracy, although spiritism also welcomed those of lowlier social extraction (Mateo Avilés 1986, 194–5). Such was the case with Domingo Soler.

Many intellectuals of Republican conviction were also attracted to spiritism. Consequently, as Amelina Correa Ramón underlines, it is not coincidental that the period that saw spiritist societies proliferate in Spain were the years from 1868 until 1875, when radical Republican ideals triumphed in the Glorious Revolution of 1868 and the First Republic (1873–4). The 1875 Restoration stymied but did not suffocate the spread of spiritism. Apart from Madrid, the greatest number of practising spiritists were to be found in Barcelona, a Republican stronghold that had undergone pronounced industrialization. In September 1888 Barcelona hosted the first International Spiritist Conference, while in 1889 the first Spanish Theosophic Society was established there, with maximum influence between 1902 and 1912 (Correa Ramón 2002, 16–19). In short, in Catalonia, Gerard Horta notes, spiritism's periods of greatest strength were those of Republican effervescence: 1868–74, 1880–1902, and 1931–9 (2004, 297).

Likewise, there were deep sympathies between spiritism and freemasonry, as Álvarez Lázaro explains. Proof of their connection was the establishment of spiritist freemasonry lodges, the diffusion of Kardec's works and translations through the lodges, the fact that many freemasons took Kardec's name as their symbolic name, and freemasonry's creation of periodicals and centres for psychological studies. Although it is not known if Domingo Soler became a freemason, her religious tolerance was certainly in keeping with her links with freemasonry. In contact with the Order of the Great Architect of the Universe, she read a poem at the Masonic wake for Ramón Chíes held on 27 November 1893 by the Assembly of Confederated Lodges of Barcelona, at which López de Ayala was also present (Álvarez Lázaro 1985, 189–91).[6]

Domingo Soler's association with spiritism, as she herself indicates, began in Madrid when she read the spiritist periodical *El Criterio* and Kardec's works. She began publishing in *El Criterio* in 1872, as well as in *La Revelación* (Alicante) and *El Espiritismo* (Seville), among many others (Domingo Soler [1912] 1990, 87, 89, 96, 121–2). Assiduously attending the Madrid Spanish Spiritist Society, she officially embraced spiritism on 31 March 1875 (119). Domingo Soler's move to Barcelona in June 1876 was at the invitation of Luis Llach, then president of the spiritist circle La Buena Nueva in the Gracia district of Barcelona (165–6). Three years later, in 1879, she founded *La Luz del Porvenir: Semanario Espiritista*, dedicated to freethinking women.[7] Remaining as editor of and contributor to this periodical for some fifteen years, Domingo Soler there published the writings of many of her freethinking sisters.

In her *Memorias* Domingo Soler refers to the birth of her spiritist weekly (a periodical dedicated exclusively to women and where only women would write), divulging that Llach and the editor Juan Torrents had urged her to create and head "un periódico espiritista dedicado exclusivamente a la mujer, donde no escriban más que mujeres" ([1912] 1990, 203). Torrents, she continues, financed the periodical, while Llach took charge of the marketing and subscriptions (203–4). The polemical nature of the publication is evident in the fact that it was suspended for forty-two weeks because of Domingo Soler's essay "La idea de Dios," published in the first issue on 22 May 1879. Reappearing on 12 June 1879 as *El Eco de la Verdad*, it ran for twenty-six issues before again being closed down due to Cándida Sanz de Castellví's article "Los obreros." When the suspension was lifted by royal decree on 29 November 1879, *La Luz del Porvenir* resurfaced on 11 December, continuing until 1894 (204). In its sixth year, on 23 May 1884, Domingo Soler took over its administration, working out of 9 Cañón Street, first floor, in Gracia, a property that Torrents had legally bestowed on her the previous day.[8]

Appearing on Thursdays and with consecutive pagination, the periodical would regularly lead with an article on a spiritist meeting and its communication with spirits or an essay on some aspect of spiritist philosophy, for which Domingo Soler was the principal contributor. Following the editorial article there would be further essays, poems, short stories, and announcements. One purpose of *La Luz* was to serve as a vehicle for collecting funds for the poor, either from the sale of spiritist books or from donations, mainly from spiritist subscribers. It also placed advertisements for jobs, as in the case of the young widow of Antonio Ras, who wished to use her knowledge of English and French to work as a governess or in a business.[9] Distributed in prisons, *La Luz del Porvenir* was, according to Domingo Soler, acknowledged by inmates as performing a redemptive function, offering them hope and consolation ([1912] 1990, 237–42).

However, the periodical mostly, but not exclusively, published contributions by women, whose articles and poems centred on the importance of reason and secular education in combating Catholic dogma, the role of women in society, and the purpose of spiritism in fashioning a more equitable world.[10] Among its contributors featured Coronado, Pardo Bazán, and Burgos.[11] An especially assiduous columnist from 1885 to 1888 was Acuña, who at times practically co-wrote the periodical with Domingo Soler. From 1889 to 1895 *La Luz del Porvenir* frequently published pieces by López de Ayala, whom Domingo Soler would assist in founding a major feminist organization, the Barcelona Sociedad Autónoma de Mujeres, to be discussed in the following chapter.[12] In *La Luz* there also appeared, especially between 1895 and 1896, poems and essays by Sárraga that bear the influence of her association with spiritist circles through Domingo Soler.[13] Likewise, Domingo Soler contributed to López de Ayala's *El Progreso* and *El Gladiador: Órgano de la "Sociedad Progresiva Femenina,"* and to Sárraga's *La Conciencia Libre.*

The purpose served by contributors as different in political, class, and spiritual affiliations as Acuña and Pardo Bazán was, as Domingo Soler attests on 17 November 1887, twofold: first, to show the periodical's female readers that rationalism had the power to cross class and political divides: "demostrar a nuestras lectoras que el racionalismo filosófico se abre paso en todas las esferas sociales, y que lo mismo las escritoras demócratas, que las aristócratas, comprenden que el culto y el formalismo de la religión católica … ha llegado al grado máximo del ridículo" (to show our female readers that the philosophy of rationalism is making headway in all spheres of society, and that female writers who embrace democracy, as well as those of aristocratic birth, equally understand that Catholicism's rites and formalities … have become ridiculous in the extreme). Second, the aim was to bond all women who work for the cause of civilization (por unir en estrecho lazo a todas las mujeres que trabajan en favor de la civilización).[14] In this sense, Domingo Soler represents a unifying freethinking perspective in her willingness to work alongside women of divergent social backgrounds and political persuasions. In contrast, López de Ayala, as will be discussed in chapter 2, was not so forgiving in her acceptance of writers such as Pardo Bazán and held views different from those of Domingo Soler on the methods by which to effect reform in Spain.

The articles published in *La Luz del Porvenir* on women's role in society offer a telling snapshot of the varying positions adopted by Spanish feminists to argue for women's education and emancipation. Often their writings utilize elements of the normative paradigm for femininity, represented by the Angel in the House, to press for women's greater participation in national life. Some contributors, such as Sanz de Castellví, vindicate the role of educated women as the moral authority in the family, laying equal importance on education and domestic obligations: "La madre digna, ilustrada y pensadora, considerada moralmente, es la primera autoridad de la familia … Los trabajos domésticos e intelectuales, son sin duda dos polos distintos que muchas mujeres desatienden el uno por seguir el otro: … haz, en cambio, que sean siempre los gemelos de tu existencia" (The honourable, educated, and freethinking mother, considered in moral terms, is the highest authority in the family … Domestic and intellectual labours are undoubtedly polar opposites and many women disregard one to pursue the other … nevertheless, ensure that both are always the twin linchpins of your existence).[15]

The tensions produced by seemingly acknowledging sociocultural models while attempting to broker more politically engaged roles for women come to the fore in Domingo Soler's long article from 1884, "Necesidad apremiante," on the need to give Spanish women a secular education because they are the soul of society. Overlaying conservative stereotypes of femininity with a more political discourse, as Sárraga would later do, Domingo Soler states that it is ignorance that prevents knowledge of the duties and rights of citizenship: "*Ignorancia* siempre producirá el mismo efecto, *la esclavitud*, el desconocimiento absoluto de los deberes y de los derechos" (113; *Ignorance* will always produce the same result: *slavery*, the total lack of knowledge of duties and rights). With a nod to convention, she underlines that, as the "ángel del hogar" (Angel in the House), Spanish women exert a powerful influence on the customs and wellbeing of nations: "influye[n] poderosamente en las costumbres y en la prosperidad de las naciones" (114). As the essay progresses, it increasingly links the necessity of educating Spanish women with Spain's desired civilization: "Mientras que la educación y la instrucción de la mujer no sea un hecho, los pueblos serán esclavos de su ignorancia, y España ocupará el último lugar entre las naciones civilizadas" (115; As long as the education and instruction of women are not realities, peoples will be slaves to their ignorance and Spain will be last among civilized nations).[16] Here abolitionist discourse and working-class concerns, captured in the allusion to "esclavos" (slaves) and "pueblos" (peoples), intersect to advocate rights for women.

In a later article that same year, Isabel Peña equates democracy with women's education, affirming that the most advanced nations free women from the "degradante yugo de la ignorancia" (degrading yoke of ignorance). The well-educated woman, she argues, occupies a central position as social actor, as the "protagonista del gran drama social" (191; protagonist of the great social drama) and the "gran obrero de la reforma social" (great worker of social reform). This more progressive role, however, is subsequently contained within the limits of the home, in accordance with woman's prescribed function as the "digna sacerdotisa del hogar" (191; worthy priestess of the home).[17] Like Peña, other female contributors to *La Luz del Porvenir* constantly emphasize the role of reason and rationalist education in women's emancipation, as is apparent in a statement by Rita Arañó y Peydro, also from 1884: "Ayer la mujer que sabía leer y escribir era una bruja, una endemoniada, hoy, es apreciada de todos; el racionalismo la deja libre y le dice: estudia, analiza, compara, y elige lo que más en armonía esté con tu razón" (Just yesterday the woman who could read and write was a witch and possessed by the devil; today she is valued by all; rationalism makes her free and tells her to study, analyse, compare, and choose what is most in keeping with reason).[18]

As in Domingo Soler's above-mentioned essay, Dolores Navas's 1888 "Carta a un amigo" treads a similarly delicate path in proclaiming women's right to equality while simultaneously attempting not to challenge too overtly established models of femininity.[19] The article contests her male interlocutor's belief that women are congenitally inferior to men and his use of theories such as those of phrenologist Franz Joseph Gall (353–4). Intellectual differences between the sexes, Navas insists, stem from differences in education, given that women possess the same faculties as men (355). These forthright statements, however, are tempered by the author's reassurances to her male addressee that women should not participate directly in political life: "No pretendo que la mujer ha de entrar en las corrientes todas de la vida y que ha de concedérsela intervención directa en la marcha del Estado, en los negocios públicos o en las agitadas esferas donde el hombre medita y persigue el mejoramiento y bienestar de las naciones" (355; I do not aspire for women to enter all spheres of life and be granted the right to intervene directly in matters of state, in public affairs, or in the tumultuous arenas where men reflect on and pursue the betterment and well-being of nations). The public sphere, she comfortingly concludes, should be left to men, with women content to wield influence indirectly: "La mujer … jamás usurpará los derechos del hombre. … En el hogar, no se abrogará derechos ni autoridades que no le pertenezcan. En la esfera social y política, ejercerá la influencia indirecta … pero encauzando la acción social por las anchas vías del progreso y la libertad" (356; Women … will never usurp men's rights … In the home they will not abrogate rights or powers that do not belong to them. In social and political spheres women will wield influence indirectly … while channelling social actions through the wide pathways of progress and freedom).

Contrary to Domingo Soler's statement that *La Luz del Porvenir* was not politically oriented,[20] from time to time contributions do deal more explicitly with political issues. One such example is the reproduction of a speech read by Domingo Soler in the Centre of La Alianza, formerly El Círculo del Progreso (The Circle of Progress), and reproduced in *La Luz* on 20 November 1884. There Domingo Soler likens the centre to a large family whose models are the democratic nations of France, Switzerland, and the United States. Social reform, Domingo Soler stresses, begins with individual reform inspired by moral and philosophical ideas; democracy and collective sovereignty are founded on personal sovereignty: "En las sociedades de los obreros y de la clase media, su ideal político es el democratismo, sistema de gobierno en que el pueblo ejerce la soberanía. Para gobernar a los demás, el hombre debe comenzar por saberse dominar a sí mismo" (201; In working-class and middle-class associations the political ideal is democracy, a system of government founded on the sovereignty of the people. To govern others, humankind must begin by knowing how to govern themselves).[21]

In fin-de-siècle Spain, however, exactly which sectors of society were encompassed by the term *pueblo* varied according to the interests of those who wielded it. As Demetrio Castro Alfín explains, at the time,

> the "people" functions to designate something amorphous and anonymous, the combined force of all those who do not possess a clearly defined, autonomous space and social identity after the disappearance of traditional structures and frameworks of identification such as the guilds, or all those who in the new liberal, individualist body remain in a subordinate position, with reduced or eliminated rights … the "people" does not serve to designate social layers or levels of income and education but to refer to all those who share the same political and moral aspirations, precisely those aspirations that set them in opposition to elite groups. (1987, 198–9)[22]

It was through this notion of shared opposition to sociopolitical elites, Castro Alfín continues, that the denomination *pueblo* was not exclusive to workers and marginalized groups but was often extended to intellectuals and liberal professionals, as evident in essays from the mid-nineteenth century onward (1987, 199). This inclusive concept of *pueblo* underlies the relationship of my three middle-class intellectuals with society's disadvantaged.

One of the political events at which Domingo Soler played a significant role was a liberal meeting scheduled for Sunday, 25 August 1895, at the Circo Ecuestre in Catalonia Square and announced in the radical periodical *La Tramontana* on Friday, 23 August. Its objective was to counter reactionary threats to an incipient democracy in Spain, "which are at war with the generous democratic spirit that with so much bloodshed has succeeded in infiltrating the legal system," with a peaceful demonstration ("the energetic but prudent protest of liberals") and organize all freethinking entities in Catalonia in a General Association for

Freethinkers. Among the members of the organizing committee headed by Odón de Buen featured Domingo Soler, López de Ayala, and Sárraga, together with Sárraga's spouse, Emilio Ferrero, Cristóbal Litrán, and the anarchist Josep Llunas, all of whom had already signed the association's manifesto on 18 August.[23] The aims of the association, subsequently reported in *La Luz del Porvenir*, were: "(A) The propaganda and defence of freedom of conscience. (B) The practice of civil acts (weddings, the registering of births, burials), and the promotion of secularism in all acts of life. (C) The defence of persons and interests against religious intolerance. (D) The creation and sustaining of centres for secular education. (E) Mutual financial aid to all members. (F) The practice of acts of charity. (G) The rewarding of meritorious, altruistic acts of solidarity."[24]

The issue of *La Tramontana* published on 30 August 1895 provided a lengthy account of the meeting, which began at 9:30 a.m. The venue was packed to overflowing with some four to five thousand persons. The third speaker was Domingo Soler, who is recorded as urging women to reject Catholicism and embrace freethinking, so that they might make their sons "enlightened men and worthy citizens, useful to the nation and humanity."[25] Her speech, "A las mujeres," was reproduced in full in the issue of *La Luz del Porvenir* on 26 September 1895. There she affirms that women are responsible for the development of freethinking in Catalonia through their influence in the family, which makes them the "dueñas" or rulers of the world (166). By educating their children in secular schools, she insists, mothers make an indispensable contribution to universal regeneration:

> ¡Mujeres! … las que tenéis la luminosa aureola de la maternidad uníos, sí, unid vuestros esfuerzos, trabajad en la organización de los libre pensadores en Cataluña llevando a vuestros hijos a las escuelas laicas, asociaos a la gran obra de la regeneración universal. … ¡Mujeres! de vosotras depende el éxito feliz de esta obra verdaderamente humanitaria. (167)

> (Women! … you who are crowned by the luminous halo of motherhood, unite, yes, combine your efforts, work in the organization of freethinkers in Catalonia by educating your children in secular schools, join in the great work of universal regeneration. … Women! on you depends the successful outcome of this truly humanitarian work.)

The participation of Domingo Soler in such political events and the coverage given to the same in her spiritist periodical should not surprise, given the sympathies of spiritism with anarchism and socialism, and its intersection with Republican values and aspirations. In the late nineteenth century, many writers who embraced utopian causes of a socialist or anarchist bent, such as Victor Hugo, Dostoevsky, and Pío Baroja, also practised spiritism (Correa Ramón 2002, 12–13, 17).

The convergences between spiritism and anarchism have been signalled by Horta, who remarks that, for both movements, their development of social projects was closely tied to paradigms of rupture with the status quo and to denouncing capitalism.[26] Like anarchism, spiritism eschewed the politics of a centralized state, opposed religion in the form of the Catholic Church, embraced civil baptisms, marriages, and burials, and placed huge importance on the secular education of the illiterate masses. Hence all spiritist centres possessed a library, many publications included a section for the contributions of the common people, and spiritist supporters included numerous teachers (Horta 2004, 120–1).

Spiritism and anarchism also found common cause in their anti-militarist ethos and pacifist stance (Sànchez i Ferré 1990, 143). In 1888 spiritists called on anarchists to support the First International Spiritist Conference, at which Domingo Soler was one of the four Catalan vice-presidents (Horta 2004, 229), alongside Llunas. The conference called for the abolition of permanent armies and the peaceful resolution of international conflicts, stating that working-class soldiers were the principal victims of war (Sànchez i Ferré 1990, 142, 217). Domingo Soler and Llunas again participated in the pacifist meeting for international peace and fraternity that took place on 14 April 1889, with representation from England, France, and Italy. Similarly, for an important meeting in Milan in 1889 against tyranny and for peace, Domingo Soler's *La Luz del Porvenir* sent a message of support, one of many from freethinking entities across the full radical political spectrum (Sànchez i Ferré 1990, 142–4). As well as her links with Llunas, Domingo Soler maintained a close friendship with the anarchist leader Claramunt. Indeed, Claramunt was buried in the same niche as Domingo Soler in a civil ceremony at Barcelona's Cementerio Nuevo on 12 April 1931 (Pradas Baena 2006, 93).

Nevertheless, where Domingo Soler differed from an extreme anarchism was in her repudiation of violence, as evident in an exchange of poems with her contemporary Carolina Coronado, published in *La Luz del Porvenir*. In "Los niños," first published in the *Diario de Barcelona* and reproduced in *La Luz*, Coronado expresses her fear of anarchism and the loss of faith in Spain (267–8). Domingo Soler's response, "Los niños del porvenir," informs Coronado that today's children are not incendiaries and calls on Coronado to awaken her reason and abandon traditional ways of thinking:

> ¡Despierta tu razón!
> Despierta Carolina.
> Olvida tradiciones,
> Porque el progreso avanza. (269)

(Awaken your reason! / Awaken Carolina. / Forget traditions, / Because progress advances.)[27]

Spiritism was also perceived as akin to socialism in its objectives, as acknowledged by Sárraga in "Espiritismo y socialismo," an essay published in *La Luz del Porvenir*. There Sárraga calls on socialists to consider spiritists not as mystical fanatics but as twin siblings in search of progress and justice. Socialism and spiritism, she exclaims, are both weapons, albeit different, against the Catholic Church in a freethinking republic: "Vuestro socialismo y lo que nosotros llamamos Espiritismo son dos hermanos gemelos que están llamados a confundirse en el camino del Progreso. ... armas diferentes del mismo ejército" (125–6; Your socialism and what we call spiritism are twin siblings destined to unite on the path of Progress. ... different weapons fighting the same war).[28]

It was precisely as the Industrial Revolution accelerated, Horta stipulates, that spiritism emerged as a popular force to deconstruct liberalism, coming to the fore in a context of tumultuous and swiftly evolving social and political changes (2004, 298). Similarly, *testimonio*, John Beverley remarks, is "a transitional cultural form appropriate to processes of rapid social and historical change" (2004, 61). How this genre, which vindicates what Ranajit Guha calls the "small voice of history" in counterpoint to master narratives (quoted in Beverley 2004, xii), can be fruitfully deployed as a lens through which to examine Domingo Soler's spiritist writings and their accounts of the dispossessed is the issue with which I now engage.

Spiritism as *Testimonio* in Domingo Soler's *Memorias de una mujer*

At first glance, spiritism, Spanish republicanism, and *testimonio* appear to be strange bedfellows. As Linda Maier indicates in her overview of the genre, *testimonio* is nowadays associated with a Third World or resistance literature that emerged in the 1960s, with a special presence in Latin America. Its hybrid texts are voiced by marginalized, oppressed members of society whose challenges to hegemonic powers represent those of their entire community (2004, 3–5). The relationship of *testimonio*, then, to fin-de-siècle spiritism and early Republican aspirations in Spain can seem tenuous, to say the least.

Nevertheless, in etymological terms *testimonio*, as Beverley asserts, signifies an "act of testifying or bearing witness in a legal or religious sense" (2004, 32) – a feature that similarly characterizes spiritist narratives. The links between spirituality and *testimonio* are evident in Mary Chamberlain and Paul Thompson's definition of the latter as "a secular spiritual testimony, telling a life, as a left-wing moral, with the overt intention of raising consciousness" (quoted in Sklodowska 2001, 253). Christian overtones are clearly present in Domingo Soler's *Memorias de una mujer*, which she describes as a history of expiation ([1912] 1990, 28). There she draws frequent comparisons between spiritism and Christ's deeds (e.g., 106–7), and the text is saturated with religious imagery of exile and redemption. Beverley's explanation of what he considers to constitute *testimonio* applies equally well to spiritist works such as Domingo Soler's *Memorias*: "By testimonio I mean a novel or novella-length narrative in book or pamphlet ... told in the first person by a narrator who is also the real protagonist or witness of the events he or she recounts, and whose unit of narration is usually a 'life' or a significant life experience. Testimonio may include, but is not subsumed under, any of the following textual categories ...: autobiography, autobiographical novel, oral history, memoir, confession, diary, interview, eyewitness report, life history, novella-testimonio" (2004, 30–1). Following Raymond Williams, Beverley reminds us that texts with elements of the *testimonio* have historically represented social actors, such as women, children, and the working classes, who were "excluded from authorized representation when it was a question of speaking and writing for themselves rather than being spoken for" (2004, 31).

In this section I explore some of the connections between the premises of spiritism, republicanism, and *testimonio*, drawing on Beverley's theoretical writings on that genre as well as on Linda Brooks's analysis of *testimonio* as a "poetics of performance" (2005). I find Beverley's position especially useful for unpacking the revolutionary potential of Domingo Soler's spiritist writings, influenced as they are by Romantic socialism and utopian philosophies, and concerned with increasing consciousness and action to remedy social inequities. Moreover, the encounters with others that her texts highlight – those who are invisible to society's gaze, whether they be the dead, women, or the down-and-out – are staged events in the sense that Brooks explores, strategically designed to arouse emotional identification and sympathy for transformative sociopolitical purposes. When they are seen as representations or performances, it becomes less relevant to situate Domingo Soler's spiritist writings with respect to their truth value and vital to perceive them in terms of their truth impact. I hence share Brooks's view that "*testimonio is* literature, that it *is* aesthetically determined, and that ... *testimonio*'s performance strategies have always defined it as a genre. Unveiled, these strategies emerge not as subversions of the genre's social message but as vehicles *of* it" (2005, 182).[29]

While all Domingo Soler's writings are dedicated to spreading spiritist thought and freethinking, her works, from essays and autobiography to poems and short stories, give voice to the worlds of poverty and hardship experienced by working-class society. I propose that Domingo Soler's spiritist writings enact the promise of union between intellectual and people symbolized through *testimonio.* As Beverley has affirmed, *testimonio* is instrumental in "defining new paradigms for the relationship between the intelligentsia and popular classes" (2004, 61). Or to restate more clearly, "the relation of narrator and compiler in the production of a testimonio can function as an ideological figure or image of the possibility of union of a radicalized intelligentsia and the poor and working classes of a country. ... testimonio gives voice in literature to a previously 'voiceless,' anonymous, collective, popular-democratic subject, the pueblo or 'people,' but in such a way that the intellectual ... usually of bourgeois or petit bourgeois background, is interpellated as being part of, and dependent on, the 'people' without ... losing his or her identity as an intellectual" (36).

Consequently, far from being an eccentric fad, spiritist writings such as those of Domingo Soler, when viewed through the prism of *testimonio*, become powerful vehicles for authorizing the emergence of Beverley's popular-democratic actor, a more progressive political model, and an empowered form of female subjectivity. In the case of Domingo Soler, I argue, the genre of *testimoni*o applied to spiritism functions in a two-way sense: it allows the dispossessed and illiterate to speak through the medium of a more educated other, and it authorizes the educated – but socially, politically, and economically disempowered – female subject to write in the public sphere, given that her words are, and are not, her own. These processes are particularly highlighted in Domingo Soler's autobiography, *Memorias de una mujer*, which weaves together memoir and spiritist writings to blur distinctions between self and other. First published in episodic form in the late nineteenth century and then posthumously as a volume in 1912, the text was republished in 1990 by a spiritist press.

In *Memorias de una mujer* Domingo Soler's narration of her life history stresses her identification with society's poor. Brought up by a mother abandoned by her husband, Domingo Soler came from an impoverished middle class driven to maintain appearances but without the means to earn a living adequately. This situation was especially applicable to highly educated women like Domingo Soler, who, once orphaned and unable to live from her writing, had to resort to taking in sewing to eke out a living. Even this means of earning a living became unviable because of her deteriorating sight. In order to pay the rent of an attic and eat once a day, she had to pawn her clothes. Near-blindness, she concludes, deprives her of value in society: "La persona que apenas ve es un cero sin valor que al parecer sobra en la suma social" (Domingo Soler [1912] 1990, 61; The person who can barely see is a worthless nobody, apparently redundant in collective society). However, even worse than sightlessness, she maintains, is the social disease of poverty, *"la gran enfermedad de la vida"* (71; *life's great illness*). Domingo Soler's circumstances became so dire that she was forced to depend on charity to eat once a day, just one of hundreds in identical circumstances: "Vi centenares de pobres de todos los aspectos ... Había pobres de todas las condiciones, muchas mujeres humildemente vestidas con su mantilla, que como yo llevaban la muerte en el alma, muchos ancianos con sus raídos gabanes que parecían espectros escapados de sus tumbas" (79; I saw hundreds of poor people of all kinds ... There were poor from all walks of life, many women humbly dressed in their mantillas, who like me bore death in their souls, many elderly in threadbare coats who looked like ghosts who had escaped from their graves). At one point she notes that she could not answer a letter for two years because she did not have enough money for a stamp (116). This brief exposé demonstrates that Domingo Soler not only experienced first-hand many of the existential conditions suffered by the working classes. She also shared with them the exclusion from full citizenship that, as Beverley points out, accompanies the notion of civil society and constitutes the subaltern (2004, 18–19).

The exclusion was not only economic but also sociocultural. The greatest problem, Domingo Soler perceives, was her unmarried state, because women, she explains, need a husband's support: "Para mí, entonces, la mujer tenía perfecta semejanza con la hiedra, tenía que enlazarse a un algo que la sostuviera, si no sus débiles ramas se romperían arrastradas por el suelo" (Domingo Soler [1912] 1990, 35; At that time I believed women to be completely like ivy; they had to cling to something that would sustain them, because otherwise their weak tendrils would break and drag on the ground). Although here Domingo Soler attributes such a need to nature, she immediately proceeds to reconceive the relationship between the sexes in terms of power, stating that the husband is "el árbitro de los destinos" (the arbiter of all fates) and that a single woman incurred social ridicule: "Estaba condenada al ridículo, a ser un juguete en la sociedad" (35; She was condemned to ridicule, to being society's plaything).[30] Another major issue, she signals, is the inadequate education that Catholic women receive, which denies them the rights of progress, reason, and freedom available to men:

> Las mujeres católicas gimen en la triste esclavitud. Para ellas … el ángel del progreso no bate sus alas de oro, para ellas su propia razón es un volcán apagado, para ellas la libertad es un nombre sin valor … Y considerando que las mujeres son las primeras figuras de la Humanidad, porque son las que educan a los hombres del porvenir, es necesario educarlas, instruirlas, conducirlas por la vía del progreso. (225)
>
> (Catholic women moan in the sorrows of slavery. For them … the angel of progress does not beat its golden wings, for them their very reason is an extinct volcano, for them freedom is a noun without meaning … And considering that women are the foremost figures for Humanity, because it is women who educate the men of the future, it is imperative to educate them, instruct them, and guide them on the path of progress.)[31]

Emphasizing the humble nature of her *Memorias* and their anonymity, Domingo Soler requests that the text be seen as representative of a community, "un libro humilde, … *las memorias de una mujer*" (39; a humble book, … *the memoirs of a woman*). Thus countering the excesses of the Romantic construction of the self, she states that her life account is not intended to privilege the individual but to function as an inspiration for a collective body of women, similarly deprived of family, material resources, and health. Domingo Soler's reference to those who suffer as members cut off from the "gran cuerpo social" (37; greater social body) and her affirmation of shared misfortune again align her text with aspects of *testimonio*, which Beverley perceives as expressing a "sense of sisterhood and mutuality in the struggle against a common system of oppression" (2004, 39). As Beverley declares, what *testimonio* does, as "something materialized in the form of a transcript or text," is "bring subaltern voice and experience into civil society and the public sphere" (2004, 19). At the same time, Domingo Soler's representation of herself as spokesperson for an entire underprivileged social body constitutes the deliberate adoption of a persona, an acting out of a part to produce in the reader/listener/spectator a fuller experience of the event to enhance emotional identification, as stipulated by Victor Turner (1991, 101) and developed by Brooks (2005, 190–1). This inclusion of the emotional, over and above the cognitive, was particularly important for not only spiritists but also, as I explore in the last section of this chapter, certain female intellectuals who, for strategic and other reasons, considered it imperative to balance reason with emotion.

Structurally, *Memorias de una mujer* is partially cast as a spiritist text. Although the bulk of it, some 222 pages, was written by Domingo Soler during her lifetime, the 10-page Spiritual Prologue and part 2, comprising 26 pages, were allegedly dictated by Domingo Soler through a medium in 1912, three years after her demise. This representation of sections of the text as dictated from another world, that of the past to the future, its present audience, in the name of a more democratic society, not only fragments the supposedly unified autobiographical subject. It also guarantees the authority of the narrative voice and echoes another principle of *testimonio.* As Beverley affirms, if *testimonio* is to construct "more heterogeneous, diverse, egalitarian and democratic nation-states," it must begin with recognizing "an authority that is not our own, an authority that resides in the voice of others" (2004, 24). There is perhaps no greater authority than one that comes from beyond the grave. By underlining the spiritist features of Domingo Soler's *Memorias*, the narrative also demands that the reader/listener suspend reality. As Brooks states, drawing on Alberto Moreiras (1996), *testimonio* invites the creation of "an interstitial middle ground where Third-World witness and First-World editor participate in an interaction that does not occur in the 'real world' … 'reality' is put in abeyance in this arena, suspended for as long as the *testimonio* process takes" (Brooks 2005, 189). Such liminal, shared spaces, Brooks continues, "pose a threat to established verities, … unhinge cultural stability and change identities" (2005, 190).

In the case of Domingo Soler's *Memorias*, the authority of its narrative voice is established on the opening page: "Bien podía haberlo dejado escrito en la Tierra, pero entonces no hubiera tenido el valor que tendrá ahora para los seres pensadores, escribiéndolo desde las alturas en que mora mi humilde espíritu" ([1912] 1990, 9; I could have written it on earth, but then the text would not have had the value that it will now have for freethinking beings, given that I am writing it from the heights where my humble spirit dwells). In turn, in the first section of the *Memorias*, entitled "Prólogo de una historia," Domingo Soler's continued writing of her life history is authorized by her first love, the deceased Álvarez, who exhorts her to serve as an example to poor women dependent on their own means: "Que des comienzo a escribir tus Memorias porque harás un gran bien a las mujeres pobres, entregadas, abandonadas a sus propias fuerzas" (26; Begin to write your memoirs, because you will do great good to poor women who have given up and who are abandoned and reliant on their own resources). Indeed, it is Álvarez, we are informed at this point, who is dictating to Domingo Soler the prologue: "Yo he querido dictarte el prólogo de tus Memorias. ¿Quién con más legítimo derecho? Nadie" (26; I have wished to dictate to you the prologue of your memoirs. Who has a greater right than I to do so? No one). Likewise, in chapter 2, another spirit, that of Father Germán, the subject of another of Domingo Soler's spiritist texts, *Memorias del Padre Germán* ([1900] 1985), tells her that she must leave her *Memorias* as an inheritance to the poor on earth (42). Thus the authorization of Domingo Soler's voice is constant, reinforcing its authority but also undercutting any notion of an autonomous, self-sufficient narrator, to suggest a collaborative narration. Such storytelling techniques are, as Brooks notes, meta-narrational, because "they guide our attention back to the teller – to her strategies, her purposes, and her directives on how she wants to be understood. Above all, they remind the audience that they're witnessing a performance" (2005, 200).[32]

Considering these framing devices as artistic choices and strategies designed to produce a desired effect allows for an alternative way of engaging with a major issue that clouds *testimonio*: the perceived manipulation of the voice of the other by the more educated writer and the resulting inauthenticity of the *testimonio*.[33] Thus Beverley asks whether *testimonio* is "an authentic subaltern voice, or ... a 'mediated' narrative in which a literary simulacrum of that voice was being staged ... for the reader, whose own position of relative authority and privilege was left uncontested in the process" (2004, xvi). One response, which is the position that I adopt on Domingo Soler's spiritist texts, is that *testimonio* is both, depending on what kind of truth is privileged: an experiential truth directed at solidarity or an allegedly objective, rational, universal truth.[34] Nevertheless, Beverley does consider that *testimonio* manifests "the agency of the subaltern" and that its goal is "not only to interpret the world but also to change it" (2004, xvi). Similarly, Horta maintains that spiritism is "a referential system peculiar to subaltern classes" and based on what he terms a cooperative Republic of work: "[Spiritism] develops according to a horizontal organization that demonstrates more than a desire to participate according to democratic principles and structures. It counters the modernizing model of the market economy to advocate rationalization, understood as the organizing force for the good of society as a whole, 'a cooperative Republic of work'" (2004, 297).

In spiritist writings, and in Domingo Soler's text, the medium is represented as being taken over by spirits and as acting as a passive conduit that allows the stories of the underprivileged to be heard. Such is the case with Eudaldo Pagés, the medium of the Barcelona Centre of La Buena Nueva with which Domingo Soler was associated, and through whom she receives much of the material that she reproduces in her writings. Domingo Soler refers to him as a "médium puramente mecánico, no recuerda jamás ni un solo pensamiento de sus discursos" (Domingo Soler [1912] 1990, 195; purely passive medium who never remembers anything he says) and affirms that she faithfully transcribes what Eudaldo relates, underscoring the truth of her writings: "Siempre en todos mis escritos ha dominado la sencillez de la verdad" (196; In everything that I have written the pure truth has always prevailed). However, undoubtedly in this two-step process the others' voices become doubly displaced, not only by the writer but also by the medium. Furthermore, their testimony is dogged by the ambiguities that Beverley sees as characterizing *testimonio*: a genre of defiance and resistance that is and is not literature, is and is not oral history, is and is not an authentic form of subaltern culture (Beverley 1992, 10). The principle of authenticity is at stake in Domingo Soler's reiterated proclamations that her text is "débil" (weak) and "humilde" (humble) (Domingo Soler [1912] 1990, 31, 39); while such affirmations of inadequate literary expertise of the female writer of the day concur with a normative paradigm of feminine false modesty, they also contribute, as Beverley states with regard to *testimonio*, to "the 'truth effect' the form generates" (2004, 33).

The overwhelming presence of women in spiritism and as mediums, Horta indicates, marks an incongruence between the often important roles that they held within spiritism and their social reality (2004, 250–1). Yet I suggest that spiritism is in keeping with women's culturally sanctioned role as the spiritual repository for society and that their role as medium conformed to society's view of women as passive conduits or vessels for the projects and voices of others. At the same time, I argue, spiritism allowed women to articulate indirectly their concerns behind the mask of another's identity. As mediums, women were granted licence to speak and represent others, and often, as was the case with Domingo Soler, to write, refuting the oppressive norm of feminine silence. Horta makes a similar point when he posits that spiritism offered women the opportunity to vent frustrations disallowed in their sociocultural life. More important still, spiritism gave women a means to express their demands for emancipation and emphasized, more than any other movement in Europe at the time, the importance of women's work in the public sphere and their intellectual production (Horta 2004, 252–3).

Another highly relevant factor that aligns spiritism with *testimonio* in a common quest for a more democratic society is their emphasis on free will. Free will is paramount in spiritist thinking, given that the acts and thoughts chosen in one incarnation determine the nature of the subsequent one. Birth becomes not an accident beyond one's control nor something preordained but an act freely chosen. Hence in her *Memorias* Domingo Soler refers to choosing to be born in Seville: "Llegué por fin a la Tierra, eligiendo la oriental Sevilla" ([1912] 1990, 44; I finally arrived on earth, choosing the oriental Seville). Indeed, the real importance of her text, she maintains, is its stress on the premise that one is arbiter of one's own fate: "De sí mismo depende ser un criminal o el redentor de un mundo" (59; Each determines whether they are a criminal or the saviour of a world). Just as *testimonio* offers the enslaved a discourse of revolution and freedom, spiritism provides Domingo Soler with the means to understand her past histories and free herself from the spiritual slavery of endless reincarnations: "Quiero saber si … me es posible libertarme de la esclavitud" (92; I want to know if … it is possible to free myself from slavery).

Still more suggestive is the indebtedness of spiritist thought to the discourse of equality that sustains democratic citizenship. As Domingo Soler relates, spiritism allows her to think of herself not as "una cosa animada, como llamaba Aristóteles a los esclavos" (an animate thing, as Aristotle called slaves) nor as belonging to "una casta inferior a la raza que habita en los pueblos civilizados" (95; an inferior caste to the race that lives in civilized nations): both definitions traditionally ascribed to women in patriarchal societies. On the contrary, spiritism decrees that Domingo Soler is "un espíritu con los mismos derechos y los mismos deberes que todos los hombres que pueblan la Tierra" (94; a spirit with the same rights and duties as all men who inhabit the earth) and that all are entitled to a voice in universal democracy: "Nadie, absolutamente nadie, podrá usurparnos nuestro puesto en el Congreso Universal" (163; No one, absolutely no one, can take away from us our place in the Universal Congress). Citizenship's discourse of rights and corresponding duties continues to be evident in Domingo Soler's announcement that spiritism provides the means to recover "nuestros perdidos derechos, comenzando por hacernos cumplir nuestros olvidados deberes" (181; our lost rights, beginning by making us fulfil our forgotten responsibilities). The study of spiritism has the power to eliminate castes and social inequalities: "Con el estudio del Espiritismo desaparecen las castas degradadas y los hijos desheredados, lo mismo que las razas privilegiadas y los seres elegidos" (181; With the study of spiritism, denigrated castes and disinherited children will vanish, together with privileged races and chosen beings). In this sense Domingo Soler's *Memorias* enacts the utopian promise of *testimonio* that Beverley specifies: "The subject that speaks in testimonio has a differential relation with the nation and the 'general will' expressed in representative democracy: it is what is not, or not yet, the nation" (2004, 18).

In Domingo Soler's *Memorias de una mujer* the subjects who speak articulate the ideals of democratic nationhood that would take another eighty-odd years to bear lasting fruit in Spain in the late twentieth century. In her text, the tensions that *testimonio* highlights between Third World and First World, colonized and colonizer, see an earlier but analogous manifestation in the social and gendered inequalities present between the privileged and the poor, man and woman, and the struggle between the forces of conservatism and the aspirations of a modern Spain. As an example of *testimonio*, Domingo Soler's *Memorias* demand that the readers/listeners of her testimony breach their cultural and political boundaries in a mutual commitment to a more equitable society and a declaration of universal solidarity. As a spiritist text, it stakes out a particular relationship of its subjects to history – one that gives a voice in the present moment of grounded narration to unacknowledged, buried pasts.

Women as Creative Subjects in Fin-de-Siècle Spain

Although Domingo Soler's *Memorias de una mujer* are couched as the memoirs of a woman and a female spiritist, even more so they chart the development of a female writing subject. The text demonstrates a curious heterogeneity, mixing observations on spiritism with autobiography and diary entries, and inserting throughout many of Domingo Soler's poems in a self-conscious display of talent. As such, it presents itself as an example of the *Künstlerroman* or portrait of the artist, a subgenre of the masculine Bildungsroman that, according to Lokke, counters the latter's traditional sociopolitical conservatism to stress "female artistry and creativity" (2004, 4). These features of Domingo Soler's *Memorias* invite it to be placed in the context of a very recent tradition of female Romantic texts highlighted by Lokke, which reject patriarchal structures to "create feminine and (proto)feminist visions of spiritual and artistic transcendence that constitute a critique of Romanticism from within" (2).

According to Simón Palmer, Domingo Soler composed over two thousand pieces throughout her lifetime (1993, 731). Domingo Soler herself confides that her vocation as a writer began at the age of ten ([1912] 1990, 214). Indeed, she emphasizes her prolific rate of production, which not only underlines her contribution to spiritism but also suggests a culturally inappropriate pride in her literary gifts. Thus in chapter 10 of her *Memorias* she relates that between November 1872 and March 1891 she wrote 1,286 pieces, encompassing poems, conference presentations, and anti-clerical writings (177). Later she reproduces a letter written by José Amigó y Pellicer, editor of Lérida's spiritist periodical *El Buen Sentido*, and published there on 15 November 1880. Saluting Domingo Soler as "the heroine of the new idea," the letter pays tribute to Domingo Soler's remarkable production, published not only in spiritist periodicals in Madrid, Barcelona, Alicante, Seville, and Lérida, but also in Mexico, Mérida de Yucatán, Montevideo, Buenos Aires, and Italy (210). In her response to the letter on 29 June 1881, Domingo Soler specifies that in 1878 she wrote 103 articles, in 1879 127, in 1880 125, and in the first half of 1881 60 (215). Lest this extraordinary creativity on the part of a woman meet with social censure, Domingo Soler represents her writings as fulfilling a culturally sanctioned maternal function in that they comfort those less fortunate, as suggested in her wish not to "dejar a mi numerosa familia huérfana de mis escritos" (261; leave my large family orphaned, without my writings).

Nevertheless, the manner in which Domingo Soler describes how she wrote in her early years as a spiritist lays claim to the masculine Romantic trope of the writer's originality and genius, given that, she states, she produced without dictionaries, grammar treatises, and reference books. She relates how she painstakingly gathered together a library, "lo más querido de la Tierra" (what is most cherished on earth) by using her dinner money to bind loose fascicles into books (122). When in 1876 Domingo Soler moved to Madrid, she complains about having to write under extremely trying conditions because she shared a room with a close female friend and the house with the latter's three children and elderly mother. Anticipating Virginia Woolf's articulated wish decades later, Domingo Soler asks God to enable her to earn enough to afford a room of her own in which to write (153). She again marks out her exceptionality on recounting how, when later that year she leaves Madrid for Barcelona, she is encouraged to write by Llach: seamstresses, he tells her, are a dime a dozen in the city, whereas what are needed are female writers (167).

The acknowledgment that Domingo Soler was breaking gender boundaries while endeavouring to preserve her femininity is intimated in a lengthy political poem by "Una Andaluza" (alias Soledad Areales). Entitled "A mi querida amiga Amalia Domingo Soler," it appeared in issue 2 of *La Luz del Porvenir* on 23 May 1895. The composition opens by portraying Domingo Soler's literary work as a virile voice that enters Areales's sanctuary while simultaneously retaining a sanctioned femininity rooted in tenderness and love:

Viril tu voz a mi retiro llega
y me embriaga con su tierno acento.
¿Qué canto es ese que en el bien se inspira,

que dulcemente se dirige al pueblo
brindándole un amor grande, sublime [?] (13)

(Virile your voice reaches my sanctuary / and enraptures me with its tender tone. / What song is this that is inspired by good, / that sweetly addresses the people / offering them a great, sublime love?)

Here the female writer is cast as appropriating a masculine Romantic discourse to seduce Areales as listener and transport her from the enclosed, individualistic space of the home into a transcendent, collective sphere represented by the "pueblo" as people and nation. This stanza, saturated with Romantic tropes, especially emphasizes those of inspiration and the sublime, alluded to in the phrases "que en el bien se inspira" (that is inspired by good) and "un amor grande, sublime" (a great, sublime love). Both concepts formed part of a Romantic aesthetic biased towards male creators. Inspiration, or, as Fay explains, "the spontaneous quality of artistic production," was attributed largely to male Romantics whose inspiration was traditionally derived from a female muse (1998, 10–11). Similarly, the revolutionary potential of the sublime, a feeling of transcendence founded on awe and associated with the highest degree of creativity, was barred to women because they were thought to function as mere mediums for men's experience of the same (7, 14). Areales's poem refers to Domingo Soler as challenging these discriminatory premises, which work to keep women from participating as creators and political actors. The final stanza again seeks to undo any rigid separation between the private and public spheres. Although the poetic voice situates Domingo Soler within the private sphere of intimate relations, addressing her as "sincera amiga" (sincere friend) and "noble hermana" (noble sister), it also places her in the public arena, proclaiming that she faithfully upholds "los grandes ideales" (great ideals) and "la vanguardia del progreso" (the vanguard of progress) (15).

Domingo Soler's aesthetic ethos is more precisely captured in a compilation of writings entitled *Sus más hermosos escritos*. First published in 1903, and then again in 1907 and 1910, the volume is a curious mix of essays by the author, posthumous biographical sketches of Domingo Soler by fellow spiritists, correspondence between Domingo Soler and other female writers, and letters among female writers reproduced by Domingo Soler. In that sense it ceases to be the amalgamation of an individual's works to become the testimony of a collective female writing subject.

Particularly striking are Domingo Soler's three letters to a young female artist. Entered erroneously in the table of contents as to "un racionalista" (Domingo Soler 1903b, 541; a rationalist), their correct title is "A una joven artista" (To a young female artist). In the first letter, Domingo Soler addresses Sofía, a budding artist whom she has known since childhood, whose need to earn a living through sewing hampers the full expression of her artistic talent. Domingo Soler represents Sofía's creativity, constrained by poverty, according to a Romantic masculine paradigm that likens the imagination to volcanic activity, in what Kirkpatrick (1991, 30) has identified as a Promethean impulse that seeks to fulfil individual male subjectivity within a hostile world: "Tu imaginación volcánica no se aviene con una existencia humilde llena de contrariedades y angustias en el ignorado rincón de tu hogar; ... Has luchado desesperadamente, y al fin has tenido que dejar los pinceles para coser un vestido ... y ocuparte en los medios de satisfacer las imperiosas necesidades de la vida" (Domingo Soler 1903b, 276; Your volcanic imagination does not accord with a humble existence plagued with obstacles and anguish in the forgotten corner of your home; ... You have struggled desperately, and in the end you have had to put down your paintbrushes to sew a dress ... and busy yourself with satisfying the imperious needs of existence).[35] In this reference to the incongruity between Sofía's creativity and her humble existence, Domingo Soler indirectly suggests that Sofía's gifts raise her above her working-class background, which should not limit her aspirations in life. Domingo Soler's avowal of a female creativity equal to that of men is reinforced in her third letter to Sofía, where she refers to Sofía's mind as harbouring the wings of genius and being pure light: "Tienes en tu mente las alas del genio y vives luchando con las apremiantes y tiránicas necesidades de una posición humilde, obscura: ¡vives en la sombra, cuando en tu cerebro todo es luz!" (287; Your mind harbours the wings of genius and you live struggling with the pressing, tyrannical needs that arise from a humble, obscure social position: you live in the dark, while in your intellect all is light!)

In the face of her material obstacles, Sofía considers, according to Domingo Soler, that she can no longer find adequate subject matter to paint (277). However, in what is an advocation of the superiority of realism over and above Romantic topoi, Domingo Soler advises Sofía that there is ample subject matter in life itself and that it is not necessary to paint "deslumbradores paisajes, históricos episodios de matanzas y exterminios, sorprender en su carrera al indómito alazán" (208; dazzling landscapes, historical episodes of killings and exterminations, the galloping, indomitable steed). Consequently, she closes her second letter to Sofía by exhorting her to paint not the monumental history of the elites but the as-yet-unrecorded stories of humanity: "Querida Sofía: la historia de la humanidad, la que no se escribe ni deja tras de sí monumentos, te dará siempre asunto para cuadros de gran efecto. El talento del artista consiste en sorprender esa historia inédita y apoderarse de su secreto" (285–6; Dear Sofía: the history of humanity, that history that is not recorded and does not leave monuments, will always provide you with material for paintings with great impact. The artist's talent consists of capturing this unwritten history by surprise and appropriating its secret). Such a history common to all becomes synonymous with democracy.

Finally, Domingo Soler's third and last letter to Sofía stresses that the essence of great art is the ability to move others and inspire compassion: "Traslada al lienzo el cuadro que te he bosquejado, y mientras no encuentres una palabra más propia, más adecuada para pintar la misteriosa atracción que aproxima a los seres, bautiza tu nueva obra poniéndole por nombre: *¡Simpatía!*" (290; Transfer to the canvas the picture that I have sketched for you, and whilst you cannot find a more personal and appropriate word for painting the mysterious force that brings people closer, baptize your new work giving it the name of *Sympathy!*) This emphasis on empathetic feeling was not only a fundamental premise of spiritism. Sympathy was also an essential element in a Romantic aesthetic that sought to balance reason with emotion. Indeed, Fay notes that "sympathy was the visible outward sign of one's awareness of others and of the community; it was a necessary emotional gift for anyone of refined temperament or sentiment" (1998, 6). As I now develop in the following pages, the virtues of feeling versus reason would constitute a major point of difference among fin-de-siècle female writers and inform their aesthetic and sociopolitical choices.

The debate over the place of feeling and reason in a remodelled femininity is a dominant theme in sixteen letters, accounting for 77 of the 537 pages in *Sus más hermosos escritos*, which Domingo Soler, Acuña, Carmen Piferrer, and Trinidad González exchanged with the mysterious Violeta, the pseudonym adopted by Consuelo Álvarez Pool (1867–1957) in her early writing life.[36] In particular, the letters dispute two epistemological modalities that were pivotal in Romantic thought: one that emphasizes reason and another that claims a privileged place for feeling, love, and the soul. The former position was upheld by Acuña and, like her, López de Ayala, as I discuss in chapter 2; the latter stance was common to writers who embraced more fully the spiritist cause: Domingo Soler, Violeta, Piferrer, and Trinidad González. Consequently, these epistolary exchanges, ostensibly among the most private of genres, delineate publicly the points of union and fracture among freethinking women on their sociocultural positions and political philosophies. They both testify to the writers' commitment to the advancement of women's emancipation through the avenues of freethinking and spiritism and also reveal their extraordinary relationships and close engagement with one another's work.

The ability of the letter to undo culturally created distinctions between the private and public spheres has been well documented by feminist scholars. In particular, Favret highlights how "the letter in Romanticism hints at a correspondence between public and private experience, and that correspondence continually revises – and disrupts – fixed images and narratives. What the individual writes, the masses read; experience is translated from the private to the public domain, and back again" (1993, 9). Literal and emotional correspondence was the necessary accompaniment to friendship, which Favret describes as "not just sympathy and understanding, but a political solidarity based on egalitarian principles ... Produced within this network of radical correspondence was a new sense of 'Union,' 'nation' and 'People'" (28). The context with respect to which Favret makes these observations was that of the numerous radical societies or "friends" for social and political reform that existed in England in the last decade of the eighteenth century, for whom "the letter was an open democratic form, predicated on a belief in negotiation between disparate and multitudinous voices" (33). Nevertheless, Favret's comments can be fruitfully extended to the friendships and correspondence among fin-de-siècle female writers in Spain who also embraced similar ideals. If the circulation of letters among these women ostensibly created a closed circle limited by gender, it must also be remembered that their exchanges were published in freethinking periodicals and circulated openly in the public sphere.

In the first of the series of exchanges, entitled "El amor," which is reproduced in Domingo Soler's text, Violeta writes to the latter addressing her as "Amiga mía" (my friend). In her opening statement, Violeta asks Domingo Soler to allow her to call her "amiga" and to address her familiarly as "tú" (Domingo Soler 1903b, 311). Through this rhetorical strategy Violeta continues the tradition of female Romantic writers, who, as Antonio Manzano Garías remarked, "without knowing one another personally maintained a frequent, affectionate exchange, greeting one another at the beginning and end of their letters with the sweet name of sister" (quoted in Kirkpatrick 1991, 88). There is, however, a subtle difference between these two generations of writers: "hermana" or sister implies a relationship predetermined by birth into a family, whereas "amiga" or friend refers to a freely chosen interaction governed by a reciprocity of feeling and ideas.

Consequently, although Violeta states that she does not know Domingo Soler and it is the first time that she writes to her, she considers that friendships are not formed by time and mutual favours but by "la comunión de sentimientos y de ideas," shared feelings and ideas that constitute a community of like-minded individuals: "Piensas y sientes como yo, y sé que existes; soy, por consiguiente, tu amiga" (Domingo Soler 1903b, 311; You think and feel as I do, and I know that you exist; hence I am your friend). In this sense Violeta's words reflect a practice adopted by female Romantic intellectuals, such as the London Bluestocking Circle a century earlier, who used letters, as Fay argues, to "create a female community of the mind"; moreover, this medium allowed them to "clothe their intellectual community with something that makes it acceptable for women to have such pursuits" (1998, 156).

In her response to Violeta, Domingo Soler opens by addressing her as "mi dulce y poética Violeta" (my sweet, poetic Violeta): an interpellation that frames Violeta within a conventional framework of femininity. Immediately, however, the letter also situates the discourse within the masculine Romantic trope of mystery and quest for identity by requesting Violeta to disclose who she is and where she is from (Domingo Soler 1903b, 317). Taking up Violeta's request that she write about love, Domingo Soler distances love from a strictly private context to remark that the essence of love is spiritism and dedicating oneself to personal and collective progress (320–1). In a second letter, Domingo Soler criticizes women who calculatingly secure their material welfare through an advantageous but loveless marriage, equating them with prostitutes. Nevertheless, these feminist proclamations are contradicted when Domingo Soler describes the ideal woman in terms that recall the self-sacrificing and clinging Angel in the House, as "apasionada, amando siempre, dispuesta al sacrificio, hiedra cariñosa que se enlaza a la vida del hombre" (324–5; passionate, always loving, ready to sacrifice herself, an affectionate ivy that wraps herself around man's life).

Violeta's second letter to Domingo Soler, entitled "Efusiones," begins with the questions concerning her identity that Domingo Soler had asked her. She affirms that it is impossible for her to say who she is because mere matter cannot contain one's essence and soul: "¡Quién soy! No lo sé, Amalia, porque los nombres no son las esencias; porque la flor no es el aroma; porque los perfiles y contornos del rostro no son el alma" (340; Who am I! I don't know, Amalia, because names are not essences; because the flower is not its scent; because the profiles and contours of faces are not the soul). With this declaration Violeta rejects being defined by linguistic form and her female body, once again suggesting that her identity exceeds predetermined moulds. Summarizing her beliefs, she explains how she became a feminist and freethinker, refusing to be enslaved by the doctrines of Catholicism: "Y de rebeldía en rebeldía, porque yo no había nacido para esclava, llegué a romper la infamante argolla que oprimía mi cerviz, y volví la espalda al dogma" (341; And from one rebellion to another, because I was not born to be a slave, I succeeded in breaking the infamous shackles that oppressed my intellect and womb, and I turned my back on Catholic dogmas). Instead of seeking guidance from the Catholic Church, Violeta places her faith in empiricism by trusting her senses, her reason, and, above all, her feelings (341).

Conversely, Violeta sardonically criticizes those male freethinkers, "los grandes hombres del racionalismo, los titanes del librepensamiento … los mesías de la libertad y de la dignidad humanas" (the great men of rationalism, the titans of freethinking ... the messiahs of freedom and human dignity), who equate freedom of thought with pure positivism and disregard feelings and faith: "En el vocabulario librepensador moderno, contemporáneo, libertad de pensar significa obligación de no creer" (342; In the vocabulary of the modern, contemporary freethinker the freedom to think is synonymous with the obligation not to believe). Violeta therefore counterposes a masculine freethinking founded on positivism and reason with a feminine freethinking that claims the supremacy of feeling. Such a vision, she affirms, is also shared by Domingo Soler: "Pero tú crees y esperas, como yo creo y espero. ... Tenemos señalado nuestro sitio entre los corazones que sienten" (343; But you believe and hope, as I also do. ... We have our place assured among those hearts that feel).

Violeta's vindication of feeling as a necessary companion to reason similarly informs her enthusiastic appraisal of a letter by Acuña published in *Las Dominicales del Libre Pensamiento*. Describing the letter as the "primera página de nuestro éxodo, primer capítulo de la dignificación de la mujer por la mujer, y de su emancipación de un dogma absurdo" (Domingo Soler 1903b, 344; first page of our emancipation, the first chapter in the dignifying of women by women, and their emancipation from absurd dogmas), Violeta nevertheless questions whether Acuña's work can forge a new temple for women's emancipation capable of housing not only reason but also the soul:

> Yo ya sé que su elocuentísima palabra será un formidable piquete para derribar el viejo templo de las supersticiones católicas; pero, ¿servirá para labrar el nuevo templo, donde en lo porvenir, el alma, segura de su inmortalidad y de su progreso eterno, adore al Dios que tan dulcemente canta Rosario de Acuña en el número 110 de *Las Dominicales*? (346)

> (I already know that your eminently eloquent words will be a formidable weapon in bringing down the old temple of Catholic superstition; but will it suffice to forge the new temple where in the future the soul, sure of its immortality and eternal progress, may adore the God that Rosario de Acuña so sweetly praises in issue 110 of *Las Dominicales*?)

Acuña's response to Violeta is given indirectly in "Una carta a Amalia Domingo Soler," which opens with Acuña addressing Domingo Soler as "estimada amiga" (353; esteemed friend). Defending herself from Violeta's charge that she does not reveal what she stands for, Acuña affirms her independence of thought and her respect for diverging opinions:

> ¿Por qué se me acosa ... para que me aliste bajo una bandera, profese en una doctrina, o fundamente una secta? ... Y yo contesto: *Librepensadora respetuosísima con el*

> *pensamiento ajeno, siempre que se encauce en la gran corriente de la vida que lleva por nombre este lema inconmovible*: "AMA A TUS SEMEJANTES." (354, 356)

> (Why am I hounded ... to enlist under a banner, profess a doctrine, or found a sect? ... My response is as follows: *I am a freethinker highly respectful of the beliefs of others, provided that they swell the great river of life that bears as its unfaltering motto*: "LOVE THY NEIGHBOUR.")

Stating that the present is unable to resolve the great problem that it faces, Acuña proclaims that the mission of fellow freethinkers is to demolish old sociopolitical structures and leave any rebuilding to future generations: "Lo que se impone entre nosotros, aunque sea triste, es la demolición, bien que tengamos que caer envueltos entre las ruinas; no usurpemos las misiones del porvenir, y derribemos" (356; What is most necessary for us to do is to destroy, even if it seems sad or we have to die enshrouded in the ruins; let's not usurp the mission of the future and let's demolish). Bringing down obsolete orders, Acuña continues, is especially important for women, who aspire to representative power in society and equal rights as one half of the human race:

> Todas ellas tienen *hambre y sed* de justicia; ... de poder representativo en el seno de las sociedades humanas. ... Hay que gritar muy fuerte para que esas almas femeninas comiencen a levantarse sobre sí propias, ... contra toda tiranía y toda absorción, y todo vejamen, y toda violencia que denigre sus incuestionables derechos de *mitad de la especie humana.* (358)

> (All women are *hungry and thirsty* for justice: ... for representative power in the bosom of human society. ... We need to shout very loudly for those feminine souls to begin to rise up of their own accord, ... against all tyranny and assimilation, against every humiliation and act of violence that deprives them of their unquestionable rights as *one half of the human species.*)

Acuña therefore calls on all women to unite, irrespective of their differences of belief, under the banner of revolutionary freethinking:

> Unámonos, llevando cada uno sus ilusiones, sus esperanzas y sus creencias, bajo la bandera del librepensamiento, y sin poner en pugna o en subasta nuestras conciencias, peleemos con denuedo, del mismo modo que los ejércitos de diferentes naciones, coligados contra un tirano o un usurpador, pelean reunidos. (359)

> (Let's unite under the banner of freethinking, bringing each and every one of us her dreams, hopes, and beliefs, and, without entering into clashes of conscience or selling

out on beliefs, let's fight courageously, in the same way that armies from different nations, allied against a tyrant or usurper, fight together.)

Domingo Soler's response to Acuña, entitled "Una gran sorpresa," follows immediately. Addressing Acuña as "señora y dulce amiga Rosario" (Madam and sweet friend Rosario), Domingo Soler proceeds to establish fundamental similarities and differences between her and Acuña's positions. Common to both, Domingo Soler affirms, is the belief that women are the most essential element in the moral progress of human societies, as a result of their influence over their children's education. Nevertheless, where she and fellow spiritists diverge from Acuña, Domingo Soler continues, is in their resistance to the total destruction of belief systems. Whatever is destroyed, she insists, must be replaced by ideals capable of sustaining the individual, the family, and society: "El que ingenuamente imagina que le es lícito arrancar unas creencias, cualesquiera que sean, sin substituirlas con otras, sean también las que fueran, se halla en gravísimo error; la substitución es ineludible, es sacratísima obligación" (363; Whoever ingenuously imagines that it is permissible to tear out certain beliefs, whatever they are, without sowing others in their place, whatever they may be, commits a grave error; replacing is unavoidable, it is a sacred obligation). Distancing herself from Acuña through the use of the formal "usted," in contrast to the familiar "tú" that she employs with Violeta, Domingo Soler stresses that this point constitutes the major difference between their respective stances: "Respecto de este particular, amiga Rosario, yo no puedo menos de declarar a usted que me hallo, con hondo sentimiento, en diametral oposición con cuanto dice respecto del fuero interno" (363–4; With regard to this matter, friend Rosario, I must tell you that I am, with deep regret, diametrically opposed to your statements on personal conscience). What is at stake, as Domingo Soler indicates, is an issue of personal sovereignty or "fuero interno."

Violeta returns to the debate with a letter entitled "A la eminente escritora Rosario de Acuña," the intention of which is to respond "de una manera digna a las benévolas alusiones de Rosario de Acuña y a la cariñosa excitación de Amalia, mi amiga del alma" (366; in a dignified manner to the kind comments of Rosario de Acuña and to the affectionate, spirited defence of Amalia, my kindred spirit). Violeta begins by proclaiming herself unworthy of Acuña's flattering evaluation of her writings, which she declares, in an avowal of false modesty, to be "obscuros trabajos" (366; humble works). She states that, as a grieving widow dedicated now for some years to the care of her son, she lacks the "gimnasia especial" (specialized mental agility) developed through suitable readings and opportunities to write to engage appropriately with Acuña's thought (367). It was this kind of self-effacing argument that had made the letter such a preferred medium for female Romantic writers, given that it was supposedly more an expression of emotion than reason and hence less reliant on the type of education, necessary for intellectual debate, that was generally proscribed to women (Fay 1998, 150). Nevertheless, Violeta's following rhetorical question repositions the discussion firmly within an intellectual terrain: for whom is Acuña's work intended? Her answer is that Acuña writes for women and for their emancipation. She is not just another freethinker, but a female freethinker whose writings are exemplary weapons of liberation for other women: "una *mujer* librepensadora, que ha dejado de ser sierva, y que armada de un talento clarísimo y de una elocuencia de fuego, viene a esgrimir estas armas contra la feroz tiranía, material y moral, de que la mujer es víctima" (Domingo Soler 1903b, 368; a freethinking *woman* who is no longer a slave, and who, armed with unquestionable talent and a fiery eloquence, wields these weapons against the ferocious material and moral tyranny of which women are victims).

However, Violeta exclaims, to pretend to win women to the freethinking cause without offering them anything that might satisfy their conscience and hopes, reveals ignorance of women's nature and needs (368). Using language that clearly foreshadows the late twentieth-century feminism of difference, Violeta maintains that women need reason to be allied with feeling – "una fe racional que llene su corazón" (369) – given that love allegedly constitutes the essence of woman's natural being: "Amar y dar la vida por los seres amados es ley moral de nuestra naturaleza femenina" (368; To love and give our lives for those whom we love is the moral law of our feminine nature). Criticizing Acuña for not explaining what she believes in when asked, Violeta states that freethinking requires the full disclosure of one's convictions; for Acuña to act otherwise is to be a freethinker by halves and to lose credibility among her sister writers: "No será librepensadora sino a medias, en menoscabo de la santa libertad de conciencia, y tanto peor para nosotras, que no podremos contar con su valiosa pluma" (372; You will only be a freethinker by halves, to the detriment of the holy freedom of conscience, which will be so much the worse for us, because we will not be able to count on your valuable pen). Allying herself with Domingo Soler, Violeta affirms that, when it comes to the revolution of freethinking, the best way to destroy what is obsolete is to revolutionize systems of ideas by reconstructing them: "Precisamente en la gran revolución de las ideas, de ninguna manera se demuele tan aprisa como edificando. … su fin [del librepensamiento] es demoler construyendo, negar afirmando" (373; Precisely when it comes to the great revolution of ideas, there is no more rapid way to demolish than to build. … the aim [of freethinking] is to destroy by constructing, to negate by affirming).[37]

Just one article later, Domingo Soler responds to Violeta's letter to Acuña with another entitled "Intimidades." There she addresses Violeta as "amiga mía"

(382; my friend), as "querida Violeta" (383; dear Violeta), and as "¡hermosa, modestísima Violeta[!]" (384; beautiful and most modest Violeta!) After praising Acuña's response to Violeta and recognizing that, thanks to her efforts, in the twentieth century women will be subjects, not objects (382; en el siglo XX, las mujeres españolas no serían *cosas*, serían mujeres), Domingo Soler warmly congratulates Violeta on her own "soberbia contestación" (superb response) and exhorts her to write, because women need to read her work (383). With shades of the rivalry endemic in masculine Romanticism, Domingo Soler states that Violeta has demolished Acuña's most established ideas with a logic steeped in humanity: "¡Cómo has triturado los más rotundos conceptos de la gran pensadora Rosario con tu lógica profundamente humana!" (384). Indeed, Domingo Soler closes by saluting Violeta as the greatest defender of spiritist women and their cause: "El Espiritismo tiene en sí la más simpática defensora de todas nosotras. Con sólo unos pocos artículos escritos por tu pluma encantadora, te has puesto a la cabeza de nuestra legión femenina" (385; Of all of us, spiritism has in you its most compassionate defender. With only a few articles written by your enchanting pen, you have gone to the forefront of our legion of women).

The following essay takes the form of a letter to Violeta, "A la adorable Violeta," from Trinidad González, who opens by addressing Violeta as "querida mía" (my dear) and repeatedly calling her "¡hermana mía!" (my sister!) because they are both widows (386). Remarking that she has read the letters that Violeta has exchanged with Domingo Soler, "nuestra maestra en el sentimiento" (our teacher of empathy), with Acuña, "la gran escritora que a todos nos admira por su valentía" (the great writer whom we all admire for her courage), and with Piferrer, "ilustrada hermana en creencias" (our enlightened sister in beliefs), González explicitly refers to these writings as a "torneo de inteligencias," employing a phrase that recalls the masculine Romantic paradigm of a jousting of intelligences. As Ross explains, this notion constituted "chivalric jousting transformed to meet the conditions of a social system in which power manifests itself no longer in physical strength but in the strength of various kinds of cognitive and metaphorical exchanges" (1988, 31). Such a shift from physical to mental prowess, I maintain, undoubtedly gave greater validation to intellectual women who desired to participate more fully in cultural and political spheres. However, whereas the reconfigured masculine model remains governed by the premise of power over one's rivals (31), in González's account this "jousting" among female writers stresses cooperation through the motif of the "concierto," which unites in harmony different spirits and emotions in a common enterprise of female emancipation: "concierto mágico de espíritus en rivalidad emocional y conmovedora" (Domingo Soler 1903b, 387; a magical harmony of spirits in a moving, touching rivalry).

Consequently, like Domingo Soler previously, González exhorts Violeta to write, describing her and her literary sisters as figurative soldiers who will destroy religious superstition (388).

The next letter that Domingo Soler reproduces is to Violeta from Piferrer. Entitled "¿Cómo te llamas?," Piferrer's letter turns on that exact question, in a tone that is striking for its refreshingly warm familiarity: "Perdóname, hermosa flor, y no te extrañe que te tutee, pues yo tengo por costumbre llamar a las flores con mucha franqueza" (389; Forgive me, beautiful flower, and don't be surprised at my familiar address, because I usually talk to flowers with great informality). Her allusion to Violeta as a beautiful flower, picking up on Álvarez Pool's adopted pseudonym, both recognizes and contradicts a conservative model of femininity that commonly used flowers to symbolize women as silent, erotic objects of male desire (see Kirkpatrick 1991, 202). Here Piferrer, by interpellating Violeta, grants her a subjectivity denied by her pseudonym, which denotes the retiring violet that hides its head under its leaves. Thus Piferrer's use of the flower functions in a manner similar to how Coronado reworked flower imagery in her poetry. As Kirkpatrick points out, Coronado made flowers convey images of women as subjects and established a shared intimacy between the poetic voice and the flower indicative of female solidarity (205).

The Romantic feminine ideal of women's enclosure in the home and invisibility in the public sphere is countermanded when Piferrer affirms that she likes to see Violeta's name in the newspapers. Protesting against Violeta's long silence, Piferrer confesses that both she and Domingo Soler have unsuccessfully asked the editor of Lérida's spiritist periodical, *El Buen Sentido*, where Violeta publishes, to tell them her name (Domingo Soler 1903b, 389). Piferrer informs Violeta that her writings have bewitched Domingo Soler, who feels for her an "inmenso cariño" (390; immense affection), and states that her own affection for Violeta is equally strong: "Pero yo no le cedo un punto en eso de quererte. Te nos has entrado en nuestro corazón como Pedro por su casa" (390; But my love for you is no less. You have entered our hearts as if you have always lived there). While Piferrer congratulates Violeta on her erudite response to Acuña, she reminds her that she cannot criticize Acuña for not revealing her beliefs, because Acuña has stated what she does not believe in without concealing her real name (391). Piferrer therefore exhorts Violeta to abandon her pseudonym and anonymity, and reveal her true identity (391). In short, she asks her to come out from behind the mask of her pseudonym and assume more openly her sociopolitical persona.[38] In this sense the masking of identity that habitually accompanies male Romantic heroes is eschewed, given that for women their hiding of identity is an unwelcome result of patriarchal restrictions and their fear of public condemnation for challenging them.

Three pages later comes Violeta's contestation, in the form of an essay, "La mujer y el librepensamiento," which opens with an exhortation to her young son to sleep so that she can write (395). Drawing on the rhetoric of honour commonly associated with male writers, Violeta notes that she writes to settle a debt of gratitude and honour with Piferrer, González, Bernabé Morera, and Domingo Soler, who have all encouraged her in her literary undertakings. Violeta states that she considers it a matter of glory that her writings circulate with theirs, because they are heroines and female knights who fearlessly enter the arena of combat for the cause of freethinking and women's emancipation. The victory of spiritism, she maintains, will grant women equal and legitimate ownership with men of the home and the world: "La mujer ... entrará por virtud propia en legítima posesión, a la par del hombre, del señorío de hogar y del señorío del mundo" (397; Through their own abilities women will, in equal measure with men, come into rightful ownership of the home and the world). Here Violeta's statement clearly demonstrates how freethinking feminists sought to expand their agency and rights beyond the domestic space and into the public sphere under the aegis of shared rights, regardless of gender. The triumph of freethinking and spiritism, she continues, will give women dignity, and the late nineteenth century will be great, not only for its democratic ideals and political victories but also because women will have attained equality with men (398–9).

The continuation of this exchange comes some one hundred pages later, towards the end of Domingo Soler's *Sus más hermosos escritos*, in the form of two letters: one from Violeta to Piferrer and a second, Piferrer's response. The first, "De Violeta a Carmen Piferrer," is prefaced by a short statement from Domingo Soler, who declares that she is copying Violeta's letter, which has made an unforgettable impression on her (507). Violeta excuses herself from revealing her name, stating that to write for a public requires a tranquillity of spirit, a deployment of logical argument, and a strength to fight that she lacks: "El que escribe para el público necesita poseer una tranquilidad de espíritu de que yo absolutamente carezco. Escribir es oponer doctrinas a doctrinas, principios a principios, hipótesis a hipótesis ... Escribir es luchar, siempre, sin treguas ... Yo no tengo resolución ni fuerzas para luchar: bastante hago con vivir" (508–9; To write for the public requires a tranquillity of spirit that I totally lack. To write is to oppose doctrines with doctrines, principles with principles, hypotheses with hypotheses ... To write is to fight, continually, without respite ... I do not have the determination or strength to fight: to live takes all my strength). Overcome by her widow's grief, Violeta asks what good it can possibly do to know her real name if her works are not going to be read (509). Anonymity, she confesses, allows her to reveal her most intimate soul in a way that would be impossible should she not be shielded by a pseudonym, likened to the veil that screens a woman's face from the outside world: "Mis melancólicas efusiones … dejarían de ser lo que son, derramientos del alma … confianzas íntimas, desde el momento que dejase caer el velo que oculta mi rostro a las miradas del mundo" (510; My melancholy outpourings … would cease to be what they are, expressions of the soul … intimate confidences, as soon as I let fall the veil that hides my face from the world's eyes).

In summary, Violeta affirms that her decision not to reveal her identity has been taken as a result of careful meditation and discussion, and has been influenced not only by considerations of personality but also by inescapable, external moral circumstances (510). She closes by informing "Carmen y Amalia, excelentes amigas mías" (Carmen and Amalia, my wonderful friends), that her column in *El Buen Sentido* is like oxygen to her soul; they therefore would not want her to renounce her writing, the only means of enjoyment and recreation, in the dual sense of that word, that she has (510).

It is clear, then, that the adoption of a pseudonym permitted writers like Consuelo Álvarez Pool to cross into the public sphere while still maintaining privacy. It allowed its bearer to create a tactical fiction that both exploited feminine conventions and enabled a performance, explicit in the donning of a forbidden rhetorical dress and the expression of censurable sentiments. The pseudonym, together with the letter, gave Violeta what Favret has elsewhere referred to "ideological drapery" (1993, 11), which concealed ambitions not authorized by hegemonic society.

Subsequent to Violeta's letter, Domingo Soler declares that she has asked Piferrer to respond, feeling too overcome to do so herself (Domingo Soler 1903b, 510). Piferrer opens by apologizing for her and Domingo Soler's indiscreet questioning and declares that Violeta has already revealed herself in her writings as the ideal modern woman, because she represents what is greatest about woman, "su amor de esposa y madre" (511–12; her love as a wife and mother). Having positioned Violeta within a normative femininity equated with the roles of wife and mother, Piferrer proceeds to acknowledge female writers as recklessly courageous, because they must contend with the discrimination of men: "Estoy además bien persuadida que la mujer que … se atreve a escribir, ejecuta un acto de temerario valor, pues los hombres que saben mostrarse indulgentes con las faltas de ciertos escritores de dudoso mérito, son siempre severos hasta la injusticia para con las mujeres que escriben" (514; I am, moreover, absolutely convinced that the woman who … dares write commits an act of reckless courage, because those men who show indulgence towards the failings of certain male authors of dubious merit are invariably severe, to the extent of being unjust, towards female writers). Although she describes her own writing skills as inadequate (514), Piferrer states that she will never cease to write for the causes of freethinking and women's emancipation; she exhorts Violeta to do the same, because she has the ability to make women conscious of their subjection when her fellow writers may fail: "En cuanto a nuestros *animosos llamamientos*, es más que probable que con ellos no consigamos sino exasperar a las esclavas que duermen perezosamente acariciando sus propias cadenas. Tú lograrás, sin duda, despertarlas de su indolente sueño, si quisieras escribir con ese objeto" (515; As far as our *spirited calls* are concerned, it is more than likely that they will not accomplish more than exasperate the slaves who slothfully sleep fondling their own chains. Undoubtedly you will succeed in awakening them from their indolent sleep, should you wish to write for this purpose). Consequently, Piferrer again exhorts Violeta to write, even if she considers it necessary to continue to do so under her pseudonym: "Calla tu nombre, amiga mía, puesto que juzgas necesario callarlo; pero escribe" (515; Keep your name to yourself, my friend, since you consider this necessary, but write).

After Piferrer's letter, Domingo Soler provides closing remarks that refer to the continuation of her and Piferrer's personal correspondence with Violeta, informed by a "sentido fraternal, íntimo, amoroso" (515; sisterly, intimate, and loving sentiment). As a whole, the letters in Domingo Soler's volume speak of the writers' complex negotiation with conventional models of femininity, their questioning and adaptation of Romantic tropes of masculine creativity, and their determination to fashion viable models of female subjectivity that would not require their assimilation into a dominant masculinity. Reflecting these premises, the last pages indirectly advocate women's full participation in the public sphere and political life. Domingo Soler proclaims that Violeta finally relinquished her pseudonym after writing a column for women for a leading Madrid Republican newspaper. Although Violeta's advocacy of spiritism, Domingo Soler states, was swallowed up by politics and popularity, she remained faithful to the spiritist cause (515–16).[39] As for Piferrer, Domingo Soler writes that she went on to give political speeches at large Republican gatherings, receiving the applause of Castelar at a political meeting in Lérida (516). These are the memories, Domingo Soler declares, of her "amigas que no olvidaré nunca, y siéntome orgullosa de haber confraternizado con ellas" (515; friends whom I will never forget and I feel proud of having had them as sisters).

Domingo Soler's *La Luz del Porvenir*, *Memorias de una mujer*, and *Sus más hermosos escritos* constitute powerful crucibles for Spanish fin-de-siècle freethinking and feminism. These works combat religious superstition and ignorance, lobby for the causes of the dispossessed, and provide a forum for female writers who sought to appropriate and redefine misogynist masculine paradigms of creativity and conduct. The sociopolitical content of Domingo Soler's writings is intensified to an inordinate degree in the writings of a younger generation of more radical writers that she mentored, of whom López de Ayala and Sárraga are representative.

In the production of López de Ayala, to whom the next two chapters are dedicated, gender and class inequalities and sociopolitical issues are constantly foregrounded. With her intense political activity, political press, and campaigning for women's and working-class rights, she stands for a new breed of Spanish women unafraid to challenge gender stereotypes and enter the rough and tumble of the public sphere.

VIDA MASÓNICA

COLUMNA DE HONOR DE MASONAS ESPAÑOLAS

Doña Angeles López de Ayala

Lámina núm. 3.

2.1 Portrait of Ángeles López de Ayala. *Vida Masónica: Columna de Honor de Masonas Españolas* 1, no. 4 (June 1926): 4. By kind permission of Spain's Ministerio de Educación, Cultura y Deporte, Centro Documental de la Memoria Histórica (M64)

2 Towards the Republic through (R)evolution: Ángeles López de Ayala (1856–1926)

¿Que de indiferencia llena
en nieve la llaga anego?
No, Amalia; ¡le arrojo fuego
para cortar la gangrena!

(You say that, completely uncaring, / I steep the wound in snow? / No, Amalia; I cauterize it with fire / to stop the gangrene!)[1]

Creo en el Dios Pueblo, todo poderoso, criador de las grandes revoluciones. Creo en el Cristo la Justicia, su única hija, que padeció debajo del poder del Poncio Pilatos de la restauración borbónica; … Creo en la resurrección de la República española. Creo en la vida espléndida de la libertad y del progreso.

(I believe in the God of the people, almighty and maker of great revolutions. I believe in Christ Justice, his only daughter, who suffered under the Pontias Pilate of the Bourbon Restoration; … I believe in the resurrection of the Spanish Republic. I believe in the glorious life of liberty and progress.)[2]

Of the three women who feature in this project, Ángeles López de Ayala was arguably the most significant in freethinking and feminist circles from the mid-1880s until her death in 1926. In this first of two chapters, I chart her life, her activism, and her sociopolitical thought, drawing this information in part from the few studies that exist but more especially, from freethinking periodicals of the day that allow a more complete picture of this remarkable woman and writer to emerge. The emphasis in my discussion here will be placed on her political and feminist activities and writings, which constantly challenged women's prescribed roles and spheres. In the second of the two chapters on López de Ayala, I engage with her more substantial pieces that have survived the ravages of time but that remain, apart from their titles, unknown by scholars and invisible in literary histories. My analysis of her life and corpus seeks to contribute to the recognition of the full import of this figure for the histories of Spanish freethinking, republicanism, and feminism.

A Political Life

Details on López de Ayala's life and publishing trajectory are patchy and dispersed, with many discrepancies in the few existing studies. Born in Seville in 1856 into the upper middle class,[3] and niece of the prolific Sevillan dramatist Adelardo López de Ayala (1828–79), López de Ayala began her literary career in 1880 with a play, *Lo que conviene a un marido*, performed at the Duque theatre in Seville (Méndez Bejarano 1922, 388). It was reportedly followed a year later by her novel *El triunfo de la virtud*, jointly awarded second prize in a literary competition held in Seville in 1881 to commemorate the second centenary of Calderón de la Barca's death.[4]

That same year, López de Ayala married her first husband, Francisco Valero de la Peña, whom she had met in freethinking circles, and with whom she moved to Madrid. A series of literary works followed in rapid succession: a second novel, unlocated, entitled *Los terremotos de Andalucía o Justicia de Dios* (ca. 1886);[5] *Cuentos y cantares para los niños* (1888); her drama *De tal siembra, tal cosecha* (1889); a third novel, *El abismo*, serialized from 5 December 1896 onward in her periodical *El Progreso*; a fourth novel, *Justicia* (1897), which has also vanished; a third play, unlocated, *Un español del siglo XV* (1897) on the subject of Don Gonzalo of Córdoba;[6] a collection of articles from her regular column in *Las Dominicales del Librepensamiento*, reportedly published in 1899 under the title *Absurdos sociales*; and a ninety-six-page pedagogical short novel, *Primitivo*, intended for students of secular schools and published in serial form in *El Gladiador* between 23 June 1906 and 30 November 1907. Of this substantial production, the only works that to my knowledge have been preserved are *Cuentos y cantares para los niños*, *De tal siembra, tal cosecha*, *El abismo*, albeit incomplete, and *Primitivo*.

Nevertheless, the plot of *De tal siembra, tal cosecha* reveals interesting parallels with the domestic marriage plot of the anonymous novella *María o el triunfo de la virtud*, held in Spain's National Library, suggesting that this latter work may be López de Ayala's disappeared novel from 1881.[7] Distinctive features of this novella are its setting in an unspecified Andalusian city that may be Seville, as well as in Madrid and Barcelona – both centres in which López de Ayala would later live – its use of pairs of characters as foils – as in *De tal siembra* and *El abismo* – the presence of an aristocratic anti-hero, Rodolfo, whose role distinctly resembles that of Carlos in *De tal siembra*, and its theme of virtuous courtship and marriage, which would reflect López de Ayala's imminent marriage in 1881 to her first husband. Aspects that work against López de Ayala as the novella's author are first, its tacit defence of the Catholic Church (although her later anticlericalism is not a theme either in *De tal siembra*); second, its anonymity, given that López de Ayala always used her own name as author; third, Simón Palmer's statement that the novel consisted of four volumes (1991, 392); and fourth, the fact that the National Library's copy was printed in Córdoba in 1904 (although this town was associated with Sárraga's *La Conciencia Libre* from 1902). However, it is tempting to see *De tal siembra, tal cosecha* as a reworked and more sophisticated version of this extant novella.

In addition to having written the known texts, López de Ayala was the author of hundreds of political essays, of which I have found 220, as well as poems and short stories, published in the many radical periodicals where she maintained an indomitable presence over a period of some thirty-five years. That these works constitute but a minimal part of López de Ayala's literary production is attested to in an article published on 28 May 1921. There López de Ayala refers to her forty years of struggle on behalf of the freethinking cause: "Cuarenta años de lucha bajo todos los aspectos que puede luchar el ser humano, descartando el de la indignidad. Lucha enérgica y enconada, por medio de la pluma, en más de treinta periódicos y en catorce novelas; por medio de la palabra hablada y por medio de las obras" (Forty years of contending with all possible odds, except indignity. A bitter, strenuous struggle waged by the pen in more than thirty periodicals and fourteen novels, and through all that I have said and written). She underlined the hardships associated with her undertaking, such as financial difficulties, censorship, political persecution, and gender discrimination, on which I will touch shortly:

> Y esto, sin que me arredrara la falta de recursos económicos, ni las censuras que, por distintos conceptos, amigos o adversarios me prodigaban, ni las persecuciones que furiosamente desalaban mi ideal político y librepensador, proporcionándome procesos y encarcelamientos a granel, a más de intentos de acabar con mi existencia.
>
> (And all this without once being daunted by financial hardships or the criticisms that, for different reasons, both friends and enemies showered on me, or by the vicious hounding that clipped the wings of my political and freethinking ideals, bringing me trials and imprisonments in abundance, as well as attempts on my life.)[8]

My archival research has revealed that López de Ayala was publishing in 1889 with contributions to the Madrid federal newspaper *Las Regiones*. Extant issues demonstrate that she published there from 25 May 1889 to 11 January 1890. She formed a more enduring relationship with *Las Dominicales del Libre Pensamiento*, where she published from 16 May 1891 to 27 June 1902. Its successor, *Las Dominicales*, also published her contributions between 19 August 1904 and June 1906. During the 1890s, other newspapers that carried López de Ayala's pieces were Domingo Soler's *La Luz del Porvenir* (July 1891 to March 1896), *La Nueva Cotorra* (Barcelona) in 1892, and *El Clamor Zaragozano* (1899, 1902). The Barcelona satirical newspaper *La Tramontana*, edited by Llunas, also covered her activities sporadically between August 1892 and February 1896. Subsequently, from 1 May 1920 until 1 February 1924, López de Ayala published assiduously in *El Motín*, the Madrid weekly founded and edited by the Republican journalist José Nakens, alongside similarly substantial contributions by Acuña. Over the course of her sporadic collaboration with this newspaper, López de Ayala published twenty-three pieces in it, with her last contribution appearing on 16 February 1924.

The majority of López de Ayala's writings, however, appeared in the four Barcelona periodicals that she herself founded and edited. As evident from their titles, they formed part of a radical literature of combat (Culla and Duarte 1990, 43–4). Regularly victims of governmental censorship, they carried frequent references to the suppression of material or temporary suspensions.[9] The first periodical was the weekly *El Progreso*, which López de Ayala edited from 28 November 1896 until 17 November 1901, the year in which, by now widowed, she remarried (Carmona González 1999, 163).[10] It was succeeded in 1906 by the monthly *El Gladiador: Órgano de la "Sociedad Progresiva Femenina,"* which ran until 1909, when it was closed down after Tragic Week.[11] Its successor was *El Libertador: Periódico Defensor de la Mujer y Órgano Nacional del Libre-Pensamiento*, which López de Ayala founded in 1910 and edited until its publication was curtailed by governmental order in 1914. A radical weekly that published contributions by well-known Lerrouxists, it advocated republicanism, the secularization of society, and the destruction of Catholicism (Ramos 1999a, 105). It was reincarnated in the fourth periodical to be founded and edited by López de Ayala, *El Gladiador del Librepensamiento: Órgano de la Federación Librepensadora de Barcelona y otros Pueblos Adheridos*. Born in 1914, this publication, more aggressive in tone than its previous version, was the mouthpiece for the Sociedad Progresiva Femenina, which López de Ayala headed. Presented in a three-page format with one page of advertisements at the end, it came out fortnightly until it was forced to close down as the result of financial pressures in March 1920.[12]

The flavour of López de Ayala's periodicals is evident in a reference to *El Progreso* in *Las Dominicales del Libre Pensamiento*, which heralds its forthcoming publication on 23 October 1896. Referring to a new weekly directed by "the invincible Ángeles López de Ayala," the announcement affirms the periodical's working-class

Año II. Barcelona 16 Enero de 1897 Núm. 8

El Progreso

PERIÓDICO REPUBLICANO

SE PUBLICA LOS SÁBADOS

PRECIOS DE SUSCRIPCIÓN

Barcelona y su llano	trimestre.	1	pta.
Provincias	»	1'50	»
Extranjero	año	10'	»
Ultramar	»	8	»

El pago por adelantado se hará en sellos de correo de 15 cts. ó en libranzas del giro mutuo; además un sello de 10 cts. por el cambio. A los corresponsales se les dará el 25 por 100 de comisión.

Dirección y Administración: Tallers, 45, 2.°, interior

Horas de Oficina: de 7 á 9 de la noche

La Correspondencia, á D.ª Ángeles López de Ayala

Anuncios y comunicados á precios convencionales

Número suelto	10	cénts.
» atrasado	20	»
Paquete de 25 números	1'75	ptas.

De los artículos firmados, responden sus autores.

¡SE APROXIMA!

¡Es ella! ¡La república!

Vedla volver hacia nuestras desventuras su mirada humedecida por el llanto del dolor... Vedla atravesar el espacio que de nosotros la separa, sobre las rosadas nubes de sus promesas fascinadoras..

Observad cómo se desciñe el rico manto, anhelosa de tenderle sobre la manigua enrojecida por la sangre de miles de hermanos que, precipitados unos sobre otros, por un puñado de mónstruos agenos al amor y á la piedad, se devoran entre sí con rencor indescriptible, con saña horripilante.

Vedla ofrecer sus brazos á los peninsulares, y á los cubanos, y á los filipinos; é invitarles á jurar una humanitaria reconciliación, en el altar de su amoroso pecho.

¡Vedla llorar por las jóvenes víctimas, sacrificadas en aras de egoísmos miserables; y consolar á las madres atribuladas, y restaurar la sangre del herido, y suspender la mortandad, y volverse airada contra las *fieras* que á tales horrores condujeron, y marcarlas con el *sambenito* de la deshonra, y castigarlas con el triple látigo de la justicia, de la humanidad, y de la civilización atropelladas!

¡Vedla! ¡es la república!

La han llamado los desaciertos restauradores, y la prevaricación de los malos demócratas.

La han hecho salir de su letárgico sueño el clamoreo que la tiranía levanta, y el ruido de la hirviente y mal contenida indignación de los honrados, y los gemidos que se escapan á través de los macizos mu- [illegible]

cree; ya se os detesta; ya todos ansian salir del fango en que les revolcasteis; ya quieren lavarse con las regeneradoras aguas de la ilustración; y abandonando las sombras de una reacción maldita secarse al sol de la libertad de la conciencia!

No os opongais al paso de las masas, si no quereis ser arrollados.

Dejad que marchen esas innúmeras legiones hambrientas de progresos; ¡dejadlas, pigmeos, ó de lo contrario, temblad ante su ya omnipotente empuje!

¡Ved, que han apretado sus filas, y que tratan de apretarlas más y más!..

¡Reflexionad en que han visto cernerse en lontananza, la sublime imagen de su ideal idolatrado; pensad que se ha rasgado el velo encubridor de vuestras concupiscencias, y de vuestras maquiavélicas intrigas, y de vuestras sordas é indignas maquinaciones!

¡Dejad el campo libre á las huestes de la luz, amigos de las tinieblas! ¡Huid que los ejércitos se aproximan guiados por vuestros manejos burdos, por vuestro afán de imposición, por vuestras humillantes torpezas!

¡No os detengais, no volvais la vista atrás, que la leyenda de la mujer de Lot, trocarase en una realidad del presente, mas, no quedareis convertidos en estátuas de sal; sino en montón de cenizas aglomeradas en la hoguera de la revolución, y diseminadas luego, por el impetuoso ciclón de las maldiciones públicas!

¡Poned en salvo vuestras vidas, ya que no podreis jamás, poner en salvo vuestras honras!

[illegible]

na, el grande hombre de Estado, el gran caudillo de la Revolución, malogrado general Prim, secundando luego la Marina y el Ejército, y unidos los partidos democrático, progresista y unionista, con el patriótico pensamiento de derribar el trono de Isabel II, quien, por *una série de lamentables equivocaciones*, se había hecho inepta para regir los destinos del noble y honrado pueblo español.

Después de unos años de gobierno de *moderados y polacos*, con el cruel Narváez, el inmoral Conde de San Luis y el cínico González Bravo, considerados como *ilegales* los partidos avanzados, obligados los progresistas al retraimiento y lanzados ignominiosamente del poder los unionistas, cuando vino la conjunción de los tres partidos, que representaban á los descontentos, ó sea la nación en masa, bastó el Manifiesto de Cádiz, seguido de la batalla de Alcolea, para arrojar del trono de San Fernando á la que entonces le ocupaba, quedando escrito, con gruesos caracteres negros, en las paredes del Ministerio de Hacienda, en la calle de Alcalá, el punto más céntrico de la Corte, el siguiente significativo y conocido epitafio de

«Cayó para siempre... etc.
Castigo justo á su perversidad».

Después del Gobierno provisional, la Monarquía genuinamente democrática del caballeroso Amadeo, y la malograda República, la traición de un general que tantas desdichas y vergüenzas ha traído á España, vino la infausta Restauración. Esta, habiendo disfrutado de veinte años de paz, ha puesto á la infeliz patria al borde del abis-

por ejemplo, ya existe su tipo ideal al que su forma debe ajustarse, y hasta podría ser percibida su forma ideal por algún vidente, si esto hubiera de tener influencia directa é inmediata en los sucesos humanos. De igual manera, antes de que llegue un acontecimiento social á su desarrollo, ese acontecimiento existe como realizado en el mundo ideal, á la manera que un arquitecto concibe y desarrolla el plano de una obra antes de ser ésta ejecutada.

» Cuando los acontecimientos están lejanos, apenas se percibe el rumor, sino por un oído fino y delicado. Con referencia á los sucesos futuros que nos atañen, si su realización estuviese muy distante, sólo por séres muy sensibles podrían ser percibidos, y esto imperfectamente y con mucha confusión de detalles; mas cuando se hallan tan próximos como ahora los tenemos, se notan en todas partes y por los más rudos entendimientos.

» Y si los acontecimientos futuros están ó no cercanos, podemos juzgar haciéndonos cargo del rumor público y del inmenso número de personas que los presiente. Se están cerniendo en la atmósfera con una intensidad cada vez mayor; parece como si se escuchara el choque de las armas, el piafar de los caballos y el estruendo de los cañones. Y tan intenso es el rumor de esa *silenciosa algazara*, que los más interesados en detener la marcha de los sucesos andan desorientados, y la turbación de sus espíritus no les deja discurrir con claridad y acierto, y así cometen cada día mayores torpezas.»

. . . .

2.2 First page of *El Progreso* 8, Year II (16 Jan. 1897): 1. By kind permission of the Arxiu Històric de la Ciutat de Barcelona (microfilm no. 245-H)

sympathies by stating that, like Sárraga's *La Conciencia Libre*, *El Progreso* will similarly defend "the cause of the Spanish working class." To subscribe, readers are invited to write to López de Ayala at 27 Planeta Street, Gracia.[13] The column also praises the energies of women like López de Ayala at a time when so many men show feminine weakness and decries the fact that this "enlightened, eloquent writer and poet" does not receive the recognition in Spain that she would in other countries such as France. Although López de Ayala, the article continues, is superior to most male journalists, she is hated and persecuted because she is a woman.[14]

AÑO I Barcelona 26 de Mayo de 1906 NÚM. 1

EL GLADIADOR

ÓRGANO DE LA "SOCIEDAD PROGRESIVA FEMENINA"

Saldrá por lo menos una vez al mes

PRECIOS DE SUSCRIPCIÓN	Pago adelantado, en giro mútuo ó sellos de 15 céntimos.
50 céntimos trimestre en toda España.	El 50 por 100 de rebaja á los corresponsales.
Una peseta en el extranjero.	**NÚMERO SUELTO 10 CÉNTIMOS**

Redactores: Las socias y protectores de la *Sociedad Progresiva Femenina.*

Colaboradores: Todos los seres de ideas adelantadas que tengan cabida dentro del amplio credo de este periódico.

Directora literaria: ÁNGELES LÓPEZ DE AYALA

Redacción y Administración: Calle de Colón, n.º 12, pral. 1.ª—Barcelona (Gracia).

Horas de Oficina: De 10 á 12 de la mañana y de 2 á 4 de la tarde. Los días festivos, hasta las 12 de la mañana solamente.

«EL GLADIADOR»

Comprendemos la extrañeza de nuestros suscritores al ver que nuestra publicación no lleva el nombre de "El Progreso" según lo había llevado siete años y según indicábamos en nuestras circulares.

Pero no hemos sido los culpables de este cambio: Al dar la notificación al Gobierno de la provincia de la salida de nuestro periódico, se nos manifestó que otras dos publicaciones nuevas se habían anticipado á la nuestra, y que ambas publicaciones se designaban con el nombre de "El Progreso"

Tuvimos, por tanto, que renunciar á nuestro propósito, titulando la nuestra "**El Gladiador**", título que, después de todo, se halla en perfecta armonía con nuestro destino, puesto que venimos á reñir sangriento combate con las terribles fieras de todos los absurdos y de todas las preocupaciones, con el mismo vigor y arrojo con que los gladiadores romanos peleaban contra las espantables bestias que el Cesar les proporcionaba.

Y para que la similitud sea más perfecta, así como aquellos históricos héroes se precipitaban desnudos en el Circo, donde les esperaban las horribles fauces de sus furiosos adversarios, así nosotros, desnudos de toda protección y valimiento nos precipitamos al Circo de esta moderna Roma, para exterminar á las fieras de la reacción, ó sucumbir entre sus garras formidables.

Queda, pues, hecha la explicación del cambio.

¡Hasta la muerte!

Hasta la muerte ocuparemos con firmeza el que para nosotros es puesto de honor.

Hasta la muerte lucharemos por la augusta trilogía de "Libertad, igualdad y fraternidad" base fundamental del expléndido edificio de la redención humana.

¿Que parece imposible que nuestros ánimos retoñen, después de haber sufrido los múltiples embates de la tempestad del infortunio privado que casi secó nuestra existencia, y del infortunio público que agosta de contínuo nuestros santos ideales?

¿Que el tiempo transcurrido y los

2.3 First page of *El Gladiador: Órgano de la "Sociedad Progresiva Femenina"* 1, Year I (26 May 1906): 1. By kind permission of the Arxiu Històric de la Ciutat de Barcelona (microfilm no. 73)

Año I — Barcelona 19 de Noviembre de 1910 — Núm. 6

EL LIBERTADOR

PERIÓDICO DEFENSOR DE LA MUJER Y ÓRGANO NACIONAL DEL LIBRE-PENSAMIENTO

SE PUBLICA LOS SÁBADOS

PRECIOS DE SUSCRIPCIÓN

Directora literaria, D.ª Ángeles López de Ayala

2.4 Heading of *El Libertador: Periódico Defensor de la Mujer y Órgano Nacional del Libre-Pensamiento* 6, Year I (19 Nov. 1910): 1. By kind permission of the Arxiu Històric de la Ciutat de Barcelona (microfilm no. 535-H)

The Republican desire to reach the working classes is evident in the issue of *El Progreso* published on 6 February 1897. There López de Ayala proposes establishing a list of sponsors to subsidize printing costs and enable its greater divulgation among the working classes, declaring, "¡¡(h)ay que popularizarle!!" (it must be for and of the people!), and stressing her resolve to create "un órgano *esencialmente popular*" (an *essentially popular* vehicle). So that the working classes might purchase it more easily, the price was reduced from one peseta to five centimes, and Republicans, freemasons, freethinkers, spiritists, and workers alike were all called on to support the periodical.[15] Republican objectives were again revealed in the issue published just two weeks later, where the lead article, by López de Ayala, calls on the people, here identified with the working classes, to use associationism as an essential weapon in sociopolitical struggles: "Le diremos que renuncie a su sistema de apartamiento de la vida política, … Que asista a las asambleas populares … y que … forme una masa compacta, inteligente y de gran resistencia" (We will tell you to renounce your habit of not engaging with political life, … to attend meetings of the people … and … form a tight-knit, intelligent, and highly resilient body).[16]

The third reappearance of *El Progreso*, frequently subject to censorship, was announced by López de Ayala in *Las Dominicales del Libre Pensamiento* on 28 December 1899. This time, however, *El Progreso* would take on a distinctly feminist purview, becoming the mouthpiece of not only the Barcelona Sociedad Progresiva Femenina but also of all women's associations in the Iberian Peninsula and of working women, whom it aimed to defend from injustice, abuse, and physical degradation at the hands of the male employers and co-workers in the

COLEGIO

DE LA

Sociedad Progresiva Femenina

Calle de Ferrer de Blanes, núm. 12, pral. 1.ª (Gracia)

Clases nocturnas a cargo de buenos profesores

MENSUALIDADES MODICAS

FABRICACION EN GRANDE ESCALA DE CUADROS Y ESPEJOS

Depósito de Molduras del País y Extranjeras

DEPOSITO DE CROMOS, MAPAS, OLEOGRAFIAS Y GRABADOS DE LAS MEJORES MARCAS

DE

ANTONIO ARTIGAS

Tallers, 44. BARCELONA

Ventas al por Mayor y Menor

Disponible

Sastrería de ANTONIO ESPLUGAS

TRAVESERA, 55 y 57, Pral. 2.ª

Buenos Géneros, elegancia y prontitud en la confección de trajes hechos segun los modelos más acreditados. PRECIOS MÓDICOS

¡NO EQUIVOCARSE! Travesera, 55 y 57, pral. 2.ª-GRACIA

ALPARGATERIA DE ZACARÍAS SARTI

Especialidad en la medida y reformadas

CALZADO DE LONA

Calle Cera, 30

D. ELADIO GARDO Y FERRER

ABOGADO

Despacho de 7 a 9 noche

Salmerón, 53, 1.º, 2.ª - BARCELONA

ZAPATERÍA

DE

José Biscarri

Gran surtido en toda clase de calzado a precios de fábrica

Calle de Argüelles, número 12.-GRACIA

INSTALACIONES ELÉCTRICAS - ILUMINACIONES DECORATIVAS - LAMPISTERÍA EN GENERAL

J. JORGE VINAIXA Y C.ÍA

Dinamos - Electromotores - Teléfonos - Timbres - Pararrayos Ascensores - Material Eléctrico, etc., etc.

OFICINAS: Diputación, 168, pral. 2.ª TALLER: Villarroel, 57, tda. (esquina Cortes)

BARCELONA

Nuevo Colegio Láico

La inteligentísima profesora láica, D.ª María Marín, ha establecido en su domicilio OLMO, 17 y 19, pral., un Colegio de niñas a mensualidades módicas, para facilitar la asistencia al mismo de las hijas de los obreros. Esperamos que estas se apresurarán a concurrir a las clases, que son diurnas y nocturnas.

EL INCRÉDULO

Preciosa obra del cultísimo escritor D. JAVIER DE ZENGOTITA

Se vende en nuestra Redacción, a 0'75 cts. ejemplar

DE TAL SIEMBRA, TAL COSECHA

Comedia en tres actos y en verso, original de D.ª ANGELES LOPEZ DE AYALA

Se vende a mitad de precio, o sea, a una peseta.

A LOS

CONCURRENTES A LAS ARENAS

Después de una tarde de sol y de entusiasmo, nada es tan agradable como saborear una rica copa de licor o un delicioso refresco, y esto puede obtener fácilmente y por precios increíbles, en el Kiosco que en la Plaza de España tiene establecido Juan Ballart.

ALLÍ ENCONTRARÁN ABUNDANCIA, ECONOMÍA, AMABILIDAD Y EXQUISITOS GÉNEROS.

RECORDADLO BIEN: ¡KIOSCO DE JUAN BALLART, Plaza de España!

The Viadin - Elixir Viadin

Para curar gástricas, tifus, irritaciones, pulmonías, viruelas, sarampión y otras enfermedades

Es el gran remedio para la baba de los niños

DE VENTA EN FARMACIAS Y DROGUERIAS!

Depósito General San Pedro Mártir, 44

NO CONFUNDIRSE

"EL GLADIADOR" DEL LIBREPENSAMIENTO

PERIODICO QUINCENAL

Órgano de la Federación Librepensadora de Barcelona y pueblos adheridos

Suscripción trimestral, Barcelona, 0'75 céntimos — Fuera, UNA peseta

Dirección y Administración: Ferrer de Blanes, núm. 12, pral., 1.º; Gracia-Barcelona

HORAS DE OFICINA: De 6 de la tarde a 7 de la noche

Se vende en los Kioscos «Franco Español» y frente a la calle del Hospital, (Rambla) y en los dos que al término del Paseo de Gracia, desembocan en la calle Mayor de dicha Barriada.—Precio de 30 ejemplares, una peseta.

factories where they worked: "[A] las que defenderá de las injusticias, abusos y atropellos de que sean objeto por parte de patronos o empleados de las fábricas donde trabajen." These objectives would be strengthened, López de Ayala adds, by the inauguration of a special section publishing contributions from men sympathetic to their causes: "*siempre que estén dentro de nuestro hermoso credo de libertad y de justicia*" (*providing they also profess our beautiful creed of freedom and justice*). López de Ayala ends by calling on women, freethinkers, freemasons, and spiritists to support *El Progreso*.

On occasions, not only were López de Ayala's periodicals subject to censorship, as noted previously, but her articles also led to her imprisonment. In 1892 she was incarçerated in the Barcelona prison on Amalia Street because of an article in *La Nueva Cotorra*. Although it was stipulated that she pay four hundred *duros* as bail for her release, she was eventually freed without payment and was put on trial for her alleged offence in February 1893.[17] While in prison she wrote at least two poems. In "Mis noches en la cárcel," composed on 13 June 1892, López de Ayala extends her own imprisonment to that of Spain as a whole and dreams of the Republican flag unfurled in her nation, which she imagines governed by reason, fraternity, and a sovereign people.[18] Yet another poem, "Desde la cárcel," written on 11 July, describes the jail as "esta Babel sin par" (this Babel without equal). Calling for the abolition of the death penalty, the poetic voice advocates compassion and education: "Ilustración y clemencia / El pueblo, a voces le clama" (Enlightenment and clemency / the people vociferously demand), and "Gobierne por la indulgencia, / Y por la instrucción bendita" (Govern with leniency, / and through the grace of education).[19]

Like Sárraga, López de Ayala's political positioning was a radical one, informed by freemasonry, republicanism, and feminism. Her association with freemasonry dates back to 1881, when she studied with noted freemason Joaquín Ponce de León,[20] and joined the Madrid Masonic lodge Orden de la Estrella de Oriente, to which her first husband also belonged. Subsequently in 1888, she became a member of the Madrid lodge of adoption, Amantes del Progreso, and the Gran Oriente de España lodge, while the following year she joined the lodge of adoption, Hijas de los Pobres (Tavera 2000, 570–1). In addition, López de Ayala belonged to the lodges of La Libertad, La Mantuana, and Comuneros de Castilla (Carmona González 1999, 162–3). On 20 October 1893, at a meeting of the Hijos del

2.5 Advertisements from *El Gladiador del Librepensamiento: Órgano de la Federación Librepensadora de Barcelona y Pueblos Adheridos* 82, Year VI, Second Epoch (3 June 1916): 4. By kind permission of the Arxiu Històric de la Ciutat de Barcelona (microfilm no. 73)

Trabajo lodge, she is recorded as criticizing the secondary role of women in society and freemasonry (Sànchez i Ferré 1990, 171). Consequently, in 1894 she entered the Barcelona Constancia lodge, a mixed lodge within the Progressive republicanism of Ruiz Zorrilla, holding the position of secretary there and reaching the thirtieth grade in the Scottish Rite (152, 159, 196).[21]

Freemasonry lodges brought López de Ayala into close contact with other free-thinking women, among them Acuña. On 4 November 1888 the Madrid Republican newspaper *El País* reported that López de Ayala and Acuña, referred to as "writers," attended a Masonic banquet in honour of the Viscount de Ros, where freemasons agreed to lobby for the removal of the death penalty for political crimes from the Civil Code.[22] Just over three years later, in April 1892, López de Ayala delivered a speech at the Inmortalidad lodge and was described by Domingo Soler in *La Luz del Porvenir* as follows: "She spoke on freemasonry with the greatest enthusiasm … with feeling and conveying that feeling; she is a true priestess for freemasonry." At the close of the meeting López de Ayala and Antonia Amat de Torrens, a secular teacher, took donations for three needy families.[23]

That López de Ayala's association with freemasonry was lifelong is verified by her address at the Barcelona Ciencia y Libertad lodge in August 1904, as well as her presence at the commemorative act for Francisco Ferrer Guardia in 1914, recorded in the September–October bulletin of the Gran Logia Simbólica Regional Catalana Balear (Álvarez Lázaro 1985, 195–6). López de Ayala's stature within freemasonry is demonstrable in the fact that on her death in 1926 the Catón lodge established its library in her home at 12 Ferrer de Blanes Street, Barcelona.[24] That same year the June issue of the journal *Vida Masónica* inaugurated its "Columna de Honor de Masonas Españolas" with her biography (see figure 2.1).[25]

As I noted in my introduction, López de Ayala's brand of republicanism was independent of any specific political party.[26] Thus in her 1906 article "Lo que somos" she rejects being defined as supporting Lerroux's Radical Republican Party or the alliance of Nicolás Salmerón's Republican Union with the regionalist coalition Solidaridad Catalana: "Detestamos las banderas … manteniéndonos en una neutralidad absoluta respecto a las divergencias de detalles, que separan a hombres valiosísimos, restando fuerzas a la gran masa democrática" (We detest flag-waving … maintaining complete neutrality with regard to small differences, which divide the worthiest men and weaken the great democratic mass) (see figure 2.6). López de Ayala's anti-Catalanist stance stemmed from her reiterated conviction that Republicans must unite to achieve their sociopolitical aims, rather than be further divided through the Catalan push for autonomy. Hence she affirms the ideological unity of republicanism: "Somos partidarios de la *idea*" (We support *ideas*) and "*somos republicanos de la república*" (*we are Republicans of the republic*).[27]

An earlier instance of López de Ayala's criticism of potential divisions within republicanism was her 1897 editorial article, "A Juan del Pueblo y a *El País*," signed

AÑO I Barcelona 25 de Agosto de 1906 NÚM. 4

EL GLADIADOR

ÓRGANO DE LA "SOCIEDAD PROGRESIVA FEMENINA"

Saldrá por lo menos una vez al mes

PRECIOS DE SUSCRIPCIÓN
50 céntimos trimestre en toda España.
Una peseta en el extranjero.

Pago adelantado, en giro mútuo ó sellos de 15 céntimos.
El 50 por 100 de rebaja á los corresponsales.
NUMERO SUELTO 10 CÉNTIMOS

Redactores: Las socias y protectores de la *Sociedad Progresiva Femenina.*
Colaboradores: Todos los seres de ideas adelantadas que tengan cabida dentro del amplio credo de este periódico.
Directora literaria: ÁNGELES LÓPEZ DE AYALA
Redacción y Administración: Calle de Colón, n.° 12, pral. 1.ª.—Barcelona (Gracia).
Horas de Oficina: De 10 á 12 de la mañana y de 2 á 4 de la tarde. Los días festivos, hasta las 12 de la mañana solamente.

LO QUE SOMOS

¿Qué es **El Gladiador?** ¿Lerrouxista ó Solidario?

He aquí la pregunta que algunos de nuestros suscriptores de fuera de Barcelona nos dirigen.

Y como nosotros no queremos hacer misterio de nuestro rumbo, y como nos consideramos educados y corteses, por lo mismo, nos apresuramos á dar la más cumplida respuesta á nuestros amigos, empleando para ello toda la franqueza que nuestra lealtad nos dicta.

No somos Lerrouxistas, ni somos Solidarios, porque entendemos que, el sólo hecho de afiliarse á una cualqu'era de estas dos fracciones, implica proclamación de personalismos que, *en ningún caso* estamos dispuestos á aceptar.

Y no los aceptamos, porque somos partidarios de la *idea* y solo consideramos como un medio de convertirla en realidad á los hombres que la encarnan.

Más claro: queremos una república honrada y justiciera, sin que nos importe el nombre de los que trabajen para su implantaaión, y si únicamente el trabajo que realicen.

"Por el fruto conocereis el arbol" dijo, según nos aseguran, Cristo: Pues bien: por el resultado que en un plazo prudencial tenga la obra de Lerroux, ó por el que en idéntico plazo tenga la de Salmerón, conoceremos cual de los dos se ha equivocado, sin temor de cometer ligerezas temerarias, y las más de las veces, censurables.

En pocas palabras: *somos republicanos de la república*, y nos merecen la más alta consideración sus hombres, pero *detestamos las banderías*, porque no queremos hacer de la hermosa capital de Cataluña una nueva Verona, con sus tristemente célebres bandos de montescos y capuletos.

Nuestra labor, pues, será la de *hacer* republicanos á los que no lo sean,

2.6 Ángeles López de Ayala, "Lo que somos," in *El Gladiador: Órgano de la "Sociedad Progresiva Femenina"* 4, Year I (25 Aug. 1906): 1. By kind permission of the Arxiu Històric de la Ciutat de Barcelona (microfilm no. 73)

by *El Progreso*. There, calling on Progressive Juan, Centralist Juan, Federal Juan, and National Juan, all of whom she describes as "amantes de la libertad, del progreso y de la República" (lovers of freedom, progress, and the republic), she states that the diversity of political parties might be good for government and state but it works against uniting the masses, making a revolution, and establishing the republic. She therefore advocates "la fusión de los republicanos, no de los partidos" (the fusion of Republicans, not of parties).[28] Further evidence of López de Ayala's identification with the Republican cause comes in an autobiographical essay published in 1916, where she refers to the fact that she was born in September, the month the First Republic came into being, that she had French, and hence Republican, blood in her veins, and that she was descended from the Comuneros.[29]

Spanish republicanism, Raymond Carr notes, was characterized by two principal diverging models that coalesced around the political survivors of the short-lived First Republic. On the one hand, there was "the tradition of romantic revolution" that would later be taken up by Lerroux and his Radical Republicans. On the other, there stood an "evolutionary tradition" of reform favoured by intellectuals of Krausist leanings (Carr 1982, 534). While, as I will develop in chapter 3, in *De tal siembra, tal cosecha* López de Ayala debates both options and ultimately shows a preference for reform, she would later decant towards a more revolutionary stance, evident in her 1901 letter to the director of the radical Madrid newspaper *El Imparcial*, subsequently reprinted in *La Publicidad* and *Las Dominicales*. There, refuting an accusation from *El Imparcial*'s Barcelona reporter that she is an anarchist, she describes herself as a freethinker and a "REPUBLICANA REVOLUCIONARIA" (revolutionary Republican), affirming her belief that only a republic established through revolution can rehabilitate Spain's political and economic systems. In support of her claim, López de Ayala refers to the testimony of "todos los republicanos, socialistas y anarquistas de Barcelona, y las campañas republicanas que he venido haciendo en más de 40 periódicos de Madrid y de provincias, y que en el día sostengo en *El Progreso*" (all the Republicans, socialists, and anarchists in Barcelona and the Republican campaigns that I have waged in more than forty periodicals in Madrid and the provinces, and that I today continue in *El Progreso*).[30]

Revolution was a constant message in the many Republican and freethinking meetings at which López de Ayala invariably played a prominent part. Many times these events brought together Republicans, socialists, and anarchists, with class boundaries swept aside by common objectives. As Duarte explains, in its more radical manifestations Catalan republicanism adopted a minority position that defended a tactical alliance between Republicans and socialists. In turn, in the 1890s the strand of Catalan socialism known as opportunistic socialism, associated with the El Obrero group and led by Josep Pàmias, declared itself Republican in an attempt to engage the working classes more fully in political life and thus give greater strength to liberalism (Duarte 1987, 84–5). As a result, the theoretical framework through which Republican parties attempted to grant cohesion to these standpoints was an eclectic, pragmatic socialism founded on three principles: first, facilitating the moral emancipation of the working classes through education, over and above their economic emancipation; second, creating a new social order by extending the right to private property; and third, ensuring that social transformations reached all classes (89). As I will elucidate in chapter 3, all these premises are foregrounded in López de Ayala's novellas *El abismo* and *Primitivo*.

As for relationships between Republicans and anarchists, evidence can be seen in López de Ayala's close involvement with leading anarchists such as Claramunt and Llunas, as I document below.[31] For Llunas the struggle for social change could not be effected only by the working classes but also had to attract the social foundation of fin-de-siècle republicanism, the middle classes, which included small industrialists, wholesalers, shopkeepers, and artists (Duarte 1987, 88).

One major event that brought together freethinkers of all persuasions was the meeting of some two thousand persons held in Barcelona at the Circo Ecuestre in Catalonia Square on 28 August 1892. Its aim was raise donations for the working classes to attend the next Conference of Freethinkers, scheduled for October in Madrid.[32] Prior to the meeting López de Ayala had written a poem, "El Congreso de libre-pensadores," which called on all Spaniards – "hermanos" (brothers and sisters) and "ciudadanos" (citizens) – to support the gathering and let freethinking unite them with America and Europe.[33] Besides López de Ayala, the speakers were well-known anarchists Gurri, Llunas, and Claramunt. Claramunt's speech centred on the need for the working classes to attend the conference in order to define what they understood by freethinking, which, for Claramunt, had to attack the clergy and the bourgeoisie, identified as the two main culprits of working-class woes. A similar anticlerical message was present in López de Ayala's speech.[34]

At the end of September, *La Tramontana* again signalled the importance of the Madrid Conference for the working classes. Stating that workers' associations were of the view that the militant proletariat must participate in the discussion on the relationship of freethinking with social inequality, the periodical affirms that freethinking depends on economically emancipating manual and intellectual workers and eliminating class boundaries: "It is a most humanitarian act to help the working class, both manual workers and intellectuals, attain economic emancipation, because only in this way can thought flourish without class obstacles and be completely free."[35]

In mid-October 1892 López de Ayala and Claramunt were among the orators at a freethinking meeting at the Principal Theatre in Tarrassa, alongside Odón de Buen, Salmerón, Llunas, and Gurri.[36] The two women also regularly attended meetings of the Gutenberg Society, a secular organization. López de Ayala spoke on women and free education at one of these society meetings on 18 June 1893 to raise funds for secular schools, while she attended another on 23 July 1893 in Barcelona's Zorrilla Theatre, together with Domingo Soler, Cristóbal Litrán, Garriga Peraira, and others.[37] Another freethinking event for which López de Ayala formed part of the organizing committee and spoke on feminism was the celebration held on Holy Thursday 1894 at the Sabadell Federal Circle (Sànchez i Ferré 1990, 130).

Like Domingo Soler and Sárraga, López de Ayala maintained an exhausting schedule of sociopolitical activities, constantly seeking to advance the causes of women and the working classes. One example was the freethinking meeting that she attended in Calella in April 1898 with four other speakers from Barcelona: Pau Isart Bula, Juan Cañellas, Leopoldo Bonafulla, and Palmira de Bruno. After a tour of the village and a coffee at the local inn, the meeting in the theatre began. Speaking last, López de Ayala focused on women and the legal system. She called on women to join the freethinking movement, stressing education as the means for them to obtain their rights. Affirming the necessity of revolution, she praised republicanism as the only political system capable of ending the present abuses and gender inequalities.[38] In 1915 López de Ayala was one of two keynote speakers, together with Francisca Benaiges, vice-president of the Sociedad Progresiva Femenina, at the freethinking meeting and banquet of *promiscuación* held on Holy Thursday at the Radical Federalist Centre in Mataró.[39] Speaking for nearly two hours, López de Ayala inveighed against false freethinkers and Republicans and against their apathy towards the church's influence over women and their disdain for women's culture.[40] The following year, in 1916, López de Ayala was the only woman among six speakers at the party celebrated by the Freethinking Association of Gracia and San Gervasio on New Year's Eve.[41]

The most high-profile political activity in which López de Ayala was involved was the campaign for which she was secretary to lobby for a review of the Montjuich trial. This campaign was organized in 1898 by the Sociedad Progresiva Femenina and the Constancia lodge (Ramos 1999a, 104, 106), associations in which López de Ayala figured prominently. On 13 February 1898 López de Ayala was the only woman on the organizing committee for an important meeting held at the Tivoli Theatre to demand a review, which was attended by Marxists, spiritists, socialists, anarchists, Republicans, and freemasons (Sànchez i Ferré 1990, 219–20).

Among other reported accounts of her campaign activities was the meeting held in Madrid on 24 June 1899. Called by the Catalan revisionists on behalf of the widows of those executed in Montjuich prison, it was attended by more than ten thousand. The prejudices with which women contended if they dared step outside a normative femininity became apparent when López de Ayala was prevented from taking the podium by Republican men, anxious at her infringement of gender conventions. In an article entitled "La señora López de Ayala en Madrid," the journalist lambasts such discrimination, signalling that her democratic commitment and political achievements far surpass those of male Republicans:

> Very few men who spoke at the meeting were as entitled to do so as Sra. López de Ayala because, while they slumbered, she soared. … While Sra. López de Ayala epitomizes those who work with righteous passion to raise up the sleeping nation, and has suffered imprisonment, denunciations due to her articles, and indescribable troubles for always meeting the powerful Jesuit order of Barcelona head-on, those grave Republican men wallowed in apathy … What they believed to be impossible – instilling again passion in the people – has been accomplished; and it has been done by the very person who can do it, the person who shares their passion and has always fought for them, despite being surrounded by indifference and disdain, Sra. López de Ayala. … none of those men who look down on her from on high have accomplished what she has, the resurrection of the spirit of democracy … nor have they succeeded in creating a movement as intense and as powerful as that for the review of the Montjuich trial, a movement born principally from the initiative of the fine Women's Society that doña Ángeles has succeeding in establishing with such effort.[42]

That these discriminatory incidents by Spanish male liberals were not isolated affairs is verified by events at a later Madrid meeting in November 1904 to review the Montjuich affair. In a stinging attack entitled "Pseudo-liberalismo," Sárraga contrasts the warm reception given to a woman wearing a white mantilla at a bullfight with the humiliation meted out by the all-male meeting to López de Ayala, prevented from speaking on behalf of more than fifty Catalan workers' societies for the freedom of imprisoned comrades. Whereas for Sárraga the first woman embodies the commodification and objectification of her sex – the "mujer-juguete, la mujer-cosa" (the plaything woman, the object woman) – López de Ayala represents "la mujer redimida, la conciencia femenina elevada a las regiones del pensamiento" (the redeemed woman, feminine consciousness raised to the realms of thought). Sárraga closes her article with a dire warning: the revolution led by freethinking politicians against reactionary forces in the church and Antonio Maura's conservative government will be in vain if they continue to encourage gender discrimination, or what she terms the "*maurismo* femenino … el enemigo formidable que dará al traste con todos vuestros proyectos de progreso y civilización" (feminine Maurism … the formidable enemy that will destroy all your plans for progress and civilization).[43]

Exactly what the product of feminine Maurism might be can be gauged from López de Ayala's fiery outburst printed in *El Gladiador* in 1906, where she denies Catholic women the category of woman and likens them to vacuous dolls:

(N)o son mujeres, son hembras, porque la mujer, compañera del hombre y como el hombre inteligente, ha de atesorar un cerebro pensador, un criterio racional, y un albedrío libre de sugestión dominadora.

Y esas muñecas de porcelana, conjunto de pintados rostros, de enguantadas manos y de crujiente seda, ni son inteligentes, ni tienen substancia gris en su masa encefálica, ni proceden, por tanto, libremente, sino a impulsos de la voluntad omnímoda, de sus amos y señores.

(They are not women, they are females, because a woman, the companion of man and intelligent like man, must have a mind that thinks, rational judgment, and a free will not subject to manipulation.

And those china dolls, an assemblage of painted faces, gloved hands, and rustling silks, are not intelligent, nor do they have any grey matter in their cranial space, nor do they thus act freely, but on the contrary, according to the absolute will of their lords and masters.)[44]

In early August 1899 López de Ayala formed part of the Barcelona Commission charged with garnering support for a review of the Montjuich trials. To this end the commission undertook a challenging lecture tour to many Catalan towns and villages. On 12 August 1899 they visited Cassá de la Selva, where López de Ayala was the last of five speakers and the only woman. The next day they visited the Republican Circle in Cassá and continued on to La Barneda, accompanied by some three hundred freethinkers. There López de Ayala and Isart Bula, the commission's president, stood as godparents at the civil registry of a baby girl, followed by an open-air banquet. Immediately afterward, on 13 August, the commission continued to Llagostera, where that same evening a meeting took place. Subsequently, López de Ayala visited Port-Bou, where she and Sárraga had been invited to speak on the topic of justice.

Part of López de Ayala's Port-Bou speech, enthusiastically acclaimed, centred on her freethinking adaptations of the Lord's Prayer and Creed. They provide telling insights into López de Ayala's sociopolitical beliefs and the Republican adaptation of religious discourse to convey political themes:

Mi "Padrenuestro"

¡Pobre Pueblo, que estás en los cielos de la inocencia! –Santificadas sean tus virtudes. –Venga a nos el tu reino. –Hágase tu voluntad aquí en la tierra, ya que poco me importa que no se haga allá en el cielo.

El pan nuestro de cada día, quitémoslo de los que nos lo roban. Perdonemos a nuestros deudores, después de haber castigado sus infamias. – No caigamos en la tentación de la misericordia, causa de nuestra ruina y de nuestra perdición. – Librémonos del mal de las monarquías, y libremos de él a nuestros descendientes. – Amén.

(My "Lord's Prayer": Wretched People, who art in the heavens of innocence! Hallowed be thy virtues. Thy kingdom come. Thy will be done on earth, because I do not care if it is done in heaven.

Let us take our daily bread from those who steal it from us. Let us forgive our debtors after we have punished their crimes. Let us not fall into the temptation of pity, the cause of our ruin and damnation. Free us from the evil of monarchies, as we in turn free our descendants. Amen.)

Mi "Credo"
Creo en el Dios Pueblo, todo poderoso, criador de las grandes revoluciones. Creo en el Cristo la Justicia, su única hija, que padeció debajo del poder del Poncio Pilatos de la restauración borbónica; que fue crucificada, muerta y sepultada en las horribles mazmorras de Montjuich; que bajó a los infiernos del olvido nacional. Creo que empieza a resucitar de entre los muertos del indiferentismo. Creo que subirá a los cielos de la libertad. Creo que se sentará a la diestra del Dios Venganza, y juzgará a los vivos y a los muertos. A los muertos que profanaron el nombre de jueces, para maldecir eternamente sus memorias; y a los vivos que prostituyeron el nombre de humanos, para que sufran el terrible merecido de sus crímenes. Creo en el espíritu santo de la confraternización universal. Creo en la comunión de los ideales progresivos. Creo en el perdón de nuestras imbecilidades y de nuestras cobardías. Creo en la resurrección de la República española. Creo en la vida espléndida de la libertad y del progreso.

(My "Creed": I believe in the God of the people, almighty and maker of great revolutions. I believe in Christ Justice, his only daughter, who suffered under the Pontias Pilate of the Bourbon Restoration, who was crucified, dead, and buried in the dreadful dungeons of Montjuich; who descended to the hell of national oblivion. I believe that her resurrection is beginning from among those dead from indifference. I believe that she will rise to the heavens of freedom. I believe that she will sit on the right hand of the God of Vengeance and will judge the quick and the dead. The dead who profaned the title of judge, may they eternally curse their reports, and the quick who debased what it means to be human, may they suffer terrible punishments for their crimes. I believe in the holy spirit of universal fraternity. I believe in the communion of progressive ideals. I believe in forgiveness for our stupidity and cowardice. I believe in the resurrection of the Spanish republic. I believe in the glorious life of freedom and progress.)[45]

As Antonio Robles Egea explains, the common deployment of religious symbolism in Republican representations of the people accorded with their equating the republic with an authentic Christianity counterposed to the corrupt interests of a Catholic Church defended by Spain's Restoration monarchy. Religious tropes, with their emotional charge and familiar narratives, were especially appropriate for reaching a largely illiterate Catholic population and hence, for furthering the inter-class aims of republicanism (Robles Egea 1994, 297). Evidently, religious narratives lent themselves easily to left-wing historical paradigms of ascension towards progress and secular truth. Equally significantly, the Republican identification of a downtrodden people with a Christological suffering and purity was used to authorize the use of violence in the struggle against oppression, as was also common in socialism and anarchism (Álvarez Junco 1987, 252–5). José Álvarez Junco underlines the synonymity of revolution with redemption in Republican culture: "With regard to national evils, the people were the Innocent Lamb ... It was necessary to breathe the Revelation of Culture/Truth into the dead people/Messiah to bring about revolution/redemption" (1990, 409–10). These themes are clearly evident in López de Ayala's Creed and would also feature substantially in Sárraga's poetry.

Two days after López de Ayala's Port-Bou address, she again spoke at a mid-afternoon, open-air meeting in Capellades, at which sixty pesetas were raised for the victims of the Montjuich trials. She exhorted the crowd not to forget the abuses of Montjuich and embrace revolution when the opportune moment arrived.[46] The next stop was Cerbere, where López de Ayala and the commission were welcomed with a dinner for democracy. Yet again López de Ayala visited Port-Bou, followed by La Escala, where she was unable to speak at the scheduled meeting because she became ill. However, the next evening, once recovered, López de Ayala did address the villagers, who turned out in force and contributed generously to the fundraising for the Montjuich victims. López de Ayala was particularly taken with La Escala and its "democratic spirit," which had produced the likes of Teresa Paradís, a Republican reporter for the Figueras newspaper *El Ampurdanés*.[47] Still more meetings took place in September: on 17 September López de Ayala was in Sabadell, while days later her speech in Caldas de Montbuy received an ovation.[48]

López de Ayala's work on behalf of the Montjuich campaign was still very much visible in 1901. On 3 May she attended a meeting in Barcelona, accompanied by Isart Bula, Emili Junoy (at that point president of the campaign), and Lerroux, to honour those shot in Montjuich prison on 4 May 1897. The event was closely monitored throughout by the police and Civil Guard. The venue, the Salón de la Serpentina, was overflowing with more than three thousand persons, with many more unable to enter. López de Ayala concluded her speech with a prayer to progress and offered her life to the cause of the Montjuich review.[49]

López de Ayala's beliefs inform her numerous poems, which furthered her sociopolitical objectives. I have recovered seventy-five compositions from the freethinking press written between 1889 and 1919, which fall into the following major thematic categories: political comments on contemporary issues, the call to the Republican battle, commemorative eulogies for significant Republican figures, poems to personal friends, and feminist matters. A full analysis of López de Ayala's poetry falls outside the scope of this study. Nevertheless, through three key poems, I will now briefly highlight how López de Ayala reframes Romantic topoi to infuse them with greater political intent. Such a rewriting of Romanticism not only sets the scene for my examination in the following chapter of her play *De tal siembra, tal cosecha,* which critically engages with the Don Juan plot. It also points to the particular slant of López de Ayala's feminist activities and thought, to be discussed in the final section of this chapter.

López de Ayala's poetic corpus builds on a Romantic tradition that privileged nature and subjectivity to promote principles of independence, freedom, and revolution. In her compositions, nature invariably becomes politicized. Two poems that illustrate this adaptation well are "A la orilla del mar" and "Ante unas hojas de rosa." The first, published at the close of 1896,[50] resorts to a tripartite structure of three blocks of four verses, in which the initial scene is rewritten twice to intensify the political content on each subsequent occasion. The first section opens by describing a seashore, a liminal space that symbolizes the limit of fixed boundaries and traditions and thus exposes a status quo to potential change. There the wild sea that comes to harmonious rest on the sands is described in a clearly gendered analogy that recalls the union of man with woman in a consensual relationship:

La superficie del mar bravío
rota en pedazos, viene a besar
la humilde arena que silenciosa
puerto le ofrece de dulce paz.

(The surface of the wild sea / whipped up by whitecaps, comes to kiss / the humble sand that silently / offers a harbour of sweet peace.)

The sea, cast as masculine through the gender of the Spanish noun "mar," and the activity assigned to it, is counterposed to the sand, feminine not only in terms of its grammatical gender but also in the markers of sanctioned femininity that accompany it: those of humility, silence, sweetness, and peace.

In the second block of verses, the windswept sea is equated with the tyranny broken by the winds of freedom, while the seashore becomes the ennobled working class to whom tyranny must inevitably yield:

Lo mismo en breve la tiranía
rota por vientos de libertad,
ante los parias dignificados
mansa y confusa se postrará.

(Similarly, shortly tyranny / broken by the winds of freedom, / before the ennobled pariahs / will bow down meek and confused.)

This inversion of roles, which sees the once-proud masculine element – sea, man, and despot – overturn custom by humbling himself before the formerly lowly seashore – symbolic now of woman and the working classes – recalls the tradition of courtly love, which set the aristocratic woman on a pedestal to belie her lack of social and legal status. Thus the poem places a love relationship, traditionally confined to the private sphere and naturalized as such, firmly within the public sphere of politics, and the oppression of gender and class.

The final section of the composition refers to how the winds of freedom, now transformed into the hurricane of progress, overwhelm the turbulent sea of despotism. The sea's previous agency, signalled by the earlier phrase "viene a besar" (comes to kiss), is now subject to the will of freedom and progress, which obliges it to unite in love with the principle of equality, represented by the beautiful beach:

Porque en los mares del despotismo
de los progresos ya el huracán,
lanza las olas para que besen
la hermosa playa de la igualdad.

(Because in the seas of despotism / the hurricane of progress is already / hurling its waves to kiss / the beautiful beach of equality.)

The taming of the masculine element in the natural and human world sits ambiguously between a message of revolution and one of reform: a hesitancy that also transpires in López de Ayala's drama, *De tal siembra, tal cosecha*, as I will discuss.

The second poem that I address, "Ante unas hojas de rosa," was published just a few weeks later.[51] The six-stanza composition draws on a familiar motif of femininity, the rose, emblematic of beauty and chaste sexuality, to open with a depiction of still life:

Desparramadas yacen por el suelo
suaves hojas de rosada flor;
desparramadas yacen, y marchitas,
sin belleza ni olor.

(Scattered there lie on the ground / soft pink rose petals; / scattered they lie, and wilted, / lacking in beauty and fragrance.)

Such a description accords completely with the type of poetry, of an innocuously domestic bent, that nineteenth-century female writers were expected to deliver, while the deployment of the past participles "desparramadas" (scattered) and "marchitas" (wilted) underlines an appropriate feminine passivity.

The next verses mark the poem as an elegy for the past beauty and lost unity of the stem of roses, emphasized by the past tenses "fueron" (they were) and "se erguían" (they would raise their heads). At the same time, specific words such as "beautiful," "sweet," "adorable," "delicate," and "blush" continue to align the discourse with a normative, shy femininity:

¡Fueron hermosas, cuando todas juntas,
en dulce y adorable confusión,
se erguían sobre el tallo delicado
cubiertas de arrebol!

(How beautiful they were, when all together, / in sweet, adorable confusion, / they would raise their heads on the delicate stem / reddened by a rosy blush!)

In the following stanza the poetic voice likens the roses to a group of entwined sisters, a human still life that formerly bewitched the beholder, into which a note of challenging discrepancy now creeps, carried by the adjective "inimitable"; meaning "incomparable" or "unable to be copied," it is hence tinged with the improper quality of originality, considered a masculine attribute:

Y es que entonces, de hermanas parecían
un grupo inimitable, encantador;
produciendo su enlace primoroso
la más grata emoción.

(And so they resembled an incomparable, / bewitching bevy of sisters; / arousing in their exquisite union / the most pleasurable emotions.)

The fourth stanza turns from the theme of past glory to the present sadness and bitterness provoked by the separated, divided roses:

En tanto que ahora tristes, divididas,
avivan la amargura y el dolor,
de todo el que entre el polvo las contempla.

(While now sad, divided, / they arouse bitterness and pain, / in all who gaze on them in the dust.)

It is suggested that the roses are no longer a casualty of time but that they have wilfully rejected unity: "ajenas a la unión" (unmindful of unity). This pathetic fallacy is rendered explicit in the following stanza, where the roses become hearts that, although beating to the rhythm of freedom, are disunited by hatreds and dishonour:

Así también, en división perpetua
en odios, en rencilla y deshonor,
viven los corazones que se agitan
de libertad al son.

(So also, perpetually divided / by hatreds, quarrels, and dishonour, / live the hearts that beat / to the spirit of freedom.)

The poem ends with a wish that the roses be reunited and bound by ties of love. The desired and imagined recomposition of the stem of roses becomes equated with re-establishing the republic and hoisting the Republican flag. The rose of feminine virginity, deflowered by internal quarrels among warring Republican factions, is transformed into the rose of socialism:

¡Quién pudiera aún a costa de la vida
unirles con los lazos del amor!
¡Quién pudiera lograr que la república
alzara su pendón!

(Who could, even risking life and limb, / unite them in the bonds of love! / Who might enable the republic / to raise on high her standard!)[52]

It is hardly coincidental that the political climate that enveloped the composition of "Ante unas hojas de rosa" was dogged by lack of unity among the Republicans, which López de Ayala critiqued in a good number of articles that also appeared in *El Progreso*. On 27 February 1897, in her lead article entitled "¡Infelices!," López de Ayala calls on freethinking citizens to bury their differences and unite: "¡Ahogad las diferencias, las pequeñeces, las mezquindades!" (Bury your differences, meanness and pettiness!) and "¡¡Unión hermanos míos!!" (Unity, my brothers and sisters!!). Adapting to her political purposes a Christological discourse that privileges the communion of spirit and body, López de Ayala reiterates her message of unity: "Todos comulgamos en las mismas ideas, ... ¿qué aguardamos para confundirnos en una sola aspiración? ... ¡Unión! ¡Unión, republicanos!" (We all take the same sacrament of ideas, ... why are we waiting to become one in the same aspiration? ... Unity! Unity, Republicans!) The inclusive, inter-classist character of the republicanism that she embraces is palpable in her call to the working classes to join Republicans against what she describes as their common slavery and oppressors: "¡Acércate a nosotros, honrado proletario que no eres republicano: somos tus compañeros de esclavitud, ... tus opresores son los nuestros!" (Come unto us, oh honourable proletariat who is not Republican: we are your companions in slavery, ... your oppressors are ours!). The unity of disparate social bodies in one through freethinking thought, she assures them, will provide firm foundations for a future republic: "Hagamos la más hermosa de las uniones, la unión del pensamiento, ... y sobre esta sólida base asentemos la república" (Let's forge that most beautiful of unions, union through thought, ... and on this solid foundation let's establish the Republic).[53]

López de Ayala's constant infusing of nature with political themes, turning nature into culture, also heralds her feminist views. In relation to her feminist activities and to her literary works, López de Ayala's brand of feminism anticipates what in the twentieth century would become known as constructivist feminism, which emphasizes the role of society and culture in the formation of gender paradigms. Given that her feminist activities span at least thirty years, undoubtedly those that I relate in the following section constitute only a small proportion of her untiring efforts to better the condition of her sex.

Feminism without Borders: López de Ayala's Feminist Spaces, Activities, and Writings

Described by Sànchez i Ferré as the most important fin-de-siècle feminist in Catalonia, in 1889, the year in which she published *De tal siembra, tal cosecha*, López de Ayala founded in Barcelona, with Claramunt and Domingo Soler, the Sociedad Autónoma de Mujeres. It first occupied premises in the Raval neighbourhood in Cadena Street, later shifting to 20 Ferlandina Street, first floor (Sànchez i Ferré 1990, 169, 172). Announcements regarding the society's meetings in Llunas's *La Tramontana* tell us that on 4 December 1892 a meeting was held at the society's locale.[54] Two weeks later the same periodical refers to a forthcoming lecture by López de Ayala on the family.[55]

In the opinion of historian Isabel Segura Soriano, the Sociedad Autónoma de Mujeres was significant in that it "broadened the range of female-gendered urban spaces that, up to that time, had consisted only of the convents and beguinages" (2006, 28). The catalyst for the emergence of these spaces, Daphne Spain signals, are periods of sociocultural and political transition that see the abandoning of traditional norms without new ones having yet been fully developed. Such a context can be said to characterize fin-de-siècle Spain, especially Catalonia. Moreover, women-only organizations, Spain continues, are important because they enhance women's access to and participation in the public sphere (Spain 2006, 31). In that sense, they contribute to forging a democratic community: "To the extent that a vital public realm is crucial for civil society, gendered spaces that usher women into public [*sic*] are important contributors to an egalitarian city" (33).

Nine years after its founding, in April 1898, the Sociedad Autónoma de Mujeres morphed into the Sociedad Progresiva Femenina, which, according to Sànchez i Ferré, maintained a vigorous presence in Barcelona life until at least 1919 (1990, 173). Described by Ramos as "the most important, and with the greatest impact, of all the nuclei of freethinking feminism," the society shared its premises with the Constancia lodge, with which López de Ayala was associated (Ramos 1999a, 104). Not long after the inception of the Sociedad Progresiva, López de Ayala wrote a long letter, dated 25 June 1898, to Lozano, director of *Las Dominicales,* which was published in that periodical just five days later. There she describes the work of the Sociedad Progresiva Femenina, which complements those societies already established in Valencia, Cádiz, Huelva, and elsewhere. The principal objective of the society, López de Ayala affirms, is "la educación y dignificación de la mujer, en cuanto con su vida íntima, moral y social se relaciona" (the education and ennoblement of women, of everything concerning their intimate, moral, and social lives). In order to effect these aims, the letter continues, the society is to offer free night classes, given by its member Paulina Manresa, to illiterate women.[56] These classes, the text states, are in addition to the fortnightly lectures on politics, positivist thought, and sociology that the association is already offering its female members, so that they might emerge from the tutelage of others into sovereign subjecthood. While for the moment the main concern of the society was female education, future plans included creating secular health clinics, refuges for orphaned girls and invalid women, cooperatives, and periodicals that would promote reason and justice.[57]

On 3 December 1899, López de Ayala published a report entitled "La Sociedad Progresiva Femenina," in which she refers to the many activities of the society in the twenty-odd months since its establishment. In this period it has set up two secular schools – a girls' day school and the above-mentioned women's night school – held lectures, evening events, and charity acts to assist the poor and infirm, and pushed for a review of the Montjuich trials. New branches of the society have been established in Sabadell, Reus, and San Martín de Provensala in Barcelona, its representatives have attended civil burials and weddings, and it has founded the Grupo Humanidad (Association for Humanity), dedicated to caring for the sick. The most recent initiative of the society has been the establishment of a mutual fund from regular payments made by members, who, in the event of illness, will have access to a doctor, a pharmacy, and a daily allowance. The report concludes with López de Ayala calling on women to form associations, because only they themselves can achieve their sociocultural redemption: "¡Ah! mujeres, alentaos y constituiros asociaciones, que sólo nosotras somos llamadas a redimirnos" (Oh women! take heart and form associations, because it is up to us to save ourselves). It also announces that, as from January 1900, the society will have its own mouthpiece, López de Ayala's *El Progreso*.[58] Once this newspaper folded, López de Ayala's subsequent periodicals would perform that function. Another important initiative of the society was the establishment of a secular version of the Red Cross, known as the Nivel Rojo, the meetings and services of which were advertised in *El Gladiador del Librepensamiento*.[59] It was first mentioned in *El Gladiador* on 1 January 1916, when J. Costa Pomés refers to the fundraising for a refuge-hospital that might attend to the sick and suffering, irrespective of their religious beliefs. The next page of the same issue carried an announcement on behalf of the Sociedad Progresiva Femenina of a meeting to be held in early February to determine the mission of the Nivel Rojo and elect its board of directors.[60] Subsequently, meetings were held on the last Sunday of each month.[61] Apparently, in 1922, just four years before her death, López de Ayala was planning to expand the organization with a secular hospital (Méndez Bejarano 1922, 389). Yet another testimony to López de Ayala's continued concern for those less fortunate in society is an article of hers, "El modelo," first published in Lerroux's *El Progreso* and reprinted in *El Motín* on 19 February 1921. There she praises a Barcelona School for the Deaf, Dumb, and Handicapped, which, as the title of the article affirms, is a model that should be imitated in cities throughout Spain.[62]

Well linked to international feminist organizations, as early as 1899 the Sociedad Progresiva Femenina sponsored two representatives, Ernestina Meunié and Paz Ferrer, to attend the International Feminist Conference celebrated in London that June. They took with them a document addressed to the conference's president and co-written on 17 June by the society's honorary president, Domingo Soler, its president, López de Ayala, and its secretary, Dolores Zea. There the signatories declare that women, half of the human species, have been labelled as "inferior in their intellectual life and nonentities in political life." Consequently, they call for the conference to establish "a formidable, sisterly female association to demand from reason and humanity the right to shake off the degrading stigma of ignorance … so as thus to obtain the ennoblement and moral esteem to which all beings endowed with the faculties of thought and reason perforce aspire."[63] The presence of these Spanish feminists at the London conference calls for a more careful evaluation of the history of Spanish feminisms, refuting Geraldine Scanlon's belief that Spain was not represented at any of the international feminist conferences held from the end of the nineteenth century onward. The activities of the Sociedad Progresiva Femenina are but one example of an organized feminism well prior to the end of the First World War, the moment when, Scanlon states, the first serious feminist associations emerged in Spain (1986, 195–6).

The society also forged ties with feminists in other countries through its mouthpiece, López de Ayala's *El Gladiador del Librepensamiento*, just as Sárraga would do with *La Conciencia Libre*. Proof of this international outreach is a letter from Hermila Galindo, director of the Mexican weekly *La mujer moderna*, written to López de Ayala on 6 August 1916 to propose that they exchange their periodicals so as to promote "an effective union and true cohesion" within the international feminist movement. There is already such an arrangement, Galindo states, with Ana Carvia y Bernal's Valencian periodical, *Redención*, as well as with feminist associations in Spain, Cuba, and the United States. On accepting, López de Ayala emphasizes the transnational purview of feminism: "Para las mujeres no deben existir fronteras: todas animadas del ideal de su redención deben laborar con decisión y sin demora en tal sentido, hasta lograr que la justicia quede victoriosa" (For women, frontiers must not exist: inspired by the ideal of their redemption, all must work decisively and without delay for such an end until justice is victorious).[64]

López de Ayala's efforts on behalf of feminism and securing civil and political rights for women are evident in the demonstration, attended by some twenty thousand Catalan women of all classes and supported by followers of Lerroux, that she organized on Barcelona's streets on 10 July 1910. Under the banner of "Down with religion and long live freedom of thought," the demonstration, which Ramos describes as the most important feminist meeting of the Restoration period (1999a, 106), urged passage of the vote to women through the revision of Article 11 of the Constitution (Méndez Bejarano 1922, 389).[65] Another major feminist demonstration organized by López de Ayala would take place in May 1917, with coverage in the 19 May issue of *El Gladiador* (see figure 2.7).[66] These events point to an organized lobbying for women's suffrage well before the commonly accepted time frame of the 1920s.

Female-gendered spaces, freethinking associations, and feminist organizations fashioned ties of solidarity and friendship among women and brought them together in a common objective of female emancipation that transcended specific interests. At an 1895 cultural evening to promote secular thought, organized by teachers Antonia Amat and José Riera and closed by López de Ayala, female students sang López de Ayala's "Himno a la igualdad," which foregrounds women's demands for equality:

> Y pues sello ninguno tenemos
> que nos marque de inferioridad;
> igualdad relativa pedimos,
> ¡¡Igualdad, igualdad, igualdad!!

Año VII — Segunda época   Barcelona 19 de Mayo de 1917   Núm. 104

EL GLADIADOR DEL LIBREPENSAMIENTO

ÓRGANO DE LA FEDERACIÓN NACIONAL DE LIBREPENSADORES

SALDRÁ LOS SÁBADOS PRIMERO Y TERCERO DE CADA MES

PRECIOS DE SUSCRIPCIÓN

En Barcelona, trimestre. . . . . 75 céntimos
Fuera . . . . 1 peseta
Año. . . . . 3 »
Fuera . . . . 4 »

Los pagos en sellos de fácil cobro, o letras del Giro Mútuo.

Directora Literaria: D.ª Angeles López de Ayala

La Correspondencia a la misma

Ferrer de Blanes, número 12, pral., 1.ª GRACIA (BARCELONA)

Extranjero, trimestre. . . . . . 5 pesetas
Un año . . . . 7 »

Número suelto 10 céntimos

La Redacción no responde de los artículos firmados

MITIN FEMENINO

En la tarde del día 6 del corriente, tuvo lugar en la "Unión Republicana Radical Graciense" el mitin femenino que para tal fecha había sido organizado.

El salón teatro en el que en un principio se temió un fracaso por el escaso público que en él había, acabó por rebosar de gente, en la que predominaba el sexo femenino, representado por numerosos grupos pertenecientes a todas las esferas sociales, y en particular a la de las obreras.

Abrió la sesión el presidente del Centro, señor Canals, el que expuso el objeto del acto, que no era otro que el de probar la existencia de elementos femeninos progresivos, ya que hay la creencia de que la mujer, en general, es reaccionaria, o cuando menos, rutinaria; por su cobardía en manifestar en público sus juicios y apreciaciones sobre los problemas sociales, y muy especialmente sobre el problema religioso.

Hechas estas breves aclaraciones, cedió la presidencia a la señora Lopez de Ayala la que concedió la palabra a la señorita Marina Valls, que no habló mucho, pero que dijo en su discurso grandes verdades, atacando al atavismo que sigue imponiendo a la desgraciada España el terrible yugo de un fanatismo irracional, perturbador y absorvente. Fué muy aplaudida.

Siguióle en el uso de la palabra la jovencita Petra Romero, que recitó magistralmente una hermosa poesía librepensadora, cosechando muchos y muy nutridos aplausos.

Francisca Benaiges, vicepresidenta de la "Sociedad Progresiva Femenina", esa obrera abnegada, consecuente y culta, cuyos alientos no están en relación con su estado delicado de salud, siguió en el orden numérico a la señorita Romero, explicándose con soltura y valentía indescriptibles. Una ovación entusiasta premió su labor provechosa, obligándosela a recitar una magnífica poesía que tambien fué aplaudida con calor.

Se levantó D.ª María Marín, que es acogida con salvas de aplausos, y habla poco, por impedírselo el mal estado de sus pulmones, pero tan elocuente y sugestivamente, que produce una verdadera tempestad de ovaciones. Se lamenta de que los asuntos exteriores traigan consigo las divisiones y los choques en el interior de España, aumentando con ésto el malestar que nos aflije, e invita a las señoras a abandonar el rutinarismo y a decidirse por la libertad de la conciencia. Grandes muestras de aprobación en el auditorio.

Al llegar a este punto, la presidenta, abandonando su puesto y avanzando hacia el proscenio, advirtió que iba a dar lectura al admirable discurso, enviado expresamente para el mitin, de D.ª Rosario de Acuña, ante cuyo nombre, dijo, debían ponerse de pié los hombres y doblar la rodilla las mujeres, por tratarse del ser que más ha luchado por redimirlas de la ignoracia y de la esclavitud. (Algunos hombres se levantan respetuosamente).

A renglón seguido, Angeles López de Ayala lee la hermosa conferencia que insertamos a continuación de estas líneas.

Al terminar la lectura, la admiración del público estalló en salvas atronadoras ofreciendo un espectáculo consolador. ¡Puede estar satisfecha la gran maestra de las multitudes! Su semilla fructifica.

Angeles Lopez de Ayala resumió, y con atrayentes palabras invitó a las mujeres a dejar de ser *hembras, diamantes enlodados, flores repletas de detritus nocibos, sol tras plomizos nubarrones*, para convertirse en seres pensantes y conscientes, en deslumbradora pedrería, en flores frescas y odoríferas, en sol espléndido y vivificador.

Terminó el acto en medio de manifestaciones entusiastas. Nuestra felicitación a la Comisión organizadora.

ANGELES LOPEZ DE AYALA

Discurso de la brillante escritora D.ª Rosario de Acuña

Sres. Don Jaime Febré y Don Vicente Delago. Presidente y Secretario de la Comisión Organizadora del mitin femenino de la Unión Republicana Graciense.

Me piden Vdes. unas cuartillas para la sección que preparan. Hé aquí lo que puedo decirles.

Hondos sufrimientos morales y fsuga, de largos días de monótonos trabajos, hicieron yá que mi espíritu se encuentre cansado.

Los confines del batallar humano con su caos de horrores y hermosura sin clasificar ni encauzar aún por ninguna filosofía, por ninguna ciencia, religión, raza, ni edad, son yá para mi yo *consciente* lejanos países.

El más allá de la muerte está cercano a mí y el sueño de paz y olvido, reparador y reconfortante, que brinda sus brazos me atrae fuertemente hácia el *inmortal seguro* que cantó el poeta.

Muy trabajosamente, por lo tanto, escribo la presente; más con la carta de Vdes, llegó a mis manos otra de una mujer qué, allá en mi juventud, conocí breves días pero cuya amistad quedó sellada con un pacto recíproco: el de vivir y morir fuera de todo dogmatismo religioso gastando nuestras energías en despertar, alrededor nuestro en cuantos seres pusiera a nuestro lado el destino, las ideas racionales de justicia, bondad y belleza, desligadas de todas las religiones dogmáticas. Como este pacto fué hecho por mujeres conscientes no puede romperse más que con la muerte, pues las almas enteras traén a la vida todo el caudal que en ella han de verter, sin que manantiales ajenos a la esencia del suyo las enturbien, ni logren desviarlas del cauce que las trazó el destino.

Esta mujer, amiga mía, que hace 30 años viene *dándose* al ideal librepensador, por encima de su propio bien, porqué ¡a cuantas más inferiores que ella en entendimiento, cultura y voluntad se las vé, como monigotes de feria, subir a los tablados de la vanidad social hasta conseguir, con buenas o malas artes, un *sitio* en los frisos de los olimpos contemporaneos!

Esta pobre, noble y mártir mujer Angeles Lopez de Ayala me ha escrito una carta suplicándome que les complaciese a Vdes. mandándoles algo para su velada.

Cumplo, pues, nuestro pacto y satisfago su deseo.

Sé por su comunicación y la carta de Angeles que van a oirme mayoría de Mujeres y que se tratará en la sesión de la libertad de pensar en materia religiosa. Pues bien, sepan que no hay para mi nada más esencial para *racionalizar a la especie humana* que el sentimiento de la religión. ¿De cuál?... De todas, incluso del ateismo, que es una religión invertida, puesto que nombra a la *Nada* en el lugar del *Todo* ¡cuestión de palabras!

Les parecerá a muchas un absurdo esta afirmación mía en favor del sentimiento religioso, más, no lo es. Todas las religiones llevan en sí un fondo de *verdad* divina. En todas se halla la idea de Dios y de la inmortalidad del alma como núcleo de su razón de ser; todas ellas persiguen un mismo fin; relacionar la vida de los hombres y de la humanidad con las leyes universales; todas pretenden conocer a Dios y sumarse a El. No hay, pues, ninguna despreciable, ni odiosa, ni agena a la capacidad pensante de la especie humana. En su *fondo* es tan respetable la judía como la mahometana o la cristiana. Todas deben tener inviolabilidad para desenvolverse en las sociedades de los hombres, y, por lo tanto, todas deben y pueden discutirse, analizarse y compararse sin privilegio para ninguna; el ser humano, cuya mente no puede pasar, por medio del raciocinio, del acatamiento de una—cualquier creencia—debe ser respetado y no odiado por todos los demás seres de las opuestas.

Esta es la pura y fundamental doctrina del librepensamiento. Otra cosa es fanatismo, superstición, brutalidad, tan funesta del lado de los racionalistas como del lado de los inquisidores.

Más, en los tiempo actuales, este transcendental estado de conciencia es imposible que subsista en España; primero porque el Estado español está adscrito a la dominación católico romana, y luego, por que a pesar de los artículos de la Constitución que aseguran la tolerancia en materia religiosa, como todas las clases directoras, desde la cumbre al fondo, son completamente adictas al Vaticano y a sus enseñanzas que tienen por *verdad verdadera*, resulta que están casi fuera de la nacionalidad, como párias a quienes no se les debe ni el pan ni el agua, todos los que dejen de comulgar en la religión oficial, considerándose una virtud dejarles la vida (en cuanto a los bienes, la honra, el respeto y el afecto, esos se les quita o merma por todos los medios posibles).

Nada de esto es extraño, pues es la consecuencia de dar a una religión supremacía sobre las demás. De aquí que la cuestión palpitante en España; la piedra angular que sostiene la ignorancia, incultura, crueldad, ódio, disgregación, miseria, estancamiento y decadencia es la cuestión religiosa. Resuelta ésta, las demás se resolverían con facilidad; ínterin la voluntad nacional no imponga todo esto—separación de la Iglesia y el Estado; el órden civil independiente de toda la religión; renovación de todos los códigos en los ambientes científicos y racionalistas de la moderna edad; el inmenso caudal de riqueza que afluye a la Iglesia y sus derivados, tales como Comunidades, Centros de enseñanza confesional, etc., etc., recojido en beneficio de la Sociedad Civil; en las escuelas oficiales enseñanza de *todas* las religiones; prohibición de toda manifestación pública de carácter religioso, y libertad completa en la prensa y en la palabra para analizar, criticar, definir y comparar *todos* los dogmas de *todas* las religiones.

Puesto en este pié de justicia el Estado español nada importaría qué, despues, cada secta extremase su celo y propaganda para aumentar sus prosélitos. La libertad para esto, tambien completa, sin más limitación que la del escándalo y el desorden.

Cuando sea dado públicamente, y en igualdad de circunstancias, desentrañar los dogmas de las religiones, investigar sus fines y expresar sus medios ¿qué mal ha de haber en que aquellos que, apesar de estas aclaraciones, no dejen su creencia sean cristianos, moros o judios? ¿acaso no estarian todos de este modo mas convencidos de su verdad? ¿No sería mejor convivir con creyentes sinceros, libres de imposiciones, que con hipócritas o cobardes, por fuera creyentes, por dentro excépticos, por fuera blancos, como los sepulcros del evangelio, por dentro llenos de la ponzoña de la mentira?

¡Ay! ¡si nuestros católicos fueran siquiera celestiales! Porque lo que caracteriza a las almas religiosas no son las ceremonias de los cultos, ni las apariencias de beatitud. El dulce ambiente de la religiosidad ha de surgir del amor al prójimo; única y segura base de todas las religiones conocidas y única base tambien de todas las que los hombre vayan inventando.

Entonces, las mujeres españolas no serían las agarrotadas de la patria, como lo son ahora, pues no hay duda de que las mujeres,—salvo contadas excepciones y contadísimas agrupaciones—sostienen este estado medioeval en que agoniza España.

La mujer tiene en sí un elemento adaptable a los manejos de toda clase de sacerdocio; este elemento es la sentimentalidad.

Dios, la inmortalidad del alma y la responsabilidad de sus actos, son los tres puntos cardinales de la personalidad femenina. Si sobre ésta idiosincrasia del alma de la mujer se extendiera una educación sólida en conocimientos, la evolución de la mujer religiosa-dogmática a la mujer religiosa-racionalista estaría hecha y los hijos del hombre beberían en los senos maternos savia de ideas sublimes y no se envenenarían con linfa extenuante, henchida de prejuicios, absurdos y terrores. ¡Ah! cuando las madres sean racionalmente religiosas de la esencia divina que inspiran todas la religiones; cuando sean intransigentes en el único y solo mandamiento-raíz en que se apoyan todas, que es el amor a sus semejantes, entonces podrá la humanidad llamarse orgullosamente racional.

Hoy, por hoy, el espíritu jesuítico está infiltrado en el alma de la mujer española y ésta es la que lanza sus hijos al medio educador que tan funestos resultados tiene. Todas las mujeres que pertenecen a las clases impulsadoras de la vida nacional envían sus hijos a los colegios de inspiración jesuíta; pues la iglesia católica, en su camino de petrificación, está entregada a ésta doctrina. Los jóvenes de sano organismo, de índole generosa, de mente equilibrada, resisten bien la influencia de todas las negaciones que se les imponen, y aún algunos se salvan del pesimismo; los jóvenes insanos, débiles, de índole cavilosa y poca o indefinida personalidad, caen, son las almas dañadas por atormentamientos recónditos e inseguridades de voluntad, y los jóvenes imbéciles, en los grados mínimo y máximo, salen a la sociedad aportando una corriente de anormalidades y estultezas que perturba y desorganiza; y todos llevan en su fondo un *átomo dañado*, el de la soberbia que se les impone bajo *formas* más u menos comedidas, átomo que les impide luego, en el resto de su vida, sumarse, como partículas infinitesimales, al plan del Universo, todo armonía y equilibrio, sin más infierno para nosotros que el de la herencia de animalidad que aún circula en la carne humana, y, sin más paraíso que la progresiva elevación de la mente, en etapas terrenales o ultraterrenales, al reconocimiento de su origen divino para secundar la obra creadora como chispa fluente de lo Absoluto-Eterno, abarcador de astros y átomos.

Poco se necesita saber de psicología para conocer la *marca* de la educación a que las madres sujetan a sus hijos. En las mismas cumbres de la intelectualidad se ven sus efectos funestos ¡cuán pocos de los ingénios que pretenden ser *Mentores* traspasan los umbrales de la pedantería, de la vacuidad, de las disquisiciones menudas, del análisis pueril y presuntuoso. Si pretenden hacer filosofía arman un galimatías de filósofos conocidos, todo sin ilación ni fundamento, de tal modo qué, al acabar de seguir sus elucubraciones, se palpa uno a sí mismo asombrado de hallarse vivo, después de la pedrea de erudición y ausencia de ideas de que hacen gala. Si hacen literatura y se les lee con intención de aprender en ellos, no hay más remedio que buscar todas las obras del clasicismo, para encender con ellas una hoguera, por enbusteras y perturbadoras; de tal modo se golrigay de versos y prosas, que nos sirven los ajesuitados, excluye toda regla sana y todo bello órden de los maestros... ¡y lo mismo pasa en todas las demás bellas artes!

En la mentalidad española salta lo nimio y común, lo presuntuoso y despreciador, el detalle del necio envanecimiento, de la soberbia disimulada, del ruin egoismo... ¡del átomo dañado que asimilaron las juventudes, durante más o menos años, en las aguas turbias que fluyen de las castas sacerdotales! Apoderados de los mitos y símbolos con los cuales la Humanidad se ha ido perfeccionando, todos los sacerdocios los han clasificado con arreglo a su ética

2.7 Ángeles López de Ayala, “Mitin Femenino,” in *El Gladiador del Librepensamiento* 104, Year VII, Second Epoch (19 May 1917): 1. By kind permission of the *Arxiu Històric de la Ciutat de Barcelona* (Microfilm no. 73)

(72; And so we do not bear any brand / that marks us as inferior; / equality in equal measure we ask for, / Equality, equality, equality!)[67]

For López de Ayala, it was incumbent on freethinking women governed by reason to exercise a particular responsibility to lead Spain out of its indifference and apathy, as she explains in "La epidemia reinante":

> Y en particular, vosotras, mis hermanas en ideas, las que os sentís con el vigor necesario ... dad un nuevo impulso a vuestra acelerada marcha por la senda de la razón, y entre todas, y entre todos los que no se desdeñen de imitar nuestra conducta, suplantemos el congelante sinflujo del harto extendido y contagioso mal, con la fe en lo grande, en lo noble, en lo sublime.
>
> (And especially you, my sisters in ideas, those who feel you have the necessary strength ... lend new energy to your rapid pace along the path of reason, and among you all, and with all those men who do not disdain to imitate what we do, let's sweep away the stagnant waters of the widespread, contagious disease with faith in all that is great, noble, and sublime.)[68]

Yet among these "sisters in ideas," as I elucidate in chapter 1, there were tangible differences on how best to create the freethinking female citizen and effect Spain's sociopolitical transformation. One was López de Ayala's antipathy towards Pardo Bazán – like her, a feminist, but dissimilar in her firm adherence to Catholicism.[69] Her critique of Pardo Bazán is evident in "Figueras," a satirical composition from 1899 that lambasts Pardo Bazán for denigrating this Catalan town:

> La perla del Ampurdán,
> la de historia peregrina,
> maltratada por la inquina
> de Emilia Pardo Bazán
>
> (The pearl of the Ampurdán, / of far-flung fame, / ill-treated by the spite / of Emilia Pardo Bazán)

Whereas, for López de Ayala, Figueras symbolizes the cradle of Catalan freedom and equality – "aquella cuna dorada / de la santa libertad, / emporio de la igualdad" (that golden cradle / of holy freedom, / the centre of equality) – Pardo Bazán, identified as "la autora de 'Insolación'" (the author of "Insolación"), has allegedly described it as "horrible y esquiva" (horrible and unfriendly) and as a "poblacho" (dump of a place). The reason for these diverging appraisals, López de Ayala states, is that Pardo Bazán embodies an old order built on aristocratic titles and wealth, to which Figueras does not pay the anticipated respect:

> Que allí no halló vasallaje
> su título o sus riquezas;
> porque allá, a tales *grandezas*,
> no se les rinde homenaje.
>
> (There she found no vassals / because of her title and wealth; / because there, such *privileges* / do not receive homage.)[70]

For López de Ayala, then, perceived differences in social class and in attitudes towards tradition override any common ground that she might have with her more famous contemporary.[71]

In comparison, there are many testimonies to a long and deep friendship between López de Ayala and Domingo Soler, despite fundamental differences. Although Domingo Soler establishes that López de Ayala is not a spiritist, she does describe her as "una buena obrera del progreso, trabajando por el libre pensamiento y por la masonería con verdadera abnegación" (a good worker for progress, labouring for freethinking and freemasonry with true abnegation).[72] Nonetheless, López de Ayala did participate in spiritist activities such as the 1892 Congreso Espiritista Iberoamericana e Internacional (International Ibero-American Spiritist Conference), where she gave a presentation entitled "Memoria sobre la conveniencia de la redención y vindicación femenina" (Horta 2004, 255). When López de Ayala was imprisoned in 1892, Domingo Soler supported a petition for international amnesty and expressly mentioned López de Ayala (Simón Palmer 1991, 739). Their passionate promotion of secular education and efforts to improve the conditions of the working classes brought them together in many activities, leading Domingo Soler to praise López de Ayala in 1895 as "un verdadero apóstol para la clase obrera y trabaja por las escuelas laicas con el mayor entusiasmo, con la mejor voluntad" (a true apostle for the working class, working on behalf of the secular schools with the greatest enthusiasm and goodwill).[73] On a more personal note, Domingo Soler refers to being accompanied by López de Ayala in 1892 on an early morning walk by the sea in Barcelona,[74] while on 10 November 1895 López de Ayala wrote a poem to Domingo Soler on the occasion of the latter's birthday, entitled "A mi querida amiga Amalia Domingo Soler en su cumpleaños." There López de Ayala affirms that time must be measured by the good deeds that one performs and not by time wasted.[75]

Surviving poems also reveal disparity in their respective visions of how best to resolve social inequalities. In López de Ayala's 1898 poem "A Amalia Domingo

Soler,"[76] she opens by rejecting Domingo Soler's criticism of her writing, which the latter perceives as encasing terrible truths in bitterness rather than sweetness:

> ¿Que en la tinta de la hiel
> estoy mojando mi pluma?
> ¿Que la verdad, cuando abruma,
> hay que envolverla con miel?
>
> (You say that in the ink of bitterness / I am dipping my pen? / That the truth, when unpalatable, / must be coated with honey?)

The composition juxtaposes Domingo Soler's admonition that injustices can be remedied by constructive action, gentleness, and turning the other cheek, with López de Ayala's affirmation of the need to combat violence or "hiel" with violence:

> Óyeme, mi amiga fiel:
> Cuando están negras historias
> escritas en las memorias,
> ¡sólo se borran con hiel!
>
> (Listen to me, my faithful friend: / When dark histories are / engraved in memories, / they are erased only with violence!)

and

> ¿Que de indiferencia llena
> en nieve la llaga anego?
> No, Amalia; ¡le arrojo fuego
> para cortar la gangrena!
>
> (You say that, completely uncaring, / I steep the wound in snow? / No, Amalia; I cauterize it with fire / to stop the gangrene!)

Until the world is governed by fraternity and freedom, it is vital, the poetic voice continues, to destroy the old in order to construct a better world:

> Mientras, no; ¿cómo seguir,
> buena amiga, tu consejo,
> si hay que derrumbar lo viejo
> para poder construir?

(Meanwhile, no; how can I follow, / good friend, your advice, / if what is old must be demolished / in order to build?)

Also at stake in these diverging world views are two models of femininity: a more conservative paradigm professed by Domingo Soler that equates women's writing with beauty and sweetness, and another avant-garde framework proper to López de Ayala that presents women as actors prepared to take unpalatable steps to create a more equal society.

Just four weeks later Domingo Soler's poetic response appeared, entitled "A la escritora librepensadora Ángeles López de Ayala."[77] Manifesting an attitude of tolerance, Domingo Soler commences by expressing her desire to engage in reasoned dialogue with López de Ayala without wanting to impose her own point of view:

Quiero, Ángeles, contestarte,
sin tener la pretensión
de que yo pueda inculcarte
mi profunda convicción;
...
Ni tú me convencerás,
ni yo te convenceré;
tus razones expondrás,
yo mis ideas expondré.

(I want, Ángeles, to respond, / without any expectation / of instilling in you / my deeply held convictions; / ... / Neither you will convince me, / nor I you; / you will set out your reasons, / I will explain my ideas.)

According to Domingo Soler, López de Ayala's passion for science blinds her to more spiritual possibilities: "Que yo te he visto dormida, / por la ciencia hipnotizada" (For I have seen you asleep, / hypnotized by science) and "Tú ves horribles efectos, / mas las causas desconoces" (You see terrible consequences, / but you are ignorant of their causes). Domingo Soler considers that the writings and actions of López de Ayala and other women similar to her create violence and intensify hatreds:

Pero en vuestra propaganda
vais los odios avivando;
al pueblo le decís: ¡anda,
anda, sí (pero matando);
tu salvación te lo manda!

(But in your propaganda / you are all inflaming hatreds; / you tell the people: go forward! / go forward, yes (but killing); / your salvation demands it!)

In her closing stanzas Domingo Soler urges López de Ayala not to write with bile but to instruct by delighting and creating empathy:

Tienes bastante talento
para enseñar deleitando;
deja tu estilo violento.
¿No es bien triste ir aumentando
el general descontento?
Haz con tu pluma sentir,
no hagas con tu pluma odiar.

(You are sufficiently talented / to marry instruction with enjoyment; / give up your violent style. / Isn't it tragic to go about increasing / the general discontent? / Arouse compassion with your pen, / don't use it to provoke hatred.)

Perhaps the freethinking writer to whom López de Ayala was closest in her views on sociopolitical transformation was Rosario de Acuña, whom she acknowledged publicly as her mentor and who contributed regularly to her periodicals, especially to *El Gladiador del Librepensamiento* between 1915 and 1918. Several documents speak of their lasting mutual support amid social censure and adversity. López de Ayala's admiration for Acuña is evident in an 1891 sonnet, "A Rosario de Acuña,"[78] which encourages the playwright to rise above the petty politics and controversy created by the Madrid performance and subsequent publication that same year of her anticlerical play, *El Padre Juan*:

Pero, ¿qué importa a tu esplendor radiante
el loco empeño y los esfuerzos vanos,
con que pretende el mísero intrigante
eclipsar tus destellos soberanos?[79]

(But why should your radiant splendour be concerned / with the unbalanced resolves and vain efforts, / with which the wretched plotter seeks / to eclipse your sovereign rays of light?)

Almost thirty years later, with both writers nearing the end of their lives, on 17 April 1920 Acuña published a long letter to Nakens, the editor of *El Motín*, to which she and López de Ayala were frequent contributors. In it she thanks Nakens for recommending that she receive the Ayuso Prize: a sum of one thousand pesetas given to anticlerical writers in need of financial assistance. The letter provides a sobering account of the financial straits endured by Acuña: the amount will serve to recover pawned jewels that had belonged to her mother and grandmother, pay outstanding bills, and purchase a much-needed pair of shoes. The remaining two hundred pesetas will buy Acuña her food supplies for the next three months and ensure that she can pay the mortgage for a year; her widow's pension, she stresses, only gives her one thousand pesetas a year, and there is no home safe from the influence of the Catholic Church and the discrimination against women from liberal men: "La hombría de los hombres de las izquierdas que ¡vaya si son *zurdos* en esto de considerar a las mujeres capaces de ser personas!" (The manliness of men on the left, how *cack-handed* they are in believing women capable of being persons!) She can only dream of a better existence: "un existir menos rastrero, menos animalizado, menos inicuo que este de los presentes días" (a less degrading, less animal-like existence, less iniquitous than my current state). In her postscript Acuña turns her attention to López de Ayala, whose health is frail and whose situation is similarly precarious, asking if her friend might be considered for the following year's prize:

> Esta mujer lleva cuarenta años escribiendo en pro del racionalismo y en contra de las supersticiones y los desmanes de esta fanática religiosidad española. Esta señora es muy anciana; de mi edad; enferma del corazón atada a un trabajo extenuante para ganar un pedazo de pan, y ayudada solo por la piedad de leales librepensadores catalanes.
>
> (This woman has spent forty years writing in support of rationalism and against the superstitions and outrages of this fanatical Spanish religiosity. This lady is very elderly, about my age, with a bad heart and tied to an exhausting job to earn a scrap of bread, and whose only support comes from the compassion of loyal Catalan freethinkers.)[80]

López de Ayala's epistolary reply, written on 22 April, is carried in the issue of *El Motín* published on 1 May 1920. Her response is particularly interesting because there she pays homage to Acuña as her mentor and inspiration:

> Además tú fuiste mi maestra; de ti aprendí a pensar honradamente; la grandeza de tus sentimientos se me *contagió*, y la que sólo contaba con el antecedente de haber leído una buena biblioteca de autores selectos … se enajenó de gozo al admirar tus dotes y corrió hacia ti como dice el poeta que "los ríos corren a la mar." … y traté de imitarte, bien que con la grosería con que un diamante falso imita al verdadero.
>
> (Moreover you were my teacher; from you I learnt how to think honourably; the greatness of your feelings was *infectious*, and she who had only previously read a good

library of select authors ... was transported with delight on admiring your talents and ran towards you, as the poet says, like "the rivers flow to the sea." ... and I tried to emulate you, although with the imperfection with which a false diamond resembles the real one.)

Featuring also in the letter are references to López de Ayala's dire financial circumstances; at the age of sixty-four, the closing down of *El Gladiador* has forced her to take a lowly position with the Barcelona Town Hall, which she obtained through the efforts of freethinking friends. The small income derived from this job is especially appreciated, López de Ayala tells Acuña, because over the last two years she has been caring for an orphaned girl: "Hoy, amiga mía, soy sólo una modestísima empleada del Ayuntamiento barcelonés ... *puesto* que he aceptado con gratitud, porque hace más de dos años que recogí a una huerfanita" (Today, dear friend, I am merely a very lowly employee of the Barcelona Town Hall ... a *position* I have accepted gratefully, because over two years ago I took into my home an orphaned girl).[81]

The straitened circumstances endured by female freethinking writers are highlighted in another article written by López de Ayala on 1 January 1921 and published in *El Motín* a fortnight later. Entitled "¡¡¡Justicia!!!" it draws attention to the plight of María Marín, whose short stories and historical and scientific articles had appeared in the Valencian periodical *El Pueblo*, as well as in *El Gladiador del Librepensamiento*.[82] Now "enferma, sola y desamparada" (ill, alone, and without protection), Marín's only son, who lives far away, cannot meet her modest expenses. Stating that the freethinking woman or "mujer racional" is an exotic anomaly unappreciated by an unjust society (una planta exótica torpemente cultivada por nuestra injusta sociedad), López de Ayala calls on her fellow journalists and editors to publish Marín's writings out of solidarity, so as to provide her with a small income: "Es la compensación de sus escritos; es el medio de sostener la materia para conservar la inteligencia que puede y debe propagar la luz; es, finalmente, la solidaridad que debe existir entre los amigos de la justicia y del progreso" (It is the due recompense for her writings; it is the means to sustain the body in order to preserve the intelligence that can and must transmit the light; it is, finally, the solidarity that must exist among the friends of justice and progress).[83]

A sense of the inequality against which López de Ayala and her literary sisters fought is encapsulated in an article published in *La Tramontana* on 28 February 1896. Its subject matter was a document drawn up by freethinking women that decried Article 13 of the Constitution for discriminating against the female sex by referring to "male citizens" and not "female citizens." Although the newspaper does not mention López de Ayala, it would have been unthinkable for her not to have participated in the elaboration of the document. Taking its bearings from the document, the column refers to women's lack of legal status and rights: "Women are subject to the will of their husbands, they cannot administer or decide anything; in the eyes of the courts, they are equal to men only as criminals; they cannot write or publish anything if their husband ... does not allow it, and indeed, in these times of democracy women have no greater rights than they did under the emperor Tiberius."[84]

The enslavement of women is a constant theme in López de Ayala's feminist poems, reflecting what Scanlon denounces in that sociohistorical context as women's actual legal slavery (1986, 126).[85] The four compositions that I now analyse set out López de Ayala's concern for women's emancipation, which she often likens to the struggle by Spain's working classes for freedom from financial hardship. In the rousing "La esclavitud" López de Ayala's poetic voice opens by affirming the freedom of nature and denouncing, in contrast, men's lack of liberty. However, the poem continues, this lack pales in comparison with the yoke imposed by the male sex on the female, disregarding the ties that bind them:

Esa esclavitud durísima
que, con egoísmo bárbaro,
un sexo impone a otro sexo,
sin ver que ambos son hermanos.

(This brutal slavery / that, with barbarous selfishness, / one sex imposes on the other, / without seeing that they are brother and sister.)

The enslavement of women by men begins with the female's parents, continues with her lover and husband, and is sustained by her children. Hence the poetic voice calls on her sisters to unite and break their chains of oppression:

¡¡Ay!! ¡¡juntémonos hermanas!!
y la noble frente alzando,
convirtamos en añicos
los hierros que nos forjaron.

(Ah! Let's unite, sisters! / And with our noble heads high, / let's smash to smithereens / the chains that they forged for us.)

Republican men are also invoked to support women's emancipation and not to imitate those who denied women a soul: "[Y] no imitarán a aquellos / que hasta el alma nos negaron." Women, the poem concludes, must educate themselves and exchange the dressing room and Catholic Church for books, so as to fight for their rights and emancipate themselves: "¡Luchemos por nuestros fueros[!]" (Let's fight for our rights!) and "¡¡¡Mujeres, a emanciparnos!!!" (Women, let's emancipate ourselves!)[86]

The domestic tyranny under which many women lived is couched as a political matter in López de Ayala's 1897 poem, "La vuelta a la vida," directed at raising personal and collective consciousness of an abusive situation. The poetic voice urges a feminized Spain, "esquilmada y maltrecha" (abused and battered), to awaken from her lethargy and become aware of her exploitation:

> ¡Despierta, pobre España,
> de tu letargo,
> y ve cómo te explotan
> hombres bastardos[!].
>
> (Awaken, poor Spain, / from your apathy, / and see how you are being exploited / by bastards!)

Deploying tropes of a naturalized normative femininity, such as the retiring violet and its subdued silence, López de Ayala implicitly draws a parallel between the situation facing Spain's working classes and her women:

> Cuál violeta que entre hojas
> su cáliz guarda,
> sin saber que su aroma
> la hace preciada,
> así tus bríos
> yacen en la hojarasca
> de tu mutismo.
>
> (Just as the violet among its leaves / hides its bud, / without realizing that its value / resides in its scent, / so too your energies / lie among the dead leaves / of your silence.)

The poetic voice demands that justice be done and that rights not be the province of the wealthy and the Catholic Church but be granted to all, so as to accompany already existing duties:

> Que enderecen la vara
> de la justicia;
> que ni ricos ni clérigos

gocen primicias;
que los derechos,
igual que los deberes,
causen respeto.

(Let them hold upright the rod / of justice; / may neither the rich nor the clergy / enjoy the first fruits; / may rights, / the same as duties, / inspire respect.)

The time has come, the poem concludes, for Spain not to delay further and to defeat tyranny:

¡Que más tiempo no pierdan,
...
que en los espacios
suena ya un ¡viva España
sin sus tiranos!

(Don't waste any more time, / ... / because across space / there already resounds a Long Live Spain / without her tyrants!)[87]

A slightly earlier composition, "¡La mujer!," centres on the imperative to educate women appropriately. Women are represented as caught between the future and the past, between modernity and an obsolete theocratic order:

"Ilústrate sin tardanzas,"
le dice el tiempo moderno;
y el Viejo, con destemplanza,
le habla sólo del infierno.

("Educate yourself without delay," / these modern times tell her; / while that Old Fogey Time, out of touch, / only lectures her on hell.)

Caught between their desire for education and fear of public censure, women feel damned if they do and damned if they do not:

En fuerza fiera, constante,
siente que el mundo le grita:
si no se instruye, "¡ignorantes!"
y si se instruyen, "¡malditas!"

(With wild, unrelenting force, / she hears the world shout at her: / if she does not educate herself, "Simpleton!" / and if she educates herself, "Be damned!")

Some of the fault, the poetic voice affirms, can be attributed to the attitude of men who deny women education while simultaneously criticizing their ignorance: "¿Le negáis ilustración / y la odiáis porque no sabe?" (You men deny her education / and you hate her for not knowing?) Men's duty, the text continues, is to help women advance, given that, as mothers, they will be the educators of their offspring: "[¡]Porque la madre ha de ser / la institutriz de sus hijos!" The poem concludes by refuting the misogynist belief in women's allegedly natural deficiencies:

Están bien organizados
su cerebro y corazón;
¡¡no hay disculpa, hombres honrados,
les debéis educación!!

(They are rationally and emotionally sound / in mind and heart; / there is thus no excuse, men of honour, / you owe them an education!)[88]

One of López de Ayala's most inspiring feminist poems is "La ola" from 1897 (see figure 2.8). Now the turbulent waves of "A la orilla del mar" have become the unstoppable tsunami of feminist revolution that is sweeping the Western world:

[¡]Al cabo, todo lo invade:
al cabo, todo lo llena,
del femenil entusiasmo
la ola gigante y soberbia!
Vedla cómo surge en Francia
y en Alemania y América,
y en Italia y Portugal
y en Austria y en Inglaterra.

(At last, it invades everything: / at last, it is everywhere, / the gigantic, magnificent wave / of women's agitation! / See how it springs up in France, / and in Germany and America, / and in Italy and Portugal / and in Austria and England.)

Enumerating all the Spanish cities that the wave has engulfed – Cádiz, Villa del Río, Madrid, Córdoba, and Reus – López de Ayala stresses that where it has gathered most strength is in *"Barcelona la seria"* (*Barcelona, the serious one*), which she describes as a progressive city of science and progress where "la mujer lucha

Año II. Barcelona 13 Febrero de 1897 Núm. 12

El Progreso

PERIÓDICO REPUBLICANO

5 céntimos — SE PUBLICA LOS SÁBADOS — Céntimos 5

PRECIOS DE SUSCRIPCIÓN

Barcelona y su llano. . . . . trimestre 1 pta.
Provincias. . . . . » 1'50 »
Extranjero. . . . . año 10 »
Ultramar. . . . . » 8 »
El pago por adelantado se hará en sellos de correo de 15 cts. ó en libranzas del giro mutuo; además un sello de 10 cts. por el cambio
A los corresponsales se les dará el 40 por 100 de comisión.

Dirección y Administración: Plaza del Sol, 27, 1.°—GRACIA
Horas de Oficina: de 7 á 9 de la noche
Los domingos, de 10 á 1 de la mañana
La Correspondencia, á D.ª Angeles López de Ayala

Anuncios y comunicados á precios convencionales

Número suelto. . . . . 5 cénts.
» atrasado. . . . . 10 »
Paquete de 25 números. . . . . 75 »

De los artículos firmados, responden sus autores.

IMPORTANTÍSIMO

Se han trasladado las oficinas de **El Progreso** á la Plaza del Sol, núm. 27, 1.°, Gracia, donde se deberá dirigir la correspondencia y hacer todas las reclamaciones.

¡CON BRAVURA!

Así hemos luchado, luchamos y lucharemos, interin nos queden esperanzas en nuestra alma, alientos en nuestro pecho, fé en nuestro corazón, sangre en nuestras venas é ideas en nuestro cerebro.

Con bravura lucharemos, hasta dar fin á esta situación anómala, enojosa, tiránica, insufrible, inquisitorial y absurda que hace 23 años nos agobia, y que amenaza con no dejar resto de nuestro tesoro, y de nuestro prestigio y de nuestra dignidad.

Porque la contemplación de iniquidades tantas nos subleva, inspirándonos el recuerdo del derecho, el sentimiento del deber, el entusiasmo de la actividad, y el ardiente deseo del triunfo, aunque para lograrlo hayamos de soportar todo género de persecuciones y torturas.

Sí, es indispensable probar á nuestros crueles adversarios y á nuestros entorpecedores los indiferentes, que nosotros no conocemos la debilidad, porque amamos el sacrificio; que no nos acobarda el sufrimiento, porque nos arrebata la abnegación; que no nos espanta el calvario, porque su cima está dorada por el sol de la justicia.

¿Que hay grandes sacudidas que desequilibran el orden social y le perturban?

¡Animo, y á restablecerle á toda costa, combatiendo siempre bajo el punto de vista del adelanto, la causa del fenómeno existente!

¿Que separa un abismo á los demócratas entre sí? Pues, ¡á trabajar para que se llene con restos de amor propio procedentes de los unos y los otros, hasta que ambas muchedumbres se confundan en el más fraternal de los abrazos! ¿Que levanta su espantable cabeza la dinamita? ¡A destrozársela por medio de un interés protector, cariñoso é ilustrativo hacia el obrero!

¿Que agoniza el comercio y la agricultura muere, y la industria se amilana? ¡á vivificarlas y fortalecerlas haciéndoles ver entre la marejada de descalabros que nos cerca, la posibilidad de que el cuerno de la abundancia de la república española, vierta muy en breve, la prosperidad en nuestro suelo!

¿Crece el despotismo? ¡A contrarrestarle!

¿Reina la arbitrariedad? ¡A destronarla!

¿Se multiplican el abuso, el chanchullo y el agio? ¡Con voluntad, honradez y decisión, se consiguen cien prodigios!

Nosotros así lo creemos, y por eso trabajamos, sin vacilaciones, sin treguas ni desmayos!

Y os aconsejamos que trabajeis también, según la medida de vuestras fuerzas, porque ya lo hemos dicho, el movimiento es lucha, y la lucha vida!

¡A entenderse en las próximas asambleas populares!

¡A unirse, republicanos!

¡Llega la hora de la prueba!

¡Se acercan los instantes difíciles: para los que se requieren harmonías, virilidad y fuerzas!

¡Terminen las rencillas! ¡Acaben las divisiones! ¡Concluyan las pequeñas batallas!

Y unisonos, generosos, ennoblecidos, potentes, salgamos de las asambleas populares armados con las palas de nuestra enérgica resolución, limpiando con ellas el lodo que dificulta el paso á la república!

Ángeles López de Ayala.

Juan del Pueblo

Á "EL PAÍS"

He leído tus consejos, *El País*, y han llegado hasta mi corazón haciéndole palpitar de entusiasmo con un rayo de esperanza.

¿Sabes por qué de nuevo pruebo levantarme é intento andar? Porque mi pecho se halla abierto á toda generosidad, mi alma á la ardiente fe y mi sér impregnado de amor á la santa libertad.

¡Tú lo has dicho, amigo del pueblo! Cien veces me han llamado, y cien veces he respondido; pero en lugar de llevarme á la lucha, cruenta sí, pero fecunda y reivindicadora de mis derechos y de mi soberanía, me hicieron servir para lo que tú me recuerdas, y yo no olvido.

¡Que me redima!! Por esto me muero ahora, y para eso iré á los *meetings* y después á otra cosa. Sí, para redimirme, pero de todos y en absoluto y para siempre.

De todos, porque ya conocen y sé cómo encauzando mi fuerza, la han utilizado para elevarse *ellos* y no para barrer la..... reacción.

En absoluto, porque empiezo ya á ver claro, y no he de atender por armoniosa que sea, la voz de nadie que como yo no sienta hambre de pan y hambre de libertad.

Y para siempre, porque si á la revolución me siguen mis hermanos, ó sucumbiremos en la contienda, redimiéndonos así la muerte, ó traeremos la República, que esta vez será hija del pueblo, sangre de mi sangre, redentora de la patria.

Sí, yo soy republicano, no soy legislador.

Allá, cuando yo, cuando el pueblo soberano envíe sus mandatarios al templo de las leyes, entonces será tiempo de que elija entre los que crean en la federación ó estimen el unitarismo, entre los que quieran una religión para el Estado ó un Estado garantizador de todas las creencias, y respecto á los derechos al trabajo y á mi pan... ¡figúrate amigo *El País*, si sabré de esto, cuando es lo que me decide á levantarme y andar!!

Agradecido á tus consejos, queda amigo tuyo,

Juan del Pueblo.

SOCIOLOGÍA

LA PROPIEDAD

Examinemos hoy este concepto bajo su aspecto industrial, y con relación á los adelantos de las ciencias.

¿Quién puede en justicia atribuirse el derecho de la propiedad particular del vapor, de la electricidad, de la fuerza hidráulica, de la dinámica, ni de las sublimes concepciones de su aplicación, producto del pensamiento del hombre?

¡Ah! Si por la levadura del egoismo, latente todavía en la humana naturaleza, las generaciones pasadas sufrieron la detentación de los derechos naturales del individuo, hoy reivindicados estos, réstale al proletario todavía conquistar el goce, la plena utilidad de las fuerzas naturales ya encauzadas, mas por su ser, de dominio universal en la misma gradación que el aire, que la luz ó que el espacio.

[illegible] que las conciencias honradas y los espíritus serenos abominen de las religiones positivas, es la simonía que sus sacerdotes hacen del dogma y del concepto de la divinidad ¿por qué ha de tolerarse sin protesta que haya quien monopolice y lucre particularmente con el destello de divinidad de los pensamientos de Gutenberg, Stephenson ó Edisson? Tan sacrílego es el sacerdote que no entierra sin estipendio al hombre muerto en la religión que él predica, como el ambicioso que reduce el salario del obrero porque el balance no arroja el tanto por ciento por su avaricia prefijado.

Las máquinas son para las fuerzas motrices, lo que el cuerpo para el espíritu. La causa de utilidad no es la máquina, es la fuerza, y la fuerza no es el hogar, ni el combustible, ni el dínamo, sinó la naturaleza que acumuló el calórico ó establece la corriente: el alma de su aplicación, no son los cálculos algebráicos ni los signos geométricos de la fórmula de un sistema de palancas ó de ejes, sinó la inteligencia que los concibió y les dió forma y les *hizo ser*.

Así pués, al lucrar un reducido número por medio del capital, utilizando en su exclusivo provecho las fuerzas de la naturaleza combinadas por el destello de agena inteligencia, es una detentación de lo inalienable, tan anti-humanitaria, tan atentatoria al propio derecho natural, que al principio supusimos ya del todo á salvo, como puede serlo el comercio de esclavos entre los pueblos semi-bárbaros ó el lenocinio en los civilizados (demos por buena la denominación)

Cuando la humanidad se da cuenta de las grandes injusticias, es que ha llegado en el tiempo y en el espacio la hora de las reparaciones.

¿Cómo tendrán lugar éstas? ¡Poco importa!

¿Qué son los menguados intereses materiales de unos cuantos egoistas, por muy elevado que sea el guarismo que los represente, ante los derechos de la colectividad al disfrute de las maravillas del intelecto de las pasadas generaciones, así como de los elementos de la madre naturaleza?

Al dolor, vibración eterna que es á la transformación universal lo que el movimiento á la vida, no podrá sustraerse el interés de cierta parte de la humanidad, en esta etapa del progreso indefinido.

En el órden natural, aun el tipo más perfecto de la escala zoológica, el propio hombre, padece desde el punto en que es concebido, hasta el instante de su muerte. Y ¿quién sabe si el dolor vibraba ya antes de la concepción, en las moléculas y en los efluvios de su sér, siendo eterno compañero de los átomos de su cuerpo y purificador constante de las facultades de su espíritu?

¿A qué vacilar, pués? Sométase la transformación social á las leyes eternas del universal progreso. Y ya que para proceder á la labor de su propia redención, tiene el pueblo, el proletariado, los medios indicados con el ejercicio de la gobernación del Estado, láncese á la conquista del poder, invierta el órden actual en el que los más están supeditados á los menos, y si su abrumadora mayoría no sabe imponerse por la fuerza del número, haciendo prevalecer la justicia de su causa, es...—¡aunque duela!—porque existen todavía en los explotadores reminiscencias del tirano, y en los proletarios sedimentos del siervo

Dósico.

LA OLA

Al cabo, todo lo invade:
al cabo, todo lo llena,
del femenil entusiasmo
la ola gigante y soberbia!

Vedla cómo surge en Francia
y en Alemania y América,
y en Italia y Portugal
y en Austria y en Inglaterra

Vedla inundar las naciones
y por virtud de su fuerza,
ahogar las bajas pasiones
que pretenden detenerla

Y sobre todo, miradla
en España, en esta tierra,
que es feudo de clericales
y monárquicas prebendas.

Aquí arrollando á su paso
cuanto estorba á su grandeza,
brama poderosa en Cádiz,
en Villa del Río truena,
en Madrid se alza potente,
en Córdoba surge fiera,
en Reus crece en empuje
y repercute en Valencia.

Pero donde más se agita,
donde adquiere más potencia,
es en la gran Cataluña,
en *Barcelona la seria;*
en este lugar que es foco
de adelantos y de ciencias
la mujer lucha y trabaja
con firmeza verdadera;

Y se une á otras mujeres,
y les encarna su idea,
y en admirable conjunto,
mutuamente al fin se alientan;
que es su divisa: *¡Adelante!*
Y adelante van serenas,
sin que las detengan cárceles,
persecución ni miserias.

2.8 Partial reproduction of Ángeles López de Ayala's poem, "La ola," *El Progreso* 12, Year II (13 Feb. 1897): 1. By kind permission of the Arxiu Històric de la Ciutat de Barcelona (microfilm no. 245-H)

y trabaja / con firmeza verdadera" (women fight and work / with true determination). In comparison with the disunity of the Republicans lambasted in other poems and articles, these feminist women draw mutual strength from their common purpose and cohesiveness:

> Y se une a otras mujeres,
> y les encarna su idea,
> y en admirable conjunto,
> mutuamente al fin se alientan.
>
> (And it gathers up other women, / and begets in them its idea, / and in admirable union, / they spur one another on to their goal.)

Now the gender tables have turned: the determined energy of freethinking women exposes their men who hang back, "rezagados": "Siempre altivas e impertérritas, / con su denodado arrojo / tan mal parados les dejan." (Always proud and unflinching, / with their resolute daring / they put their men to shame.) Described as heroines, they conserve all the attributes of femininity – tenderness, grace, modesty, and docility – while infusing them with a new, uncompromising fierceness:

> ¡Gloria al libre pensamiento
> que heroínas tales crea:
> con sus hijos adorados,
> arrulladoras y tiernas[!];
> Con sus padres, gacelillas;
> con sus hermanos modestas,
> palomas con sus esposos,
> y con sus tiranos … ¡fieras!
>
> (Glory be to freethinking / that creates such heroines: / with their beloved children, / cooing and tender!; / With their parents, gazelles; / with their brothers, modest, / doves with their husbands, / and with their tyrants … wild beasts!)

In the final two stanzas the poetic voice urges her "sisters" forward in their "*colosal* empresa" (*colossal* endeavour) and exhorts them not to give up: "¡Adelante hermanas mías! / ¡No hay descanso ni tregua!" (Onward, my sisters! Without rest or respite!) It is their unity that will put an end to their slavery: "[Y] gritemos a una todas: / ¡¡Ya se acabaron las siervas!!" (And let's all shout as one: / We won't be slaves anymore!!)[89]

As López de Ayala was well aware, any transformation of the national body into a viable democracy depends on concomitant reforms in the domestic sphere, unseating patriarchal power, and addressing women's position within civil society. These are themes that she continues to take up in her drama *De tal siembra, tal cosecha* and, to a lesser extent, in her incomplete novella, *El abismo*. This text also engages, like her didactic novella, *Primitivo*, with the plight of the working classes and the duty of the upper-middle classes to assist them to rise out of their degradation and impoverishment through education and thus empower them financially. My next chapter examines these works to highlight the fact that, for López de Ayala, the personal or domestic is always political.

3 Domestic Politics, National Agendas: López de Ayala's Literary Works

No entiendo esa obligación
que en tiranizar consiste,
ni ese derecho que asiste
para tal imposición.

(López de Ayala 1889, 65)

(I do not understand that duty / that consists of being a tyrant, / nor that right that aids / such an imposition.)

The engagement with the tenets of Romanticism that Domingo Soler's and López de Ayala's texts display, as discussed in chapters 1 and 2, is not fortuitous, given that Romanticism, as Labanyi emphasizes, constitutes the "literary expression of liberalism" (1995, 8). That literary and political movement, however, was constructed according to terms that rendered it difficult for women to participate in culture and society as full subjects: the consolidation of the private/public divide, gendered as feminine and masculine and justified by biological theories on sexual difference, the foregrounding of the individual, which clashed with the self-sacrificing ideal of the Angel in the House, and the emphasis on desire, an emotion disallowed in paradigms of respectable womanhood. At the same time, Romanticism also depended on qualities traditionally aligned with femininity such as introspection, sensitivity, and compassion, valued by an emerging middle class that eschewed an aristocratic culture of heroism in pursuit of economic and political tranquillity.[1] It was these ambiguities that would enable women to negotiate their entry into the public sphere as writers, and later, political subjects.

Underlying Romanticism is what Kirkpatrick calls a discourse of psychological response that assigned women the authoritative voice in matters of love (1991, 18).

This discourse and its implications for liberal political life are played out in López de Ayala's neglected early feminist play, *De tal siembra, tal cosecha.* Rewriting clearly identifiable aspects of José Zorrilla's late Romantic play from 1844, *Don Juan Tenorio* (2002), it challenges the ethos of a conservative liberalism. Part 1 of this chapter traces how López de Ayala reformulates the paradigms of masculinity and femininity displayed in Zorrilla's text to contest a liberal political model based on a social contract that positioned women as unequal stakeholders in civic life and the public sphere. Crucial to the social contract are the concepts of honour, obligation, and the promise, which are all foregrounded in *De tal siembra, tal cosecha.* By proposing a revised model of gender politics for the liberal upper-middle and middle classes, López de Ayala arguably paves a tentative path towards a vision of democracy that diverges from mainstream Restoration liberalism.

In parts 2 and 3 of this chapter I address the way in which López de Ayala's two novellas, *El abismo* and *Primitivo,* which I discovered only recently, engage more directly with hierarchical social systems. Shifting from the upper-middle-class concerns of *De tal siembra, tal cosecha,* they vindicate the necessity of alliances among the upper-middle, middle, and working classes to effect sociopolitical transformation. Both works promote Republican values among an inter-classist reading public and demonstrate the writer's dedication to forging the modern citizen and woman.

De tal siembra, tal cosecha: Reforming Don Juan and the Liberal Subject

The Don Juan theme has played a prominent role in representing and shaping Spanish cultural politics. It first appeared with Tirso de Molina's drama *El burlador de Sevilla y convidado de piedra* (ca. 1630), where Don Juan's assault on moral laws and social hierarchies is punished by God and king. There the plot upholds a sociopolitical order founded on divine authority, dynastic right, and a patriarchal culture. In mid-nineteenth-century Spain, however, the transgressions effected by Zorrilla's Don Juan Tenorio embody the Romantic individualism and the desire for freedom from sociopolitical restraints that are important for affirming new forms of political governance removed from dynastic succession and inherited blood. Nevertheless, the disorder that he sows must be curbed to safeguard the nation's unity and its domestic economy, as implied by his repentance and redemption through Doña Inés. The import of Don Juan for sociopolitical matters continued, evident throughout the first third of the twentieth century, when he frequently featured in discussions on Spain's vitality, such as José Ortega y Gasset's *El tema de nuestro tiempo* (1923), Gregorio de Marañón's "Notas para la biología de Don Juan" (1924), and Ramiro de Maeztu's Nietzchean interpretation in "Don Juan o el poder" (1925) (see Mandrell 1992, 237–43).[2]

As James Mandrell elucidates, any rewriting of the Don Juan theme constitutes a *refundición*: a text that builds on previous versions to infuse it with the particular imprint of the author's originality and context, providing "a critical and aesthetic reevaluation" (90). In the case of Zorrilla, the rivalry between Don Juan and Don Luis Mejía in the interrelated arenas of love and war is transformed, Mandrell continues, into "a confrontation between two texts in which *one version* of the *same story* will be granted privilege over the other" (99). The thematic repetitions and doublings do not simply reproduce the story but re-inscribe it differently in a process effected by both author and audience (111).

Not all rewritings of the Don Juan plot, however, are by male authors. As Johnson has explored, a number of texts featuring a female Don Juan and created by female modernist writers such as Sofía Casanova, Blanca de los Ríos, and Burgos appeared in the early twentieth century, at a time when feminist issues in Spain were gathering momentum. Critiquing the politics of gender and building on seventeenth-century works by Ana Caro and María de Zayas, these representations of the traditional Don Juan story see Don Juan either defeated or domesticated, and they vindicate women's rights (see Johnson 1998). The significance of such modifications is indicated by Geoff Dyer: "Only ... where women are the undisputed property of men – where men act and women appear – is he [Don Juan] a subversive force. He cannot flourish where women themselves are struggling for emancipation, since his promise is, ultimately, an intense expression of patriarchal power" (quoted in Mandrell 1992, 270). López de Ayala's *De tal siembra, tal cosecha* constitutes a precursor of those later feminist texts, as I develop in my reading.[3]

The feisty reforms sought by López de Ayala in Restoration Spain reveal a sociopolitical system uneasily poised between aspirations to democracy and its reluctance to abandon an old order of naturalized privileges. It is this struggle that is played out in *De tal siembra, tal cosecha*, a play in verse in three acts set in contemporary Spain. While act 1 takes place in Seville, López de Ayala's birthplace and the city most associated with Don Juan, acts 2 and 3 see the action move to Madrid. The plot revolves around a love triangle, in which the protagonist, Rosa, is desired by both her cousin, Carlos, and her fiancé, Julio. When Julio attempts to kill Carlos and must flee Seville for Madrid to escape arrest, Rosa elects to elope with him. Although the married couple's relationship is initially idyllic, it is marred by Rosa's questioning of traditional models of femininity and by Julio's unfounded suspicions regarding his wife's fidelity, spurred on by Carlos's reappearance in Madrid. Unjustly accusing Rosa's parents of connivance in her alleged adultery, Julio challenges her father, Don Antonio, to a duel, which the latter avoids. Another duel with Carlos is averted only through Rosa's intervention and the imminent arrival of the police. The play ends with Carlos's departure for France, the reconciliation of the couple, and the re-establishment of harmony within the family.

De tal siembra, tal cosecha was first performed in Barcelona at the Circo Theatre on 14 May 1889 (Méndez Bejarano 1922, 389). Reviewed in *El Clamor Zaragozano*, to which López de Ayala contributed and where she had sent a copy of the drama, the comedy was found to be "good" and "not difficult to act," and was praised for its "morality and pure Spanishness," in contrast to "the vulgarities of foreign theatre and especially those of French modernist theatre."[4]

Despite being thought to represent the essence of Spain, *De tal siembra*'s real interest lies in the modifications introduced into more traditional Don Juan versions and their implications for subverting gendered sociocultural hierarchies and fashioning a democratic society. Clearly the rivalry between Julio and Carlos for Rosa's affections echoes that between Don Juan and Don Luis in Zorrilla's drama. However, that is but one of the multiple elements in *De tal siembra* that refract Zorrilla's *Don Juan Tenorio*. López de Ayala begins her play by evoking Zorrilla's opening scenes of the wager between Don Juan and Don Luis in the public sphere of the tavern, now transformed into a card game among the family members of an upper-middle-class home: Rosa's father, Don Antonio, her mother, Doña Dolores, Rosa herself, Plácida, her widowed cousin, Carlos, and Julio. Like Zorrilla's protagonist, Julio is described as having "visos de calavera" (López de Ayala 1889, 8; the appearance of a rake), now suggestive of the decadence of Restoration Spain,[5] while Zorrilla's drama is again recalled in Antonio's later statement that "quizás no falte un Tenorio" (12; perhaps a Casanova will appear).

More striking still is López de Ayala's account of the clandestine meeting between Julio and Rosa, which rewrites aspects of Zorrilla's famous sofa scene between Don Juan and Doña Inés at his property on the banks of the Guadalquivir River. As Don Juan does with Doña Inés, López de Ayala's Julio, portrayed as a Romantic character,[6] opens his rendezvous with Rosa by placing her within the normative paradigm of bourgeois femininity, embodied by the figure of the Angel in the House: "Ángel mío, ídolo amado" (27; My angel, beloved idol). Inviting her to see, like him, their love through rose-tinted glasses, Julio exclaims that Rosa serves as a mirror that returns only positive images to him: "No hay desdicha para mí, / cuando me miro en tus ojos" (28; There exists no misfortune for me, / when I see myself reflected in your eyes). These words parallel Don Juan's description of Doña Inés as the mirror that gives light to his eyes: "Espejo y luz de mis ojos" (Zorrilla 2002, v. 2215; Mirror and light of my eyes). Similarly, just as Zorrilla's Don Juan prostrates himself before Doña Inés (Zorrilla 2002, v. 2218), so too does Julio kneel before Rosa: "Mírame a tus pies, hermosa" (López de Ayala 1889, 31; Here I am at your feet, beautiful woman).

In Zorrilla's play, Doña Inés's feelings are so fanned by Don Juan's words that she professes her adoration of him, bringing her perilously close to acting upon her desire. At this point, the author prevents her from infringing upon sanctioned feminine codes of behaviour by having Don Juan immediately reposition her in conventional terms as his soul and avow his intention of asking for her hand in marriage (Zorrilla 2002, vv. 2252–83). In comparison, López de Ayala initially follows Zorrilla's plot by having Rosa's reason overcome by Julio's passion, leading her to exclaim,

Basta, que ya el corazón
tu enfermedad ha sentido
y al verse de ella vencido
detesta la reflexión.
Que ni ya el temor le aterra,
ni ya le aterran las faltas.

(López de Ayala 1889, 31–2)

(Stop, because now my heart / has felt your illness / and realizing that it has been conquered / detests reflection. / Because now not even fear terrifies it, / nor do shortcomings.)

Here Rosa likens Julio's love to a contagious illness, a metaphor that recalls Doña Inés's representation of Don Juan's amorous breath as a poison – "tu aliento me envenena" (Zorrilla 2002, v. 2255). Earlier, Rosa had expressed her passion and desire for Julio in Romantic terms, declaring that she loved him "con delirio; / Eres mi dicha, mi sueño" (López de Ayala 1889, 6–7; deliriously; / You are my happiness, my dream). Hence the sociocultural ideal of nineteenth-century bourgeois femininity, characterized by female passivity and asexuality, is countervened by Rosa's articulation of her desire.

Nevertheless, authorial criticism of a love that refuses to acknowledge reality is implicit when Rosa states that her affection cannot calm her doubts:

En vano el cariño intenta
calmar mi justo desvelo;
¡ay! ¡si se nubla ese cielo!
¡ay! ¡si ruge la tormenta! (28)

(In vain affection attempts / to calm my justified worries; / Ah! What if that sky clouds over! / Ah! What if that storm howls!)

Unlike Julio's desire, depicted as disrupting the peace and order of the domestic economy, feminine desire is shown to be tempered by reason, as when Rosa rapidly recontains her passion and begs Julio to display "prudencia" (prudence) and "compasión" (32; compassion). Indeed, invoking reason, Rosa calls on Julio four times to curb his passion, as exemplified in the following quotation: "Julio, hablemos en razón, / con menos fuego y más calma" (28; Julio, let's talk reasonably, / with less passion and greater calm).

López de Ayala's portrayal of feminine desire is pertinent to her critique of the patriarchal gender models inherent in liberal thought. As Carole Pateman has indicated, any "reconstruction of democratic theory has to reach into the heart of the conventional understanding of sexual identity as well as into the structure of the state" (1985, 194). Within Romantic plots and liberal economies, desire is represented as only proper to masculine subjects, whose utopian visions ostensibly enable humanity's progress (Kirkpatrick 1991, 269). In contrast, feminine desire constitutes the linchpin that justifies liberalism's exclusion of women from the public sphere. As women are considered to lack reason and thus the ability to curb bodily passions, qualities deemed necessary to become civil individuals, they are perceived as naturally subversive of sociopolitical order and restricted to the domestic sphere (Pateman 1988, 94, 96, 100). This prejudice is exemplified in *De tal siembra* through Doña Dolores, who, when she declares herself to be governed by her emotions – "Soy mujer … / y a mis impulsos atiendo" (I am a woman … / and I heed my impulses) – is met by her husband's response: "No bastan para juzgar" (López de Ayala 1889, 14; They are useless for judging). Consequently, for liberal thought, as Pateman declares, "women's relations to the social world must always be mediated through men's reason; women's bodies must always be subject to men's reason and judgments if order is not to be threatened" (1988, 100–1).

Forming the basis of liberal civil society is the social contract. Given that liberalism affirms that all individuals are born free and equal, rendering sociopolitical freedom and equality natural rights, any relationship of subordination must be established through mutual agreement founded on contract (Pateman 1988, 39, 82, 112). However, the premises according to which individuals enter into social contracts have varied historically for men and women. The contract made available to women is the marriage contract, through which women agree to exchange their person, together with feminine obedience and subservience, for male protection (58). Hence the rights and duties considered incumbent on women differ from those of men, being founded on concepts of inequality, and reinforce the division between civil and political society. As Teresa Brennan and Pateman emphasize, "women, more specifically married women, constitute a permanent embarrassment and problem for liberal political theory" (1998, 93).

As most of the action in *De tal siembra* focuses on what happens after Rosa's marriage to Julio, marriage is not presented in traditional terms as the ultimate corollary of a woman's life but is instead the beginning of a complex negotiation with the patriarchal politics that inform liberal societies. Dominating act 2 is López de Ayala's critique of the gendered, hierarchical division of society into public and domestic spheres. Her concern with this dichotomy is significant because, as Susan Moller Okin signals, its persistence "enables theorists to ignore the political nature of the family, the relevance of justice in personal life, and ... a major part of the inequalities of gender" (1998, 118). In scene 1 Rosa is unwilling to accept that Julio must leave domestic marital bliss to attend to neglected business interests, affirming that she does not wish to be parted from him for an instant: "No puedo vivir / ni un momento separada / de tu lado" (López de Ayala 1889, 39; I can't live / for a single moment away / from your side). In contrast, Julio upholds conventional thought that decrees separate spheres based on allegedly natural laws: "Son leyes / y debemos acatarlas" (40; These are laws / and we must heed them). In accordance with the Angel in the House paradigm, a wife's duty, he retorts, is to sacrifice her own desires for the good of her household:

> Pues debieras
> sacrificarte en las aras
> de tu nuevo estado, Rosa;
> porque una mujer casada
> debe violentar sus gustos
> si en bien no son de su casa. (39)

> (So you should / sacrifice yourself on the altar / of your new state, Rosa; / because a married woman / must act contrary to her own wants / if they do not bring benefit to her home.)

The discomfort manifested by Rosa with the gendered division of public and domestic spheres is taken further in scene 3, where Rosa and Plácida articulate differing positions on the subject. Their discussion adopts the form of the *querelle des femmes* (debate among women), a traditional vehicle for examining paradigms of femininity and contesting women's sociocultural subordination.[7] The more conventional stance is taken by Plácida, who defends differentiated paradigms of being for men and women, with their correspondingly separate spheres. She considers that home life, while ideal for women, becomes suffocatingly monotonous for men: "[Y] una vida siempre igual / le [*sic*] es a los hombres monótona" (42; And a life that is always the same / is monotonous for men). Declaring that a wife, if overly demanding of her husband, runs the risk of boring him – "y es el mayor de los males / una casada mimosa. / No aburras a tu marido" (44; and the greatest of all evils is / a demanding wife. / Don't bore your husband) – Plácida advises Rosa seemingly to conform to norms of femininity to achieve what she wants; in particular, Rosa should not cry, since weeping makes women ugly, and men's love is conditional on feminine beauty: "Ven sólo el exterior / de las mujeres que adoran" (43; They have eyes only for the appearance / of the women they adore) and "la mujer, por fuerza / debe aparecer hermosa" (43; women have no alternative / but to look beautiful).[8] Plácida's perspective echoes that of Jean-Jacques Rousseau, one of liberalism's founding fathers, who recommends in *The Social Contract*, as Pateman explains, that women's "education [emphasize] appearances" and that women "use deceit and cunning to gain their desires within the family" (Pateman 1985, 158). Moreover, Plácida considers that Julio's bad character, as part of his nature, cannot be transformed, since "genio y figura, nacen / y mueren con la persona" (López de Ayala 1889, 44; disposition and figure remain unchanged / from cradle to grave). Any attempt to change him, she stresses, would constitute a "prueba peligrosa" (45; dangerous experiment). In short, the possibilities of altering the status quo, Plácida concludes, are slim, since historical accounts demonstrate that reformers, especially female ones, face an inordinately difficult task: "Según enseñan las crónicas, / no sirven reformadores, / cuanto más, reformadoras" (44; According to the teachings of history, / if male reformers are no use, / even less so are female ones).

In contrast, Rosa's argument deploys liberalism's premise of natural law to critique sociocultural paradigms based on inequality. While society allows men, animals, and birds to show their true emotions, women, she remarks, are obliged to be hypocrites: "¿Por qué sólo a la mujer / le han de mandar ser hipócrita?" (43; Why are only women / ordered to be hypocrites?) Subsequently, Rosa subverts the contemporary discourse of domesticity, which culturally defined women as wives and mothers, thus limiting them to the domestic sphere (Nash 1993, 588), when she states that it is small wonder that women are protective of their rights in these roles, since they are ordained by society: "Además, nuestra misión / según nos dicen, no es otra / que ser esposas y madres" (López de Ayala 1889, 43; Besides, our mission / so they tell us, is purely / to be wives and mothers). By implying that women's roles are culturally decreed – "según nos dicen" – Rosa stresses that they are open to reform:

La mujer no es más que amor,
sólo sabe ser esposa;
si el hombre así no la quiere
¡que haga en su vida reformas! (44)

(Woman is nothing more than love, / she knows only how to be a wife; / if man does not want her like that / let him make changes in his life!)

Considering that marriage has already changed Julio for the better, Rosa proposes to test his perceived transformation and allow the results to speak for themselves: "Me conformarán los hechos" (45).

Rosa's desire that gender laws and the marriage contract, premised on feminine subordination and acquiescence, be reformulated is palpable when she directly challenges Julio's wish that they attend a ball. Instead, Rosa advocates that they remain at home, she sewing and Julio reading to her. Such an image combines usefulness with pleasurable illustration to offer an upper-middle-class ideal of marital harmony and critique empty frivolity. When Julio insists that she accompany him, Rosa's opposition to her husband's wishes intensifies his intransigence in the remaining scenes in act 2. Rosa's apparent capriciousness in testing Julio's love takes on broader implications when read against Mariano José de Larra's 1836 essays on Alexandre Dumas's drama, *Anthony*. There, as Kirkpatrick notes, Larra had attacked the French writer's application of liberal revolutionary ideas to relationships between the sexes. Questioning the limits of the Spanish liberal revolution and the relationship between government and people, Larra had warned the people that, by demanding greater freedom and rights, they were behaving as destructively as a rebellious wife (Kirkpatrick 1991, 59–62).

Nevertheless, the episode in *De tal siembra* also represents men as indirect victims of socialization, since Julio silently attributes the violence of his reaction to feeling obliged to prove continually that he is a man of character: "Yo soy hombre de carácter / y debo probarlo siempre" (López de Ayala 1889, 47). Tellingly, as was revealed in act 1, Julio's character is flawed because his father catered to his every whim (15), demonstrating the negative ramifications of patriarchy's privileging of the male. Julio's sense of obligation to an established gender paradigm can be read in terms of what Pateman calls pre-existing obligations, which bind individuals and characterize a liberal society. In contrast, the proper functioning of a democracy requires self-assumed obligations that individuals create, consent to, and uphold voluntarily through reason (Pateman 1985, 29–30).

The issue of obligation becomes more important in act 3, scene 2, where Julio's perspective is alternately contrasted with Rosa's standpoint. Again, the discussion highlights the defects inherent in patriarchal models that justify hierarchical relationships according to allegedly natural essences. Consequently, Julio states, being a man obliges him to impose his will on his wife, making masculinity dependent on domination:

El hombre, debe ser hombre
o lo que es lo mismo, amo.
No puedo dejar que siga
dominándome a su modo;

soy varón antes que todo
y a imponerme, esto me obliga.

(López de Ayala 1889, 65)

(Man must be man / or what is the same thing, master. / I cannot allow her to continue / dominating me as she does; / above all I am a man / and this obliges me to impose my authority.)

Conversely, Rosa's response draws on feminist arguments, in that she cannot comprehend duties that mask tyranny and rights that help to impose such abuse:

No entiendo esa obligación
que en tiranizar consiste,
ni ese derecho que asiste
para tal imposición. (65)

(I do not understand that duty / that consists of being a tyrant, / or that right that aids / such an imposition.)

Questioning the absurd gendered hierarchies determined by society – "El mundo necio, / ¿por qué a una da el menosprecio / y a otro da la preferencia?" (Why does this foolish world / despise one sex / and favour the other?) – she echoes feminist Mary Astell on signalling the incongruence of calling women mistresses when in reality they are attributed the status of slaves: "¿Por qué causa engañadora / llama a la mujer señora / debiendo llamarla esclava?" (66; For what deceitful reason / do they call woman a lady / when they should call her a slave?)[9] Rosa defends equality between men and women on the grounds that each sex forms half of one being in marriage and is thus naturally entitled to equal rights:

Siendo el hombre y la mujer
dos mitades de un ser solo,
¿qué ley ordena, o qué dolo
que una se haya de imponer? (66)

(Given that man and woman / are two halves of the same being, / what law or fraudulent act orders / that one half must impose his authority?)

Here Rosa's words capture the political implications of the marriage contract as formulated by Hegel, who held that marriage makes husband and wife "one person": members of an association that fosters mutual recognition, unity, and self-enrichment (Pateman 1988, 174). For Hegel, Pateman explains, marriage provides insight into "the differentiation and particularity of civil [economic] society and the unity and universality necessary to membership in the state" (175). However, Pateman continues, Hegel did not challenge the patriarchal division of society into a masculine public sphere and a feminine domestic sphere, as is evident in his declaration that "husbands and wives play out … the dialectic of mutual acknowledgment that characterizes relations among *men as makers of contracts* in civil society and as citizens in the state" (177; my emphasis). On the contrary, he maintained that woman's sexual difference rendered her rationally different and hence unsuited to social contracting and participation in public life (176–7).

Women's lack of rights equal to those of men is nowhere more evident than in patriarchal concepts of honour. Essential to conventional renderings of the Don Juan plot, they demarcate clearly the cultural separation between public and domestic spheres. In masculinist societies, honour accrues to men through what they possess, and depends on both "honra" or material wealth, and "honour": the social prestige derived from birth, wealth, and sexual and military prowess. In contrast, woman's honour stands as guarantor of man's honour, name, and reputation, requiring her to conform to a model of femininity characterized, as Peter Stallybrass notes, by "the enclosed body, the closed mouth, the locked house" (1986, 127). Within the wider context of nineteenth-century liberal politics, the preoccupation with honour was paramount in the "quest for an appropriate marriage of liberty and order – two classic nineteenth-century ideals that defined the struggle to forge a liberal state everywhere in modern Europe.… an intensely moralizing language of honor pervaded the often violent disputes over the appropriate civil, political and economic organization of the nation" (White 1999, 233–4).

Such concepts come to the fore in López de Ayala's drama in act 3 when Julio, convinced that Rosa has betrayed him with Carlos, becomes increasingly authoritarian in his attitude to her. Now Rosa's containment within the domestic sphere is no longer merely ideological but real, with Julio forbidding her to leave the house and expelling Plácida and Rosa's parents from it: "Rosa es mi mujer / y de esta casa no sale" (López de Ayala 1889, 62; Rosa is my wife / and she does not leave this house). Here both house and wife, deemed the husband's possessions, are presented as legally subject to his will. Resolving to obtain the information that he seeks through the unequal rights that patriarchal law has granted men rather than through reason – "¡Basta de contemplaciones! / ¡Voy a usar de mi derecho!" (66; I've had enough of being indulgent! / I am going to wield my rights!) – Julio asks Rosa if she has respected his honour and name through her virtue: "[¡]Ah! dilo: ¿mi honor de hombre / le ha guardado tu virtud? / … ¿Qué: qué has hecho de mi nombre?" (66; Well, tell me: has your virtue / defended my manly honour? … / What, what have you done to my name?)

However, Rosa refuses to act as the silent vessel of masculine honour, taking Julio to task for his "irreflexiones" (thoughtlessness), his "despego constante" (constant indifference), and his "orgullo insultante" (66; insulting pride). Although Julio inwardly concedes that Rosa's words are informed by reason, he admits that he is not prepared to relinquish his male privileges, which give him prestige:

Tal vez le asiste razón,
mas no debo posponer
a su pensar, de mujer,
mi prestigio de varón. (67)

(Perhaps she is right, / but I must not put / her woman's way of thinking / before my masculine prerogatives.)

Attempting to contain Rosa's voice, he reprimands her for answering him back and states that her duty is to answer him within precise boundaries: "Tu deber es contestarme / con estricta precisión" (67). Although Rosa recognizes that such a requirement is humiliating – "¡humillante condición!" – she tells herself that she must master her feelings rather than be overwhelmed by them – (67; debo dominarme) – again signalling her ability to overcome emotion through reason and hence refute patriarchal thought.

Notions of honour are also at stake in the giving of one's word through verbal and written contracts. As Mandrell explains, honour "inheres in the actions and words of men, and the code is then extracted from those manners of comportment. Honor is ... articulated most openly when one speaks. At a second remove is the written word, which supplements the notion of honor implied in the making of an oral contract" (1992, 78). In Zorrilla's rewriting of the Don Juan story, a crucial component in Don Juan's conquests is his mastery of the word, both oral and written. There, Mandrell remarks, "words take on critical importance; they are more meaningful than the deeds they supposedly represent" (99). Particular emphasis is placed on the written document, evident in the enumerations that Don Juan and Don Luis provide of their military and amorous exploits, as well as in the missive sent by Don Juan to Doña Inés in the convent. Mandrell asserts that, in effect, the letter represents "sure proof" (123), providing an accurate tally of the alleged honour or worth of the male contenders, and confirming Don Juan's love for Doña Inés.

Nevertheless, the letter also raises the question of authenticity, given that the written word, as Mandrell indicates above, is removed from the self, substituting presence for absence, the empirical for the abstract, and, by extension, the physical for the transcendental and the feminine for the masculine. Significantly, López de

Ayala's drama discredits the motif of the letter to shift the focus from the written word to verifiable actions. Hence Carlos's love letter to the married Rosa is de-authorized by being repeatedly prevented from reaching its intended destination. It is intercepted first by Rosa's mother, Doña Dolores, and then by Julio when it falls from her hand (López de Ayala 1889, 60), in a scene that reframes the moment when Don Juan's letter falls from Doña Inés's breviary (Zorrilla 2002, vv. 1586–8). When Julio accuses Don Antonio of being complicit in Rosa's supposed adultery, the father states that he will provide him with material proof of his and Doña Dolores's good faith in the matter of the letter (López de Ayala 1889, 70). Subsequently, Rosa's alleged dishonour is revealed as founded on circumstantial evidence and not on fact, in a refutation of judging honour according to mere appearances.

As act 3 unfolds, the patriarchal concepts of honour reproduced in canonical Don Juan texts are increasingly challenged, as when Julio and Carlos prepare to duel over Rosa's supposed infidelity. Despite Carlos swearing to Julio on his honour that Rosa is innocent (80), Julio discredits his rival's honour, retorting that men's honour is an arbitrary notion:

¡Honor! ¡fantástica idea!
comodín del hombre, cosa
que si conviene se endiosa,
y si no, se pisotea. (80)

(Honour! A fanciful concept! / A weak excuse for men, a thing / that when convenient is exalted, / and when not, is trampled on.)

He queries what honour means if it requires destroying women's virtue and innocence, and staining one's conscience:

Si se abusa del candor,
si se ultraja la inocencia
y se mancha la conciencia,
¿qué se entiende por honor? (80)

(If virtue is abused, / and innocence offended / and if one's conscience is stained, / what does honour mean?)

Here his words echo and negate the value of statements such as those delivered by Zorrilla's Don Juan and Don Luis, who each boast in turn:

La razón atropellé,
la virtud escarnecí,
a la justicia burlé,
y a las mujeres vendí.

(Zorrilla 2002, vv. 501–5, 612–15)

(I violated reason, / I mocked virtue, / I flouted justice, / and I pimped women.)

The content of Zorrilla's verses is similarly negated by Carlos when he responds:

Ni del candor he abusado,
ni la inocencia ultrajé,
ni mi conciencia manché,
ni el honor he falseado.

(López de Ayala 1889, 80)

(I have not abused virtue, / nor offended innocence, / nor stained my conscience, / nor feigned honour.)

In Zorrilla's *Don Juan Tenorio*, the duels not only highlight Don Juan's betrayal of friendship, as when he kills Don Luis, but also his disregard for family authority, as in his shooting of Doña Inés's father (Zorrilla 2002, vv. 2603–12). In comparison, in López de Ayala's play the duel is repeatedly averted, as when Don Antonio refuses to fight Julio, exclaiming that the matter is better resolved through reason: "No hay que obrar tan de ligero: / hagamos la luz primero" (López de Ayala 1889, 53; We must not act so rashly: / let's think this through first). Offending another without cause, he states, is not behaviour that befits heroes: "A mi juicio, / ultrajar al que no ultraja / no es un rasgo de heroísmo" (69; In my opinion, / to offend someone who has not offended / is not a trait of heroism). In another instance, the duel between Carlos and Julio is initially prevented through female agency when Rosa steps between them (81). When it does finally take place, Julio's aim is inaccurate and the duel is again curtailed by Rosa's action when she shoots at Carlos to defend her husband and, by extension, a union created through voluntary consent (83).

At this point, however, the feminist revolution implied by Rosa's words and actions until now appears to go into reverse. Like Zorrilla's Doña Inés, who risks her soul to save Don Juan from damnation through her selfless love, López de Ayala's Rosa exclaims to Julio that she loves him more than her soul (83), and promises to submit her will to his in a spirit of unlimited self-sacrifice:

Para probar este amor
pide, manda sin reboso,

ni me importan sacrificios
ni me detendrán escollos. (84)

(To test this love, / ask, order without restraint, / no sacrifice is too small / nor will obstacles stand in my way.)

Rather than declaring, as before, that differences between the sexes are created by sociocultural factors, Rosa now avows that such differences stem from egotism: "Las diferencias creadas / a causa del amor propio" (84). Indeed, she goes so far as to declare that the time for women's equality with men is not yet ripe:

Aun no es tiempo de igualarnos
sin causar grandes trastornos;
si frívolas no adquirimos
saber, discreción y aplomo. (84)

(The time for equality has not yet come / without causing great upheavals; / unless we frivolous women acquire / knowledge, prudence, and level-headedness.)

What is needed, as she had declared earlier, is for each sex to be taught its respective duties and rights, in an extension of citizenship into the home:

Mostráranse a cada uno
sus deberes y derechos,
y no tuvieran lugar
resultados tan funestos. (71)

(If both were taught / their duties and rights, / there would not be / such disastrous outcomes.)

Nevertheless, Rosa's voluntary embracing of feminine selflessness is important in that it leads Julio to promise publicly to reform his character:

De hoy más prometo ser otro
...
Reprimiré mi carácter,
emplearé todas mis fuerzas
en educarme de nuevo. (85)

(From now on I promise to be different / ... / I will control my temper / and dedicate all my energies / to re-educating myself.)

Through reason, he states, he will embrace an ethos ambiguously poised between the complementarity of the sexes and their equality:

> Haré que de mi cerebro
> no se aparte la creencia
> de que el hombre y la mujer
> los crió naturaleza
> tan igualmente precisos
> que uno sin otra, no fuera,
> y así que entre ambos no exista
> esa injusta diferencia
> de superior e inferior,
> que tanto mal acarrea. (85)

(I will ensure that my mind / always holds present the belief / that man and woman / were made by nature / so equal in exact measure / that one without the other could not be, / hence ensuring that between them there does not exist / that unjust difference / of superior and inferior / that causes so much harm.)

The significance of Rosa's and Julio's respective promises can be understood when approached from Pateman's distinction between two different kinds of promise, each of which implies a particular political system. On the one hand, the promise to obey, which women traditionally give in the marriage contract, is integral to the liberal social contract and state, in that "substantive political freedom and equality, necessary if citizens are to create their own political obligations, are given up or exchanged for the protection of the liberal state" (Pateman 1985, 169–70). On the other hand, the promise as self-assumed obligation underpins democratic conceptions of the nation, implying the right to disobey and create new relationships not previously defined by others (162).

Rosa's promise to obey Julio uncomfortably recalls the inequalities of a liberal Restoration Spain plagued by caciquism and widespread illiteracy that, in 1889, was still one year away from granting universal suffrage to men. At the same time, in that her promise is freely given, it suggests the concept of true consent, which can exist only between individuals recognized as free and equal.[10] Moreover, as Jagoe points out with respect to another nineteenth-century character, Benito Pérez Galdós's María Egipcíaca, the wife's duty "to redeem is ultimately to reform, to recreate; that is, to usurp a masculine privilege" (1994, 80). Julio's validation of Rosa's equality and his commitment to change point to López de Ayala's affirmation of the transformations required within the domestic sphere to fashion a more democratic Spain: a shift from a patriarchal family and society to more egalitarian structures. Rosa's reform of Don Juan in *De tal siembra, tal cosecha* reveals the flaws in liberal thought and heralds the hesitant emergence of a more progressive present and future forged through dialogue and reason.

El abismo: Between Feminist Treatise and Social Critique

López de Ayala's determined unpicking of the Romantic fabric that dressed a conservative liberalism and encumbered women's forward movement into sociopolitical life is also evident in *El abismo*. One of only two novellas by López de Ayala that I have been able to locate, *El abismo* was published in the Republican periodicals that she herself founded and edited in Barcelona. An incomplete feuilleton of melodramatic characteristics, it first appeared in *El Progreso* from 28 November 1896 onward, with the last instalment available on 24 April 1897.[11] Subsequently, it was republished in *El Gladiador: Órgano de la "Sociedad Progresiva Femenina,"* where it replaced *Primitivo* from 30 November 1907 onward. While this republication provides pages from missing issues of *El Progreso*, once again the novella is incomplete, since extant copies of *El Gladiador* do not go beyond 1 February 1908. There was a third publication of *El abismo* in *El Libertador*, of which the sole surviving issue is from 19 November 1910. The incomplete version of *El abismo* used for the present discussion has been assembled from these three sources.[12]

Given the difficulty of establishing with certainty whether a literary work was simultaneously published as a feuilleton in periodicals, in serialized form, or as a bound volume, Leonardo Romero Tobar includes the feuilleton within the category of the popular novel (1976, 29–30). In the case of *El abismo* it first appeared as a feuilleton in *El Progreso* within its library, running in two-page blocks along the bottom of pages three and four of the four-page issue; thus, its pages would undoubtedly have been collected by readers to eventually constitute a novel.[13] From its later publication in *El Gladiador* from 1907 onward, it appears, from the work's duplicated cover, that it had already come out that same year in a single volume as a "novela original," printed in the Gracia district of Barcelona by the press of José Miguel's widow at 7 Junqueras Street, which also printed *El Gladiador* (see figure 3.3).

Significantly, each reproduction of *El abismo* employed a different typeface. As Jean-François Botrel notes, a larger typeface, evident in the reproduction of the novella in *El Gladiador*, was commonly used if the intended reading public were less literate or lacked adequate lighting to read (1974, 119). In comparison, the earlier reproduction of *El abismo* in *El Progreso* reveals a smaller typeface, while an even more reduced one characterizes those pages available from *El Libertador*. A more compressed layout, however, need not indicate a more advanced literacy level. It could also refer indirectly to the cost of paper and the pressure on the

28 Biblioteca de El Progreso

titánicos por verse libre, cuidando desesperadamente de que permaneciera oculto su semblante.

Pero el borracho que ante la contrariedad sentia nuevos impulsos y se esforzaba más y más en realizar su empeño, le sujetaba entre sus brazos como entre dos barrotes de hierro, y había logrado desgarrar gran parte de su vestido, dejando al descubierto la abundante y perfumada cabellera, y los magníficos ojos negros de la joven, á vista de lo cual exclamó con alegría:

—Eres tan bonita como arisca, picarona;— y procuró acercar sus impuros labios al rostro de la inocente niña, que estuvo á punto de gritar, pero que no lo hizo, por temor al escándalo que necesariamente había de producirse, contentándose con evitar por medio de hábiles y exasperados movimientos, el contacto de los labios de aquel estúpido vicioso.

Este, sin soltar su presa, pareció reflexionar alguna cosa y al cabo dijo con acento conciliador:

—Vamos, chiquilla, todavía me queda un duro en el bolsillo y ese portal donde te guarecías es el de mi casa, donde un cuarto de soltero y una cama bien blandita, pueden servirte por esta noche... ¿no dices nada? ¿qné te parece la idea? Porque yo creo que no serás ninguna santa Teresa, cuando tan joven y tan guapa andas solita por las calles á estas horas.

La joven, reprimió su indignación justa y terrible, porque comprendió que de ella no podía sacar partido y procurando serenar su voz, dijo sencillamente:

—Y bien, ¿puede usted abrir la puerta?

—Ves tú como al fin te amansaste, fierecilla. Si no hay cosa como ofrecer un columnario... Además, que yo no soy despreciable todavía, y que allí dentro hallaremos pan, salsichón, queso y algunas pasas que echarémos á perder con los dientes, remojándolo todo con la sangrecilla valdepeñera de una bota fenomenal, qne es mi compañera de á diario. ¿Qué tal? ¿qué tal la proposición, graciosa perdidilla?

Angélica que había estado disimulando los extremecimientos producidos por la ira en tanto mordía sus frescas labios hasta hacerse brotar sangre, respondió aparentando una tranquilidad que estaba muy léjos de sentir.

«El Abismo» 25

con el pie el casi inanimado cuerpo de su hija que le impedía la entrada en el gabinete, se lanzó precipitadamente hacia la puerta.

El momento fué supremo..... Dos hombres corrian envueltos en la absoluta obscuridad de aquellos intrincados laberintos... el uno joven y sereno; y el otro viejo y afectado; pero desconocedor del terreno aquel, y gran conocedor éste... ¿qué sucedería? De pronto, un horrible estampido obligó á lanzar un ¡ay! agudo á la desventurada Angélica que casi perdió la conciencia de cuanto sucedía, y poco despué don Gonzalo se hallaba frente á su hija, que aún permanecía postrada, y mirándola con chispeantes ojos, le preguntaba lleno de furor:

—¿Has implorado de Dios el perdón de tu infamia, miserable?

Angélica no contestó; con las mejillas lívidas, con los labios blancos con los ojos extremadamente abiertos y sin brillo; parecía próxima á agonizar... Su padre insistió:

—Si no has rezado, reza... pero sé muy breve, porque vas á morir en el acto... ¡Sí, sí, á morir, á morir como un perro; porque sólo á costa de tu mengüada vida, podré lavar la deshonra de mis canas.....

¿Nada respondes, vil profanadora de mi honor? Pues; que termine tu infausta y mísera existencia... Y el anciano levantó el desmayado y frío cuerpo de su hija entre sus brazos, é iba á estrellarle contra el duro pavimento, cuando sintió que su lacerado corazón latía con extraordinaria violencia.

Entonces volvió á colocar en el suelo el cuerpo de lo joven, y haciendo un exfuerzo sobrehumano para dominar su terrible emoción, dijo con acento espantable por lo solemne:

—Vete, vete desgraciada, vete de esta casa que de hoy más no es la tuya... Huye... pero al punto, antes que de nuevo me ciegue la indignación, porque entonces no respondo de mis hechos.

¡Huye, aparta de mi presencia, para siempre, maldita enlodadora de mi honra!....—Y el caballero con el brazo derecho extendido en dirección á los pasillos, lanzó una mirada imperiosa y significativa á la afligida víctima, qué comprendiendo la imposibilidad de resistir al cruel mandato, lanzó un gemido doloroso, y con la respiración anhelante y entrecortada, con la boca oprimida por una contracción dolorosa, y agarrándose á las paredes para no perder el equilibrio, desapareció lentamente entre las sombras.

3.1 Pages from Ángeles López de Ayala's *El abismo*, in *El Progreso* 7, Year II (9 Jan. 1897). By kind permission of the Arxiu Històric de la Ciutat de Barcelona (microfilm no. 245-H)

editor to make the publication financially viable.[14] Nevertheless, the sophisticated vocabulary and syntactic structures present in López de Ayala's novella suggest both more educated readers, such as middle-class Republicans, and the writer's desire to elevate the reading level of the working classes.[15]

Just as the content of López de Ayala's periodicals was invariably oriented towards furthering the interests of republicanism, so too were her feuilletons. The use of the feuilleton for political purposes characterized its very beginnings in mid-nineteenth-century Spain, where democratic and Republican periodicals reinforced their ideological platforms by serializing French novels such as Hugo's *Les Misérables* (1862) and Eugène Sue's *Le Juif errant* (1844–5), which promoted a historical vision derived from progressive liberalism, utopian socialism, and anticlericalism (Zavala 1971, 83, 86–7). Although French feuilletons continued to dominate in Spanish periodicals between 1860 and 1908, significant national writers also emerged, such as Wenceslao Ayguals de Izco and Manuel Fernández y González. While most feuilleton writers were male, López de Ayala was but one

4 EL LIBERTADOR

COLEGIO

DE LA

SOCIEDAD PROGRESIVA FEMENINA

CALLE DE SAN PEDRO MÁRTIR, NÚMERO 4, BAJOS (GRACIA)

Clases Diurnas y Nocturnas, á cargo de buenos profesores

MENSUALIDADES MODICAS

Taller de Carpintería del Ramo de Electricidad

DE

MAGIN PRUNERA

Se hacen toda clase de trabajos concernientes al ramo de Electricidad á precios sumamente reducidos

Calle Doménech, número 1, bajos (Gracia) Barcelona

EL LIBERTADOR

SEMANARIO ÓRGANO DEL LIBREPENSAMIENTO NACIONAL Y DEFENSOR DE LA MUJER

Suscripción trimestral. . . . 0'75 céntimos

Dirección y Administración: Doménech, 1 bajos (GRACIA) BARCELONA
Horas de oficina: Desde las 10 de la mañana á las 6 de la tarde y desde 8 á 10 de la noche

Los Vendedores y Kioscos pueden dirigirse para los pedidos de la capital á P. Latre, Kiosco de periódicos, Plaza de Palacio, frente al Gobierno Civil.—Precio de 30 ejemplares 1 peseta

LINEA PINILLOS

SERVICIO AL BRASIL-PLATA

Viajes rápidos con salidas fijas cada 22 días

Para Santos, Montevideo y Buenos Aires

Saldrá de este puerto el día 22 de Noviembre el vapor español de 7.500 toneladas

BARCELONA

el día 14 de Diciembre el vapor VALBANERA | el día 27 de Enero el vapor BARCELONA
» » » Enero » » CADIZ | » » » Febrero » VALBANERA

Admitiendo carga y pasajeros para dichos puertos.

Servicio quincenal á las Antillas y Estados Unidos

Para Puerto Rico, Santiago de Cuba, Habana, Matanzas y New Orleans

Saldrá de este puerto el 12 de Noviembre el vapor de 5.000 toneladas

MIGUEL M. PINILLOS

Para Puerto Rico, Mayagüez, Ponce, Santiago de Cuba, Habana, Cienfuegos y New Orleans

Saldrá de este puerto el día 26 de Noviembre el vapor de 6.000 toneladas

CONDE WIFREDO

Admitiendo carga y pasajeros para dichos puertos y para Las Palmas, Tenerife y Santa Cruz de la Palma.

También admiten carga dando conocimiento directo para los puertos de Sagua, Caibarién, Nuevitas, Puerto Padre, Gibara, Banes, Nipe y Guantánamo, con trasbordo en la Habana y para el de Baracoa con trasbordo en Santiago de Cuba.

La carga se recibe en el tinglado de la Compañía (muelle de las Baleares).

Prestan este servicio magníficos vapores de gran marcha, con espaciosas cámaras de 1.ª y 2.ª clase sobre cubierta.—Camarotes de lujo y de preferencia.—El pasaje de 3.ª clase se aloja en amplios departamentos.—Alumbrado eléctrico.

Consignatario: RÓMULO BOSCH Y ALSINA, Plaza Antonio López, 15, principal

GRAN SASTRERIA

— DE —

HERMENEGILDO BASI

Especialidad en la medida * Gusto y economía

CALLE MAYOR, NÚM. 23

GRACIA-BARCELONA

Sastrería y Novedades

DE

Ignacio Torrents

8, Calle Goya, (antes Junqueras), 8

BARCELONA-GRACIA

ZAPATERIA

DE

JOSÉ BISCARRI

Gran surtido en toda clase de calzado á precios de fábrica

Calle de Arguelles, número 12

Reparaciones de todas clases de obras

Prontitud * Perfección * Economía

MARIANO CIURANA

Bajada de Santa Eulalia, 4.—BARCELONA
Calle Bolívar, 17.—GRACIA

LA PLANETA GRACIENSE

Sombrerería, Corbatería y Fábrica de Gorras al por mayor y menor

DE

JUAN FUSTÉ

Planeta, núms. 9 y 11
GRACIA-BARCELONA

DISPONIBLE

24 Biblioteca de EL LIBERTADOR

—Lo he resuelto, y lo haré sin que me detengan objeciones... y luego que el disparate y la imperdonable torpeza sería quedarme aquí, imposibilitando la huida, que ahora la facilitaré derribando de un pistoletazo al criado que guarde el lado del edificio por donde voy á salir; esto sin contar con que más honrada quedas así, que si me descubren en tu aposento, y que es preciso, de toda precisión, que yo vea el amanecer desde otra parte...

—¡Don Alonso, don Alonso! Si sale usted y todo se descubre, créame, se pierde usted, y me pierde irremisiblemente!

—Me es imposible retroceder; mi plan está formado. El marido... quise decir mi perseguidor, es terrible y para vengarse del único modo que puede, no sosegará un ápice en el camino del escándalo y necesariamente, este escándalo es el que yo debo evitar, aún á costa de los mayores sacrificios.

Adiós, pues, Angélica...

—¡No, no; no saldrá V. de esta casa hasta que el peligro disminuya—suplicó la infeliz niña pretendiendo detener con su alabastrino y delicado brazo á don Alonso, que oprimiendo ligeramente contra su pecho á la linda criatura, la besó en su pura frente y empujándola con suavidad comenzó á correr presuroso hacia el pasillo.

Angélica quiso detenerle evitando su fuga; pero apenas dió el primer paso para realizar su intento, quedó petrificada y como helada de terror.

Maquinalmente, sus ojos se habían fijado en la luna de un espejo, y sus labios se contrajeron convulsivamente lanzando un grito de agonía.

La desalmada liviandad con que don Alonso había terminado la anterior escena, había tenido por testigo nada menos que al severo, al terrible D. Gonzalo, que con el rostro desencajado, erizado el blanco pelo y los miembros agitados por un temblor horrible, parecía la más acabada imagen de la venganza.

La desgraciada niña solo tuvo fuerzas para caer de hinojos á las plantas de su padre, cuyo semblante lívido anunciaba una conmoción indescriptible.

Al fin la reacción tuvo lugar en el ultrajado caballero y empu-

EL ABISMO 31

Verdad que sólo en aquel sitio podía considerarse á salvo de cualquier eventualidad, pues el dormitorio era tan blanco, tan pequeño, y le bañaba tan de lleno la luz del gabinete, que á la primera ojeada, cualquier intruso hubiera sido descubierto.

Julia, trató de reponerse tras aquella nueva temeridad y dirigiéndose á su amiga que permanecía anonadada exclamó:

Como supongo que tu no has de dormir, se me ha ocurrido la idea de ocultarle en tu lecho, ya que en él estará más seguro que en ninguna otra parte... ¿opinas lo mismo?

Angélica permaneció callada; parecía no haber comprendido el sentido de las frases de su amiga. Esta, que interpretó aquel silencio por una respuesta afirmativa prosiguió:

—Ten ánimo, querida mía; recuerda aquel adagio que nos dice; "á lo hecho, pecho" y procura únicamente espiar los movimientos de tus padres, como de los criados, para aprovechar el más ligero descuido... Ya sabes: no hay que evitar más que el escándalo, si queremos ser honradas en la opinión de la sociedad...

La joven fué interrumpida por la llegada de una doncella que inclinándose respetuosamente le dijo.

El lacayo me ha rogado manifieste á usted, que espera recibir sus órdenes.

—Perfectamente,—dijo Julia levantándose; y pidiendo á la doncella su abrigo y su sombrero, abrazó afectuosamente á su amiga diciéndole por lo bajo: ¡Valor y serenidad! Ten presente, que si se descubre la estancia de un hombre en tu aposento, tu perdición ha de ser inevitable. Compón tu rostro, y saluda á tus padres como tienes por costumbre hacerlo todas las noches antes de recojerte á descansar. Pero todo esto con aplomo, sin que en tí se trasluzca novedad alguna.

Y al terminar las anteriores frases, desapareció rápidamente, sin apercibirse siquiera de la mirada suplicante y angustiosa que la pobre é inocente víctima de tan extraños y deplorables acontecimientos le lanzaba. Antes que se apercibiera el ruido del coche de Julia sobre el empedrado de la calle, el rodar de otro carruaje, hizo retumbar hasta en sus cimientos el antiguo y espléndido edificio.

Este coche conducía al altivo, grave y severo padre de Angélica que volvía á su morada á la hora de costumbre.

3.2 Pages from Ángeles López de Ayala's *El abismo*, in *El Libertador* 6, Year I (19 Nov. 1910): 4. By kind permission of the Arxiu Històric de la Ciutat de Barcelona (microfilm no. 535-H)

— 4 —

—El autor de este libro tiene razón; la mujer necesita de un sostén contínuo que le ayude á caminar por entre los mil abrojos que se le presentan... ¡Ay! Quién será mi sostén, ¡Dios mío! ¿si á nadie he confiado mi secreto? Dos ó tres veces he estado á punto de descubrirlo todo, especialmente á mi madre; pero, ¡es tan severa conmigo, que me ha faltado valor para manifestarme á ella! ¡Ha repetido tantas veces que su hija no tendrá novio hasta que pase de los veinte años! ¡Y yo, apenas si cuento diez y seis! En cuanto á mi padre... ¡Jesús! si mi padre llegara á sospechar alguna cosa, no sé lo que me sucedería. Le quiero mucho; pero á decir verdad, su carácter me obliga á que le tenga más miedo que cariño.

¡Aqui llegaba el razonamiento de la jóven, cuando un nuevo personaje se le acercó de puntillas y por la espalda, le puso las manos sobre los ojos y le dijo, reprimiendo una alegre carcajada:

—¿Me conoces?

La persona que acababa de llegar era una muchacha de diez y ocho á veinte años,

EL ABISMO

NOVELA ORIGINAL

DE

Ángeles López de Ayala

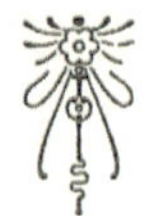

BARCELONA

IMP. DE LA VDA. DE JOSÉ MIGUEL.—JUNQUERAS, 7.-GRACIA

1907

3.3 Pages from Ángeles López de Ayala's *El abismo* in *El Gladiador: Órgano de la "Sociedad Progresiva Femenina"* 26, Year II (21 Dec. 1907). By kind permission of the Arxiu Històric de la Ciutat de Barcelona (microfilm no. 73)

of several female writers who also cultivated the genre: among them, Sinués de Marco, Enriqueta Lozano de Vilches, Julia de Asensi, and Grassi (Lecuyer and Villapadierna 1995, 26–31).

In keeping with the intention of López de Ayala's novellas, the feuilleton published in Spanish periodicals in the second half of the nineteenth century was generally aimed at middle-class women and a working-class readership that had only recently acquired literacy skills and lacked the financial means to buy books (Magnien 1995, 7, 9). The context in which López de Ayala writes her feuilletons, that of late nineteenth- and early twentieth-century Restoration Spain, sees a resurgence of the genre after the marked rise in literacy levels among these groups;[16] moreover, the feuilleton was the part of the newspaper intended for women and often the only section that most read (Seoane 1996a, 178). The content of *El abismo*, heavily focused on gender and class, suggests such a mixed reading public and the possibility of establishing empowering alliances among its different sectors. Especially interesting is the feminist content of *El abismo*, which distinguishes it from the predominant focus of the feuilleton on working-class issues.

Set in contemporary Madrid, the plot of *El abismo* follows the fortunes of its female protagonist of aristocratic birth, the sixteen-year-old Angélica. Forced to flee her home to escape being killed by her father, Don Gonzalo, who erroneously considers the family honour besmirched on discovering a mysterious man in her bedroom, Angélica ends up on the streets. There she is plunged into the physical and moral quandaries that beset working-class girls, only to be saved from hunger and rape by a night watchman, who takes her to Doña Petra's boarding house. After declaring herself an orphan, Angélica takes ill, overcome by a "congestión cerebral" (stroke) (López de Ayala [1896] 1907, 40). However, she is rescued from death by the charity of a young, handsome, and wealthy doctor, Carlos (43–4), portrayed as possessing an "elevada estatura" (lofty stature), an "agradable fisonomía" (pleasing appearance) and a "mirada inteligente" (39; intelligent gaze). To enable Angélica to recover, Carlos gives Doña Petra one of his seven houses and 250 pesetas a month, so that she may close her lodgings to care for Angélica, with the assistance of Tomasa, an ex-prostitute and one of her tenants (45, 47). Furthermore, Carlos adopts Angélica as his putative sister and potential wife, desiring to redeem her from her unfortunate state: "Estoy comprometido a ser su hermano, y a redimirla del estado de abyección en que sin duda no se halla sumergida del todo" (48; I am committed to being a brother to her and to redeeming her from the state of abjection into which evidently she has not yet totally sunk).

Undoubtedly, the narrative reveals many of the topoi common in popular contemporary serialized novels, such as the orphan, poverty, persecution, the reconquest of a lost state, and final liberation (Ferreras 1972, 254). Carlos, the representative of a secular, scientific society, embodies a hero typical of the serialized novel, where doctors enjoyed an unsullied prestige (Romero Tobar 1976, 134). Moreover, characters in *El abismo* reveal sociopolitical dualisms similar to those in serialized novels, whereby a young woman, usually a poor orphan and always beautiful and tender, is the victim of a traitor or symbolic enemy, from whom she is rescued by the young, handsome hero, her eventual husband (Ferreras 1972, 270). Nevertheless, whereas in serialized novels these dualisms usually support the status quo, in *El abismo* they undermine it and promote a more egalitarian society in accordance with Republican values. López de Ayala's *El abismo* critiques the outmoded, decadent values of the upper classes, casts the working classes in a favourable light, and suggests the possibility of inter-class alliances through Carlos's support of Doña Petra and through the romance that promises to unfold between Carlos and Angélica, believed to be of working-class origin.

What is also unusual about *El abismo* is the overtly feminist content of its initial pages, which clashes with more sensationalist elements in the text. The opening scene offers contrasting views on women's education through Angélica, her friend

Julia, and Angélica's mother, Doña Aurora. Reading alone in the garden, Angélica reflects on her book, musing that women need constant support if they are to successfully navigate the countless obstacles that life presents: "La mujer necesita de un sostén continuo que le ayude a caminar por entre los mil abrojos que se le presentan" (López de Ayala [1896] 1907, 4). She considers that she lacks such guidance; in love, she cannot confide in her severe mother, who has forbidden her to have a fiancé until she turns twenty, or in her father, whom she fears (4). Angélica's long soliloquy constitutes an authorial digression, which, as Romero Tobar explains, aims to clarify intentions or fulfil a didactic function either directly or indirectly, through long speeches by key characters (1976, 153–4).

On Julia's arrival, the narrative turns more definitively to women's education, a matter on which Angélica and Julia take up opposing positions. In this sense, they recall the characters of Rosa and Plácida from *De tal siembra, tal cosecha*, who similarly serve as foils to contrast models of femininity. Whereas Angélica maintains that women's education is the linchpin of society's future – "es tan precisa a mi juicio, que acaso de ella depende el porvenir de la sociedad" (in my opinion it is so necessary that the future of society may depend on it) – Julia states that she is the "enemiga declarada de la ilustración de la mujer" (López de Ayala [1896] 1907, 5; avowed enemy of women's education). According to Julia, and in keeping with fin-de-siècle reservations about educating women, the knowledgeable woman risks being labelled a bluestocking or "sabionda" (7), and losing her feminine distinctiveness: "La mujer conseguiría, por todo resultado, aparecer bajo un aspecto … indiferente, por no decir ridículo" (8; All that women would achieve would be to lose their apparent distinctiveness and seem ridiculous). Furthermore, Julia argues, by remaining "las niñas de la sociedad" (society's little girls), women are free to do as they please, since their relative ignorance renders them less accountable (6). This conservative model of femininity is refuted by Angélica, who advocates that women must abandon Romantic paradigms and avail themselves of education and reason to take full responsibility for their actions: "Es que la mujer ilustrada se haría más fuerte, más reflexiva y menos romántica. Caminaría no con pies de hada, sino de plomo, y por consiguiente, podría responder de cuanto hiciera" (6; The educated woman would become stronger, more reflective, and less romantic. She would not walk with fairy shoes but leaden ones, and would thus be accountable for everything she did).

Nevertheless, the contrasting stances theorized by Angélica and Julia are complicated by López de Ayala's accounts of their behaviour. On hearing a strange sound in the garden, Julia's immediate reaction is to investigate it, since she perceives it as "una aventura de las más interesantes" (7; a most interesting adventure). Conversely, Angélica considers that to do so will compromise their honour as upper-class women: "Somos dos jóvenes decentes y estamos comprometidas"

(7; We are two decent young women who find themselves in a compromising situation). Hence, although Angélica defends women's education, she reveals herself in practice as far more conventional than Julia. Indeed, Angélica's very name evokes the Angel in the House paradigm. This figure's passive suffering and silent beauty pervade a description of Angélica: "Sus hermosos ojos dieron paso a un raudal de ardientes lágrimas. Después inclinó la graciosa cabeza con muestras de gran abatimiento" (20; Her beautiful eyes welled up with a flood of burning tears. Then she bowed her graceful head with signs of great dejection). Conservative nineteenth-century models of femininity also portrayed women's supposed physical and moral weakness as illness, while conversely their alleged moral superiority was depicted in terms of spirit.[17] These paradoxical notions sit in uncomfortable juxtaposition in López de Ayala's somewhat parodic representation of Angélica's later illness: "Aun se hallaba un tanto ojerosa, detalle que la hacía más interesante y espiritual" (86; She still had dark shadows under her eyes, which made her seem even more interesting and spiritual). In comparison, Julia, described as possessing great initiative and a "carácter emprendedor y atrevido" (20; enterprising and daring spirit), also clearly manifests characteristics of the New Woman vindicated by fin-de-siècle feminism.[18]

The debate about the appropriateness of conventional models of femininity is continued through Angélica's and Julia's interactions with Doña Aurora, a woman between forty-eight and fifty years old. According to Doña Aurora, young Spanish women must not imitate the overly liberal conduct of their French counterparts but rather quell their desires and obey their elders: "Las jóvenes, especialmente en este Madrid que, imitando al mono, trata de plagiar las torpezas y extravagancias de la nación vecina; en Madrid, repito, las jóvenes deben vivir sin voluntad propia, o como dicen las reglas de la más famosa congregación, vivir muertas, para todo lo que no sea obedecer a sus superiores" (12; Young women, especially in Madrid, where all ape and try to copy the stupidities and outlandishness of our neighbouring country; in Madrid, I repeat, young women must live without any free will or, as the doctrine of the Catholic Church states, as if dead in all respects except for obeying their superiors). Whereas Julia remarks on the inflexibility of such a stance, Angélica defends it. She declares that their elders are simply protecting them from the deleterious consequences of emotional whim, to which women are allegedly more subject on account of their "natural" docility: "¿Quién respondería de los resultados si nuestros superiores no se opusieran a los muchos y perjudiciales caprichos que se apoderan de nosotras? ... nuestra misma docilidad hace que nos inclinemos con doble vehemencia hacia aquello que sentimos" (12; Who would be answerable to the outcomes if our superiors did not oppose the many harmful whims that take possession of us? ... our very docility disposes us doubly towards our emotions). Doña Aurora's respect for authority and Angélica's essentialized view of gender, both of which underpin inherited, naturalized cultural and political systems, are here counterposed with the more liberal, modern values symbolized by the French Republic.

This discussion of conventional gender roles mirrors the furore that raged in fin-de-siècle Spain over women's position in society. For most men, including freethinkers, women's roles were to be ideally limited to those of wife and mother. Women's increased participation in the public sphere would only result, many believed, in bolstering reactionary forces and the Catholic Church, given that they were seen as more susceptible to the latter's influence. What was therefore considered of primary importance was the education of women, in order to allow their greater incorporation into civil society rather than the political sphere. This objective was of strategic concern to female freethinkers within a Progressive republicanism (Duarte 1987, 63), such as López de Ayala, Domingo Soler, Palmira de Bruno, and Sárraga. The weightier, more philosophical content of the first twelve pages of *El abismo* thus appears directed at a liberal upper-middle- and middle-class female reading public, which is invited to meditate, like Angélica and Julia, upon contrasting models of femininity.

The remainder of the novella, however, is quite different in its subject matter and more sensationalist tone, depicting a world with which lower-class readers would be more familiar and that all readers are indirectly called on to change. Concentrating on action and class, the text exposes the appalling conditions in which the destitute live: the figurative abyss intimated by the title. This critique is especially channelled through López de Ayala's portrayal of Doña Petra's boarding house and its inhabitants, many of whom constitute the dregs of Madrid society. The boarding house itself is described as a "miserable morada" (wretched abode) and a "vivienda de insectos" (dwelling overrun with insects), full of "polvo" (dust) and "humedad" (damp), with an air that is "escaso, viciado y nauseabundo" (López de Ayala [1896] 1907, 33; lacking in oxygen, foul, and nauseating). Tenants live in rooms depicted as "reducidísimos, atestados de camastros y de gente" (extremely small and crowded with makeshift beds and people), while Angélica's bed is a "jergón cubierto por una sucia y remendada manta y por algunos trapos amarillentos y aún manchados" (35; straw mattress covered with a dirty, patched blanket and yellowish, still-stained rags). The motifs of filth and stench similarly predominate in the initial description of Doña Petra, characterized by her "negra, callosa, sucia y hedionda mano" (34; blackened, calloused, dirty, smelly hand), while Tomasa, thirty-six years old, is introduced as the "símbolo de la abyección y la impudicia" (35; symbol of abjection and wantonness).

Nevertheless, it is through Doña Petra and Tomasa that the narrative stresses the innate goodness and charitable impulses of the working classes and their potential for social redemption if empowered to do so by the middle and upper-middle classes. Beneath their coarse exteriors, the text insists, lie rough diamonds, as intimated by the description of the two women as "espíritus nobles encubiertos por las más groseras formas" (54; noble spirits under the coarsest of appearances). With regard to Doña Petra, her "exterior grosero, sucio y hablador" (rough, dirty, and garrulous exterior) conceals "una delicadeza de sentimientos excelente" (41; a wonderful delicacy of feeling), hence belying the imagined dangerous excessiveness that patriarchal society attributes to its feminized others and must contain. Likewise, in the case of Tomasa, she herself recognizes that she has a good heart: "No tengo mal corazón" (54).

Of greater relevance for López de Ayala's reformist objectives is that poverty and amorality are not portrayed as essential to the lower classes but as rooted in specific socioeconomic circumstances. Moreover, the revelation of these factors is often not articulated by an omniscient narrator of upper-middle-class extraction but by the working-class characters themselves, who are presented as explaining their situation from their own perspective. It is due to Doña Petra's widowed state and lack of education that she is obliged to take in the down-and-out: "viuda de tres maridos, pobre, ignorante, acostumbrada a vivir entre la verdadera chusma … en contacto con lo más perdido de Madrid" (46; thrice widowed, poor, ignorant and used to living among hardened rabble … in contact with Madrid's most down-and-out). Her illiteracy is conveyed through her inkwell and pen, which she has so that others can write on her behalf: "Tengo un tintero y una pluma … que compré … no porque yo sepa escribir, sino para que alguien hiciera el favor de escribir en nombre mío" (40; I possess an inkwell and pen …, which I bought not because I know how to write but so that others might write on my behalf). In this sense Doña Petra is representative of two-thirds of Spain's fin-de-siècle population.[19]

López de Ayala's social message is further underlined through Tomasa, for whom prostitution is her only means of survival. After she was left an orphan on her mother's death, her moral fall was caused by an unfortunate love affair, "unos malditos amoríos" (57). Stating that prostitution does not pay well, Tomasa recognizes that her working life, conditional on her good looks, will be short-lived: "Los condenados hombres, huyen de las caras amarillas y ojerosas, y de los cuerpos flacos y extenuados por la debilidad. … Y luego, que hay días de suerte, pero los más son de desgracia; y ¡ya se ve! … una ya no es un *pimpollo*, y … la vida que se pasa no es de las más buenas que digamos" (56; Those wretched men flee from sallow-faced women with dark shadows under their eyes, and from thin, feeble, exhausted bodies. … And while there are lucky days, the majority are full of misfortune; and it's quite clear! … one is no longer a *pretty young thing*, and … life is not what one might call the best). Like the upper-middle-class characters in *De tal siembra, tal cosecha*, Tomasa redefines honour, stipulating that it depends on having sufficient skills to earn one's living differently: "Para ser honrada, se necesita tener qué comer, o haber aprendido algún oficio con qué ganárselo" (57; To be honourable you need to have enough to eat or to have learnt a trade to sustain body and soul). Hence López de Ayala's novella stresses that moral emancipation cannot take place without improved financial conditions.

When Doña Petra invites Tomasa to assist her in caring for Angélica by cleaning and sewing in the home that the doctor has symbolically sold to her, Tomasa accepts, but only after a battle between spirit and matter, as the text expresses it: "¡Cuán grandiosa fue la lucha que sostuvo su espíritu con su materia! ¡cuán gigantescos, cuán titánicos los esfuerzos llevados a cabo por aquella alma pura, ansiosa de triunfar de aquel cuerpo corrompido!" (58; What a tremendous battle her spirit waged against her body! What gigantic, titanic efforts that pure soul made, eager to overcome that corrupt body!) It is important that Tomasa's moral redemption is not only facilitated indirectly by an upper middle class represented by the doctor but also by a lower social class incarnate in Doña Petra. This coalition of actors from disparate social sectors in the creation of a more caring world can be read as an allegory of the need for upper-middle- and middle-class Republicans to forge alliances with working-class movements to better achieve mutually held objectives. Such a socially committed attitude comes to the fore in *Primitivo*, where the education of the lower classes is the primary theme.

Primitivo: Social Elevation through Secular Education

In fin-de-siècle Spain, Republicans, and freethinkers in general, saw a secular, scientific education as the key to personal dignity and the foundation of individual freedom. The extension of education to all sectors of society would enable Spain to be self-governing, according to democratic principles (Duarte 1987, 54–5). Similarly, education was the fundamental weapon in the class struggle from the viewpoint of the working classes, who defended a holistic, secular education inspired by utopian socialism and Marxist principles (Delgado 1979, 30–1). This inter-class concern for educating the nation is readily understandable in the context of the calamitous state of education in fin-de-siècle Spain. Referring to J. Jimeno Agius's study on primary education in Spain in 1880, Botrel specifies that just over half of all children then received schooling, and of these, 27 per cent were enrolled in schools but did not attend. As for schools, 61 per cent were insufficiently equipped. Only 59 per cent of teachers, paid approximately half a labourer's wage, were qualified. Despite an increase of 16.35 per cent in the number of enrolled pupils between 1880 and 1908, the proportion of teachers in public education grew by only 11.55 per cent, resulting in overcrowded classrooms and appalling learning conditions. Nevertheless, that rise in pupils still represented only 47.7 per cent of children between the ages of six and fifteen in 1910 (Botrel 1993, 321–3).

López de Ayala's fierce criticism of mainstream Restoration education is highly evident in *Primitivo*, a ninety-six-page novella preserved in its entirety. Intended for students of secular schools, it affirms, like her earlier short story, *Cuentos y cantares para los niños* (1888), the ability of the lower classes to better themselves through education and contribute to the regeneration of society. Appearing in *El Gladiador* between 23 June 1906 and 30 November 1907, its duplicated cover, featured in the inaugural issue of the periodical alongside its first instalment, proclaims it to be a "moral, entertaining novel" and a "reading suitable for students of secular schools" (see figure 3.4).[20] In accordance with *Primitivo*'s didactic message, the language employed is much simpler than that in *El abismo* and the characters are drawn with broader strokes, to enable ready comprehension by novice working-class readers. Reviewed in 1916 in *El Gladiador del Librepensamiento: Órgano de la Federación Librepensadora de Barcelona y otros Pueblos Adheridos*, there the transformative intent of the novella transpires in its description as "much more than a novel for children. It is a book that makes us think specifically about the ills besetting our Spain and suitable ways of remedying them."[21]

The plot of *Primitivo* centres on the vicissitudes and strivings of its eponymous twelve-year-old, lower-class hero to overturn the disadvantages of class and educate himself against all odds, to become a rationalist school teacher. A Bildungsroman that charts the protagonist's path to maturity, the text is also a quest romance, whose hero is tested by numerous obstacles only to emerge triumphant. The story unfolds according to a tripartite structure, mirroring the three phases of separation, initiation, and return through which the hero must pass, as has been noted by Joseph Campbell (1973, 30, 36–8). These consist of an initial stage in which Primitivo's attempts to study meet with frustration; a second, intermediate period when he studies at a boarding school and passes his exams; and a third stage that marks his successful career as a rationalist teacher and founder of schools. The bulk of the narrative is taken up with the first and second stages.

The authorial account of the initial stage highlights the seemingly insurmountable difficulties that Primitivo faces to fulfil his aspirations and his dogged determination to succeed. First and foremost are the barriers of class. Primitivo is the eldest child of six in a poor family, whose members "contaban con escasísimos medios para vivir, toda vez que el padre era un modesto empleado, y lo que él ganaba, los únicos ingresos que había en aquel humilde hogar" (López de Ayala 1906–7, 22; had only the most meagre of means to live on, since the father was a modest employee, and what he earned was the only income in that humble home). Primitivo's vocation to become a teacher meets with his parents' opposition, due to the low regard in which society holds teachers and the pitiful recompense that they receive for their labours (4); thus his father perceives teachers as "tipos extravagantes y ridículos que arrastran una vida anémica, empleada en dar voces a una docena de chiquillos, para olvidar el hambre que les devora" (46; eccentric,

— 8 —

y hermanos, y dió comienzo á la tarea de aprender los párrafos que de cada libro le habian sido señalados, y que él pretendia saber á la perfección al día siguiente.

Pero el niño, poco habituado al estudio, ignoraba lo rebelde que es la atención aún del más juicioso, cuando el que la posee trata de encaminarla á un punto determinado, en tanto que los que le rodean la conquistan en fuerza de cien incidentales impresiones, que el oido lleva al cerebro del que lee, y de las que no puede sustraerse no obstante recurra á los más vivos esfuerzos de su voluntad.

¡Ah! ¡Qué tormento hubo de pasar Primitivo aquella noche, y qué de corazón envidió á los niños que disponen de una habitacioncita en la que nadie les molesta, y en la que pueden dedicarse tranquilamente á adquirir conocimientos útiles por medio de los buenos libros!

A pesar de todo, como el niño no era de los que se desanimaban facilmente, insistió tanto y tanto en su lectura, hizo tales maravillas de dominio de sus facultades intelec-

PRIMITIVO.

NOVELA RECREATIVA Y MORAL

DE

Ángeles Lopez de Ayala

Lectura adecuada para los alumnos de las Escuelas Láicas

3.4 Page 8 from Ángeles López de Ayala's *Primitivo* and advertisement of that novella, in *El Gladiador: Órgano de la "Sociedad Progresiva Femenina"* 1, Year 1 (26 May 1906): 12. By kind permission of the Arxiu Històric de la Ciutat de Barcelona (microfilm no. 73)

ridiculous types who lead miserable lives shouting at a dozen or so kids to forget the hunger that devours them). Primitivo can study only at night, since his day is occupied with helping his mother and running errands. His study is further hampered by the fact that he has to work at the dining-room table surrounded by his noisy brothers and sisters, because the family's means are insufficient to allow him another candle to study elsewhere (8). As the story progresses, the setbacks experienced by Primitivo increase: his parents curtail his attempts to study in the quiet hours of the early morning because he is not sleeping enough (16), and his mother tears up his book and forbids him to read when Primitivo accidentally drops his little sister, whom he is tending while studying (20). Finally, when Primitivo takes up a position at the office where his father works, to help his family's precarious situation, his depression at not being able to study overcomes him (26–9).

It is significant that, just as in *El abismo*, the text accentuates the role of the upper-middle and middle classes in assisting the progress of the socially disadvantaged. Consequently, Don Filiberto, Primitivo's wealthy neighbour, champions Primitivo's cause in the face of his parents' opposition, offering to coach him and provide him with the necessary books to achieve his aims (5). When Primitivo's inability to study sees him succumb to illness, his doctor also fosters his ambition, sponsoring with Don Filiberto the boy's studies at a boarding school.

The second stage of the narrative deals with Primitivo's year at the school, his two years at a teaching college, and his subsequent experience as a teaching assistant prior to his becoming a teacher in his own right. The context of the boarding school permits López de Ayala to expand further on class issues through Primitivo's acquaintance with two fellow students, Simplicio and Generoso. The names of all three characters are clearly allegorical. Whereas that of Primitivo refers indirectly to his humble class origins, those of Generoso and Simplicio allude to dominant qualities in those characters, recalling the anarchist practice, signalled by Murray Bookchin, of naming offspring after moral and political ideals (1977, 57).

Through Simplicio, López de Ayala underlines that material privileges do not guarantee spiritual wealth. While he is handsome and from a comfortable family background, Simplicio is also represented as arrogant and convinced that the world owes him a living: "Pagado de su talante y en la confianza de que sus padres poseían una regular fortuna, creía que a su paso por el mundo todas las puertas las hallaría de par en par, juzgando inútiles sus estudios y por consiguiente la adquisición de una carrera" (López de Ayala 1906–7, 65; Overly complacent about his talents and convinced that his parents were well off, and believing that the world would throw wide open all its doors to him, he saw studying and forging a career as useless). In contrast, Generoso, from a very poor family and physically unattractive, possesses a keen mind and desires nothing more than to finish his studies and become a teacher: "Generoso, hijo de familia extremadamente pobre, de presencia poco atractiva y de cerebro bien organizado, deseaba ardientemente concluir sus estudios preparatorios y abrir clase" (65).

Despite his material and physical advantages in life, Simplicio is revealed as a bully in his conduct towards Generoso and a nest of fledglings (66–7). Although Primitivo manages to dissuade Generoso from taking retribution against Simplicio, through his mastery of the classical skills of rhetoric and logic – "poseía el don de la elocuencia, y la empleaba con argumentos tan lógicos cuanto persuasivos" (71; he possessed the gift of eloquence, which he used in arguments that were not only logical but also persuasive) – he informs the school principal about the incident to prevent recurrences, with the result that Simplicio is expelled (72–3). López de Ayala's insistence that intelligence and the right to education are not conditional on material wealth and class is again evident when Primitivo subsequently proves himself to be the best student in the examinations: "Eclipsó a los demás alumnos, obteniendo la calificación de sobresaliente en distintas asignaturas, y en otras la de notable" (74; He surpassed the other students, obtaining A grades in several subjects and in others, high Bs).

The third and final stage of the narrative, composed of some twenty pages, constitutes a defence of rationalist schools. The text clearly states that the school that Primitivo establishes, financed initially by don Filiberto and the doctor, is a rationalist institution, dedicated to a scientific, secular education: "Sin duda el título de 'Escuela Racionalista' con que había sido denominada la recientemente establecida, sirvió para alejar de ella a los ignorantes rebeldes a la ilustración, en tanto que atrajo a los partidarios de la luz que es la ciencia" (76; Undoubtedly the label of "Rationalist" attributed to the recently established school served to put off all those who were ignorant and against education, while it attracted those advocates of the light that is science).

Essential for understanding this emphasis on rationalist education in *Primitivo* are López de Ayala's own links with rationalist schools. Throughout her life she constantly promoted them, often in conjunction with Domingo Soler and Sárraga, as seen on the occasion of the inauguration of the Sócrates schools in Barcelona on 24 November 1894, which she covered in three consecutive pieces of writing: two poems and a prose account, all published in *Las Dominicales del Libre Pensamiento*. One poem, "En el acto de la inauguración de las Escuelas laicas 'Sócrates' (Invitación)," written on the same day as the inauguration, calls on citizens to attend the opening seen as the consecration of a "templo a la ciencia" (temple to science). Through secular education, heaven and God have been replaced by science and human conscience: "El mejor cielo es la ciencia, / y que Dios es ¡la conciencia, / innata en la humanidad!" (The best heaven is science, / and God is the conscience / innate in humanity!)[22]

The article, "De enhorabuena," written just two days after the event and addressed to Lozano, describes how the school hall was already full at 8.30 p.m. The event itself began at 9.30 p.m., opened by the president, who then handed over to Domingo Soler, flanked on her right by Sárraga, the teacher in the girls' school, and on her left, by López de Ayala. Attending the gathering were also representatives of various freethinking, Republican, and Masonic centres. After the children had recited poetry and enacted a dialogue written by Sárraga for the occasion, Domingo Soler and Sárraga, among others, gave readings. López de Ayala affirms that the inauguration of the Sócrates schools demonstrates that Catalonia "se emancipa de la tiranía religiosa, porque ha comprendido que por religión se toma la anulación de la razón, la preterición del buen sentido, la obcecación en el absurdo" (is freeing itself from religious tyranny, because it has understood that religion means the disappearance of reason, disregard for common sense, and defending the absurd at all costs). She also foregrounds the fact that the school for girls opened first, signalling the importance given to wresting women from ignorance and the grip of the Catholic Church.[23]

The second poem, "Carta-reseña," written on 29 January 1895 and published on 1 March, provides details not given in the prose account. Taking the form of a missive addressed to Lozano, it informs readers that the Sócrates school for young girls is run by Antonia Amat, while the boys' school is under José Riera, a Mason. At the inauguration both López de Ayala and Domingo Soler received roses and a dedication from a seven-year-old girl, Adela Rodríguez, a freemason's orphan.[24] Later that year, on 11 July 1895, Domingo Soler refers to an evening function offered by the pupils of Amat's secular school. There the young girls sang songs – among them, López de Ayala's aforementioned "Himno a la igualdad" – and recited poetry. According to Domingo Soler's account, López de Ayala closed the function, showing herself to be "un verdadero apóstol para la clase obrera" (a true apostle for the working class).[25]

Crucial also for the context of *Primitivo* was the influence of the Institución Libre de Enseñanza. As Delgado has explored, its founder, Francisco Giner de los Ríos, was closely connected with Barcelona at the turn of the century. Even more important was the impact of the Modern School, established by Francisco Ferrer Guardia in Barcelona in 1901 (Delgado 1979, 67). López de Ayala's relationship with Ferrer Guardia is corroborated by the fact that he was among the Spanish contingent who accompanied López de Ayala and Sárraga to the International Conference for Freethinking in Rome in 1904 (de Buen 2003, 71). The growth of rationalist schools that followed Ferrer Guardia's model received impetus from prominent Republicans and freethinkers with whom López de Ayala was associated, such as Cristóbal Litrán, Odón de Buen, and Lerroux, as well as from the parties in which Lerroux was instrumental: the Republican Union (1903) and Radical Republican Party (1908) (Delgado 1979, 183–7). In 1906, just one year before the publication of *Primitivo*, López de Ayala gave an address at the Federal Republican Centre on the occasion of the examinations of students from the Modern School of Villanueva y Geltrú.[26]

According to rationalist principles, co-education of the sexes and classes was fundamental for bringing about the emancipation of women and the equality necessary for building democratic societies (Delgado 1979, 104–5). Consequently, education in Primitivo's school is likewise mixed (López de Ayala 1906–7, 76). As for the school curriculum, its subjects include natural history, mineralogy, zoology, science, anatomy, and anthropology (75–8), and even theories of evolution: "Luego [Primitivo] trataba de los cuadrumanos, que son los monos, poniendo de relieve su semejanza con la del hombre; los descubrimientos hechos sobre sus costumbres, la calidad de ascendientes nuestros que lógicamente se les atribuye, y otras importantes cosas con ellos relacionadas" (78; Next [Primitivo] turned to the quadrumanes or apes, stressing their similarities with humankind, the discoveries about their habits, how they are logically considered to be our ancestors, and other important, relevant matters).

To a large extent, the subject matter taught in Primitivo's school and equally promoted in López de Ayala's *Cuentos y cantares para los niños* is typical of the curriculum found in rationalist schools: geography, mineralogy, zoology, physics, chemistry, history, mathematics, drawing, and music (Delgado 1979, 112). The fact that anthropology and evolution feature is even more significant. Only fifteen years prior to the publication of *Primitivo,* the University of Barcelona had established in 1892 a chair in anthropology, occupied by López de Ayala's friend Odón de Buen, who defended Darwinian theory. Forced to withdraw pedagogical texts banned by the Vatican in 1895, he retained his chair only after protests in which Domingo Soler, López de Ayala, and Sárraga figured prominently, as I discuss in chapter 4.

Another subject taught in Primitivo's school is hygiene, which, as Delgado remarks, was considered an indispensable component of a modern, scientific education, contrary to the norm in fin-de-siècle Spain, where schools bred infection and disease (1979, 104–6). Indeed, Primitivo's school, the text affirms, reflects the rationalist principle of hygiene, together with the premise of beauty in usefulness: "Un hermoso e higiénico local, que fue decorado con un mobiliario tan útil como elegante" (López de Ayala 1906–7, 75; A beautiful, hygienic place, furnished with objects both useful and elegant). Similarly in keeping with the premises of rationalist education, as outlined by Delgado (1979, 150, 175), are the recreation periods, "para que en ellas se refrescaran los cerebros de los estudiantes" (López de Ayala 1906–7, 83; so that students' minds might be refreshed), and the field excursions, "con el doble objeto de hacer que respirasen gran cantidad de oxígeno, y de que recreándose, oyeran ciertas explicaciones" (84–5; with the dual purpose of allowing them to breathe in copious amounts of fresh air and listen to educational explanations while enjoying themselves). That Primitivo's school concurs with a utopian blueprint for secular schools can be seen in a column from López de Ayala's *El Gladiador*: "The best school will be the one with the BEST TEACHER, most space and fewest walls so as to allow the free passage of the sun and air."[27] Primitivo also holds weekly lectures for the wider public: "Pues se celebraban conferencias instructivas públicas y semanales" (López de Ayala 1906–7, 81; Weekly public educational talks were held). These talks are reminiscent of the Sunday seminars or "science masses" given by freethinking intellectuals associated with the Modern School and intended to attract the working classes to republicanism (Delgado 1979, 106–7, 185).

The incredible success of Primitivo's school evokes the rapid expansion of rationalist institutions in fin-de-siècle Barcelona: from ten in 1901 to forty-three in 1905 (Delgado 1979, 183).[28] Just one year after Primitivo establishes his school, he is working with two male teachers and three female, in order to cater to the astonishing rise in student numbers (López de Ayala 1906–7, 77). Shortly afterward, he expands his staff still further and opens branches in all areas of town, as a result of the school's excellent academic reputation: "Los niños y niñas ...

adquirían conocimientos tan sólidos y precisos en todos los más importantes ramos del saber, que en breve hubo que aumentar el personal de profesores, abriendo sucursales en todas las barriadas de la población, todas ellas regidas por el mismo orden que se observaba en la primitiva" (80; The boys and girls acquired such sound and precise knowledge in the most important fields of learning that within a very short time the number of teachers had to be increased and branches opened in all areas of the town, with all the schools governed by the same order that reigned in the first one).

On the third occasion that Primitivo takes on additional teachers he is joined by Generoso, who, disenchanted with the inadequacies of mainstream education, has become a rationalist (82). In turn, Generoso employs Simplicio to assist him in his branch of Primitivo's schools, rescuing him from his intention to commit suicide because of his family's loss of fortune (88–90). Simplicio's repentance, reform, and redemption, then, clearly constitute a secular version of the biblical narrative of the prodigal son, made possible by the beautiful principle of fraternity that underpins true freethinking: "El hermoso principio de la más verdadera fraternidad" (83).

The didactic quality of the novella, centred throughout on the theme of pedagogy, reaches a crescendo in the final chapter. Here the narrative voice, focalized through Primitivo, elaborates on the value of rationalist education for the nation's democratic future:

> A convertir a todos los alumnos … en verdaderos seres pensantes y conscientes, que sirvan de base a la sociedad del porvenir, facilitándoles la adquisición del conocimiento de su valor: individual y colectivo, y los principios democráticos, justos y fraternales en que deben fundar todas sus aspiraciones, e informar todos sus actos. (93)

> (To transform all its pupils … into truly thinking, conscious beings who will be the backbone of the society of the future, empowering them to become aware of their value, both individual and collective, and of the democratic, just, and fraternal principles on which they must found all their aspirations and acts.)

Teachers, therefore, in forming the consciousness and intelligence of their pupils, become the creators of a "mundo sabio, justo y feliz" (94; wise, just, and happy world). The quasi-religious overtones that habitually inform the discourse of freethinking are palpable in the allusions to the "gran obra" (great work), the "sublime tarea" (sublime task), the "formidable masa de adeptos" (formidable mass of followers), the "misión impuesta" (necessary mission), and "la redención que sin duda habrá de fructificar en cercanos días" (93–5; the redemption that undoubtedly must come to pass in the near future). It is relevant that Primitivo, Generoso, and Simplicio all eventually have families (95), suggestive of the closely knit national family that freethinking hopes to engender.

López de Ayala's extant novellas offer enlightening perspectives on the substantial contributions by female intellectuals and writers to forming an ideal Republican nation in consonance with their feminist values. Her constant vindication and enactment of inter-class alliances point to her acute awareness of the links between the subordinate status of women and that of the lower classes and the need for such groups to unite behind commonly held sociopolitical objectives. Yet López de Ayala's front-line profile in freethinking circles during the late nineteenth and early twentieth centuries, her prolific writings, and her unrelenting activism on behalf of republicanism, feminism, and the working classes, are barely recorded, if at all, in the annals of Spanish republicanism or in literary and cultural histories, built on the achievements of founding fathers and canonical texts.

A similar oblivion has shrouded another figure of comparable stature: Belén Sárraga, the subject of my fourth and final chapter. Like López de Ayala, Sárraga's political engagement and feminist activities are truly impressive. However, whereas López de Ayala's efforts were focused primarily on Spain, Sárraga, a federal Republican with strong anarchist sympathies, sought to establish a transnational freethinking association of republics. In pursuit of this dream she travelled extensively not only in Spain, but also in Algeria, Europe, and Latin America, and was even more directly involved in political events and parties. Chapter 4, then, will attempt to broker just recognition for a remarkable woman in turbulent times.

LIBERTAD JUSTICIA

LA CONCIENCIA LIBRE

FRATERNIDAD

¡Guerra á la hipocresía y á la ignorancia! ¡Paso á la ciencia y á la verdad!

BELÉN SÁRRAGA DE FERRERO

Directora de LA CONCIENCIA LIBRE

4.1 Image of Belén Sárraga on the first page of *La Conciencia Libre*, Year I (24 Oct. 1896): 1. By kind permission of the *Ateneu Enciclopèdic Popular*, Barcelona

4 Federal Republicanism, Feminism, and Freethinking in (Trans)national Arenas: The Sociopolitical Poetics of Belén Sárraga (ca. 1873–1950)

Y tú, Belén, intrépida viajera,
queridísima hermana en ideales,
que a través de las iras clericales
llevas enhiesta la inmortal bandera;
si ese pueblo que sufre comprendiera
lo que debe a tu amor y patriotismo

("A mis hermanas en ideas," Una Andaluza [Soledad Areales])

(And you, Belén, intrepid traveller, / dearest sister in ideals, / who amidst the ire of the Catholic Church / bears on high the immortal banner; / if that suffering nation understood / what it owes to your love and patriotism)[1]

Teresa Mañé's (Soledad Gustavo) *La Revista Blanca* is acknowledged as one of the foremost anarchist periodicals in early twentieth-century Spain.[2] Yet prior to that publication, another periodical, also edited by a female friend of Mañé's, emerged as a beacon for left-wing political ideals harnessed to feminism and working-class objectives. The periodical in question was Belén Sárraga's *La Conciencia Libre*, to which Domingo Soler and especially López de Ayala also contributed. Like her Republican sisters, through her life and creative writing Sárraga played a protagonist role in fashioning the foundations of Spanish democracy. Like them also, she had all but vanished from historical studies until the pioneering scholarship of Ramos and Sanfeliu in the Spanish context, and of Vitale and Antivilo Peña with regard to Latin America. While Sanfeliu's book concentrates on Sárraga's association in Valencia until 1898 with Blasco Ibáñez's radical Republican movement, Ramos provides essential documentation on Sárraga's life and sociopolitical affiliations. The enormous scope of Sárraga's activities throughout Latin America is evaluated in Vitale and Antivilo Peña's painstaking and invaluable amassing of evidence, as well as in Antivilo Peña's 2011 article.

Building on these scholars' works, in part 1 I round out the picture of Sárraga's role as a major player in radical Republican politics on national and transnational levels by drawing on references to her in leading freethinking periodicals of the day and her contributions to them. This biographical overview will foreground how Sárraga set out to forge alternative paradigms of female subjectivity that argue for women's political agency and privilege a truly cosmopolitan ethos. Part 2 will examine Sárraga's more literary works, and in particular her poetic compositions and essays, barely addressed in historical studies, and which serve at all times as vehicles to promote her vision of sociocultural and political transformation. As in Domingo Soler's and López de Ayala's works, anticlericalism and the defence of the working classes are prominent themes in Sárraga's writings, especially in connection with the Montjuich imprisonments and the Spanish-American colonial war. Sárraga's poems and essays, however, grant greater political importance to the figure of the mother and seek to place a maternal ethics of care at centre stage in state affairs.

In Search of the Freethinking Nation and Cosmopolitan Ideal

A secular teacher, journalist, essayist, poet, and indefatigable defender of human rights, Sárraga was born into a middle-class liberal family in Valladolid in approximately 1873, the year that saw the birth of the First Republic. She spent her early years in Puerto Rico, given that her father, a member of the military, was a citizen of that Spanish colony.[3] By the time Sárraga published *Minucias* with a popular press in Málaga in 1901, she was already a well-known writer and political actor, formed by her studies in medicine and the humanities at the University of Barcelona, as well as by her affiliation in 1893 to the Madrid federal Centro Instructivo Obrero Republicano (Republican Workers' Educational Centre), directed by Eduardo Benot (1822–1907). According to Ramos, the centre, a meeting place for many anarchists, held talks and debates on social issues, women's emancipation, and sexual freedom (2002a, 133).[4]

Sárraga's unremitting sociopolitical activism on behalf of freethinking, federal republicanism, and feminism was channelled through three overarching endeavours: the weekly *La Conciencia Libre*, the Asociación General Femenina, and the Federación Malagueña de Sociedades de Resistencia. While these initiatives were born in Valencia and Málaga, urban centres with strong Republican identities, Sárraga promoted freethinking ideals throughout the nation and abroad, representing Spain at international conferences and embarking on lengthy lecture tours in Latin America. In this sense, she is the most cosmopolitan of the three writers in this study. I now turn to chart salient features of Sárraga's life and her core contributions to freethinking goals.

Sárraga succeeded in combining her work in the public sphere with her roles as spouse and mother. In 1894 she married, in a religious ceremony that ran counter to her anticlerical beliefs, the Republican freethinker Emilio Ferrero Balaguer, from whom she would later separate in South America (Ramos 2005a, 76). With him she would have at least three children: a son, Rafael, a daughter, Libertad, born on 8 January 1897, only to die just eight years later in 1905, and a second son, Volney Víctor, who was born on 26 May 1902.[5] The names of Libertad and Volney denote their parents' left-wing ideals. According to *La Conciencia Libre*, Volney's name, after the French freethinking philosopher and historian, was controversial, given that the local judge refused to register the child under that name.[6] At the time, Sárraga was suffering from ill health and her husband was in prison.[7]

Also inflecting Sárraga's ideals was her association with the interlinking worlds of spiritism, secular education, and freemasonry. Regarding spiritism, Ramos maintains that Domingo Soler was responsible for Sárraga's entry into the literary arena (2005a, 78), publishing her poems and essays in *La Luz del Porvenir* between 23 May 1895 and 23 April 1896, as already mentioned in chapter 1.[8] However, what also undoubtedly would have brought Domingo Soler and Sárraga together was their mutual involvement in secular education, which, in Sárraga's case, began with her experience as a teacher at the Sócrates secular school for girls, inaugurated in Barcelona on 24 November 1894, details of which were given in the previous chapter. Between May 1895 and April 1896 further insights into Sárraga's activities as a teacher are provided through columns in *La Luz del Porvenir* such as "¡Los prometidos! (A Concha)," where Domingo Soler describes a "velada infantil que celebró mi compañera de redacción la joven profesora laica Belén Sárraga de Ferrero" (children's evening organized by my editorial companion, the young secular teacher, Belén Sárraga de Ferrero).[9] Sárraga's unstinting dedication to teaching is palpable in Domingo Soler's appraisal that "Belén trabaja cuanto sabe y cuanto puede, y cree ... que sus esfuerzos son recompensados por sus alumnas, que se desviven por su profesora ..." (181; Belén works as hard as she knows how to and can, and believes ... that her efforts are rewarded by her female students, who are devoted to their teacher). During the evening Sárraga's young son Rafael read a poem by his mother, "A mis discípulas," which reveals Sárraga's commitment to rationalist education:

Esto es la enseñanza pura,
Racional y razonada,
Siempre en la verdad basada
Sin engaño ni impostura. (182)

(This is the essence of education, / Rational and reflective, / Always based on truth / Without deceit or lies.)

Sárraga's enjoyment in her profession is captured in the following verses: "¡Ah! no sabéis lo que gozo / Cuando en una inteligencia, / Voy inculcando la ciencia" (Ah! You don't know how much I rejoice / when in a mind / I instil scientific knowledge). As the self-proclaimed intellectual mother of her pupils or "las hijas de mi alma" (daughters of my soul), she is conscious that she is forming the Woman of the Future:

Y vuestros vuelos
Me hagan mañana decir
Con razón, que hice surgir,
De la instrucción bajo el peso,
En la escuela del "Progreso,"
[¡]La Mujer del Porvenir! (183)

(And may your accomplishments / Bring me to say tomorrow / Quite rightly, that I brought about the birth, / Through the power of education, / In the school of "Progress," / of the Woman of the Future!)[10]

Sárraga's advocacy of rationalist education as essential in the emancipation of humankind is the subject of a long speech, "La instrucción libre como base de la regeneración humana," delivered to the Ateneo Obrero (Workers' Society) in Gracia, Barcelona, in early 1896 and published over two issues of *La Luz del Porvenir*.[11] There Sárraga lambasts the historical coalition of the Catholic Church and aristocracy in oppressing the "people." Presenting a scientific education as the most effective means of countering tradition and fanaticism, Sárraga presents her working-class audience with clear choices:

Es preciso escoger, pues, o continuar en la ignorancia siendo dominados por la hipocresía y la mentira, o romper abiertamente con la tradición proclamando a la ciencia única soberana de nuestro entendimiento. … Ahora bien, vosotros ¿qué preferís? ¿queréis a vuestros hijos imbéciles o ilustrados, hipócritas o leales? si lo primero, llevadlos a las escuelas católicas, si lo segundo, mandadlos a las escuelas libres. (395, 398)

(It is necessary to choose, then: either to continue in ignorance, dominated by hypocrisy and lies, or to break openly with tradition proclaiming science as the sole sovereign of our minds. … Well now, what do you prefer? Do you want your children to be stupid or educated, hypocritical or trustworthy? If the former, send them to Catholic schools; if the latter, send them to freethinking schools.)

Secular education, she exhorts on summing up, will deliver the next generation from slavery and foster a free nation: "No marquéis a vuestros hijos desde que nacen con un sello de esclavitud, dejadlos que crezcan libres ... Dadles pues ciencia, mucha ciencia, mucha moral, mucha educación, pero no les deis religión" (399; Don't brand your children from birth with the seal of slavery, let them grow up free ... Give them, then, science, science, morals, and education in abundance, but don't give them religion).[12]

1896 also appears to have been the year in which Sárraga was initiated into freemasonry, joining the Severidad lodge.[13] Later, she would become a member of the mixed international Masonic order El Derecho Humano, in which she attained grade 33 and represented the Virtud lodge in Málaga at the 1906 Universal Conference for Freethinkers in Buenos Aires, as I develop below.[14] Moreover, Ortiz Albear documents Sárraga's continued association with Andalusian freemasonry: she is recorded on the List of Honour of the Fe lodge in Seville in 1901 and was connected with the Cádiz lodge of markedly feminist orientation, Hijas de la Regeneración, in which Amalia and Ana Carvia were highly influential – sisters with whom Sárraga would respectively found *La Conciencia Libre* and the Asociación General Femenina (Ortiz Albear 2005, 224–5, 243).[15] In later years Sárraga moved in freemasonry circles in Portugal, Argentina, Chile, and Uruguay (Ramos 2000, 225). Indeed, as Vitale and Antivilo Peña substantiate, on Sárraga's lecture tours throughout Chile and Argentina she was invited by and spoke at the Masonic lodges (2000, 108, 120). According to Ortiz Albear, Sárraga was even expelled from the Supremo Consejo Mixto Order in Argentina, supposedly for her "rather unorthodox behaviour" (2005, 89).

In 1896, at the age of twenty-three, Sárraga established in Valencia, with Amalia Carvia and López de Ayala, the weekly *La Conciencia Libre*, the name of which attests to its espousal of freethinking.[16] Achieving runs of twenty thousand, the periodical was frequently closed down by government order for alleged censorship infringements (Rivera 1913, 168).[17] Consequently, its chequered publication history was divided into two epochs: the first, which saw it published in Valencia in a four-page format, ran from the summer of 1896 to July 1898; during the second, more intermittent epoch, the periodical appeared in Málaga from 1899 until 1902, and throughout 1905–6. There is also reference to it being published from Córdoba from 1902 by Soledad Areales, Amalia Carvia, and Sárraga.[18] In 1907, its final year, it was published in a twelve-page format from Gracia, Barcelona, where Sárraga and her family were again living, before her departure for Uruguay in 1908.[19]

Until at least the end of 1902 the front-page banner of the weekly was embellished with the motto "Liberty, Justice, Fraternity" and the Masonic symbols of the triangle, square, and compass. Flanking the publication's name were two sets of figures (which vary slightly from the earlier depictions in figure 4.1): on the left, symbolizing the importance of secular education in the creation of a new society, stands a woman with a young boy and girl, who listen attentively to her teachings; under this group the caption reads, "¡Guerra a la hipocresía y a la ignorancia!" (War on hypocrisy and ignorance!) On the right, a lower-middle-class man is seated on a bench inscribed with the words "El trabajo es ley para todos" (Work is law for all). Waving his cap in the air with his right hand, he holds an anvil in

LA CONCIENCIA LIBRE

REVISTA SEMANAL

ÓRGANO DEL LIBREPENSAMIENTO INTERNACIONAL

¡Guerra á la Hipocresía y á la Ignorancia! ¡Paso á la Ciencia y á la Verdad!

SEGUNDA ÉPOCA Año II Núm. 59	Redacción y Administración: Sta. Madrona, 1, Barcelona -- GRACIA La correspondencia á Amalia Pérez Conjiu	BARCELONA Marzo 16 de 1907

Cristo en la picota

4.2 Cover image from *La Conciencia Libre* 59, Second Epoch, Year II (16 Mar. 1907): 636. By kind permission of the Arxiu Històric de la Ciutat de Barcelona

his left hand, while at his feet lie a scythe and spanner: all items that denote the publication's alliance with the lower-middle class and rural and industrial working classes. The caption beneath this image reads, "¡Paso a la ciencia y a la verdad!" (Make way for science and truth!) By 1907, however, the image on the editorial page is that of a nubile woman in the art nouveau style, a modern Liberty representing the values of Progressive republicanism. She bears in one hand a banner and in the other holds aloft the globe, pointing to the international purview of the publication, as does its subtitle, which denotes it as the "Órgano del Librepensamiento Internacional" (Mouthpiece for International Freethinking) (see figure 4.2).

While more than 273 issues of *La Conciencia Libre* appeared over the ten years during which it was published, I have managed to locate only twenty copies.[20] Nonetheless, these issues allow us to evaluate the radical tenor of the weekly, its frequently satirical content (see figure 4.3), and the sociopolitical matters debated in its pages. Revealing its progressive tone, a diversity of radical political sympathies, and an engagement with the most advanced ideas, past and present, from within Spain and beyond, the periodical featured articles and quotations

4.3 Satirical images from *La Conciencia Libre* 111, Year III (28 July 1898). By kind permission of the *Ateneu Enciclopèdic Popular*, Barcelona

by reporter Alfredo Calderón, Hugo, Claramunt, Peter Kropotkin, Leopoldo Bonafulla, Luis Bonafoux, Nakens, Joaquín Dicenta, John Locke, Gumersindo de Azcárate, Darwin, Lerroux, Lord Macauley, Blasco Ibáñez, Max Nordau, Horace, Castelar, and Pi y Margall.

It is worth providing a more detailed account of the contents of the issue of *La Conciencia Libre* that has survived from March 1907, to give an idea of the variety of columns that it contained and the kinds of issues debated.[21] Anticlericalism is the dominant theme in the first seven pages, over half the issue. The lengthy editorial of two and a half pages, by Sárraga and entitled "Cristo en la picota," rails against the Catholic Church's appropriation of Christ's utopian teachings (636–8). In the following three and a half pages, an article entitled "Un fraile al descubierto" reports on the scandal that occurred in San Juan, Argentina, from the discovery of a priest's sexual abuse of young girls and women (638–41).[22] López de Ayala's ensuing article continues the anticlerical critique, decrying the Catholic Church's economic monopoly, which she presents as the major cause of the emigration of Spain's poor (642).

The Literary Section consists of a poem, "La Sentencia" by Domingo Soler (643), whose renewed collaboration with the weekly is acclaimed in a small article, "Una más":

> Amalia Domingo y Soler, doyen of freethinking Spanish women, who has spent forty years of her life fighting for rationalist ideas, dedicating her pen to consoling those who are "hungry and thirsty for justice," the venerable old woman who has guided the first steps of us all on the path of promoting the freethinking cause, once again, after several years of absence due to her broken health, returns to contribute to our periodical.
>
> Her sweet, persuasive words will be most valuable to convince women's hearts.
>
> Her name, respected and loved by all, brings glory to all us women through its presence in the columns of this periodical. (646)

Of special interest is the International Section (643–5), part of which relates a freethinking evening held in Azul, Argentina, in the Teatro Español, where an Argentinean teacher, Alicia Moreau, and Sárraga were among the four speakers. While Moreau blamed the Catholic Church for promulgating theories on women's alleged inferiority and lack of soul, Sárraga's address denounced the church as "el mayor enemigo que ha tenido la mujer en todas las edades" (the greatest enemy of women throughout the ages). What women need, she exclaims, is to be "más ciudadanas y menos religiosas; menos siervas del clericalismo y más compañeras del hombre" (better citizens and less religious; less servants of the Catholic Church and better companions to men). Sárraga's speech, the article remarks, was "the most brilliant and courageous speech ever delivered in the Teatro Español" (644). A second part of the International Section reports on Sárraga's visit to the Santa Catalina estate to gauge the wealth of the pampa, and her visit to an Indian settlement. There she learned about Indian customs from an indigenous woman and took notes for a book on Argentina that the article indicated Sárraga would publish shortly (644). Whether or not Sárraga did publish this book cannot be ascertained, as it is not mentioned in existing studies on her nor does it feature among her surviving publications.

Through *La Conciencia Libre*, Sárraga entered into dialogue with freethinkers in a host of countries. Testimony to its transnational reach is a poem by Lázaro Tadeo Blue from El Tocuyo, Venezuela, published in 1897 in *Las Dominicales del Libre Pensamiento*. Addressed to "the passionate freethinker Sra. D.ª Belén Sárraga de Ferrero, editor-in-chief of *La Conciencia Libre* and to her worthy female editorial colleagues" and in turn dedicated by Sárraga to her "distinguished friends and fellow freethinkers, señoras doña Ángeles López de Ayala y doña Amalia Domingo Soler," the poem opens by describing Sárraga and her colleagues as

> Sabias mujeres que con noble ejemplo
> predicáis la virtud y el patriotismo,
> demoliendo del rancio fanatismo
> el tenebroso y carcomido templo.

> (Wise women, who, by noble example / proclaim virtue and patriotism, / demolishing rank fanaticism's / dark and rotten temple.)

The author affirms his admiration for the courage demonstrated by the publication of this free periodical: "Ese valor jamás vencido, / que aun siendo con fiereza perseguido / un periódico libre fundar pudo" (That unconquerable courage, / which even when fiercely persecuted / successfully founded a freethinking periodical).[23]

Yet another column in the March 1907 issue of *La Conciencia Libre* is the Feminist Section, which reports on feminist activities in Italy, Washington, and London. The news from Italy centres on the parliamentary debates on the right of women to vote and be elected for administrative, municipal, and political positions – debates that have resulted in the first proposition being accepted and passed on to a committee. Similarly, the report from London announces the imminent introduction of a bill for women's suffrage to the House of Commons (646). Here what is highly interesting is the attention paid in the periodical to developments concerning women's right to vote at a time when suffrage was not considered to have been a focus of concern for Spanish women. Such a promotion of feminist issues in *La Conciencia Libre* appears to have been constant, as seen in the issue of 8 November 1902. It had alluded to the feminist periodical *Nosotras* in La Plata, Argentina, with which *La Conciencia Libre* would be exchanged.[24] The final page of the 1907 issue is dedicated mainly to advertisements promoting freethinking endeavours. It informs readers that the editor of the weekly is Belén Sárraga de Ferrero; the administrator, Amalia Pérez Conjiu; and contributors Domingo Soler, Amalia Carvia, López de Ayala, Consuelo Álvarez (Violeta), Lady Prado, María del Pilar Cañamaque, María Marín, Soledad Areales (Una Andaluza), and Victorina del Mar; regular foreign contributors are Ida Altman (Germany), Leon Fournemont (Belgium), Nicolás Estevanez (Cuba), William Heaford (England), Sebastiano Puccio (Italy), Zenon Luzchewsky (Russia) and Charles Fulpius (Switzerland) (647).[25]

Social equality and its necessary companion, secular education, continued foremost in Sárraga's activities when, in July 1897, one year after the founding of *La Conciencia Libre*, she established in Valencia, not without legal difficulties, the Asociación General Femenina, together with fellow freethinker and freemason Ana Carvia y Bernal.[26] Other centres soon followed in Catalonia and Andalusia. As Sárraga, the association's president, and Carvia, its secretary, declared in their manifesto, "La mujer española despierta," written in Valencia on 10 July 1897 and published five days later in *Las Dominicales del Libre Pensamiento*, the first objective of the association was "la instrucción y la educación de la mujer" (the instruction and education of women). The tautology inherent in the use of these two terms is apparent, since, as Ballarín explains, *educación* and *instrucción* refer to two differentiated concepts: *educación*, directed at cultivating the heart, was traditionally considered appropriate for women, while *instrucción*, aimed at cultivating the mind, was thought to corrupt them (1993, 601). Hence the intention of Sárraga's association was to educate women's minds and emotions, conforming to the holistic ethos expressed in the letters contained in Domingo Soler's *Sus más hermosos escritos*.

A second, parallel objective was to forge "hermosas corrientes de solidaridad y mutuo apoyo" (splendid ties of solidarity and mutual support), not only among women but also between the sexes, described as divided by a culturally created abyss. Consequently, the manifesto calls on men, "nuestros hermanos" (our brothers), to support the association's aspirations in the interests of the nation, because they will "acelerar en nuestro pueblo el triunfo anhelado de la razón" (hasten in our nation the yearned-for triumph of reason). It is the association's education of women, Sárraga stipulates, that will empower them to participate on an equal footing with their male companions in forging the Spanish people's self-respect and dignity: "Esta Asociación surge potente para dar al sexo femenino torrentes de luz intelectual ... penetrando en las imaginaciones, hoy por el fanatismo oscurecidas, ... poniéndolas en condiciones de poder compartir con el hombre, su compañero, su hermano, mas no su señor, la sacratísima misión de dignificar a los pueblos" (This association emerges, powerful, to bring to the female sex torrents of intellectual light ... penetrating imaginations today darkened by fanaticism, ... enabling women to share with men, their companions and brothers, not their masters, the most sacred mission of bringing dignity to nations).[27] To accomplish these ends, the association set up day and night secular schools for girls and women and created a public library illuminated with electric light.[28]

Some time in 1897 Sárraga and her family left Valencia and relocated to Málaga, where Emilio Ferrero, employee of a foreign company, had been transferred (Ramos 2000, 221; 2002a, 151).[29] There they would remain until 1907, when they returned to Barcelona for almost two years. Andalusia, with its unequal distribution of landed wealth and deep social divisions, was fertile soil for anarchist and socialist movements and demands for rural workers' empowerment. It was on these that Sárraga drew when, at the end of 1897, she founded the Federación Malagueña de Sociedades de Resistencia.[30] Its president was Ferrero and its mouthpiece, *La Conciencia Libre*. A form of trade unionism, the federation formed, according to Ramos, the radical left wing of freethinking republicanism in Málaga (2002a, 132).[31] During its period of greatest strength from 1897 to 1903, as Mateo Avilés indicates, the federation had eighty-one branches and some thirty thousand members, drawn from workers' societies, farm workers' associations, freemasons, freethinkers, anarchists, undecided socialists, cooperativists, spiritists, and feminists. This complex composition was due to the diversity of the federation's sociopolitical program (Mateo Avilés 1986, 173). It also indicates how republicanism created in both rural and urban contexts an intense network of relationships between the middle classes and broad popular sectors that lasted until well into the twentieth century (Suárez Cortina 1994, 161). Sárraga's impact on Málaga can be gauged from the issue published on 14 April 1938 of the Falangist newspaper *Boinas Rojas*, which inaccurately describes her as "the first Marxist microbe introduced into Málaga ... that poisoned workers" (quoted in Ramos 1986, 67).

As a result of her association with anarchists such as Claramunt, Anselmo Lorenzo, and Trinidad Soriano, and her activities through the federation, some studies have recorded Sárraga as an anarchist (García-Maroto 1996, 240; Scanlon 1986, 103). This categorization, however, disregards the historical links forged between anarchism and bourgeois revolution in Andalusia between 1868 and 1872. It also overlooks anarchism's affinity with key premises of federal republicanism: their common antipathy to the Catholic Church, their rejection of a national standing army, and their defence of mass scientific education, associationism, and workers' rights.[32] Regarding Sárraga's feminist views, on which I expand below, her advocacy for democracy in the family aligns her with anarchism's attack on the authoritarian family (García-Maroto 1996, 175), while her privileging of the mother as educator in the home also echoes Republican concepts of women's mission. Where Sárraga clearly diverges from anarchist ideals is in her aspiration to establish a federal republic and decentralized state in Spain, as opposed to the anarchist objective of overthrowing the state completely. Another difference from extreme anarchism was Sárraga's conviction, following Pi y Margall's ethos, that social revolution must be forged not through violence but through education and culture, as manifest in her declaration from 1933: "Es insensato resolverlo (el problema social) por la violencia. La solución que algunos quieren a plazo fijo, vendrá por la superposición de conquistas que harán de evolucionar códigos y costumbres" (It is senseless to resolve [the social problem] with violence. The solution that some want by a set date will come about as a result of conquests that will bring changes in laws and customs).[33]

Some of the activities undertaken by the federation are recorded in issues of *La Conciencia Libre*, such as the conditions proposed for workers in the 1902 grape harvest, which stipulated the hours of work, the rates of pay (equal for men and women), the periods of rest, and even the quality of food.[34] Although the federation's desire to garner the support, participation, and betterment of the working classes led to conflict with local socialism (Mateo Avilés 1986, 173), some socialists did advocate a fusion of their movement with the federation in the interests of greater strength, as the letter from one José López Cano from Nerja published in *La Conciencia Libre* reveals. Addressed to Sárraga, it alludes to the creation of the federation and its common cause with socialist objectives:

> I, who have seen established here two workers' associations with 1,500 determined, courageous men, who have demanded reforms in the regulation of food taxes, and the Town Hall has had to give way to the fair demands of a people who have gathered around the socialists, asking for all that is just, I, who see these two associations with the same aspirations, don't I have a right to ask a thousand and one times why they don't combine? Isn't it splendid to want to combine strengths for the social work underway? . . . What reasons are there for us all not to commune in the same idea and shelter under the same roof, thus avoiding quarrels and unpleasantness, and loving one another like conscientious socialists?[35]

In late December 1902 the Málaga Federation was one of six major federations, also comprising those of Almería, Cádiz, Córdoba, Granada, and Huelva, that proposed amalgamating to form the Confederation of Andalusia. Covering five provinces, the envisaged confederation is described in the lead article in *La Conciencia Libre* on 20 December 1902 as constituting "six formidable armies that have just prepared themselves intellectually for the work of redeeming and bringing culture to the people." Among its defined purposes was the advancement of modernity and the working classes: "To build with the combined strength of all free men of good will an impregnable stronghold from where to defend the great ideas of modernity and generate all the impetus … that might lead us to redeem the proletariat within a short time." Another objective of the confederation was to be inclusive in political orientation, envisaging Republicans, socialists, and anarchists as pulling together for common goals:

> That Andalusian Confederation … attentive to the betterment of all, unites instead of dispersing, attracts rather than repels, and far from wounding partisan interests, makes ample room in its program for all the honourable desires of the people … to walk together, from the Republican who works only for the next victory, the introduction by the people of a people's government, to the honourable anarchist who dreams of a perfect society that is as just as it is free and happy.[36]

Until Sárraga's departure from Valencia for Málaga, all three of her undertakings, *La Conciencia Libre*, the association, and the federation, played a significant part in the Valencian Republican movement led by Blasco Ibáñez and known as *blasquismo*. Formed in 1895 as a result of Blasco Ibáñez's separation from the modality of federal republicanism defended by Pi y Margall, one of the four presidents of the First Republic and Sárraga's professor at Barcelona University, *blasquismo*, as Sanfeliu notes, provided a potent means to unite the different Republican sectors in a social block of urban, progressive character, bringing together the proletariat, the radical petit bourgeoisie, and intellectuals with modernizing aspirations (2005, 27). The mouthpiece for *blasquismo*, the periodical *El Pueblo*, lent its support to *La Conciencia Libre* and the association, perceiving their importance for its Republican movement. Sárraga's strategic value for the Blasquist movement is clear in that she was an invited orator at many of its events.[37]

Despite her relatively brief connection with *blasquismo*, Sárraga's ongoing political affiliation was to federal republicanism, evident in her membership in the Federal Republican Party founded by Pi y Margall (Rivera 1913, 168). Indeed, a column in *La Conciencia Libre* from December 1902 recounts the celebration in honour of Pi y Margall that Sárraga attended as a federal Republican and honoured guest at Málaga's Progressive Republican Casino.[38] However, as her words from 1906 make clear, her concept of federal republicanism was advanced for her day, imbued with workers' demands, and feminist and pacifist objectives: "Soy republicana federal, pero mis ideas van más lejos en el orden social, político y económico. Mi actuación se vincula al movimiento obrero para la obtención de conquistas; como la protección del trabajo de la mujer y del niño. Preconizo la paz mundial, y como medio de llegar a ella la supresión de los ejércitos" (quoted in Vitale and Antivilo Peña 2000, 55; I am a federal Republican, but my ideas go further in social, political, and economic matters. My actions are linked to the workers' movement to win victories, such as protecting the working woman and child. I advocate world peace and, to this end, the abolition of armies). Sárraga's constant faith in Pi y Margall's federal republicanism is attested to in her declaration from her Eighth Lecture on "Clericalismo y Democracia" published in 1913: "Veo destacarse la España del futuro, la España del porvenir, ... aquella España de Pi y Margall, la España levantada por el Libre Pensamiento" (Sárraga 1913, 141; I see emerging the Spain of the future, the upcoming Spain, ... Pi and Margall's Spain, the Spain forged by freethinking).[39]

According to Ramos, Sárraga spent from 1909 until 1931 outside Spain, an exile motivated by Ferrero's professional transfer to South America and the pull of the South American republics (Ramos 1986, 67). However, Vitale and Antivilo Peña maintain that Sárraga had already left Spain for Uruguay in 1908, accompanied by her grandmother and her two sons, Volney and Demófilo (2000, 35). From 1908 until at least 1910 Sárraga would reside in Montevideo, where she directed the freethinking periodical *El Liberal* and wrote its editorial column almost daily. While in Uruguay she travelled throughout the republic, founding associations for freethinking women.[40]

In 1909 her Republican sympathies and feminist commitment also took her to Portugal, then on the verge of becoming a republic. There she possibly participated in the Conference for Freethinkers in Lisbon and helped establish the first Portuguese feminist organization, the Republican League of Portuguese Women. In October 1911 Sárraga returned to Portugal to celebrate the first anniversary of the proclamation of its First Republic. In December 1913 she also contributed with a theosophical article to the journal *A Madrugada*, edited by feminist and freemason María Veleda (Ramos 2000, 226).

An intrepid traveller, as the epigraph to this chapter attests, Sárraga traversed Central and South America on several occasions.[41] She had already visited Argentina in 1906 for the Thirteenth Conference for Freethinking, to be discussed below. She would return again in May 1910, as the delegate for Uruguay's liberal women's associations, for the International Feminist Conference in Buenos Aires, at which she was vice-president (Antivilo Peña 2011, 415). In 1930, prior to her return to Spain, Sárraga was in Mendoza, previously visited in 1906 and 1918, to give three lectures: "El momento actual," on the international situation after the First World War, "La mujer en la evolución de nuestro siglo," and "El hogar y la escuela" (Vitale and Antivilo Peña 2000, 120–1). Sárraga also spent periods in Mexico, where she would witness the Mexican Revolution in 1912,[42] while on two occasions she travelled to Cuba. Sárraga's first visit occurred in February

1912, when she participated in the Workers' Conference of Unificación de Cruces (Las Villas), chaired by the anarchist Emilia Rodríguez, whom Sárraga knew from her time in Andalusia. Twelve years later, in 1924, Sárraga returned to Cuba to establish the Anticlerical League, accompanied by Rodríguez and Julio Antonio Mella, founder of the Cuban Communist Party in 1925.[43]

From 1912 until 1913 Sárraga undertook a lengthy lecture tour that took her to Mexico, Guatemala, Costa Rica, Panama, Cuba, Puerto Rico, Venezuela, Colombia, Peru, and Brazil, establishing freethinking associations wherever she went (Vitale and Antivilo Peña 2000, 55–8). In January 1913 she arrived in Santiago de Chile, where, before packed audiences in the National Theatre, she delivered her nine *Conferencias* or Lectures. Published that same year in the freethinking daily *La Razón* in an edition of ten thousand copies, they were republished in 1915 in Mexico. From Santiago Sárraga proceeded in early February to Valparaíso and then on to Iquique in the salt lands of northern Chile, arriving there in March 1913. According to a radical local periodical, *El Despertar de los Trabajadores*, from 9 to 18 March she gave several addresses to a packed municipal theatre: "Evolución religiosa," "La mujer como entidad social," "La moral," "La familia y la confesión," "Los pueblos y las congregaciones religiosas," and "El jesuitismo y el porvenir de América."[44] As one witness reports, Sárraga "electrified the most fervent liberals, as well as us socialists," while *El Despertar* informs readers that the Francisco Bilbao and Fraternidad y Progreso lodges offered her an homage. As a result of her stay in Iquique, anticlerical centres were established: among them, in May, the Anticlerical Centre Belén de Sárraga, which in 1915 became the Belén de Sárraga Centre for Freethinkers. On 19 March Sárraga visited Negreiros to give an address and then left Iquique for Antofagasta, where she remained until 4 April, attending a banquet in her honour and founding the Belén de Sárraga Centre for freethinking women.[45]

According to Antivilo Peña, in addition to these centres in Iquique and Antofagasta, Sárraga established at least a third Anticlerical Women's Centre Belén de Sárraga in Valparaíso. All active into the 1920s, the associations were pivotal for the development of working-class feminism in Latin America (Antivilo Peña 2008, 100–2). After her northern Chile tour, Sárraga embarked on a similarly frenetic schedule throughout the south of the country, speaking at Concepción, Talcahuano, Chillán, Victoria, Temuco, and Valdivia before returning to Valparaíso and, from there, to Uruguay (Vitale and Antivilo Peña 2000, 103–7).

A second lengthy lecture tour through Chile would follow in 1915, subsequent to Sárraga participating in a freethinking conference in Buenos Aires that same year. This time, as a result of pressure from the Catholic Church and conservative sectors, Sárraga could give only three lectures in May in Santiago: "El Problema de América," La iglesia en la política," and "La guerra y la religión." In June, she was in Iquique, Negreiros, Pisagua, and Antofagasta, going on to Bolivia in July and back to Punto Arenas in November. Yet again, in 1930, Sárraga toured Chile, prior to continuing to Buenos Aires, as mentioned above (Vitale and Antivilo Peña 2000, 108–21).[46]

Sárraga would not return to Spain until 1931, when the Second Republic came into being. In 1933 she stood unsuccessfully as Málaga's candidate for the Federal Republican Party, gaining 1,117 votes (Ramos 1986, 66), and was the party's vice-president on going into exile in France after the victory of the Nationalists in the Civil War (1936–9).[47] From France, Sárraga would depart for Mexico on board the *Flandre*, listed as Belén de Zárraga and by profession, a writer: one of 312 Spanish refugees who arrived in Veracruz on 21 April 1939 (Rubio 1977, 1059).[48] By 1942 Sárraga had joined the Ateneo Pi y Margall, which relates that Sárraga, then seventy years old, was "totally without resources and had to earn her living working like a twenty-year-old girl. She has given talks on the radio and written articles that have paid her late and badly, she has worked as a shop assistant and in other jobs completely inappropriate for her age and circumstances."[49] Hence in May 1943 she was one of the elderly who received financial assistance (46.50 pesos) from the Comisión Administradora del Fondo de Ayuda a los Republicanos Españoles (CAFARE), the successor of the Junta de Ayuda a los Republicanos Españoles (JARE) (Rubio 1977, 1154).[50] This mention is the last available on Sárraga, who, as Antivilo Peña has verified, died in Mexico in poverty on 11 September 1950 (2011, 409).[51]

Like that of Domingo Soler and even more so, López de Ayala, Sárraga's visibility in political matters and skilled public oratory demonstrated that women could, and did, assume prominent roles in spheres traditionally reserved for men, countermanding the self-effacement and silence prescribed for femininity. Already in 1895, at the age of just twenty-two, Sárraga had revealed her gifts as a public speaker at a meeting that she, López de Ayala, and Palmira de Bruno convened on 17 October in Barcelona's Federal Republican Casino to urge women to join their voices to freethinkers' protests against the removal of Odón de Buen from his university chair for defending Darwinian theory. As a result, his treatises on geology and zoology had been placed on the Catholic Index of banned books.[52] According to the coverage of this event provided by Domingo Soler's *La Luz del Porvenir* on 7 November 1895, López de Ayala presided over the meeting, which enjoyed speeches by Bruno, Claramunt, and Sárraga.

Sárraga's speech, "¡Ciudadanos! ¡Ciudadanas!," reproduced in full in *La Luz del Porvenir*,[53] bears witness to the impassioned nature of her oratory, not so evident in the more academic *Conferencias* published in 1913. She calls on all those present, male and female citizens, to protest against Odón's removal from his chair and for Republicans to overcome their reluctance to take a stand on this matter:

> ¿Es este el modo de proceder de un pueblo libre? De ninguna manera. No se rechazan las imposiciones y las tiranías con indiferentismo, antes al contrario, el pueblo sabe que es el soberano y único árbitro de sus leyes en circunstancias como las presentes. … ¿Es pues por derecho propio, por lo que los gobernantes pueden decidir e imponer a su antojo su voluntad? Este derecho se lo da el pueblo … El puesto, pues, de todos los ciudadanos sin distinción de sexos, al ver como en los actuales momentos, pisoteados sus derechos, es en las calles, en las plazas, manifestando con su imponente protesta que no impunemente se pretende atropellar sus libertades. (219)

> (Is this the way for a free people to act? Not at all. Demands and tyrannies are not fought with apathy; on the contrary, the people know that they are the sovereign and sole arbiter of their laws in circumstances like the present. … Do, then, those in power have the right to decide to impose their will at whim? This right is granted them by the people … The place, then, of all citizens, regardless of their sex, seeing how their rights are being trampled underfoot at this very moment, is in the streets and squares, showing in a powerful demonstration that their freedoms cannot be abused with impunity.)

Evoking history, and in particular, the founding myth of modern Spain, the rebellion of the Spanish people against Napoleon's troops in 1808 (Álvarez Junco (2004, 144), Sárraga justifies the anticipated revolutionary action of her fellow Republicans in the name of the will of the people:

> Tras el momento de indecisión lanza el pueblo un rujido de rabia y de amenaza, y sin preparación, sin armas, sin fusiles se lanza sobre el enemigo para recobrar su independencia. ¡Meeting! entonces en España no se conocía la palabra; ¡reunión! ¿para qué? cuando los hechos se imponen, las palabras sobran; … ¿Jefes? Nadie: la voluntad del pueblo … y sobre los despojos del contrario proclaman nuestros antepasados su libertad y su independencia. (220)

> (After a moment's indecision the people let out a roar of rage and menace, and without any preparation, weapons, or guns they throw themselves on the enemy to regain their independence. A meeting! In Spain at that time the word was unknown; a meeting! What for? When events demand it, words are superfluous; … Leaders? No one: the will of the people … and over the enemy's corpses our ancestors proclaimed their freedom and independence.)

Asking the men at the meeting if they need encouragement and example, Sárraga reiterates the Latin proverb "Mori potius quam foedari" to affirm that she and her fellow female speakers are prepared to defend liberty and justice to the death rather than live in shame:

> Y vosotros, ciudadanos, … ¿que necesitáis alguien que os anteceda y que os anime? pues haced vuestras mis palabras … ved en las débiles mujeres que esta noche tienen el honor de dirigiros la palabra, ciudadanas dispuestas a marchar delante de vosotros siempre que tratéis de defender los sagrados derechos de libertad y justicia, aún cuando la defensa de estos derechos pudiera costarnos la muerte, porque entendemos y así os lo hacemos presente que vale más morir con honra que vivir con el rostro encendido por la vergüenza. (221)
>
> (And you men, citizens, … do you need someone to go before you and encourage you? Well, make my words yours … see in the weak women who tonight have the honour of addressing you, themselves citizens ready to march before you, provided you attempt to defend the sacred rights of freedom and justice, even when the defence of these rights might cost us our lives, because we understand and hereby declare that it is better to die with honour than live with the blush of shame.)

Sárraga's fame as an orator would later attract multitudinous gatherings, begging comparison with the ability of prominent communist Dolores Ibárruri to pull in the crowds in the 1930s. When Sárraga visited the Spanish colony of Orán in Algeria for several days in late May 1899, she gave a lecture to more than three thousand in the Circo de Nouvantés, speaking against the "régimen jesuítico y clerical que sufre España" (the rule of the Jesuits and Catholic Church under which Spain suffers). Other issues covered in her speech were the Spanish-Cuban war, which had seen Spanish youth embark "falta de pan y de fusiles y provista de escapularios y rosarios, armas insuficientes para batir a los yankis" (without bread or guns but provisioned with holy crosses and rosaries, inadequate weapons to defeat the Yankees), and the need for women, the foundation of the family and, by extension, the people, to reject religious fanaticism. *Le Petit Fanal Oranais* waxed lyrical in its report on Sárraga, an "apostle of Spanish feminism," stating that "we have witnessed one of the rarest examples of oratory that we have been privileged to see in our entire career in the public sphere."[54] As a result of Sárraga's visit to Orán, a Spanish-French freethinking society was founded with more than three hundred members, of whom more than two-thirds were women.[55]

Judging from the glimpses provided by newspaper columns and, as illustrated above with the Latin American tours, Sárraga's schedule as a public speaker was highly demanding. With respect to the Spanish context, prior to her visit to Orán Sárraga had been in Alicante. There on 20 May 1899 she attended a banquet in her honour at the Iborra hotel, where more than 150 guests from all Republican factions proclaimed their support for the Republican Union.[56] September 1899 found her in Asturias, where, on 8 September, she spoke in Trubia, on 9 September in Oviedo, on 10 September in La Felguera, on 11 September in Gijón, and on 12 September in Mieres. The newspaper reports that "the enthusiasm was incredible," with Asturian workers joining freethinking associations established in the province. Subsequently, Sárraga visited Valladolid, Salamanca, and Madrid, before returning to Valencia, from where, it was stated, she would embark on a tour through Andalusia.[57]

Accounts of Sárraga's Andalusian journey reveal the controversy that she frequently provoked. Details are provided in the editorial, "Revolución en las conciencias," published in *Las Dominicales del Libre Pensamiento* on 16 November 1899, which covers Sárraga's activities in Linares, Bailén, La Carolina, Córdoba, Málaga, and Mahón. As a result of Sárraga's stay in Málaga, a Catholic newspaper there insulted her, provoking attacks on its premises, while her passage through Linares also caused a similar incident. Such displays of popular support, the article states, are testimony of the revolution that is taking place in the Spanish people:

> Wherever Belén Sárraga goes, faced with the real, undivided enthusiasm aroused by her words, clearly freethinking and clearly against the Catholic Church, ... our wretched scholars must awaken from their living sleep and see and touch the profound revolution that has taken place in the consciousness of Spain's working class. ... And what the people want is what Belén Sárraga proclaims: the disappearance of all oppressive philosophies and all exploitation by those who live without working at the expense of the people's sweat.[58]

Further details of Sárraga's activities in Málaga surface in the following issue of *Las Dominicales del Libre Pensamiento*, where we read that Sárraga was honoured at a banquet for 150, while the meeting had to take place in the bullring to accommodate the crowd, among whom there were many women. The column concludes by affirming the inter-classist nature of republicanism: "Under the folds of the freethinking banner there can shelter the entirety of Spanish democracy, from the simple labourer to the lawyer and the most learned professor."[59]

From Málaga Sárraga continued to Almería, where she met members of the socialist Republican group Germinal, and to Granada (21–26 October), accompanied by Salmerón, ex-president of the First Republic (Ramos 2000, 221).[60] There her stay aroused confrontations between freethinkers and Catholic reactionaries. From Granada Sárraga went on to a meeting in Seville with Lerroux and to Valencia (López Martínez and Ortiz Villalba 1990, 462–8).

Sárraga was again to join forces with Lerroux at another meeting on 10 June 1902, also held in Málaga's bullring. Extensive coverage of the event is given in the 14 June issue of *La Conciencia Libre* in a three-page lead article entitled "El mitin republicano revolucionario."[61] Republican MPs Lerroux and Rodrigo Soriano arrived from Algeciras to be greeted by a crowd of eight thousand. The speakers were Ferrero, Gómez Cestino, Sárraga, Soriano, and Lerroux. Blasco Ibáñez was prevented from participating because of his son's illness. Sárraga, herself convalescent from a serious illness, gave an address against political and religious caciquism and in favour of the republic, "el gobierno del pueblo por el pueblo mismo" (2; the government of the people and by the people). Lerroux reportedly praised Sárraga in his typically grandiloquent style:

> We have here a lady whom I consider to be the honour of an educated Spain and the example that Spanish women must follow on their path to redemption. ... Thus, this martyr, sweaty from the deserts of politics, is being tossed and turned by the hurricane of caciquism and the brutal ignorance of Spaniards, suffering shackles, imprisonment, and persecution while always remaining indomitable.
>
> (quoted in Mateo Avilés 1986, 179)

In late August 1902 Sárraga spoke at Vélez in the Málaga province, from where she left for Arenas on horseback, the only means of transport in that area.[62]

Another account of a speech given by Sárraga on 7 March 1905 to a meeting in Herrera refers to the captivating power of her oratory: "She electrified us, keeping us hanging on her words as if hypnotized for an hour and a half." The next day, 8 March, Sárraga travelled to Écija: a journey of three hours on a road lined with precipices. The meeting in the crowded theatre lasted for three and a half hours, after which Sárraga visited the Republican Centre and workers' casino, returning to Córdoba the following afternoon.[63] Shortly afterward, as reported by her friend Soledad Areales in *Las Dominicales* on 28 April 1905, Sárraga was in the Cordoban village of Villa del Río, where again she spoke for an hour and a quarter.[64]

Sárraga's commitment to democracy through the freethinking newspaper and associations that she created, as well as through her ceaseless public promotion of Republican ideals, confirms her unflagging belief in the power of association to eradicate sociocultural and political ills. The enormous importance that she placed on the right of association and its benefits becomes apparent in her following statement:

> He ahí mi crimen: Decirle al pueblo: en las leyes hay escrito un derecho que desconoces y por lo tanto no usas; el de asociación. Asóciate, no para asesinar a los hombres, sino para combatir las ideas perjudiciales al progreso; asóciate, no como los bandoleros en cuadrilla, sino como los apóstoles en comunidad.
>
> (quoted in Mateo Avilés 1986, 176)

> (My crime is the following: Telling the people that in the laws there is written a right that you do not know about and hence do not use; the right of association. Join an association, not to murder men but to fight against ideas harmful to progress; join an association, not like a gang of bandits but like a community of apostles.)

It is through freethinking associations, Sárraga maintains in her First Lecture, "Trayectorias Humanas," delivered in Chile, that a *Patria* of science, progress, and justice can be formed: "Inmensa, porque recoge a todas las patrias; infinita porque recoge todas las grandes ideas … la Patria del ideal, … la Patria de la Ciencia, … la Patria del Progreso, … la Patria de la Justicia, … la Patria del Pensamiento Libre" (Sárraga 1913, 8–9; Immense, because it encompasses all nations; infinite because it embraces all great ideas … the Nation of Ideals, … the Nation of Science, … the Nation of Progress, … the Nation of Justice, … the Nation of Freethinking).

As Sárraga's words suggest, members of freethinking associations were conscious of forming part of international communities that ideally transcended national, ethnic, class, and gender boundaries in a truly cosmopolitan, democratic enterprise. In this sense they confirm the necessary connections between the transnational thrust of cosmopolitanism, the public sphere, and democracy that Habermas has explored and that Michael Scrivener explains in *The Cosmopolitan Ideal*:

> One of the important preconditions for political cosmopolitanism both then and now is an open, tolerant and intellectually fearless public sphere with transnational currents. Only a public sphere in the special Habermasian sense of the phrase – private people coming together as a public to subject the prevailing norms to critical examination and discussion – can move society towards a deliberative democracy that achieves legitimacy through uncoerced and open discussion. (2007, 2)

Not only were the newspapers founded and edited by Domingo Soler, López de Ayala, and Sárraga, and the associations in which they participated, examples of national and often transnational spaces of sociability in which fellow freethinkers from within Spain and from abroad debated issues of concern. So too were the international conferences of freethinkers that brought together attendees from all over the Western world, including López de Ayala and Sárraga. The transnational aims of these conferences, celebrated regularly since the inception of the International Federation of Freethinkers by prominent philosophers, scientists, and politicians in Brussels in 1880, were encapsulated in their desire to create "an immense movement for intellectual and social emancipation that sweeps along with it all nations, so as to put an end to dogmas and churches."[65]

Sárraga played prominent roles in the International Universal Conferences for Freethinkers held in 1900 (Paris), 1902 (Geneva), 1904 (Rome), and 1906 (Buenos Aires) (Rivera 1913, 171).[66] With respect to the Geneva conference of 14–17 September 1902, calls for donations, and a list of those received, to cover the travel costs of Sárraga and her husband, who were representing the Málaga Federation, could be seen regularly in issues of *La Conciencia Libre* from 5 July 1902 onward. Points for the delegates to take through for discussion at the Geneva conference were put forward at the federation's public Sunday meetings.[67] At the conference Sárraga and Ferrero were accompanied by three other Spanish delegates: Lozano, politician Rodrigo Soriano, and J.I. Lapuya, journalist for *El País* (Ramos 1995, 123).

Coverage of the Geneva conference featured in *Las Dominicales*, which published expressions of support, such as Acuña's letter to Lozano in heartfelt support of the conference and its role in fashioning a Spain free from religious dogmatism, hatreds, and intolerance.[68] *La Conciencia Libre* also provided coverage, such as Sárraga's lead article in issue 263, "El congreso de Ginebra."[69] Following Sárraga and Ferrero's return to Málaga, the federation called a public meeting to make known the agreements reached at the conference, as related in the column "Por el Congreso de Ginebra." The account tells how the federation's premises, able to hold two thousand people, were packed to overflowing, with representation from all its eighty-one societies. While both Ferrero and Sárraga addressed the crowd, it was Sárraga's speech that is accorded the most space in the column. There she stresses that the importance of the conference for Spain was that the Spain that was revealed to the civilized world was not "la España de Montjuich, la España monárquica, frailuna o inquisitorial, ... sino la España verdad, la España popular que siente amor al progreso y ansia de vindicaciones sociales" (the Spain of Montjuich, the monarchical, monkish, or inquisitorial Spain, ... but the true Spain, the Spain of the people that loves progress and is eager to right social wrongs).[70]

The most comprehensive account that exists, however, is Sárraga's report on the conference, which was reportedly published in a special issue of *La Conciencia Libre* in 1903 and has been reproduced by Ramos (1995).[71] As Ramos notes, it privileges the importance that the "feminist question" assumed in the conference debates (122). As such, Sárraga's account warrants close attention for the unprecedented insights that it offers into her views on feminism and the struggle for women's rights. From the outset Sárraga positions herself as a feminist intellectual by confirming that she is one of a number of female delegates who are all well-known intellectuals and feminists: Mme Gatti de Gamond, the Belgian teacher; Mme Pognon, representing French feminists; Ida Altman from Germany, and the Swiss sculptor and painter Elisabeth Gross-Fulpius, wife of the freethinker Charles Fulpius, one of the contributors to *La Conciencia Libre* in 1907, as mentioned above (124).

It is the Second Session, for which Sárraga was vice-president, that receives the greatest attention in her report. Its topic for discussion, the relationship between freethinking and positivism, and practical ways for combating authoritarianism, delivers a series of propositions to counter the oppression of the church and state. However, they do not take into account, as Swiss delegate Mme Starkorf notes, the patriarchal authoritarianism in the home suffered by wives and children. Sárraga's words immediately place such a point within the discourses of equal citizenship, feminism, and women's rights, while also sardonically critiquing the limited liberalism of the freethinking male delegates:

> Algunos sabios graves miran con recelo a aquella ciudadana que así se revuelve contra la injusticia social; quizás no habrán contado con que las reclamaciones del feminismo, robasen tiempo a las discusiones filosóficas ... Las mujeres nos preparamos al combate; hay que arrancar a aquella representación del mundo intelectual científico y progresivo la sanción de nuestros derechos. (125)

> (Some wise, serious men look suspiciously at that female citizen who rebels against social injustice in this way; perhaps they have not taken into account that feminist demands might take time away from philosophical debates ... We women are getting ready for the fight; we have to wrest authorization of our rights from those representatives of the progressive, scientific, and intellectual world.)

Declaring that the inequality of the sexes constitutes "la gran cuestión, la que produce hoy los mayores desequilibrios morales y por lo tanto sociales y políticos" (the great question, the one that today causes the greatest moral imbalances, and hence social and political ones), Sárraga also emphasizes that, despite the impatience of women like her on the radical left, the gaining of women's rights will be a gradual process dependent on generational change: "Las que pudiéramos considerar en la izquierda del feminismo lo quieren todo; ... olvidan que la conquista de la dignificación femenina no es obra de un instante, ni de una generación siquiera" (126; Those women whom we might consider to be on the feminist left want it all; ... they forget that the conquest of women's dignity is not the work of a moment, nor even of a generation).

That for Sárraga women's rights pertain not only to their sex but, more especially, to the nation as a whole becomes apparent when, on being invited to speak, she describes her address as representing the aspirations of an intellectual Spain, on which rests the dignity of the entire nation: "Tengo la alta misión de ayudar a la dignificación de mi patria ante Europa ... Había vuelto mi alma hacia España y puestos los ojos en el mundo de los intelectuales" (126; I have the lofty mission of contributing to dignifying my nation in the eyes of Europe ... I had turned my soul's gaze towards Spain and the world of the intellectuals). The root of all authoritarianism, she declares, is the patriarchal family, which establishes the culturally upheld superiority of men and binds women to roles of obedience and servitude. Such relationships engender in the political sphere absolutism, "la voluntad de uno sobre todos" (the will of one over all), instead of socialism, "cambio mutuo de deberes" (127; the mutual exchange of duties). Therefore, Sárraga enjoins, abolishment of such a regime in the domestic sphere goes beyond feminist issues and the granting of natural rights to become a human necessity that will benefit men and women alike:

> Creedlo, ciudadanos; la abolición de *una autoridad* en la familia, es algo más que una aspiración del feminismo; es un beneficio social, es una necesidad humana. ... Y no lo dudéis, ciudadanos; el reconocimiento por vuestra parte de esos naturales derechos, hará más que beneficiarnos a nosotras, beneficiará a vosotros mismos. (127–8)
>
> (Believe me, citizens; the abolishment of *a single authority* in the family is much more than a feminist aspiration; it is a social benefit, a human need. ... And do not doubt, citizens; your recognition of those natural rights will do more than benefit us women, it will benefit you.)

Feminism, Sárraga is at pains to stress, does not mean inverting the current hierarchical relationship to give women superiority over men; on the contrary, it is a matter of justice and natural law: "Es de justicia y ésta es ley universal. ... no [es] bandera de odio y combate contra el hombre sino de amor y de justicia social bajo la cual se atienda más que a la diferencia de sexos a la igualdad y verdadera comunión de espíritus" (128–9; It is just and hence a universal law. ... it is not a banner of hatred and war against men but of love and social justice, according to which greater attention is paid to equality and the true communion of spirits rather than to differences between the sexes). Sárraga's intervention was fundamental to the session's approval of the following additional points, which secured the principle of equal rights and duties in the home, enforceable by law: "The conference hereby censures all authoritarian traditions in family life; it demands equality between men and women and recognizes between parents and children only the existence (subject to inspection by the law) of equal and common parental duties of protection and moral and intellectual guidance that guarantee children the free development of their reason" (130).

It is political rights for women that come to the fore in Sárraga's account of the Fourth Session. Noting the reluctance of many Spanish male democrats to share political roles with women, she remarks on "esos prejuicios que aun hoy existen entre muchos de los hombres que figuran en el campo de la democracia española y que juzgan su dignidad de hombres herida, a la sola idea de compartir con nosotras los trabajos de dirección y organización de las fuerzas populares" (131; those prejudices that even today still exist among many men of import in Spanish democracy, who consider their manly dignity wounded at the mere idea of sharing with us women the labours of leadership and the organization of popular movements). Sárraga also dwells on the debate concerning the proposal that women be granted equal rights in French and Belgian Masonic lodges – rights that Sárraga is at pains to point out already exist in Spanish lodges (133). Critiquing the misogynist backwardness of Spanish male politicians in comparison with their French and Belgian counterparts, Sárraga vindicates the value of women's political contributions to the Spanish nation: "Cuando esas brillantes diputaciones francesas y belgas reconocen la conveniencia de interesar a la mujer en las luchas políticas ¿cómo, sin sentirse avergonzados por la propia pequeñez de criterio, podrán los políticos motejarnos a las que intentamos cooperar a la obra política de nuestra patria?" (134; When those brilliant French and Belgian delegations acknowledge the desirability of interesting women in political struggles, how then, without feeling ashamed of their own narrow-minded judgment, can our politicians mock us women who attempt to contribute to the political work of our nation?)

As a result of the debates on women's rights, the Geneva conference established a permanent international committee for women's emancipation, which included Sárraga and determined eleven points to secure women's equality. Of these, three stand out for their implications for women's full participation in the public sphere: "(4) Grant women full political rights, (5) Regulate salaries by applying the principle 'For equal work, equal pay,' and (8) Share with women leadership in all economic, philosophical, and political matters" (Ramos 1995, 133).

The Geneva conference brought about the decision to strengthen the International Federation of Freethinkers, then composed of independent national committees with representatives in Parliament, with a National Committee for Freethinkers in Spain. Sárraga was the only woman on this committee, alongside Lozano, Odón de Buen, Calderón, Lapuya, Rodrigo Soriano, Blasco Ibáñez, Lerroux, and Fernando Gasset. The objectives of the committee were the secularization of Spain and the defence of civil rights. To these ends it invited the members of the Parliament of all the Latin American Republics to join them so as to constitute "in our nation a freethinking parliamentary body of considerable significance," capable of bringing on board the working classes or "masas populares." All popular groups were encouraged to support the committee in a common inter-classist endeavour: "In addition to the freethinking associations that will form part of the Spanish Freethinking Organization, all people's associations, whatever they may be, committees, workers' societies, Masonic lodges, rationalist societies, workers' clubs, periodicals, secular schools, trade unions, all here who stand for freedom, must join forces with the committee."[72]

Sárraga assumed an even more salient role in the International Conference for Freethinkers in Rome, 20–2 September 1904, defiantly held in premises opposite the Vatican and attended by some four thousand persons. She participated as the only woman on Spain's National Committee for Freethinkers, composed of the above-mentioned members as well as Salmerón. Other national committees came from Austria-Germany, North America, England, the Republic of Argentina, Belgium, France, Italy, Peru, and Switzerland, with additional representation from the Republics of Paraguay, Uruguay, Chile, San Salvador, Bolivia, Colombia, Guatemala, Venezuela, and Brazil.[73] Accompanying Spain's national committee were more than two hundred other freethinkers, among them López de Ayala, who left at least two poems referring to the Spanish expedition: "España en Roma" and "La vuelta del *Mallorca*."[74] They left Barcelona for Civitta Vecchia on board the steamer *Mallorca*, financed by donations from the Barcelona Casa del Pueblo (de Buen 2003, 71). Later coverage of the conference shows a photograph of Sárraga and others on a tour of the Palatino, as well as two images of the *Mallorca*.[75]

That Sárraga was seen as championing the aspirations of all freethinking Spanish women, regardless of their class, is evident in an article by Amalia Carvia published just prior to the Rome conference where she exhorts working-class women to send in donations to finance the travels of Sárraga and the women accompanying her:

> Es bastante con que acuda la masa obrera, las mujeres que tienen corazón y conciencia, y sienten ansias de libertad, sed de justicia y hambre de dignidad. Vengan pronto, miles y miles de adhesiones femeninas para el Congreso de Roma. ... De este modo podrá Belén Sárraga, y las valientes propagandistas que la acompañen, llevar una verdadera representación de la España femenina, que hacía así patente su rencor contra el Vaticano.
>
> (The support of the working classes will suffice, of those women with hearts and conscience who long for freedom and hunger for justice and dignity. Let them come soon, thousands upon thousands of women's pledges for the Rome conference. ... As a result Belén Sárraga, and the brave supporters who accompany her, can truly represent Spanish women who, in this way, clearly express their rancour against the Vatican.)[76]

In Rome Sárraga specifically addressed the issues of educating the Spanish people and their Republican hopes in a speech on the separation of the Catholic Church and state, delivered on the second afternoon of the conference, 21 September, which received a standing ovation from an audience of 2,000 to 2,500.[77] The account provided in *Las Dominicales* on 4 November 1904 again highlights Sárraga's consummate rhetorical skills: "Her flexible, delicate body leans over towards the audience, she speaks with her eyes, her arms, her whole body, and there is no one who does not understand that language, perfected in these many ways, and which transforms ideas into living, beating words."[78] The impact of her speech was still being felt in December 1904 when, in an article entitled "Belén Sárraga de Ferrero," Enrique Portillo y Jiménez from

Vélez, Málaga, lauds her performance in Rome, describing her as "the renowned *leader* of freethinking feminism in Spain."[79]

Shortly after returning to Spain, in mid-October 1904, Sárraga reported on the Rome conference to a meeting of some six thousand persons organized by the Republican Union Party in Seville, whose province she had represented in Rome. Sárraga's speech advocated freedom of thought and conscience, and returning the republic by revolutionary means. As always, her schedule of engagements was frenetic: speeches in the Seville Republican centres of the first, second, sixth, and eighth districts, a conference in the centre of the ninth district, evening functions in the centres in the eighth district and Triana, a tour, and a musical homage.[80]

At the Rome conference it had been decided that the gathering in two years' time would be in Barcelona, and another would take place in Buenos Aires a year later. The decision to name Barcelona as the next host city was especially due to the Republican circles of Barcelona's Gracia district, who had substantially funded the Spanish contingent's travels to Rome.[81] However, Spanish freethinkers, deferring to the wishes of their Argentine counterparts, agreed to postpone the Barcelona conference so as to fully support the one in Buenos Aires, scheduled for 20–23 September 1906. At that same time Buenos Aires was also to host the Masonic Conference for South America.[82]

Consequently the Thirteenth Conference for Freethinkers, attended by 130 delegates, was held in the Teatro Argentino. Sárraga's international profile is evident in the fact that she was the only woman among six elected vice-presidents: Dr Benjamín da Motta from Sao Paulo, Brazil; Fournemont from Belgium, secretary-general of the International Federation of Freethinkers; Temístocles Zona, professor of astronomy and physical geography at Palermo University; Giovanni Michelli, leader of the Italian rationalists and journalist for the Milan newspaper *Il Secolo*; and Lozano, who represented various Spanish rationalist centres. Representing the Málaga lodge Virtud, Sárraga spoke on the first day, 20 September, in defence of feminism and the emancipation of women.

Two days later, on 22 September, Sárraga participated in a debate on the separation of church and state, together with three male colleagues. That same day, her speech on the suppression of standing armies, "Estudios más eficaces para obtener la supresión de los ejércitos permanentes," met with enthusiastic applause.[83] There Sárraga proposed a motion that the conference declare its opposition to war and militarism, and work to replace the teaching of such principles in schools with premises of altruism and universal fraternity. In turn, Michelli proposed the expansion of that motion, asking the conference to support international arbitration to resolve disputes among nations.[84] These proposals resulted in the second of forty resolutions approved by the conference: "In the name of fraternity among men [the conference] condemns militarism and recommends that this message be energetically communicated within the army to arouse soldiers' abhorrence of war. It recommends the suppression in all freethinking homes of whatever may directly or indirectly contribute to initiating boys in ideas of destruction. … It decrees that mothers in the home and teachers in schools should enforce the following principle of moral education: 'The right to life is sacred and any infringement constitutes an offence.'"[85] The principles endorsed to promote international peace echo Kant's theories on cosmopolitanism, especially those elaborated in his 1795 essay, *Perpetual Peace.* For Kant, as Fine explains,"the primary aim of the cosmopolitan condition … is to put an end to war between states and establish perpetual peace. Seeing war as the most serious threat to Republican liberty, he envisaged a pacific future in which standing armies would be abolished, no national debt would be incurred in connection with military costs and no state would forcibly interfere in the internal affairs of another" (2007, 24–5).

Sárraga's antiwar stance was not new. It was already evident in poems in *Minucias* that condemned the 1896–8 Spanish-American War, to be discussed below, and in an article, "Doctrinal," published on 12 May 1906 in *El Clamor Zaragozano*, to which López de Ayala had also contributed between 1899 and 1902. There Sárraga exhorts readers:

> Seamos enemigos de las monarquías que fundan su poder en la conquista de territorios, enemigos de las religiones en cuanto santifican la guerra para amordazar las conciencias y acallar la razón … apartemos de nuestra vista cuanto pueda recordarnos ese triste período de la historia humana en que las sociedades honradas y aun cristianas, levantan en nombre de la justicia un cadalso para el asesino y condecoran al hombre por méritos de guerra. Hagamos, sí, labor de paz sin tregua ni descanso. (3)

> (Let's oppose the monarchies that base their power on the conquest of territories, the religions that consecrate war to gag consciences and silence reason … let's remove from our sight everything that might remind us of that sad period in the history of humanity when honourable, and even Christian, societies erect a scaffold for the murderer in the name of justice and decorate men for courage in war. Let's work for peace tirelessly, without respite.)

Other approved resolutions that Sárraga initiated at the Buenos Aires conference were for freethinkers to send their support to Ferrer Guardia and Nakens, on trial in Barcelona, to convey enthusiastic greetings to freethinkers fighting in Russia for freedom and justice, and to express their admiration of the Russian women who were risking life and liberty to further the sociopolitical progress of their nation. Sárraga and her five vice-presidents also voted for the International Committee of the Federation to oppose the Vatican by founding in Rome a transnational weekly supported by all freethinkers.[86]

Following the conference, Sárraga participated in the Conference of the Republican Leagues in America, giving a speech at the banquet. Held in the Spanish Republican Centre in Buenos Aires on 29–30 September, the conference was attended by delegates from Puerto Rico, Cuba, Brazil, Mexico, Chile, Paraguay, Uruguay, and all parts of Argentina. It determined that the only way for Spain to counter the despotism of church and monarchy was through revolution.[87] In December 1906 Sárraga, "that *star* of freethinking," brought to a close a seven-month stay in Argentina, during which she had founded Associations of Freethinkers in every province and promoted freethinking and feminist ideals: "Revolutionizing consciences and organizing a feminist movement without precedent in America and the world."[88]

Sárraga's *Minucias*: Gendering Politics and Politicizing Gender

The premises that Sárraga lived, breathed, and acted on inform her collection of poetry, *Minucias* (1901). Its somewhat disparaging title, "Trifles," concurs with the convention of false modesty with which so many female writers felt obliged to comply. Yet the themes debated in Sárraga's poetic compositions are anything but trivial, revealing her alignment with the sociopolitical causes defended by a radical liberalism. The tone is set in her handwritten Dedication of *Minucias* to the editorial board of the periodical *Germinal*. More specifically, in her Dedication to her husband, Sárraga declares that the poems reflect "todo el amor que siento hacia la causa de los humildes y oprimidos" (5; all the love that I feel for the cause of the humble and oppressed).[89] By proclaiming her desire to write for the causes of the people, Sárraga positions herself as divorced from those Spanish intellectuals whom she criticizes in her poem "Ciencia para todos." Stating that they are guilty of intellectual snobbery, she calls on them to couch their message in words that might be easily comprehended:

> Cumplid vuestro deber, hablad al pueblo,
> desarrollad su ruda inteligencia,
> no escribiéndole libros primorosos
> ...
> para que así ninguno los comprenda,
> sino haciendo llegar hasta su mente
> con sencillas palabras, las bellezas. (159)

(Do your duty, talk to the people, / polish their rough intelligence, / not by writing exquisite books / ... / that no one can understand, / but by presenting to their minds / in simple words, beauty.)

Sárraga's aim in *Minucias*, as she continues in her Dedication, is to use the emotive properties of poetry to inspire rational thought and, by inference, action: "Hacer que la poesía ... sirva para algo más que para hacerle (al hombre) sentir: sirva para inducirle a pensar" (7; To have poetry ... do more than awaken feelings: to induce humanity to think). Consequently she situates her verses within the "masculine" spheres of reason and public action, thus challenging the nineteenth-century perception that women should confine their writings to the expression of emotion and domestic affairs.

A veritable leitmotif among Republican intellectuals after Spain's loss of its last colonies in 1898 was the call to the Spanish people to rouse themselves from the torpor of religious obscurantism (Álvarez Junco 1994, 284). Sárraga's opening poem in *Minucias*, "A los hijos del pueblo," illustrates this preoccupation well. There her poetic voice urges the Spanish people to awaken and listen to the messages of progress, fraternity among nations, justice, and freedom that are being heard elsewhere in the Western world. In keeping with the ethos of federal republicanism, Spain is represented as identified with not only the Spanish people but also a wider Iberian community; hence the nation is described both as "hijos de la España" (children of Spain) and also as "hijos de Iberia" (children of Iberia) and the "pueblo Ibero" (Sárraga 1901, 9, 11; Iberian people).[90] What is keeping the nation from the light of progress and a democratic future is the darkness cast by religious fanaticism and absolutist monarchies, as indicated by the "templo oscuro" (dark temple) and "negro absolutismo" (black absolutism). Secular education, the poetic voice states, is the key to obtaining "derechos, / cultura, paz y amor" (12; rights, / culture, peace, and love). The Christian subtheme of resurrection is here recast in radical sociopolitical terms, with the Spanish people envisaged as casting aside the "triste cruz" (11; sad cross) of a figurative Calvary and affirming its capacity for sovereign action and self-redemption: "Que el hombre se redima" (13; May humanity redeem itself).[91]

Such sentiments are heralded in an article by Sárraga from 1894 entitled "¡Pueblo, despierta!" The awakening of the people, Sárraga acknowledges, is difficult, because their symbolic sleep is due to avarice and tyranny: "El letargo vergonzoso en que te sumió el mortífero veneno que en tu seno derramaron la avaricia de los hipócritas y la tiranía de los poderosos" (The shameful apathy into which you were plunged by the deadly poison that the greed of hypocrites and the tyranny of the powerful poured into your breast). A nationalistic counter-history, Sárraga argues, represented by the Asturians who repulsed the Moorish invasion and by the heroes of the War of Independence, serves as the mirror that will inspire the people to rise against their internal oppressors and pursue the redemptive ideal of liberty: "¡Viva la Libertad, que trae a los pueblos la sacrosanta Redención!" (Long Live Freedom, which brings nations their sacred Redemption!)[92]

As these texts illustrate, many of Sárraga's works rewrite Christian themes, imagery, and symbolism, in keeping with the anticlerical stance common among Republican freethinkers, their unrelenting critique of the political, economic, and social power wielded by the Catholic Church, and the adaptation of Christian and evangelical discourse by Fourierist utopian thought. In an early article published in 1895 Sárraga represents the ideal of the republic in quasi-religious terms as Virgin ("hermosa virgen de nuestros ensueños" [beautiful virgin of our dreams]), Holy Mother ("cual amorosa madre" [like a loving mother]), and Mother of Compassion, who will bring down the Catholic Church and monarchy and restore freedom to the people: "¡¡Abajo los tronos y las mitras que nos esclavizan, y al amparo de la bendita República, recobre el pueblo su anhelada libertad!!" (Down with the thrones and mitres that enslave us and, protected by the blessed republic, may the people recover their longed-for freedom!)[93]

Sárraga's critique of what she perceives as the unholy alliance between Catholic Church and monarchy is patent in "¡Levántate y anda!," where she refers to "los viles verdugos de cruz y corona / que matan a España" (Sárraga 1901, 48; the vile executioners, the church and Crown / that are killing Spain). Now the narratives of Christ's Calvary at Golgotha and Lazarus's paralysis are presented as allegories of a moribund Spanish people who must seize their opportunity for resurrection and recovery. Exactly how Sárraga envisages the path to that goal, however, is uncertain, in that her poetic voice borders on radical militancy by making revolution part of the freethinking discourse of progress, as evinced in the following pronouncement by a personified Revolution:

> Yo soy del progreso, la forma atrevida,
> ...
> ... si en sangre por fuerza algún día
> se tiñe mi espada,
> con ella los pueblos manchados de afrentas
> los rostros se lavan,
> ...
> y si hago una víctima, en cambio liberto
> naciones esclavas. (Minucias 49)

> (I am the daring form of progress, / ... / ... if out of necessity one day with blood / my sword is tinged, / in that blood those nations stained by offences / will bathe their faces, / ... / and if I am responsible for victims, I also free / enslaved nations.)

A similar justification of armed revolution is revealed in "Los ejércitos del hambre," where Sárraga's poetic voice shows herself as aware of class oppression within a Marxist framework on referring to the "hambrientos proletarios" (hungry proletariat) and calling on the ragged and exploited working classes:

> [¡]Marchad! y que el sañudo
> instrumento de muerte, haga su oficio;
> conteste vuestro golpe seco y duro
> al enemigo golpe. (78)
>
> (March! And may the cruel / instrument of death do its work; / may your sharp, hard blow counter / the enemy's blow.)

In general, however, Sárraga advocates revolution effected through education and science. Hence "Ascensiones," a poem written on the religious festival of Ascension Day, stresses that the means for workers to ascend to a better life lies in their desire to educate themselves, their rebellion against exploitation, and their search for scientific knowledge, progress, and freedom (17–18).

That Sárraga's quarrel was not with the figure of Christ but with the Catholic Church as institution is patent in "Jesús y sus ministros," a long essay written from the Gracia district in Barcelona over Easter and published in two parts in *Las Dominicales del Libre Pensamiento* on 24 April and 1 May 1896. In part 1 Sárraga describes Jesus as a forerunner of the principles of freethinking:

> Aquella inteligencia privilegiada, aquel cerebro dispuesto para la concepción de las grandes ideas, debe considerarse ... no como el único, pero sí como uno de los bienhechores de la Humanidad ... y como precursor de los muchos sabios y moralistas que, a través de todas las edades, han traído hasta nosotros el soplo de la civilización. Bajo este punto de vista la figura de Jesús se eleva grande y majestuosa allá en el pasado como anuncio y bosquejo de los ideales de fraternidad, libertad y justicia, que más tarde otros han delineado con más perfección inculcándolos en la generación presente.
>
> (That exceptional intelligence, that mind endowed to conceive great ideas, must be considered ... not as the only one, but definitely as one of those who brought great good to humanity ... and as a forerunner of the many wise men and moralists who, throughout the ages, have brought us the breath of civilization. From this perspective the figure of Jesus rises up there in the past, great and majestic, as the prophecy and prelude of the ideals of fraternity, liberty, and justice that others have later perfected, instilling them in the present generation.)

However, with the passing of time Christ's teachings, Sárraga contends, have been channelled into two contrary paths: on the one hand, the Catholic Church, "con sus sofismas, sus engaños y sus ídolos" (with its sophisms, deceptions, and idols); on the other, freethinking, with its "fortísimas columnas ... afianzadas en la investigación científica, en la Razón suprema, en la Fraternidad universal" (extremely strong columns ... securely supported by scientific research, the supremacy of Reason, universal Fraternity).[94] In part 2 of the essay Sárraga rails against the clergy, oblivious to Spain's troubles and its maimed from the Spanish-American conflict: "¿No ven las desdichas de la patria? ¿No ven las aflicciones de sus hijos? ¿No esperan ver llegar a España mayor número de lisiados cada día?" (Can't you see the nation's misfortunes? Can't you see your children's afflictions? Don't you expect to see an ever greater number of maimed soldiers arrive daily on Spain's shores?) She closes her article by juxtaposing Jesus, "el reformador sublime de lo antiguo" (the sublime reformer of the obsolete), to the clergy, "el cáncer que corroe y envenena las fibras que componen el cuerpo de la sociedad actual" (the cancer that corrupts and poisons the fibres of today's social body).[95]

A slightly earlier essay, "Contrastes," from March 1895, paints a similar picture. There Sárraga compares Jesus's life, "una completa abnegación, un completo olvido de sí mismo por amor a la Humanidad" (completely self-sacrificing and oblivious of self for the love of humanity), with Christ's representative on earth, Pope Leo XIII, who is not "bueno ni caritativo, pues que, lleno de riquezas, deja morir de hambre a doscientas familias casi a las mismas puertas de su palacio" (good or charitable, because, drowning in riches, he lets two hundred families die of hunger almost at his very palace doors). Consequently, she labels the clergy "traficadores de conciencia" (traffickers in consciences),[96] in keeping with the common anticlerical representation of the Catholic Church as a huge commercial enterprise (Caro Baroja 1980, 212). This theme is likewise reiterated throughout *Minucias* in references in "En el Día de Ánimas" to "el tráfico de oraciones" (the traffic in prayers) and to God as a "ruin usurero" (miserable usurer), while in "Los eternos negociantes" priests are cast as "los vampiros de la tierra" (the vampires of the earth) (Sárraga 1901, 71, 125).[97]

The founding narratives of Spanish democracy represented their struggle through a clear adaptation of the tropes of Christ's soldiers and a holy war. In Sárraga's "¡Resurrección!" revolution by the people is described in terms of "benditas conmociones" (blessed upheavals), "santas rebeliones" (holy revolutions), and "las santas energías" (holy energy), all directed towards what Sárraga casts in "¡Montjuich!" as "la santa democracia" (27, 22; sacred democracy). The poetic voice envisages the Spanish people as utopically freeing itself from tutelage:

Y dueña de sí misma
conoce su grandeza;
y ya a pensar empieza,
y empieza ya a sentir. (26)

(And master of themselves / they recognize their greatness; / and they are already beginning to think, / and already beginning to feel.)

Similarly, in "Ascensiones" the poetic voice urges her fellows, described as "soldados del adelanto" (soldiers of the vanguard), to wage with her a battle against their mutual enemy, the "fantásticas religiones" (16, 17; fanciful religions). "Ascensiones" concludes by evoking the theme of Judgment Day, when an enslaved humanity will ascend, through its own efforts, to the heavens of freedom:

Que se aproxima el gran día
en que atrevida levante
su voluntad de gigante
la hoy esclava humanidad. (18)

(The great day is coming / when daringly will rise up / the gigantic will / of today's enslaved humanity.)

The envisaged path to that ascension, as Sárraga clarifies in her Sixth Lecture, "El Problema de la Educación," is freethinking, which, in contrast to the hatred allegedly fomented by the Catholic religion, promotes happiness among peoples: "[¡]Y si la religión divina mata y establece el odio en el mundo, el Libre Pensamiento une, forma la felicidad de los pueblos!" (Sárraga 1913, 102; And whereas religion kills and sows hatred in the world, freethinking unites nations and fosters their happiness!)

Within freethinking circles, anticlerical sentiment formed part of a gendered politics directed at liberating all those supposedly oppressed by the Catholic Church and the Spanish state. Hence for Progressive Republicans, as Álvarez Junco notes, religion was seen as "the Monster that held captive the Lady/Spain" (1990, 407). The theme of the alleged enslavement of a feminized Spanish people by a dehumanized Catholic Church, in connivance with Restoration governments, is apparent in Sárraga's aforementioned poem "¡Montjuich!" There she denounces the indiscriminate imprisonment by Cánovas's government of left-wing suspects from the working and middle classes, as a result of the anarchist bombings in Barcelona in 1893 and 1896.[98] The Montjuich fortress is described anachronistically as an instrument of the Inquisition, outlawed in 1834:

Montjuich, por los sayones convertido
en vil inquisición, abre sus puertas
como las fauces de insaciable monstruo
que carne humana con placer husmea.

(Sárraga 1901, 20)

(Montjuich, transformed by the Catholic Church / into a vile Inquisition, opens its doors / like the jaws of an insatiable monster / that takes pleasure in sniffing out human flesh.)

Carr indicates how the Montjuich tortures aroused left-wing protests within not only Spain but also other European nations, fashioning "a modern version of the Black Legend, of the Spain of the Inquisition" (1982, 441). Reminiscences of the blood of Christ's Passion and the piercing of his side by the soldier's lance are evident in Sárraga's depiction of the tortures to which prisoners are subjected: "Chocan los hierros al herir el pecho, / brota la sangre de la abierta vena" (Sárraga 1901, 20; The chains clang when chests are wounded, / blood flows from the opened vein). In accordance with Republican renditions, the Montjuich fortress in Sárraga's poem is portrayed as a Spanish Bastille or "Nueva Bastilla" (New Bastille), which the people will bring down on a political Judgment Day: "Prepara silencioso la piqueta, / esperando ese día de justicia" (22, 23; They silently prepare the pickax, / waiting for that day of justice).[99]

Also at the heart of the relationship between the Spanish people and Catholic Church in Republican anticlericalism was the perceived ideological and economic hold of priests over women through confession. As María Pilar Salomón Chéliz explains, even freethinkers considered that women were, by nature, more susceptible to the clergy, a situation exacerbated by a deficient education: "According to a stereotype widely accepted in anticlerical and secular circles, women's attitude to religion was always due to the seductive powers of the clergy, by whom they were easily influenced. Women's weak, credulous nature, their excessive religious tendencies and lack of education make them especially vulnerable to the clergy's influence" (2005, 105).[100] This prejudice was responsible for the resistance to giving women greater participation in the public sphere through female suffrage and would come to the fore in 1931 during the Second Republic in the parliamentary debate between Clara Campoamor and Victoria Kent, Republicans who took up opposing positions on the very issue of granting women the vote (see Scanlon 1986, 276–8).

Anticlerical thought went so far as to posit that the man who held most sway over married women was not their husband but the priest through confession, a liturgical process proscribed to other men. It was through wives that priests could exercise moral control over husbands in the areas of sexual intimacy and the education of offspring (Salomón Chéliz 2005, 106). Sárraga's poem "¡Ven!" takes up this theme to lambast the interference of the clergy in the intimacy of the couple: "Que el confesor siempre ha sido / siniestro abismo extendido / entre el hombre y la mujer" (Sárraga 1901, 45; The confessor has always been / a sinister abyss / between men and women). However, Sárraga's composition pushes the consequences further, beyond the sphere of the private and into the realms of domestic and even national economy. The poetic voice tells her female addressee that she is guilty of giving the church, at the priest's instigation, the money earned by her hardworking spouse and destined to her family's well-being:

Siempre en Dios tus ojos fijos,
das con cuidados prolijos
lo que, perdiendo el reposo,
conquistó tu honrado esposo
para mantener tus hijos. (43)

(Always on God your eyes fixed, / you give with great care / what, sacrificing his rest, / your honourable spouse earned / to support your children.)

Indeed, Sárraga's text accuses women of placing the church's interests ahead of national concerns:

Antes la hueste extranjera
habrá muerto a la nación,
...
que habrás dejado de dar
dinero a tu religión. (43)

Foreign hordes / will have slaughtered the nation, / ... / before you cease giving / money to your religion.)

Such conduct, as Sárraga stipulates in her Fourth Lecture on "La Moral," constitutes an "inmoralidad social" (1913, 62; social immorality).

Rather than have them worship in the Catholic Church, Sárraga's poetic voice urges women to preside over the temple of progress, incarnate in the freethinking home: "[Y] está el progreso llamando. / ¡Ven! que otro templo está alzando / del que eres sacerdotisa" (Sárraga 1901, 45; And progress is calling. / Come! Another temple is being built / in which you are the priestess).[101] The text argues that it is the mother's role as educator of future generations, in accordance with freethinking principles, that will bring about social redemption:

Piensa en la generación
que nace y has de educar,
y en la que puedes sembrar
el gérmen de redención. (46)

(Think of the generation / that is being born and you must educate, / and in which you can sow / the seed of redemption.)

Sárraga's vindication of the mother's sociopolitical utility, in accordance with freethinking values, explains her critique of the nun in "A una monja," a theme common in anticlerical discourse. The poem denounces the nun's neglect of her maternal mission to infuse it with class issues, emphasizing her parasitical existence at the expense of a hardworking Spanish people, identified with the lower and middle classes: "Lo que tú disfrutas / lo arrancas al sudor de todo un pueblo" (60; What you enjoy / you wrest from the sweat of an entire nation). This representation concurs with the premise of federal republicanism that social worth was not contingent on ancestry and wealth but on who worked and contributed the most, given that the law of equality demanded that all be useful (López-Cordón 1975, 346). By not working, the poetic voice declares, the nun transgresses a fundamental law of nature that requires all citizens to contribute to the common good:

¿No sabes que el trabajo es ley de vida?
¿No ves, mujer, cómo trabaja el pueblo(?)
...
¿Quién te dijo que puede un ser terreno
infringir esa ley de la Natura[?] (Sárraga 1901, 59)

(Don't you know that work is the law of life? / Can't you see, woman, how hard the people work? / ... / Who told you that an earthly being can / infringe upon that law of Nature?)[102]

As Sárraga elaborates in her Ninth Lecture on "La Iglesia y el Trabajo," work propels dynamic movement and change, contributing to the collective enterprise of constructing a different nation and world: "El trabajo es una ley de vida, es una ley de la naturaleza que rige en nosotros en la vida colectiva y universal. ¡Todo trabaja, todo se agita, todo tiene movimiento y acción, todo contribuye para realizar la labor de un pueblo, de un continente, de un mundo[!]" (Sárraga 1913, 150; Work is a law of life, a law of nature that governs our collective and universal life. Everything works, moves, engages in movement and action, everything contributes to the work of a people, continent, world!)

Instead of the Catholic religion, Sárraga proposes the religion of the home as the faith for society and, by intimation, that women and mothers replace Catholicism's priests. She outlines this position in her Second Lecture, "La mujer como entidad social": "Para las nuevas Sociedades a que aspiramos, la mujer puede, la mujer debe formar el corazón de la humanidad. … Hay otra religión que llama a la mujer y es la religión del Hogar, es la religión de la Sociedad" (Sárraga 1913, 21, 28; For the new societies to which we aspire, women can and must be the heart of humanity. … There is another religion that is calling women and that is the religion of the home, of society). For women to fulfil their role in the new societies envisaged by freethinking, it is imperative, Sárraga asserts, to attend to their intellectual formation to produce the female citizen: "La mujer es un tipo humano enfermo y enfermo por el misticismo religioso, de exceso de sentimentalismo … Curemos a la enferma y tendremos entonces a la ciudadana" (24; Woman is a human species that is ill, ill because of religious mysticism and excessive sentimentality … Let's cure the patient and we will then have the citizen). While Sárraga recognizes that men and women are not equal before the law – "El hombre tiene hoy día una personalidad jurídica, que no ha alcanzado la mujer" (Men today have a legal status that women still have not attained) – she insists that freethinking will provide women with legal equality: "La mujer se ha redimido siempre, por la voluntad del Libre-Pensamiento, que proclama la igualdad del derecho humano" (23, 27; Women have always been redeemed through the ideals of freethinking, which proclaim equal human rights). The intimate link that Sárraga draws between domestic and social politics is pushed even further into the political arena in her Third Lecture, "La Familia," where she declares the freethinking family to be the very embodiment of the liberal state: "El Estado no puede ser sino el reflejo de la familia … La familia … es la más alta y única representación del estado liberal" (38; The state cannot help but mirror the family. … The family … is the highest and only representative of the liberal state).

In an earlier hard-hitting article from October 1906 entitled "Femeninas: ¡Esas son las madres!," Sárraga had criticized the kind of mother that conservative Spain bred and the daughter that resulted from a deficient physical and intellectual education: "La madre por atavismo, por tradición, porque *así se lo enseñaron*, educa a la niña para delicada muñeca" (Mothers, from atavism and tradition, because *they were taught to do so*, educate their daughters to be delicate dolls). Calling on sociologists and thinkers to implement an equal education for both sexes so that women might contribute to the social good and the betterment of peoples, Sárraga warns that maintaining the status quo creates unbalanced, depraved citizens: "¿No? Pues entonces seguiréis como hasta aquí, elevando a la dignidad de madres a unas pobres histéricas cuyos hijos sólo pueden dar a España la triste ciudadanía del desequilibrio y la depravación" (No? Well then, you will continue as up until now, attributing the dignity of mothers to poor hysterical women whose children can only provide Spain with a sad, unbalanced, depraved citizenship).[103]

The tussle between the sanctioned discourse of female domesticity and the bolder proclamations of feminist thought permeates Sárraga's "¡Ven!," where her verses tread an ambiguous line between women's revolution and feminine conformity. While Woman, the poem states, is Man's "ariete de redención" (battering ram of redemption), her mission is to be accomplished as "esposa y madre" (Sárraga 1901, 42; wife and mother). She is the "palanca" (lever), but "palanca bendecida" (blessed lever); the "fuerza que impulsa" (driving force) but "escondida" (concealed).[104] Clearly, Sárraga's articulation of a feminist agenda within a discourse of gender difference is shaped by feminist debates in late nineteenth-century Spain and the first quarter of the twentieth century, which privileged the political value of the maternal role, considered to bring moral rectitude to the public sphere.[105] Thus intellectuals such as Concepción Arenal formulated a new model of charity in which women became "social mothers," to acquire, as Ramos explains, "the role of active, ... 'political' subjects, without losing in the process their excellence – or rather, their virtue – as women" (2005b, 36). These debates echo contemporary English and North American feminist thought, which also strategically deployed dominant traditional concepts of the maternal figure to affirm women's moral superiority.[106]

Like Sárraga, anarchist Mañé (Gustavo) sought to expand women's opportunities through their mission as educators within the home. Gustavo argued, however, for not just an equal education but one even more substantial than that given to men: "Precisan una educación e instrucción, no tan sólo igual, sino más sólida y provechosa que la del hombre, ya que el guiar a la humanidad a ella concierne, inculcar ideas de moralidad a ella atañe y a ella pertenece el conducir las generaciones a la libertad y al progreso" (Women need an education and instruction that is not just equal to but even more substantial and useful than what men receive, because women are charged with guiding humanity, instilling concepts of morality, and leading generations to freedom and progress).[107] Central to these concepts of the social and national virtues of the educated and educating mother are Republican values of motherhood, which saw the mother as fundamental for creating sovereign citizens rather than oppressed subjects. Nevertheless, such ideals, as Joan Landes indicates, delivered to women only a partial revolution and denied them full citizenship (1988, 138).

Sárraga's substantial early article "La mujer ante el progreso social," published in *La Luz del Porvenir* in July 1895,[108] just two years before she founded the Asociación General Femenina, allows greater insights into how she conceived of the role of women in forging a progressive society. The article opens by declaring that historically women have been kept in a state of ignorance by religion and patriarchy, which has prevented them, with few exceptions, from fulfilling their "sagrada misión de madre" (sacred mission as mother) as the educator of their children and being the "sacerdotisa del hogar doméstico" (78; high priestess of the home). Affirming the theoretical equality of men and women, "enteramente iguales en espíritu" (completely equal in spirit), Sárraga draws on a conventional discourse of gender to argue for the complementarity of the sexes: "El hombre creando, acaparando; la mujer conservando, distribuyendo; el hombre luchando, frente a frente, con las penalidades de la vida, la mujer suavizando, con su amor y su dulzura, las asperezas de su camino" (78; Man creates, commands; Woman preserves and distributes; Man battles, head on, life's hardships; Woman tempers, with her love and sweetness, the ruggedness of his path). The discussion then moves to its central premise: the duty of men as fathers and husbands to educate women so that they might be truly knowledgeable companions capable of educating their children to become tomorrow's citizens.[109]

As the article advances, however, it turns from more normative premises to attacking the inadequacies of the law to protect women's natural rights. Sárraga remarks that it is not only women's lack of education and their consequent inability to earn an independent living that condemn them to remaining in abusive relationships. Also at fault is a legal system that defends those men who perpetrate financial, psychological, and physical harm on their spouses:

> ¿Qué mujer digna podría resistir el cúmulo de humillaciones que para ella reserva el hogar doméstico? ¿qué es en él la mujer sino un ama de llaves del hombre? él tiene el derecho de gastar sus bienes sin que la perjudicada, que es la mujer, tenga el de quejarse; él puede impunemente insultar de palabra y de obra a la madre de sus hijos, delante de estos mismos, ... y estos hechos no son atendidos por la ley a no ser que la víctima haya recibido un golpe del cual quede señalada, y este hecho haya sido *ejecutado ante dos testigos.* (82–3)

> (What honourable woman could withstand the burden of humiliations that the home reserves for her? What are women in the home except men's housekeepers? Men have the right to spend their assets without women, who are the ones harmed, having the right to complain; men can with impunity insult in word and deed the mother of their children, and in front of their offspring, ... and these acts are not answerable before the law unless the victim has received a blow that marks her and this act has been *carried out before two witnesses.*)

Contesting the law that states that all property belongs to men, Sárraga grants women's domestic work equal status with men's work and argues for women's role as effective administrators of the family income: "¿Cómo y por qué los bienes habidos en el matrimonio son del hombre? Si él los gana con su trabajo, ¿no trabaja la mujer también dentro de su hogar, administrando, distribuyendo estos bienes del mejor modo posible, a fin de aumentarlos?" (83; How and why is it that matrimonial assets belong to the man? If he earns them with his work, doesn't the woman also work in the home, administering and distributing these goods as well as possible so as to increase them?) Moreover, as Sárraga exhorts her male readers/listeners to observe, the shameful enslavement of women – "la vergonzosa esclavitud de la mujer" (83) – crosses classes, affecting not only bourgeois women but even more so those from the working classes, condemned to labouring day and night while their husbands relax in the tavern: "¡Qué anomalías! para el hombre, para el fuerte y robusto, el descanso después del trabajo; para la mujer, para el débil, no hay descanso ni de noche ni de día. … Todas, pues, iguales, lo mismo la modesta obrera que la encopetada dama, sufren la imposición tiránica del hombre" (84; What anomalies! Men, strong, robust men, rest after their work; for women, for the weak, there is no rest day or night. … All women, then, whether the humble worker or the upper-class lady, suffer from men's tyranny).

Next Sárraga calls on women to study science, law, philosophy, and letters for two reasons: to become the true companions of men but also, and more importantly it is implied, to become cognizant of the law so as to reclaim their rights from tyrannical males: "Por el conocimiento de las leyes hacer valer vuestros derechos ante el hombre que pretenda ejercer tiranía sobre vosotras" (85; Through your knowledge of the laws, reclaim your rights from those men who want to be tyrants to you). As for young women, she encourages them to undertake university studies, like their northern European and North American counterparts and a few Spanish women, which will empower them to forge an independent future that does not necessarily imply marriage.

Sárraga's gradual insertion of women into the public sphere leads her to address the question of women in politics, indirectly alluding to men's fear of being supplanted in this terrain: "Se ha dicho que una vez ella [*sic*] a la altura que se desea colocarla tenderá a inmiscuirse en el terreno del hombre mezclándose en política y acaparando para ella los puestos del estado como ya ocurre en algunas poblaciones, americanas" (85; It has been said that, once she has attained the desired position, she will tend to interfere in men's terrain, meddling in politics and taking over political positions, as already happens in some American countries). While indicating that such an occurrence would be exceptional in Spain, in the same breath Sárraga argues against gender discrimination and for giving women the same opportunities as men: "No obstante descuella entre las mujeres un genio, no se corte a este las alas por la sola razón de vestir faldas y déjesele volar en buena hora, por la misma razón que se haría si fuera hombre" (85; Should, however, a genius stand out amongst women, don't clip her wings just because she wears skirts, and allow her to fly with good grace, as would be the case if she were a man). Finally, Sárraga insists, education will allow women to reclaim their rights before the law, the corollary of which will be her participation as a full citizen through universal suffrage: "Estudie, pues, la mujer e instruida, reclame a las leyes sus derechos, hasta hoy desconocidos en la práctica, para poder más adelante obtener su participación en la sociedad como ciudadano, por medio del sufragio universal (como ya se trabaja para ello en los Estados Unidos)" (86; Let women study, then, and educated, let them reclaim their rights before the law, until today unknown in practice, so that later they may participate in society as citizens through universal suffrage (for which they are already working in the United States).[110] Consequently, I posit, Sárraga's essay departs from a more conservative position that tactically aims to attract the male freethinkers to whom the initial sections are addressed. When the discussion veers towards addressing her female audience more explicitly, the discourse becomes more openly feminist and pushes more directly for women's involvement in the public sphere.

In her evaluation of the history of feminism in the late nineteenth and early twentieth centuries, Nash has stressed the need to look beyond linking the emergence of feminism with suffrage movements exclusively. She maintains that what was more important for early Spanish feminists than overt political demands was realigning the discourse of domesticity, and using gendered differences to vindicate a political citizenship for men and a social citizenship for women (Nash 1994, 153–63). Sárraga's works, however, blur this distinction. As I have argued, they highlight that, for female freethinkers, social citizenship cannot be divorced from political citizenship, nor can the domestic sphere be separated from the public realm. Moreover, as Sanfeliu emphasizes, what feminist discourses around women's rights to citizenship demand is a questioning of a concept of politics as historically defined by men. In many cases, she points out, women's political consciousness and their actions in the public sphere have arisen precisely out of their exercising their maternal and domestic duties (Sanfeliu 2005, 124).

Domestic affairs are constantly interwoven with national concerns in many of Sárraga's poems. While they consistently foreground the importance granted the mother in freethinking thought as educator and redeemer of society, many compositions give the mother still greater significance by rendering her the symbol for an ethical state synonymous with Republican principles. This social and political value is especially privileged through Sárraga's poetic representations of relationships between mother and child. More often than not, however, the mother is dead, and the orphaned child attempts to remember and act on her advice in an uncaring, inequitable society. This topical narrative not only connotes the unacknowledged matricide at the root of patriarchal society (Irigaray 1993, 36). It also becomes analogous to what Republicans perceived as the abandonment by Restoration governments of a maternal ethos of social care and justice, associated with the First Republic. Hence in "El niño descalzo," a poverty-stricken, orphaned boy calls on Christ in the temple to give him succour in his destitution, as his dead mother had advised him to do. His pleas, however, prove in vain, as he is rejected by wealthy parishioners and clergy alike, emblematic of a Catholic Church of exclusivity (Sárraga 1901, 29–34).

A similar vein of thought runs through "¡¡Una limosna por Dios!!," which again criticizes the lack of real charity shown by Restoration society towards its most vulnerable. In a Madrid of gaiety, wealth, and a vaunted liberalism allegedly at the service of the nation, as indicated by the periodicals advertised by street vendors – *El Liberal* and *El País* – an orphaned, working-class girl begs for charity on the streets, only to be ignored and perish in the bitter cold (54). While the *patria* is supposedly an "amante madre" (loving mother), with self-proclaimed Christian citizens and thousands of charitable organizations, its maternal ethos is denounced as empty rhetoric (57). Sárraga's critique of charity becomes still more acute in "¡Abajo la caridad!," where she exposes charity as antithetical to the principle of equal rights:

> Por lo tanto, si el rico, el millonario,
> de su caudal un óbolo presenta,
> ...
> no da limosna, no, tenedlo en cuenta;
> pues que da lo que suyo nunca ha sido,
> lo que haciendo injusticia ha retenido. (91)

> (Thus, if the rich man, the millionaire, / offers from his great wealth a small coin, / ... / bear in mind that he is not giving charity, not at all; / because he is giving what has never been his, / what he has retained by committing injustices.)[111]

The theme of the dying mother and her vulnerable young daughter is again present in Sárraga's poem "¡Cuidado!,"[112] where it highlights the patriarchal exploitation of women and the working classes. Like Domingo Soler and López de Ayala, here Sárraga takes issue with the gender and class inequalities that underpin a masculine, upper-class Romantic tradition. Written in octosyllables, "¡Cuidado!" reworks the Romantic premises immortalized in José de Espronceda's canonical 1837–40 text, *El estudiante de Salamanca* (1978), to critique the social fabric of contemporary Spain. The uncaring individualism of Espronceda's male protagonist, a Don Juan figure who uses and abuses women, is portrayed in Sárraga's composition as endemic of a masculinist society that prostitutes women and the lower classes. The poem opens by establishing clear parallels with Espronceda's initial description of a deserted, silent, ghostly Salamanca in the depths of night:

> La noche, triste y negra;
> los encendidos faroles

lanzan su luz macilenta
y en vano alumbrar pretenden
las solitarias aceras.
Todo es callado, tan solo
rompe el silencio que impera,
allá en la vecina torre,
de un reloj la voz intensa
cuyas lentas campanadas
copia el eco por doquiera. (Sárraga 1901, 161–2)

(The night, dismal and dark; / the lit street lamps / throw out their wan glow / and in vain try to illuminate / the deserted pavements. / Silence prevails, only / the silence that reigns is broken, / there in the neighbouring tower, / by the loud tolling of a clock, / whose slow strokes / echo everywhere.)[113]

Now, however, Espronceda's aristocratic Don Félix de Montemar gives way in Sárraga's rendition to an anonymous working-class girl barely covered in rags, who does not roam the snow-bound streets in search of adventure but out of dire necessity to procure food for her mother, dying of hunger. In her beauty and innocence she recalls Espronceda's Doña Elvira, whom Don Félix seduced, abandoned, and drove to suicide:

¿Qué busca la triste niña
cuando en noche como aquella
corre sola, por las calles
pálida, harapósa y yerta?
¡Infeliz! y ¡es tan hermosa!
La luz que su faz refleja
deja ver sus negros ojos,
deja ver su faz correcta
y su alabastrino cuello,
y su frente de azucena. (162–3)

(What does the sad girl seek / when on such a night / she runs alone, through the streets / pale, ragged, and frozen stiff? / Poor wretch! And she is so beautiful! / The light that reflects her face / shows her dark eyes, / her harmonious features / and her alabaster throat, / and her lily-white forehead.)[114]

In Sárraga's rewriting of Espronceda's work, Don Félix's trampling on Doña Elvira's innocence becomes emblematic of the wider abuse perpetrated against the vulnerable by those in positions of authority and power. Thus the civil guard, charged with protecting his fellow citizens, assumes that the girl is a prostitute. Despite her protestations, he drags her off to prison through dark streets that again resemble those that Don Félix traverses:

> [Y] por las desiertas calles
> la arrastra mas que la lleva[,]
> cruzan [una] solitaria plaza,
> llegan al pie de una puerta,
> atraviesan un portal
> sumido en negras tinieblas. (164–5)

(And through the deserted streets / he drags her rather than leads her, / they cross a solitary square, / they arrive at a door, / they cross an entrance hall / immersed in dark shadows.)[115]

The ghostly women whom Don Félix must defiantly confront in the labyrinthine passages of a Gothic mansion become, in Sárraga's poem, the prostitutes whose hellish company is responsible for the girl's fall from grace:

> Mujeres de tipos varios,
> fuman, chillan, cantan, juegan,
> ...
> y a sus pintadas mejillas
> dan sombra negras ojeras.
> ...
> con mil preguntas la acosan,
> atrevidas la rodean.
> ...
> La joven, que aún no ha podido
> comprender donde se encuentra,
> ...
> y como cuerpo sin vida
> sobre el pavimento rueda. (165–6)

(Women of different ilk / smoke, scream, sing, gamble, / ... / and their painted cheeks / are tinged by dark shadows under their eyes. / ... / with a thousand questions they harass her, / insolently they surround her. / ... / The young girl, who has still not succeeded in / understanding where she is, / ... / like a lifeless body / tumbles to the ground.)[116]

The justice that the girl hopes might be delivered by a judge is not forthcoming and, when she is released a day later, her mother is dead.

In her closing stanza, Sárraga's poetic voice inveighs against those for whom order is an empty principle and who justify incarceration in the name of morality:

¡Ah! ¡Los *amigos del orden*,
los que en su nombre gobiernan
y a título de moral
la triste mujer apresan! (167)

(Ah! The *friends of law and order*, / who in their name govern / and, claiming the moral high ground, / imprison sad women!)

Rather than women's presence on the streets being a matter of defiant choice, as is the case with Don Félix's wanderings, in Sárraga's recasting it originates in the misery, hunger, and pain that arise from social inequalities and sanctioned abuse:

Mientras en España
reina solo la miseria
y haya frío y haya hambre,
y haya dolor y tristeza (167)

(While in Spain / only misery reigns / and there is cold and hunger, / and pain and sorrow.)

The figure of the mother is used not only to legitimize Republican thought and discredit Restoration politics on the domestic front. Invariably, Sárraga positions maternal morality in opposition to the colonial policies of a corrupt Spanish state, a stance consistent with the pacifist ideals of federal republicanism. According to Ramos, Sárraga began her peace campaign, endorsed by the attendees at the 1899 International Women's Conference at the Hague, as soon as the colonial war (1895–8) broke out (2002a, 127–8). In 1896 her antipathy to the Cuban war was palpable when *La Conciencia Libre* published articles that urged Spanish mothers to demonstrate against the conflict and forecast Spain's defeat. As a consequence, Sárraga was imprisoned and placed on trial in Valencia (Sanfeliu 2005, 98–9). Indeed, Sárraga's poem "Desde la sombra" was written from Valencia's prison (Sárraga 1901, 63–8).[117]

In "Ante la repatriación," subtitled "Al terminar la guerra hispano americana," Sárraga represents the Spanish-American colonial war as a monster or "bestia feroz" that has sacrificed the Spanish working classes, "carne de cañones" (cannon fodder), in the interests of self-serving oligarchies: "Sangre que se ha agotado / por dar vida al odiado / poder de unos bandidos en la altura" (36, 37; Blood that has been shed / to give life to the hateful / power of bandits on high). By underscoring the class discrimination that determined the recruitment of soldiers for the colonial conflict, Sárraga's attitude is consistent with that adopted by many male Republicans, who, as Sanfeliu remarks, defended equality among all male citizens and hence, equal participation in the war by all classes (Sanfeliu 2005, 120).[118]

This position also accords with internationalist and cosmopolitan premises. For these movements, as Antonio Elorza points out, nationalism was associated with the bourgeoisie. In the fin-de-siècle crisis, the Socialist Party's position on discrimination in military service, like the Republicans' attitude, was "either all or none." As for the anarchists, their position fluctuated between pacifism (since the fight for independence meant the birth of new states, seen negatively) and active solidarity with the rebels' push for independence (Elorza 1996, 56).

Spanish Republicans clothed their discourse of equal participation in the colonial war in a maternal rhetoric, as was the case with Blasco Ibáñez and his party. Their defence of the right to equality of politically discriminated sons rested on the premise that maternal love does not recognize differences among human beings (Sanfeliu 2005, 120–1). In this sense, by habitually inserting Republican women's political activities within traditional feminine paradigms, the Blasquists downplayed women's political agency (99). However, in Sárraga's case, her condemnation of the international policies of the Spanish state and their impact on the working classes deploys the traditional association of mothers with the preservation of life to further political objectives laced with a feminist agenda. She denounces the Spanish state that sent its soldiers to war with pomp and ceremony to avert rebellion: "Entonces era fuerza en halagarles, / pretender engañar es / para evitar la rebelión temida" (Sárraga 1901, 37; Then it was necessary to flatter them, / to try to deceive / to avoid the feared rebellion). This same state does not offer the maimed compensation on their return, transforming the "patriota en pordiosero" (patriot into a beggar).[119] Such a Spain, the poetic voice denounces, is a "madrastra impía," an unholy stepmother who has usurped the place of the people's rightful "birth mother," the republic, and is the object of criticism from other nations (39).

In Sárraga's poem, the true "motherland" is represented by the sorrowing working-class mothers who await the return of their crippled or dead sons. Symbolic witnesses of a people's suffering, in Sárraga's text they become "la madre afligida" (39; sorrowing mother) or *Mater Dolorosa*, a common representation of Spain during the nineteenth century (Álvarez Junco 2004). Sárraga's poetic voice calls on these mothers to defy the gender prescriptions of their time by turning feminine passivity or "femenil espanto" into uncharacteristic demands or a "viril protesta"

(Sárraga 1901, 39; virile protest). Hence the poem challenges essentialist readings of women as silent mothers to portray them as articulate subjects whose maternal role grants them the courage to overturn established structures and bring about political change. This upheaval of gender norms is couched as part and parcel of a wider sociopolitical revolution in which the dispossessed of voice, life, and limb will reclaim their natural rights.

Like Sárraga, other female freethinkers such as López de Ayala would also critique the sending of working-class soldiers to Cuba through the theme of the natural rights of mothers over the alleged rights of the state. In López de Ayala's "La madre del soldado" from 1896, the poetic voice assumes the mother's voice to exclaim:

> ¡Que a defender va la patria! …
> ¡Que es su madre! … ¡No, insensatos!
> ¡Su madre soy yo, yo sola!;
> yo, que mi sangre le he dado;
> yo, que a besos le comía,
> durmiéndole con mis cantos.
>
> (He is going to defend his country! … / Which is his mother! … No, fools! / I am his mother, I alone!; / I, who have given him my blood; / I, who have smothered him with kisses; / putting him to sleep with my lullabies.)

The natural mother asks for her son to be returned to her, because she and her soldier son have received from the state only tyranny, taxes, and unspeakable violence: "¡Opresión, impuestos bárbaros, / cargas de caballería / y otras cosas que me callo!" (Oppression, barbaric taxes, / cavalry charges / and other things that I keep quiet!)[120] López de Ayala's indignation against the waste of working-class lives in the war continued to be heard in 1898, when, in her article "¡¡Doscientos mil hombres!!," published in Sárraga's *La Conciencia Libre*, she criticizes the drafting of two hundred thousand men by the minister of war, Antonio González de Aguilar y Correa (1824–1908): "Los españoles también … tendremos para sufrir resignados nuestras penas cuando el ministro vea logrado su propósito y 200.000 madres se hayan quedado sin sus hijos" (We Spaniards will also … have to suffer our sorrow with resignation when the minister achieves his purpose and 200,000 mothers have been left without their sons).[121] Consequently, Sárraga's and López de Ayala's stance exemplifies their political commitment and determination to affect public opinion. The involvement of female freethinkers in the debates around the Spanish-American war is just one of the issues in fin-de-siècle culture that demands further investigation.

The ethics of social care that Sárraga displays in her publications was apparent from very early adulthood in her medical studies. However, curing bodies was superseded by her vocation as a secular teacher, and her dedication to ridding minds of superstition and ignorance. As combative as López de Ayala, Sárraga takes women's political participation to another level, playing a major role in international conferences, working to consolidate feminism and workers' causes in Spain, Portugal, and the Latin American republics, and becoming a leading figure in Spain's Federal Republican Party. Honed by the mentorship of the likes of Domingo Soler and López de Ayala, Sárraga's intense political activism stands as a measure of their combined success in gaining women entry into the public sphere. Like them, a journalist and editor, Sárraga above all defined herself as a writer: the category under which she was listed on going into exile.

Final Reflections

Amalia, Ángeles, Belén,
Y todas las que escribiendo,
la luz estáis difundiendo
de las ciencias y del bien.
...
grato es veros avanzar
dando ejemplo de energía,
a aquellos que en su apatía
no se atreven a luchar.

(María Trulls Algué, "A las obreras del progreso")

(Amalia, Ángeles, Belén, / and all you women who, by writing, / are spreading the light of the sciences and good. / ... / It is pleasing to see you advance, / setting an example of energy, / to those men who, in their apathy, / do not dare to fight.)[1]

In 1889, the year in which López de Ayala's play *De tal siembra, tal cosecha* was first performed and she and Domingo Soler established the Sociedad Autónoma de Mujeres, their contemporary, D. Juan P. Criado y Domínguez, wrote:

> Another very great virtue that we observe in Spanish women writers, besides their adherence to the Catholic religion, is their aversion to politics with its unrelenting struggles, consuming agitations, hateful suspicions and distrust, mean and dark intrigues; the exotic breed of woman devoted with overwhelming passion to the pervasive internal conflicts of active politics is, thankfully, unknown in Spain; so if ... our illustrious ladies from time to time intervene in the lofty affairs of State, which concern everyone, they have never stooped to enter the burning arena of journalistic grandstanding and debate. (1889, 59–60)

Such a comment denies the growing participation of women in freethinking press during the 1880s, a prominent instance of which was Domingo Soler's *La Luz del Porvenir*. It also ignores the groundswell that would result in the following two decades in an explosion of female intellectuals participating in the freethinking press and the birth of the periodicals headed by López de Ayala and Sárraga.

This study has attempted not only to engage with statements such as Criado y Domínguez's but also to respond to the glaring lacunae identified in histories of the Spanish press, republicanism, and feminism. Nevertheless, it opens up many more questions than it answers. Reconstructing the lives of female fin-de-siècle intellectuals and hunting down their literary legacies is crucial for reorienting the masculinist bias of historical, cultural, and national narratives. That project, however, is a challenging one; as Fay points out with regard to British Romanticism, "The real impediment to the feminist goal of inclusion is the loss of information, letters and journals, manuscripts, and even published texts by or about these other writers" (1998, 20). In the apparent absence of material evidence, it is all too easy to accept given accounts.

Most histories of Spain's liberal political movements and their intellectual players barely mention women at all, let alone political protagonists of the stature of López de Ayala and Sárraga. Duarte's *El republicanisme català a la fi del segle XIX*, for instance, dedicates a paragraph to Domingo Soler, Sárraga, Claramunt, and Mañé (1987, 63); Álvarez Junco's study of Lerroux, *El Emperador del Paralelo*, gives a footnote each to Sárraga and López de Ayala (1990, 250n69, 392n54); cultural histories such as Serge Salaün and Carlos Serrano's edited book, *1900 en España* (1991), which covers the fin-de-siècle press, education, and the Montjuich trial, do not include them. Were it not for the historians of Spanish and Catalan freemasonry and feminism indicated in my discussion, the names of Domingo Soler, López de Ayala, and Sárraga might have vanished forever. It is time to bring them back from the margins and into the main text of Spain's liberal heritage.

Equally disturbing is the omission of the female intellectuals represented by the writers in my project from the literary and cultural movement contentiously known as the "1898 Generation." Itself a retrospective fiction created by Ortega y Gasset and Azorín (José Martínez Ruiz) from the vantage point of 1913, the Generation's inclusion of only men speaks volumes of the prejudiced determination of cultural elites to overlook the significant engagement of contemporary women with the problems of Spain that characteristically defined that group: their critique of the Spanish-American war, the need to counter religious superstition and social inequalities with a scientific education, and their deep concern for the calamitous situation of the working classes. Far more than this study has had space for, the Spanish-American war in particular was the subject of many pieces in the press by López de Ayala and Sárraga, as well as by their contemporary, Acuña. Although Domingo Soler chronologically predates those writers traditionally listed as belonging to the "1898 Generation," I consider that the thematic concerns of her writings and her quest for spirituality, as well as the public events and acts in common with López de Ayala, Sárraga, and others, indeed align her with the "spirit of 98" that José Luis Abellán (1973, 22) and Donald Shaw (1989, 259) argue for.

So why Azorín and Pío Baroja instead of Sárraga, given their similar birthdates and their anarchist and socialist sympathies? Why Blasco Ibáñez and not Sárraga, in view of their ideological affinities and association with Valencia? Did Sárraga and Blasco Ibáñez coincide in Argentina or Mexico? Why Leopoldo Alas ("Clarín"), born just four years before López de Ayala, and not the latter or Acuña? Why have the protests against the Montjuich affair of Miguel de Unamuno, Azorín, and Ramiro de Maeztu been acknowledged (Bernal Muñoz 1996, 127), and not the far lengthier commitment of López de Ayala? In his questioning of the label of the "1898 Generation," Michael Ugarte rightly asks, "Why aren't there any women in the Generation of 1898[?]" (1994, 262). This study has attempted to respond to that cry by suggesting that we have been looking in the wrong places, seeking female writers' similarities with that group's male members at the expense of their considerable and felicitous differences. I also hope to have engaged with and provided some answers to Johnson's statement that "the '98 Generation stands out as a desert for women writers of any kind, and the reasons for their disappearance from the Castilian literary scene for a period of some 30 years have yet to be sorted out" (1993, 12–13).

Perhaps because, as Kirkpatrick has indicated, the "1898 Generation" marked out its aesthetics as virile against early modernism's supposedly feminine agenda (1999, 119), this delineation has also resulted in the exclusion of the Generation's female intellectuals. However, these women were also steeped in philosophical and literary influences similar to those that José Luis Bernal Muñoz attributes to the male members of that Generation (1996, 120–1). Other reasons undoubtedly pertain to what Mary Lee Bretz has described as the "patriarchal, Castilian tradition" that the Generation revered (2001, 20) – an element absent from the contexts of my writers – and the preference of many male members of that group to seek the remedy to Spain's sociopolitical problems in philosophy rather than direct action and substitute social revolution for a radical aesthetics (Johnson 1993, 9, 11). Their shift from a belief in social intervention to an embracing of myth and a disenchantment with democracy (Abellán 1973, 27–9) is certainly not the case with Domingo Soler, López de Ayala, and Sárraga's constant, grounded engagement with sociopolitical issues and their relentless pursuit of the democratic dream. Unlike their male colleagues, they had to put their theories into practice because they had so much more at stake: political citizenship, sociocultural equality, the right to move in the public sphere, and the authority to speak, write, and be heard.

It has also invariably been noted that the intellectual activities of male fin-de-siècle writers, also journalists like my authors, were fostered through literary gatherings and public forums from which women were usually excluded (Johnson 1993, 13; Ugarte 1994, 263). However, as I have illustrated, the freethinking associations and press that flourished in progressive social sectors in late nineteenth-century and early twentieth-century Spain did include women and sought their participation, seeing them as the linchpin in the secular education of the Spanish nation. Freethinking gave female intellectuals the necessary foothold that they then used to extend their action beyond the home and into the rocky and demanding terrain of public politics.

The lack of attention paid to the intense activity of Domingo Soler, López de Ayala, and Sárraga, whether as contributors to the freethinking press or as editors of their own periodicals, is still more striking when the longevity of their production is taken into account. Domingo Soler's *La Luz del Porvenir* ran for some fifteen years, publishing many pieces of intellectual depth on topics of the day by prominent freethinkers. She herself, as she proudly reports, published prolifically in her own and numerous other spiritist periodicals within and outside Spain. Likewise, López de Ayala's journalistic career spanned at least thirty-five years, from her first extant pieces in 1889 to her last in 1924. For eighteen of those years she headed four major freethinking newspapers and was in constant communication with liberal thinkers throughout Spain and beyond. As for Sárraga, her writing and public speaking career encompassed her entire adult life, giving her protagonist roles not only in Republican and workers' movements in Valencia and Andalusia in fin-de-siècle Spain, but also in the creation of feminist and workers' movements throughout Latin America. How is it, then, that these astonishing women, so active in the public sphere during their lifetime, have been, in general, so overlooked?

The oblivion that shrouds their lives and writings can be attributed to several reasons. First, Domingo Soler, López de Ayala, and Sárraga were undoubtedly women who contravened sanctioned models of femininity and, in so doing, aroused discrimination, not only from conservative sectors of society but also, as recorded, from male freethinkers. A second factor is the already noted androcentric bias of liberal histories and literary canons. A third reason is the demise of republicanism in Spanish politics in the first two decades of the twentieth century, in the face of the strength of the anarchist movement and the growing profiles of socialism and communism – all movements that, by comparison, have recorded the presence of women in their ranks, such as Claramunt, Virginia González, and

Ibárruri, respectively. Staunch Republicans, Domingo Soler, López de Ayala, and Sárraga were, throughout their lifetimes, suspect outsiders for mainstream Restoration politics and conservative gender norms. Later, the Franco regime (1939–75) would contribute to this disregard in its determined obliteration of Republican histories. However, even now that Spain's twentieth-century Republican past has been reclaimed and recaptured, this has not been the case with the lives, actions, and voices of the freethinking women who helped lay the foundations of that democratic experiment.

Only Domingo Soler's production has managed to survive, albeit marginally, into the present, reprinted in the mid-1980s and early 1990s by minority presses in Spain. It is perhaps not surprising that the revival of Domingo Soler's works occurred during the years that propelled the memory boom in Spain, which broke with the official pact of amnesia considered essential to guarantee Spain's successful transition to democracy after the Franco dictatorship. Domingo Soler's communications with ghosts from her past resonate with the post-Franco recovery of the spectres of Spain's recent national past, which, if not granted a voice, will continue to haunt the present, as Labanyi warns (2000, 66).

Common to all three writers is their development of alternative paradigms of female subjectivity that challenge the bourgeois, gendered division of private and public spheres. Hence their works reveal their awareness and renegotiation of the Romantic topoi that inform and reinforce that movement's conceptual edifice, infusing the debt that the 1898 male writers have to Romanticism with greater critical weight.[2] Their engagement with dominant representations of women recognizes what Landes so accurately expresses: "The transformation of modern modes of discursivity becomes a fundamental task for feminists. This most obviously involves the authorization, through language, of women's legitimate participation in the public realm and their status as political actors in their own right" (1988, 206). The prescribed silence, modesty, self-effacement, and lack of desire of the sanctioned ideal of the Angel in the House are features that are all challenged in the literary output of my writers.

In the case of Domingo Soler, her *Memorias* and the reproduced letters circulated among her cultural cohort vindicate women's right and ability to be writing subjects with all the attributes of their male counterparts. As letters also published in the freethinking press, they do not so much function as intimate exchanges but, as Fay puts it, as a means for their authors "to win a public voice" (1998, 53). Countering the excesses of Romantic individualism is their emphasis on the values of empathy, community, and support, through transnational movements such as spiritism and the formation of a sisterhood of mentors. Domingo Soler therefore conceives of her writings as performing a maternal function in society through their protective and nurturing properties.

With respect to López de Ayala, she recognizes that any assault on the public/private division must begin at home, whether by discrediting the accepted values in canonical Romantic texts such as Zorrilla's *Don Juan Tenorio* or advocating that women's revolution must begin with men's domestic reform. As discussed in chapter 3, the Don Juan theme assumes special relevance in fin-de-siècle Spain, especially in works by members of the "1898 Generation." Consequently, Johnson affirms, Don Juan "comes laden with a confusing variety of national meanings ... [and] became a significant site on which both male and female writers could locate their considerations of gender roles in modern Spain" (2003, 111–12).[3]

As for Sárraga, her attempt to endow the maternal figure with a public purview recovers the mother that Romanticism had customarily rendered either mad or absent so as to stress the imaginary self-creation of the Romantic genius and the autonomy of the modern sociopolitical (male) subject (Fay 1998, 92). Even more so than López de Ayala, Sárraga's essays and poems vindicate a notion of feminist social citizenship that works to situate the home at the centre of political action and places women's domestic labours on a par with men's public works.

To a large extent the work of these feminists within the fields of secular education and social care concurred with dominant feminine roles that male liberals did sanction: the mother as educator of her children and carer. However, by extending those roles beyond the home into civil society, freethinking women like Domingo Soler, López de Ayala, and Sárraga represent the transformative ethos of civic republicanism, which conceives the power of democracy, as Dietz explains, "in its capacity to transform the individual as teacher, trader, corporate executive, child, sibling, worker, artist, friend or mother into a special sort of political being, a citizen among other citizens" (1985, 14).

Scholars like Anne Phillips have contended that civic republicanism reinforces the division between the public and the domestic spheres precisely because it affirms "the centrality of the specifically political" (1993, 79). In this sense, Phillips states, "republicanism and feminism appear to be diametrically opposed" (1991, 49). At the same time, however, the concept of citizenship is synonymous with the promise of equality, given that it "deliberately abstracts from those things that are particular and specific ... the task is to ensure that no group is excluded by virtue of its peculiarities and position, and that equal citizenship is extended to all" (81).

I have argued that the brand of feminist politics evident in the writings of Domingo Soler, López de Ayala, and Sárraga represents an attempt to resolve this theoretical difficulty. It embraces the transcending principle of equality while also arguing for the extension of the political into all recesses of society. Their political perspective, grounded in active participation and popular empowerment, has much in common with that of late twentieth-century theorists like Sheila Rowbotham and Pateman, who posit, as Phillips explains, that democracy cannot be effective unless its ideals are enacted in every area of human existence, including the domestic sphere (1991, 76–80). The issues that all three of my writers address highlight the ways in which, as Homi Bhabha puts it, "the recesses of the domestic space become sites for history's most intricate invasions. In that displacement, the borders between home and world become confused; ... the private and public become part of each other" (1994, 9).

Domingo Soler, López de Ayala, and Sárraga were acutely aware that the struggle of women for greater rights and emancipation was intimately linked to the working-class fight against exploitation and social inequity. Although all three intellectuals came from upper-middle- or middle-class backgrounds, and were thus equipped with more than a minimal education, they were also highly cognizant of the appalling deficiencies in the education that most contemporary women received. Hence a common endeavour for all was their creation and promotion of secular schools, which would free women and men from religious obscurantism and foster the rational citizens of a future republic. References to their activities in the arena of education, whether as teachers in or promoters of secular schools, are constant in their own and other contemporary freethinking periodicals.

The freethinking periodicals that these women founded and edited, and to which they contributed, constitute but one of the many public, inter-classist spheres in which they participated: freemasonry lodges, Republican gatherings, women's associations, and international conferences. Their sociopolitical acts confirm the public sphere, as Scrivener notes with regard to recent research in this field, as "multiple public spheres, not a single one" (2007, 44). In particular, however, I here wish to draw attention again to the associations that Domingo Soler, López de Ayala, and Sárraga established: the Sociedad Autónoma de Mujeres founded by López de Ayala, Domingo Soler, and Claramunt on the centenary of the French Revolution – which would become the Sociedad Progresiva Femenina – and the Asociación General Femenina created by Sárraga and Ana Carvia. These organizations were not only spaces that sought women's sociocultural empowerment. As I have developed, they also possessed a much more political agenda, evident in the role played by López de Ayala's Sociedad Progresiva Femenina in the campaign for a review for the Montjuich trial and in the fact that the mouthpieces for López de Ayala's and Sárraga's associations were the periodicals that they headed, with marked political and feminist content. Most notably, Sárraga's *La Conciencia Libre* was also the vehicle that promoted the radical ideology of the Federación Malagueña de Sociedades de Resistencia. Even Domingo Soler's *La Luz del Porvenir* had considerable political content, publishing contributions that reflect a broad spectrum of left-wing affiliations, including anarchism. She herself was closely allied with leading anarchists such as Claramunt and Llunas, and worked publicly alongside Republicans and socialists to promote a democratic Spain.

As my study has signalled, all the associations sought to improve conditions for the working classes by setting up financial support, mutual funds, health care, and freethinking libraries. The periodicals of all three writers were frequently closed down because of their perceived attacks on the Catholic Church and Restoration governments, while López de Ayala and Sárraga both suffered imprisonment for the same reason. Hence the associations headed by Domingo Soler, López de Ayala, and Sárraga were quite different from the more moderate women's organizations in fin-de-siècle Spain that Scanlon describes (1986, 200).

In turn, the concern of anarchism and socialism for women's situation in society and the need of these movements to strengthen their position through attracting women would also undoubtedly affect the socialist and anarchist leanings of all the periodicals examined in this study. These periodicals had a mixed readership of both sexes, sought to appeal to the middle and working classes of liberal persuasion, and were in close contact with international and transatlantic freethinking communities, linked through their common objectives of republicanism, pacifism, and women's emancipation.

It is this sense of community that perhaps most characterizes the cohort of female freethinkers of which Domingo Soler, López de Ayala, and Sárraga formed part. Despite their divergences on how best to achieve their social, cultural, and political aspirations – whether through revolution or evolution – what stands out is their emphasis on the need to foster unity while respecting differences. The democratic Spain envisioned by fin-de-siècle freethinkers, and parties and groups on the left of the political spectrum, was far from a reality and beset by political rifts, competing factions, and individualistic opportunism. In contrast, Domingo Soler's spiritism, López de Ayala's republic of ideas, and Sárraga's federal republicanism provide sociocultural and political platforms with the capacity to bring together productively quite diverse perspectives.

Nowhere is this harmonizing force more apparent than in their awareness and cultivation of their own "sisterhood," founded not simply on their gender but more significantly on their sociocultural and political ethos, committed to creating sovereign citizens and a nation built on equality. An exchange from December 1895 between Amalia Carvia and female freethinkers in Cádiz with Domingo Soler and Sárraga in Barcelona provides a fitting corollary to the many other instances of mutual support and mentoring that this study has highlighted. In their letter "Cádiz a Barcelona," Carvia and her companions address Domingo

Soler and Sárraga as "nuestras hermanas en el progreso" (our sisters in progress) and confirm their joint struggle for the betterment of society and women:

> No estáis solas en la brecha, denodadas defensoras de los derechos humanos, vuestra protesta contra la tiranía y los absurdos que se cometen, vuestras frases de rebelión contra los sucesos que lamenta hoy la España libre, las hacen suyas todos los femeninos corazones que sienten amor por la libertad, respeto hacia la justicia y afán por esa regeneración de que está tan necesitada una sociedad ... la regeneración social en que está comprendida la dignificación de nuestro sexo.
>
> (You are not alone in the struggle, courageous defenders of human rights, your protest against tyranny and the stupidities that are committed, your words of rebellion against the events that today a freethinking Spain laments, are those in the hearts of all women who feel love for freedom, respect for justice, and yearning for the regeneration that society so badly needs ... the social regeneration that includes the ennoblement of our sex.)[4]

The response from Domingo Soler and Sárraga comes in the form of a poem, "Barcelona a Cádiz." Addressed to "nuestras hermanas del librepensamiento Amalia Carvia y demás compañeras" (our freethinking sisters, Amalia Carvia and companions), it exhorts a "legión de mujeres" (legion of women) to combat religious dogma and be "librepensadoras, / activas, trabajadoras, / dignas hijas de la luz" (freethinkers, / active, hardworking, / worthy daughters of the light).[5]

This study has barely scratched the surface of the remarkable histories and writings of the many freethinking women that remain to be rescued from the extant archival press. I hope to stimulate further scholarship in this area and secure the place of female writers in a revised account of fin-de-siècle culture and politics in Spain. The pioneering research of José Bolado (2007–9), which stresses the amazing volume, richness, and intellectual depth of Acuña's work, and the anthology of Spanish feminist thought by Johnson and Maite Zubiaurre (2012), which features both Acuña and Sárraga, are important contributions to this collective process. Nevertheless, as Vitale and Antivilo Peña compellingly urge (2000, 150), still pending is the considerable challenge to complete the gathering of Sárraga's writings through a transatlantic research team and publish her collected works. A similar task awaits with regard to López de Ayala's huge output.

Courageous, tenacious, and committed, Amalia Domingo Soler, Ángeles López de Ayala, and Belén Sárraga shared a truly revolutionary trajectory that shattered obsolete paradigms of femininity, demonstrated women's capacity for creativity, and led by example in women's more complete integration into the public sphere.

Anticlericalism and the defence of secular education, women's rights in the private and public spheres, the unflinching critique of inherited sociopolitical, cultural, and literary traditions, the quest to empower those who suffered discrimination through their gender, their class, or their political beliefs, and the privileging of local, national, and transnational associations in pursuit of such objectives are constant themes in their intellectual corpus.

Resurrecting the works of Domingo Soler, López de Ayala, and Sárraga from the archives allows us to contest dominant accounts and understand how minority left-wing movements in Spanish politics and culture depended heavily on and derived strength from the significant but largely unacknowledged input of female intellectuals. More importantly, the materials rediscovered also demonstrate that these women were not mere accessories in sociopolitical life but full players who wagered all the consequences that men faced and more. It is incumbent on this generation of feminist scholars to recover their legacies, reshape known cultural narratives, and reposition these writers in their rightful place as dynamic sociopolitical protagonists in forging freethinking, republicanism, feminism, and democracy in Spain and beyond. Their dreams of transnational cooperation, the elimination of war, poverty, and discrimination, and an ethics of care in all aspects of the public sphere serve as telling reminders of how far our global society still has to go. Although a century apart from this contemporary context, Domingo Soler, López de Ayala, and Sárraga are indeed our own sisters in ideas.

Notes

Introduction

1 Regarding the paradigm of the Angel in the House in the Spanish context, see Bridget Aldaraca (1982). For its dominance in working-class as well as bourgeois households, see Mary Nash (1993, 590–1).
2 María Dolores Ramos alludes to Amalia Domingo Soler's mentoring of Belén Sárraga (2005a, 78), while Ángeles López de Ayala acknowledges Rosario de Acuña as her mentor in "Señora Doña Rosario de Acuña" (*El Motín* [1 May 1920]: 1). Their connection is evident, for instance, in the fact that at least nine of the thirty-nine poems that Sárraga published in *Minucias* had previously appeared between 1895 and April 1896 in the spiritist weekly edited by Domingo y Soler, *La Luz del Porvenir*, to which Acuña and López de Ayala were also assiduous contributors.
3 In particular, I draw attention to Catherine Jagoe's *Ambiguous Angels* (1994) on the figure of the Angel in the House in Benito Pérez Galdós's novels, to Susan McKenna's study of Emilia Pardo Bazán's short fiction (2009), and to Akiko Tsuchiya's focus on Galdós, Pardo Bazán, and Leopoldo Alas (alias "Clarín") in *Marginal Subjects* (2011).
4 All translations throughout are my own. For passages from all primary literary works, I provide both the original and the English translation. For secondary sources in Spanish and Catalan, I give only the English translation.
5 Regarding the contradictions in the nineteenth-century construction of the Angel in the House in the Spanish context and how it was used to justify women's actions in the public sphere, see Jagoe (1994).
6 For the debates on women's education in nineteenth-century Spain, see Geraldine Scanlon (1986, 15–50).
7 On Concepción Arenal's importance for the debates on women's roles and education, see Lou Charnon-Deutsch (2001).

8 For an excellent overview of female freethinkers' associationism in Spain, see Ramos (2002b).

9 On the links between freemasonry and liberal revolution in nineteenth-century Spain, see María José Lacalzada de Mateo (1990). For a thorough explanation of the relationship between freemasonry and freethinking, and of freemasonry with politics and republicanism in the Catalan context, see Pere Sànchez i Ferré (1990, 95–146, 177–230, respectively).

10 On the attitudes of freemasonry towards women's education, see Natividad Ortiz Albear (2005, 321–44, 382).

11 Indeed, Margaret Jacob indicates that "the earliest known European women's lodge had been held in The Hague in 1751," forming part of a mixed lodge (2006, 104). Regarding the Spanish lodges of adoption, see Ortiz Albear (2005, 47–69); for mixed lodges, see Lacalzada de Mateo (2006, 78–9, 158–74). The suggestion that women also had their own lodges is inherent in López de Ayala's following statement from 1890: "Hoy, la mujer, según acuerdo de grandes e ilustrados orientes, puede constituir logias con los mismos derechos y bajo las mismas condiciones que las de los hombres están constituidas" (quoted in Álvarez Lázaro 192; original: *La Humanidad*, 20 April 1890; Today, women, according to great and distinguished Masons affiliated to the Orient lodge, may establish lodges with the same rights and under the same conditions as men's lodges).

12 For a more exhaustive discussion of cosmopolitanism, see Robert Fine (2007). The complexity of the field is evident from Chris Rumford's remark that "there is not just one version of cosmopolitanism. As such, it is preferable to talk of cosmopolitanisms, in the plural ... cosmopolitanism signals that there are now many models for imagining the world, and the place of the individual in it, and that these models coexist and may be conflictual" (2007, 2).

13 Jacob defines "civil society" as "a metaphor for all the activities people undertake within social circles outside the home, generally informal but especially organized and sometimes formal. ... The cohesiveness, vitality, and integration of such groups, have come to be seen as barriers to the impulse for control" (2006, 42).

14 Fine enumerates these social forms of right as follows: "First, the idea of right itself and its division into property rights, civil rights and rights of political participation; second, the 'moral point of view' that declares that individuals should look inward to determine what is right and wrong; third, family and private life in which rights of love and friendship are meant to take pride of place; fourth, the rights of civil society and its constituent elements – the market, the system of justice and civil and political associations; and, finally, the rights of the nation-state and its constituent elements – the constitution, the sovereign, the executive, the legislature and the judiciary" (2007, xi–xii).

15 In 1888 there were 104 Republican newspapers: 50 of undetermined politics, 22 Progressive Democratic, 18 Possibilist, 12 federal, and 2 socialist (Sánchez Sánchez 2001, 197).

16 For an account of Spanish newspapers of different political tendencies during the Restoration period up until 1898, see María Cruz Seoane (1996a, 262–75). For an analysis of Republican periodicals from 1898 until 1914, see Seoane (1996b, 98–115).
17 Regarding the imbrication of *Las Dominicales del Libre Pensamiento* with freemasonry, see Pedro Álvarez Lázaro (1985, 107–52).
18 For specific details of press censorship laws from 1874 until 1923, see Joan B. Culla and Àngel Duarte (1990, 44–8).
19 In the 1890s, Antonio Cánovas's Liberal Conservative Party was in power from July 1890 to December 1892 and March 1895 to August 1896. Cánovas was assassinated on 8 August 1897 (see Carr 1982, 356–7n2, 386).
20 For an analysis of the hesitant emergence of socialism in Spain, see Paul Heywood (1990).
21 Article 213 of the Napoleonic Code, for example, states, "The husband owes protection to his wife, the wife obedience to her husband," while Article 215 stipulates, "The wife cannot plead in her own name, without the authority of her husband." As for Article 1421, it decrees, "The husband alone administers the property of the community" (Mason and Rizzo 1999, 341, 346). On women's legal rights, see also Cristina Enríque de Salamanca (1998).
22 Seoane, for example, dedicates nine lines to López de Ayala's periodicals, which she describes as feminist (1996b, 195). Carmen Ramírez Gómez's compilation of twentieth-century female writers in the Andalusian press provides entries on Domingo Soler (2000, 133–4), López de Ayala (202–4) and Sárraga (316). Adolfo Perinat and María Isabel Marrades offer six lines on Sárraga, spelling her surname as Segarra (1980, 37).
23 Regarding María del Pilar Sinués de Marco, Ángela Grassi, and their contemporaries, see also Jagoe (1994, 33–5).
24 For the position of women in Charles Fourier's thought, see Gloria Espigado Tocino (2002).
25 See, for example, Martha Ackelsberg (1991, 99–107) and Jesús María Montero Barrado (2003).
26 For Acuña's condemnation of the discrimination against women by male freethinkers, see Christine Arkinstall (2009, 75).
27 Indeed, Michael Scrivener stipulates, with regard to the late eighteenth- and early nineteenth-century British context, that periodicals often functioned as virtual political associations, in which readers were writers in the same (2007, 45) – a situation that also holds for freethinking periodicals in fin-de-siècle Spain.
28 See López de Ayala, "La epidemia reinante," *Las Dominicales del Libre Pensamiento* 729 (24 July 1896): 2.
29 Regarding these fin-de-siècle French feminists, see Ramos (1999b, 78–9).
30 Regarding Acuña, see José Bolado's multi-volume edition of her writings (2007–9).

31 According to Carlos Rivera, Sárraga's tour encompassed Mexico, Brazil, Cuba, Puerto Rico, Venezuela, Costa Rica, Peru, and Chile (1913, 172). Further details on Sárraga's lecture tours in Latin America are given in chapter 4.
32 Regarding the presence of the working classes in federal republicanism, see Pere Gabriel (1994, 371).

1. Transcribing the Past, Writing the Future

1 *La Luz del Porvenir* 44, Year XVII (5 Mar. 1896): 370–1. In all subsequent notes, this periodical will be given as *La Luz*. Throughout I have chosen to modernize the Spanish and the punctuation when quoting from late nineteenth- and early twentieth-century primary texts.
2 See María del Carmen Simón Palmer (1993, 732).
3 For Domingo Soler's collected poetry, see in particular *Ramos de violetas* ([1903] 1985b), *Sus más hermosos escritos* (1903b), and *Flores del alma* (1909). Regarding her defence of spiritism and anticlerical stance, see her tome, *El espiritismo refutando los errores del catolicismo romano* (1880). Spiritist texts include *Memorias del Padre Germán* ([1900] 1985a), *Consejos de ultratumba: Historia de dos almas* (1903a), *¡Te perdono! Memorias de un espíritu* ([1904] 1991), and *Cuentos espiritistas* ([1926] 1989).
4 For an excellent overview of Allan Kardec's life and the development of spiritism in the French context, pertinent also to Spain, see John Warne Monroe (2008, 96–149), and especially Lynn Sharp (2006, 49–90).
5 At the first International Spiritist Conference held in Barcelona in 1888 it was determined that spiritism was "a positive, experimental science" (quoted in Horta 2001, 195).
6 According to Amelina Correa Ramón, Domingo Soler was affiliated to the La Humanidad lodge (2002, 169).
7 On Domingo Soler and *La Luz*, see Marie-Linda Ontega (2008). For other spiritist publications in Catalonia in the second half of the nineteenth century, see Horta (2004, 140).
8 Domingo Soler provides this information in *La Luz* 2, Year VI (4 June 1884): 12, and in her *Memorias* ([1912] 1990, 219).
9 *La Luz* 10, Year VI (31 July 1884): 80.
10 For a fairly exhaustive list of female contributors, although not entirely complete, see Simón Palmer (1993, 743–4). However, there was the occasional male contributor, such as Romualdo A. Espino, Salvador Sellés, José C. Fernández, José Cembrano, and Fernando Lozano.
11 Carmen de Burgos contributed regularly to *La Luz del Porvenir* between 4 November 1886 and 3 May 1888, mainly in the form of articles with the occasional short story. Issues that carry her pieces are, from 1886, nos 24, 39, 44, and 49; from 1887, nos 14 and 20, and from 1888, nos 33 and 50.

12 López de Ayala's support of spiritism is evident in a lead article published in *El Gladiador* in 1906. There she protested against the exclusion of spiritists at the international conference for freethinkers held in Buenos Aires that year, at which Sárraga would play a key role (see chapter 4). López de Ayala writes, "[A] todos nos consta que han existido y existen espiritistas dignísimos, emancipados de toda religión positiva ... Es más, muchos de nosotros nos honramos con la amistad de espiritistas ilustrados y justos ... a quienes consideramos compañeros de trabajo y sacrificio, en la gran obra que realizamos, consistente en la ... desfanatización del pueblo" ("Carta abierta," *El Gladiador* 9, Year 1 [22 Dec. 1906]: 1; We all recognize that there have always existed and continue to exist very worthy spiritists, free from the influence of all absolute religions ... Furthermore, many of us feel honoured by the friendship of educated, just spiritists ... whom we consider our companions in our work and sacrifices, in our great enterprise of freeing the people from fanaticism).

13 See, for example, Sárraga's poems "A Kardec," "Las fiestas del Progreso (En el centro espiritista barcelonés)," "Pluralidad de mundos," and "Paso a la verdad," all of which were later republished in her 1901 volume of collected poetry, *Minucias*. Sárraga's 1895 article "Recuerdos de ultratumba" recounts a spiritist meeting (see *La Luz del Porvenir* 2, Year XVII [23 May 1895]: 9–13). In 1896 Sárraga was present at the celebration, held at the premises of the Serpentina Society, of the forty-eighth anniversary of the birth of American spiritism and the thirty-seventh anniversary of Kardec's "desencarnación" or passing. There Sárraga read her poem "Pluralidad de mundos," published in *La Luz* 50, Year XVII (16 Apr. 1896): 419–20.

14 See *La Luz* 26, Year IX (17 Nov. 1887): 202.

15 "Consejos a una niña," *La Luz* 5, Year VI (26 June 1884): 37–8.

16 *La Luz* 15, Year VI (4 Sept. 1884): 113–17.

17 "La Mujer," *La Luz* 24, Year VI (6 Nov. 1884): 191.

18 "La Mujer," *La Luz* 6, Year VI (3 July 1884): 48.

19 *La Luz* 44, Year IX (22 Mar. 1888): 353–6.

20 See Simón Palmer (1993, 742).

21 *La Luz* 26, Year VI (20 Nov. 1884): 201–6.

22 On the semantic flexibility of *pueblo*, see also José Álvarez Junco (1994, 282).

23 For these details and the Articles of the Manifesto, see *La Tramontana* 675, Year XV (23 Aug. 1895): 1–3. For details regarding the organizing committee, see "A los partidarios de la libertad de conciencia," *La Luz* 20, Year XVII (26 Sept. 1895): 162.

24 *La Luz* 20, Year XVII (26 Sept. 1895): 165.

25 *La Tramontana* 676, Year XV (30 Aug. 1895): 2, 4.

26 At the First International Spiritist Conference in 1888, which Domingo Soler attended, capitalism was denounced: "Since 1789 Capital has become Marquis and Count, the aristocracy of the times; capitalism decimates production, usurps all rights, and opposes the valid claims of workers" (quoted in Horta 2004, 231).

27 *La Luz* 34, Year VII (14 Jan. 1886): 268–71. In a speech that Domingo Soler delivered in 1884 to the Centre of *La Alianza* she states, "Es necesaria una reforma en España, sí; pero una reforma seria y profunda; no es cuestión de gritos subversivos, de motines y de asonadas pidiendo que suba *éste*, y que baje *aquél*, no" (*La Luz* 26, Year VI [20 Nov. 1884]: 204; Yes, reform is needed in Spain, a serious, far-reaching reform; it is not a matter of cries of subversion, riots, and disturbances, demanding the instatement of *this one* and the removal of *that other*, not at all).

28 *La Luz* 15, Year XVII (22 Aug. 1895): 124–8.

29 Elzbieta Sklodowska makes a similar point when she states, "[I] have always seen testimonial texts as a peculiar mixture of experience, creation, manipulation, and invention, more akin, perhaps, to a novel, than to a scientific document" (2001, 256).

30 Later Domingo Soler insists that the lives of married women are always full of suffering: "La vida de la mujer siempre es dolorosa aun dentro de su hogar, rodeada de su marido y de sus hijos. Por regla general son más las veces que llora que las que sonríe, por la debilidad de su organismo, por los disgustos que le dan sus hijos, por las continuas enfermedades de éstos, por el carácter más o menos cariñoso de su marido" ([1912] 1990, 59–60; A woman's life is always painful, even within her home, surrounded by husband and children. As a general rule she weeps more than she smiles, due to her weak constitution, the troubles caused by children, her offspring's continual illnesses, and the varying affections of her husband).

31 In a long speech that Domingo Soler delivered in 1885 at a meeting of the Confederación Española de Enseñanza Laica (Spanish Confederation for Secular Education) she presents secular education as a national duty and cites Victoria, Australia, as a model (*La Luz* 33, Year VI [8 Jan. 1885]: 259–60).

32 Linda Marie Brooks's following comment also serves to illuminate the complex motivations behind Domingo Soler's *Memorias*: "The pervasiveness of acting and storytelling techniques in *testimonio* shows clearly that the genre is more than a hyper-personalized political tract … It is about imparting lessons, explaining the significance of one's life, clarifying an aspect of one's community that would otherwise remain obscure, realizing a desired self-image, resolving issues … that are irresolvable in real life, even explaining the cosmos" (2005, 203).

33 This debate gathered force with the publication of David Stoll's *Rigoberta Menchú and the Story of All Poor Guatemalans* (1999). For an excellent introduction to the controversy that Stoll's work aroused, see Arturo Arias's edited volume (2001).

34 See Claudia Ferman's reflection on Richard Rorty's discussion of "truth" (Ferman 2001, 164).

35 While Susan Kirkpatrick's analysis addresses works by the Duque de Rivas and José de Espronceda, the representation of masculine desire through volcanic activity is especially prominent in José Zorrilla's late Romantic work from 1844, *Don Juan Tenorio* (see Zorrilla 2002, vv. 1680–5).

36 According to Simón Palmer, Consuelo Álvarez Pool contributed to *La Luz* in 1891 and 1892 (1993, 743). However, in *Memorias de una mujer* Domingo Soler states that she too, before becoming a spiritist, contributed to *La Luz* under the pseudonym of "Violeta" (1990, 122). For biographical details on Álvarez Pool, see María Victoria Crespo Gutiérrez (2013), who is completing a book on this figure.
37 The epistolary relationship between Violeta and Acuña was still apparent in 1918, when Acuña published her "Carta abierta: A Violeta." Praising her article on the mortality rate of children in orphanages, Acuña addresses Violeta as "Mi estimable compañera" (My esteemed companion) and signs as "Su amiga" (Your friend) (see Bolado 2009, 445–6; original: *El País* [21 June 1918]: 1).
38 Regarding López de Ayala's view that female writers should not use a pseudonym, see "A Punt," *El Gladiador del Librepensamiento* 92, Year VI, Second Epoch (4 Nov. 1916): 1.
39 Ortiz Albear also documents Álvarez Pool as affiliated to the Ibérica lodge in Madrid from 1911 to 1915 (2005, 107).

2. Towards the Republic through (R)evolution

1 López de Ayala, "A Amalia Domingo Soler," *Las Dominicales del Libre Pensamiento* 813, Year XVI (27 Jan. 1898): 2.
2 López de Ayala, "Doctrina racional," *Las Dominicales del Libre Pensamiento* 898, Year XVII (14 Sept. 1899): 1.
3 However, according to Francisco Cuenca, López de Ayala was born in 1858 (1921, 192).
4 For extensive coverage of this event, at which López de Ayala received a gold cross as her prize, see the Sevillan periodical *La Enciclopedia: Revista Científico-Literaria y de Intereses Generales* 20, Year V (7 June 1881): 159–60.
5 Susana Tavera (2000, 572) gives 1886 as the publication date, but the literary historian and critic D. Juan P. Criado y Domínguez, López de Ayala's contemporary, declares it to be 1887 (1889, 117). I conjecture that the subject of the novel was the earthquakes that devastated the provinces of Granada and Málaga in 1884 and 1885. López de Ayala may well have written this work to assist in the reconstruction of the devastated areas; such was the purpose of cultural contributions by prominent writers and artists – among them Pedro Antonio de Alarcón, Arenal, Coronado, Pardo Bazán, Pérez Galdós, and Zorrilla – that feature in the work *Andalucía: Colección literaria y artística formada por la prensa española con la cooperación del Círculo de Bellas Artes de Madrid*, held at the National Library in Madrid.
6 This play was performed on 21 February 1897 in the Zorrilla Theatre of the Gracia district in Barcelona (see *El Progreso* 13, Year II [20 Feb. 1897]: 3). It was reviewed in *El Progreso* 14, Year II (27 Feb. 1897): 2–3.

7 See *María o el triunfo de la virtud* (Córdoba: Imprenta del Diario, 1904).
8 "¡¡Cuarenta años!!," *El Motín* 22, Year XLI (28 May 1921): 2.
9 References to the censorship of *El Progreso* can be found in López de Ayala's articles "Los pueblos bárbaros" (*El Progreso* 5, Year I [26 Dec. 1896]: 1) and "El Progreso" (*El Progreso* 11, Year I [6 Feb. 1897]: 1). With regard to the censorship of *El Gladiador*, see López de Ayala's article "La mudez por decreto" (*El Gladiador del Librepensamiento* 86, Year VI [5 Aug. 1916]: 1) and "El cuento del abuelo" (*El Gladiador del Librepensamiento* 107, Year VII [7 July 1917]: 1).
10 With regard to the Barcelona *El Progreso*, the year of 1891 given by Mario D. Méndez Bejarano for its inception appears to be incorrect (1922, 388), as its first issue came out on 28 November 1896. However, in 1901, López de Ayala also states that she founded *El Progreso* in 1891: "semanario que vengo dirigiendo desde su fundación, que tuvo efecto en 1891" ("Carta de Doña Ángeles," *Las Dominicales* 15, Year I [24 May 1901]: 2; a weekly that I have edited since its inception in 1891). López de Ayala's *El Progreso* should be distinguished from the Madrid periodical of the same name, the mouthpiece for the Progressive Democrats headed by Ruiz Zorrilla, Nicolás Salmerón, and Figueras, and published from 1881 to 1887 (Álvarez Junco 1983, 8). According to Sánchez i Ferré, López de Ayala's second husband, also a Mason, was Joan Pou i Angelet (1998, 6), who, Méndez Bejarano notes, died soon after they married (1922, 389).
11 Intended to replace *El Progreso*, *El Gladiador* was unable to use the former publication's title because two other periodicals bore the same name (see *El Gladiador* 1, Year I [26 May 1906]: 1).
12 Regarding López de Ayala's periodicals, see also Joan B. Culla i Clarà (1986, 443), Culla and Duarte (1990, 43, 105), Ramos (2010), and Seoane (1996b, 195). *El Gladiador del Librepensamiento* had its premises, open 5–7 p.m., at 12 Ferrer de Blanes Street, first floor, in the Gracia district of Barcelona. The three-month subscription within Barcelona cost seventy-six centimes, while outside the capital it was one peseta. López de Ayala refers to the reasons for its closure in March 1920 as follows: "Dejó de publicarse, debido a la subida del papel y los jornales y a la indiferencia de muchos librepensadores" ("Señora Doña Rosario de Acuña," *El Motín* 17, Year XL [1 May 1920]: 1; Its publication ceased as the result of the rising cost of paper and wages, and the indifference of many freethinkers).
13 Later, for subscriptions to *El Progreso*, readers were also asked to contact the administrator, Dª Dolores Zea, 2 Séneca Street, 2°, 2ª. The cost of the subscription was fifty centimes per trimester, ten centimes for a single issue, and two pesetas per annum. It was indicated that whether or not the newspaper appeared fortnightly or monthly would depend on the volume of subscriptions (see "Nueva publicación catalana: ¡¡¡*El Progreso*!!!," *Las Dominicales del Libre Pensamiento* 913, Year XVII [28 Dec. 1899]: 4). The newspaper's success was demonstrated by the fact that it did become a weekly.

14 "Energías femeniles," *Las Dominicales del Libre Pensamiento* 743, Year XIV (23 Oct. 1896): 2.
15 "El Progreso," *El Progreso* 11, Year II (6 Feb. 1897): 1.
16 "Preparados," *El Progreso* 13, Year II (20 Feb. 1897): 1.
17 For details regarding López de Ayala's imprisonment, see *La Tramontana* 575, Year XII (5 Aug. 1892): 2. For reference to her trial, see *La Tramontana* 604, Year XIII (24 Feb. 1893): 3.
18 *Las Dominicales del Libre Pensamiento* 509 (24 June 1892): 3.
19 *La Nueva Cotorra* 25, Year I (22 July 1892): 2.
20 Regarding López de Ayala's studies with Joaquín Ponce de León, see Simón Palmer (1991, 391). For many years Ponce de León would head the Málaga lodge Virtud (Álvarez Lázaro 1985, 146), with which Sárraga was associated.
21 For López de Ayala's association with freemasonry, see also Álvarez Lázaro (1985, 191–6), Ortiz Albear (2005, 102, 139–42, 301), and Lacalzada de Mateo (2006, 174–6, 200).
22 See *El País* (4 Nov. 1888): 1. Acuña and López de Ayala also spoke on women's emancipation on the occasion of the inauguration of the Colegio del Grande Oriente Nacional de España on 24 June 1888 (Ortiz Albear 2005, 27).
23 See *La Luz* 48, Year XIII (14 Apr. 1892): 399, and 19 (21 Apr. 1892): 401.
24 This event was communicated in a letter from the lodge's president, José Bertamen, to the Fraternidad lodge in Barcelona on 16 May 1926, as recorded in file 50.401 on López de Ayala, compiled under the Franco regime in June 1949 and held in Salamanca at the Centro Documental de la Memoria Histórica (Documentation Centre for Historical Memory).
25 See *Vida Masónica* 1, no. 4 (June 1926): 60–2.
26 However, Mónica Moreno Seco states that López de Ayala belonged to the Radical Party (2005, 8n32).
27 *El Gladiador: Órgano de la "Sociedad Progresiva Femenina"* 4, Year I (25 Aug. 1906): 1–2. Nicolás Salmerón, former president of the First Republic and leader of the Republican Union from 1903 to 1906, stood for a centralist, reformist republicanism, whereas Lerroux's politics were more extreme and marginal (Sanfeliu 2005, 149). When Salmerón joined Solidaridad Catalana in 1906, that move split and ended his unitary Republican Party (Carr 1982, 533–4). López de Ayala's links with Lerroux probably stem from the aforementioned Montjuich campaign, which Lerroux used to increase his popularity among the working classes (see Culla i Clarà 1986, 17; Álvarez Junco 1990, 254). What would have provided further common ground with López de Ayala was Lerroux's concern for working-class issues and his anticlerical and anti-Catalanist stance (Seoane 1996b, 108). By the turn of the twentieth century, newspaper columns frequently reported on Lerroux's and López de Ayala's joint presence at political gatherings in Barcelona, where Lerroux had arrived in April 1901.

28 *El Progreso* 13, Year II (20 Feb. 1897): 1.

29 "Por cortesía," *El Gladiador del Librepensamiento* 87, Second Epoch (19 Aug. 1916): 1. The Comuneros, who from 1520 to 1521 rebelled against what they saw as Charles V's abuse of Castilian law, held special significance for those nineteenth-century liberals who pursued decentralization (see Arkinstall 2009, 40).

30 "Carta de Doña Ángeles," *Las Dominicales* 15, Year I (24 May 1901): 2. López de Ayala's support for change through revolution can be seen in her following comment from 1897: "Alegan los evolucionistas que tampoco es posible una revolución. ¿Por qué? ... Veremos cómo es factible, fácil y sobre todo justa, la revolución" (*El Progreso* 22, Year II [24 Apr. 1897]: 1; The evolutionists maintain that a revolution is not possible either. Why not? ... We will see just how feasible, easy, and, above all, just, revolution is). However, one article in which López de Ayala comes out against violent acts is "No queremos dinamita," *El Gladiador: Órgano de la "Sociedad Progresiva Femenina"* 2, Year I (23 June 1906): 1.

31 Regarding López de Ayala's links with Claramunt, see Laura Vicente Villanueva (2006, 107, 113–17, 152). References to López de Ayala's appearances with Claramunt and Llunas can be found in the following articles and issues of *La Tramontana*: "A favor del Congrès de Lliurepensadors," no. 579 (2 Sept. 1892): 3; no. 637 (13 Oct. 1893): 3; no. 674 (16 Aug. 1895): 3, and "A los partidarios de la libertad de conciencia," no. 675 (23 Aug. 1895): 1–2.

32 Representatives from López de Ayala's Sociedad Autónoma de Mujeres were also to attend the Madrid conference, which was closed down by police after the Third Session (Sànchez i Ferré 1990, 129, 127).

33 *Las Dominicales del Libre Pensamiento* 519, Year X (2 Sept. 1892): 3.

34 See "A favor del Congrès de Lliurepensadors," *La Tramontana* 579, Year XII (2 Sept. 1892): 2. López de Ayala's anticlericalism is apparent in numerous articles; see, for example, her column "Orla negra," which appeared in practically every issue of *El Progreso* between December 1896 and March 1897.

35 "Relaciones del Librepensamiento con la cuestión social," *La Tramontana* 583, Year XII (30 Sept. 1892): 2.

36 *La Tramontana* 637, Year XIII (13 Oct. 1893): 3.

37 Regarding the June meeting, see Sànchez i Ferré (1990, 137). For coverage of the July meeting, see *La Tramontana* 625, Year XIII (21 July 1893): 3.

38 López de Ayala's account takes the form of a letter addressed to Lozano, the director of *Las Dominicales del Libre Pensamiento* (see "En Calella," *Las Dominicales del Libre Pensamiento* 824, Year XVI [16 Apr. 1898]: 4).

39 According to the *Diccionario de la Lengua Española*, *promiscuación* refers to the practice of eating meat and fish together at the same meal at Lent and on other occasions when it is forbidden to do so by the Catholic Church. It constituted a means for Republicans and freethinkers to state their opposition to Catholicism.

40 "En Mataró," *El Gladiador del Librepensamiento* 55, Year V (17 Apr. 1915): 3.
41 "Noticias," *El Gladiador del Librepensamiento* 96, Year VII (6 Jan. 1917): 4.
42 *Las Dominicales del Libre Pensamiento* 887, Year XVII (30 June 1899): 1.
43 *Las Dominicales* 196, Year IV (25 Nov. 1904): 1. Antonio Maura, leader of the Conservative Party from 1907 until 1909, was eventually forced to resign as a result of the events of Tragic Week and the furore over the execution of Francisco Ferrer Guardia, founder of the Modern Schools and falsely accused of provoking Tragic Week (Carr 1982, 481–6). Both López de Ayala and Sárraga knew Ferrer Guardia.
44 "No son Mujeres. ¡Son Hembras!," *El Gladiador* 9, Year I (22 Dec. 1906): 2–3.
45 López de Ayala's article "Doctrina racional," dated 15 August 1899 in Port-Bou, together with other details concerning the Port-Bou visit, was published in *Las Dominicales del Libre Pensamiento* 898, Year XVII (14 Sept. 1899): 1.
46 "El meeting de Capellades," *Las Dominicales del Libre Pensamiento* 894, Year XVII (17 Aug. 1899): 1–2.
47 See *Las Dominicales del Libre Pensamiento* 896, Year XVII (30 Aug. 1899): 1.
48 See "Telegrama importante," *El Clamor Zaragozano* 21, Year I (21 Sept. 1899): 1, and "Meeting revisionista en Caldas," *Las Dominicales del Libre Pensamiento* 900, Year XVII (28 Sept. 1899): 3, respectively.
49 See "El meeting de anoche," *La Publicidad* 8128, Year XXIV (4 May 1901): 2.
50 See *El Progreso* 4, Year I (19 Dec. 1896): 2.
51 See *El Progreso* 7, Year II (9 Jan. 1897): 2.
52 The motif of the rose, symbolic of the republic, is continued in López de Ayala's composition "La espina enconada." Here the hearts of Republicans, pierced by the thorn of dissent, are implicitly likened to the roses of Christ's wounds and can be cured only by extracting that thorn (*El Progreso* 11, Year II [6 Feb. 1897]: 2).
53 *El Progreso* 14, Year II (27 Feb. 1897): 1. A similar call to unity in the face of approaching elections is heard in another of López de Ayala's lead articles, "¡Con bravura!" There she deploys the working-class motif of the spade that will clear the way for the Republic: "¡A unirse, republicanos! … (¡)Y unísonos, generosos, ennoblecidos, potentes, salgamos de las asambleas populares armadas con las palas de nuestra enérgica resolución, limpiando con ellas el lodo que dificulta el paso a la república!" (*El Progreso* 12, Year II (13 Feb. 1897): 1; Unite, Republicans! … And as one, generous, dignified, and powerful, let's leave the people's meetings armed with the spades of our energetic resolve, clearing away the mud that impedes the republic's path!)
54 *La Tramontana* 592, Year XII (2 Dec. 1892): 4.
55 *La Tramontana* 594, Year XII (16 Dec. 1892): 3.
56 This night school, which bore the society's name, was held at 12 Ferrer de Blanes Street, first floor, in the Barcelona district of Gracia.
57 "La Sociedad Progresiva Femenina," *Las Dominicales del Libre Pensamiento* 835, Year XVI (30 June 1898): 2.

58 See *Las Dominicales del Libre Pensamiento* 910, Year XVII (7 Dec. 1899): 3.
59 Isidro Sánchez Sánchez notes that although the church was suspicious of the Red Cross, maintaining that true charity could not exist without faith, there was a considerable increase in the number of Catholics in that organization in fin-de-siècle Spain (2001, 171, 194).
60 See *El Gladiador del Librepensamiento* 72, Year VI (1 Jan. 1916): 2–3.
61 See *El Gladiador del Librepensamiento* 83, Year VI (17 June 1916): 4.
62 See "Un modelo," *El Motín* 8, Year XLI (19 Feb. 1921): 3–4.
63 "Congreso Feminista Internacional," *Las Dominicales del Libre Pensamiento* 887, Year XVII (30 June 1899): 3.
64 "De nuestros amigos," *El Gladiador del Librepensamiento* 89, Year VI (16 Sept. 1916): 1–2.
65 According to Sànchez i Ferré, however, the purpose of the meeting was not to lobby for female suffrage but to protest against the interpretation of Article 11 in relation to freedom of worship (1990, 174).
66 See "Mitin Femenino," *El Gladiador del Librepensamiento* 104, Year VII, Second Epoch (19 May 1917): 1.
67 *La Luz* 9, Year XVII (11 July 1895): 71–2. A full report of the evening was given by Domingo Soler in this same issue (71–6).
68 *Las Dominicales del Libre Pensamiento* 729 (24 July 1896): 2.
69 For a compendium of her feminist texts and thought, see Pardo Bazán's *La mujer española y otros artículos feministas* (1976).
70 *Las Dominicales del Libre Pensamiento* 910, Year XVII (7 Dec. 1899): 4.
71 It is also highly likely that López de Ayala knew Carolina Coronado personally, given that, like López de Ayala, Coronado contributed to Domingo Soler's *La Luz*. Moreover, earlier, in June 1866, in the context of the San Gil revolution, Coronado had given refuge in her home to several liberals, among whom figured López de Ayala's uncle, the dramatist Adelardo López de Ayala (see Valis 1991, 36).
72 Domingo Soler, "Días de lucha," *La Luz* 26, Year XVII (7 Nov. 1895): 214.
73 *La Luz* 9, Year XVII (11 July 1895): 73–4.
74 *La Luz* 49, Year XIII (21 Apr. 1892): 402.
75 *La Luz* 30, Year XVII (28 Nov. 1895): 259.
76 *Las Dominicales del Libre Pensamiento* 813, Year XVI (27 Jan. 1898): 2.
77 *Las Dominicales del Libre Pensamiento* 817, Year XVI (21 Feb. 1898): 4.
78 *Las Dominicales del Libre Pensamiento* 448, Year IX (16 May 1891): 3. The composition was republished in *La Luz* 20, Year XIII (1 Oct. 1891): 172.
79 Regarding Acuña's *El Padre Juan*, see Arkinstall (2009, 54–82).
80 "Carta abierta," *El Motín* 15, Year XL (17 Apr. 1920): 1–2.
81 "Señora Doña Rosario de Acuña," *El Motín* 17, Year XL (1 May 1920): 1.

82 María Marín contributed to *El Pueblo* with her "Conferencias femeninas" from 1908 until 1910, as well as to *La Conciencia Libre* in 1905 (Sanfeliu 2005, 113–14).
83 *El Motín* 3, Year XLI (15 Jan. 1921): 3–4.
84 *La Tramontana* 702, Year XVI (28 Feb. 1896): 4.
85 It should be noted that John Stuart Mill's *Subjection of Women* (1869) had already appeared in Spain in 1891, translated by Pardo Bazán as *La esclavitud femenina* (Jagoe 1994, 125). The enslavement of women was a constant motif in writings by freethinking women, as attested to by an article published in 1871 in the freethinking periodical *La Humanidad*: "We have always been slaves and we still have not broken our chains … What have we been? Slaves. What are we? Slaves. What will we be? Free, as free as you men, who until now have been our oppressors" (*La Humanidad* 29, Year II (22 June 1871): 229, quoted in Sànchez i Ferré 1990, 164).
86 *Las Dominicales del Libre Pensamiento* 531, Year X (18 Nov. 1892): 3.
87 *Las Dominicales del Libre Pensamiento* 805, Year XV (2 Dec. 1897): 2.
88 *Las Dominicales del Libre Pensamiento* 719, Year XIV (17 May 1896): 2–3.
89 *El Progreso* 12, Year II (13 Feb. 1897): 1–2.

3. Domestic Politics, National Agendas

1 For a full discussion of these Romantic premises, see Kirkpatrick (1991, 11–24).
2 Regarding Gregorio de Marañón's and Ramiro de Maeztu's works on the theme of Don Juan, see also Isabel Paraíso (1998) and Genara Pulido Tirado (1998), respectively.
3 Roberta Johnson has suggested (communication with the author 2012) that *De tal siembra, tal cosecha* may also constitute, to a certain extent, a rewriting of Jose María de Pereda's canonical novel, *De tal palo, tal astilla* (1880). Unlike the liberal tone of López de Ayala's work, Pereda's writing is highly conservative, reflecting the writer's Carlist sympathies and anti-Republican stance. The very metaphors in each work's title speak of two different world visions: whereas Pereda's image intimates vertical, hierarchical relationships built on inherited paradigms and force, López de Ayala's conveys principles of receptivity, premises of cause and effect, and the manual labour of a rural working class.
4 See "*De tal siembra, tal cosecha*," *El Clamor Zaragozano* 6, Year I (30 July 1899): 2–3. The work was still being advertised for sale at half price – one peseta – on the back page of *El Gladiador del Librepensamiento* in May and June 1915 (see *El Gladiador del Librepensamiento* 56, Second Epoch, Year IV (1915): 4, and no. 59 (1915): 4).
5 Such a reading of the *calavera* or libertine is given by Johnson for Blanca de los Ríos's protagonist in her 1907 novel, *Las hijas de Don Juan* (1998, 227).
6 Julio's Romantic features are apparent in Rosa's description of him as "voluntarioso" (willful), "vehemente" (impetuous), and "exaltado" (hot-headed) (López de Ayala

1889, 11), while Rosa's cousin Carlos likens him to a "bandolero" (bandit) and "infame asesino" (infamous murderer) (22) – portrayals that conform to a model of the Romantic hero as alienated outlaw.

7 Regarding the *querelle des femmes* and the *querelle des sexes*, see Gisela Bock (2002). Julie Campbell notes that the rise in *querelle* topics during the sixteenth and early seventeenth centuries could be explained by the changes that occur then in the status of women and their greater participation in intellectual life (2006, 8–9), conditions also applicable to López de Ayala's context.

8 Plácida later reiterates such an opinion in act 3, stating that women's apparent conformity to traditional norms of femininity is the key to dominating men: "Hay que entender a estos bravos, / decirles siempre que sí, / tributarles cien halagos, / no lloriquear por nada, / aprobar todos sus actos, / y así, sin que ellos lo sepan, / se convierten en esclavos" (López de Ayala 1889, 82; You have to understand these machos, / always say yes to them, / pay them a hundred compliments, / not snivel over anything, / approve of all their deeds, / and thus, without them realizing it, / they will become your slaves).

9 In 1700 Mary Astell asks, "If *all Men are born free*, how is it that all Women are born slaves?" (1996, 18). Likewise, Acuña also represents the state of women in terms of slavery; in a letter written to the Constante Alona lodge on 3 July 1885 she refers to her "condición de mujer [es decir, de esclava]" (quoted in Álvarez Lázaro 1985, 340; state of being a woman [that is, a slave]).

10 As Carole Pateman states, "If a wife's subjection to her husband has a 'natural' foundation, she cannot also be seen as a 'naturally' free and equal individual. Only if women are seen as 'free and equal individuals' is their consent relevant at all" (1989, 74).

11 On the third reappearance of *El Progreso* in 1899, López de Ayala states that the periodical will continue to publish *El abismo*, begun in previous issues, because subscribers had appreciated it so much. Moreover, collections of previous instalments of *El abismo* could be purchased for two pesetas from López de Ayala at 27 Planeta Street, Gracia, Barcelona (see "Nueva publicación catalana. ¡¡¡*El Progreso*!!!," *Las Dominicales del Libre Pensamiento* 913, Year XVII [28 Dec. 1899]: 4).

12 The sources for *El abismo* are as follows: pages 3–8 from *El Gladiador*, pages 9–20 from *El Progreso* (numbered from page 7 onward); pages 21–4 from *El Libertador*, and pages 25–64 and 81–8 from *El Progreso* (page references will be placed in the text). Missing altogether are pages 65–80 and those subsequent to page 89. All extant issues of the three periodicals are available on microfilm at the Arxiu Històric de la Ciutat, Barcelona.

13 Regarding this practice, see Jean-François Botrel (2003, 32).

14 The correlation between solvency and the feuilleton is corroborated by the fact that *El abismo* coincides on the last page of the periodicals with advertisements so as to call the readers' attention to the novella, as was the practice of the day (Seoane 1996a,

180; see also figure 3.1). The precarious existence of minority periodicals is demonstrated by López de Ayala's repeated calls to subscribers to pay up, as evident in "Aviso" (*El Progreso* 10, Year II [30 Jan. 1897]: 1) and "A nuestros abonados" (*El Progreso* 15, Year II [6 Mar. 1897]: 1).

15 Readers of serialized novels came from all social classes; see Juan Ignacio Ferreras (1972, 27), Jesús A. Martínez Martín (2003, 58), and Seoane (1996a, 179). As far as periodicals were concerned, their readership could not be gauged from the number printed of any one issue; a single Republican paper might be read aloud and debated in a wide variety of public spaces, such as taverns, barbershops, workers' societies, and Republican centres (Culla and Duarte 1990, 30). In upper-class liberal households, it would often be passed on to the servants' quarters (Botrel 2003, 33).

16 See Marie Claude Lecuyer and Maryse Villapadierna (1995, 25, 43) and Leonardo Romero Tobar (1976, 206). In 1900 more than 25 per cent of Spanish women were literate, with greater levels of literacy in urban centres (McKenna 2009, 26–7).

17 For the supposedly innate illness and spirituality of nineteenth-century women, see Bram Dijkstra (1986, 3–63).

18 For the New Woman in the Spanish context, see Charnon-Deutsch (1994). Within a more general context, see Elaine Showalter (1990, 38–58).

19 In 1900, 11,867,455 out of a total population of 18,618,086 were illiterate (see Botrel 1993, 309, figure 7).

20 *El Gladiador* 1, Year I (26 May 1906): 12.

21 Arístides, "Bibliografía," *El Gladiador del Librepensamiento* 89, Year VI, Second Epoch (16 Sept. 1916): 3.

22 *Las Dominicales del Libre Pensamiento* 645, Year XII (21 Dec. 1894): 3. Similarly, López de Ayala's 1892 poem, "A los sostenedores de las escuelas laicas," also describes secular schools in religious terms, praising the teachers and parents who send children to "ese templo sacrosanto" (that sacred temple) and "ese lugar sagrado / donde el mortal se redime" (that sacred place / where mortals are redeemed) (*Las Dominicales del Libre Pensamiento* 536, Year X [23 Dec. 1892]: 4).

23 *Las Dominicales del Libre Pensamiento* 643, Year XII (7 Dec. 1894): 2.

24 See *Las Dominicales del Libre Pensamiento* 655, Year XIII (1 Mar. 1895): 2.

25 *La Luz* 9, Year XVII (11 July 1895): 71–4. Further references to López de Ayala's activities are I. B.'s piece "En Sabadell," which refers to her speaking at the prize-giving of a secular school (*El Progreso* 7, Year II [9 Jan. 1897]: 2–3) and López de Ayala's column "Crónica," where she recommends to freethinkers Julia Aymat's secular school at 124 Hospital Street, Barcelona (*El Progreso* 12, Year II [13 Feb. 1897]: 3).

26 See Adelaida Molero, "La Escuela Moderna de Villanueva y Geltrú," *El Gladiador* 4, Year I (25 Aug. 1906): 5.

27 "Escuela," *El Gladiador* 8, Year I (24 Nov. 1906): 4.

28 However, in 1906 an article published in López de Ayala's *El Gladiador* states that Barcelona still needs one hundred schools for its working classes ("Muchas escuelas," *El Gladiador* 6, Year I [6 Oct. 1906]: 5).

4. Federal Republicanism, Feminism, and Freethinking

1 This poem was read by Eugenia Areales at the Ciro Theatre in Córdoba, 6 November 1899, and reproduced in *Las Dominicales del Libre Pensamiento* 908, Year XVII (23 Nov. 1899): 2.

2 As Ackelsberg notes, *La Revista Blanca* was published in Madrid by Juan Montseny and Teresa Mañé from 1898 until 1906 and in Barcelona from 1923 to 1936 (1991, 191n34).

3 Ramos gives Sárraga's birthdate as 1872 and 1874 (2005a, 76), while Rivera states that it is 1873 (1913, 166). For details regarding Sárraga's parents, see Luis Vitale and Julia Antivilo Peña (2000, 29).

4 Hence Vitale and Antivilo Peña state that Sárraga was steeped in anarchist and socialist theories and read Menéndez Pelayo, Ramón Menéndez Pidal, and Miguel de Unamuno (2000, 33).

5 Details regarding the birth of Sárraga's daughter, who was registered civilly, feature in *Las Dominicales del Libre Pensamiento* 757, Year XV (8 Jan. 1897): 2, while news of her death in 1905 is given in an article by Amalia Carvia. There Carvia states that Libertad's secular burial on 2 August in Burjasot was attended by commissions from various casinos and societies in Valencia and Burjasot ("Niña malograda," *Las Dominicales* 234, Year VI [18 Aug. 1905]: 1–2). Sárraga's young son is referred to in Amalia Carrión's poem "Al niño, Volney Ferrero Sárraga," whom she hopes will continue "por el camino que ves abrir / a tus valientes y amantes padres, / que tanto luchan por el progreso" (*Las Dominicales* 218, Year IV [28 Apr. 1905]: 2; on the path that you see / your courageous and loving parents forge, / who fight so hard for progress. Vitale and Antivilo Peña (2000, 35) and Ramos (2006, 694) also refer to a son named Demófilo.

6 Constantin François de Chassebout, Count of Volney (1757–1820) assumed the name of Volney from the amalgamation of Voltaire and Ferney, the town where Voltaire lived between 1759 and 1778, and renamed Voltaire-Ferney after the French Revolution in Voltaire's honour.

7 See "Avisos" and "De todo y de todas partes," *La Conciencia Libre* 240, Year VII (7 June 1902): 3.

8 However, Sárraga had begun to contribute to *Las Dominicales del Libre Pensamiento* the previous year with her article "¡Pueblo, despierta!" (no. 641 [23 Nov. 1894]: 4). Up until 1 April 1896 she regularly published many poems and several articles there, usually before they appeared in *La Luz del Porvenir*.

9 *La Luz* 22, Year XVII (10 Oct. 1895): 181–8.

10 On 18 March 1896 Rafael Sárraga again participated in a poetry reading alongside his mother and Domingo Soler as part of a cultural evening offered for the poor by the Sociedad Altruista (Altruist Society) in Pueblo Seco, Barcelona (see *La Luz* 44, Year XVII [5 Mar. 1896]: 371).

11 See *La Luz* 47, Year XVII (26 Mar. 1896): 389–96, and no. 48, Year XVII (2 Apr. 1896): 397–9.

12 For further references to Sárraga's activities to promote secular education, see Luz Sanfeliu (2005, 98, 101).

13 See *La Antorcha Valenciana* 296 (21 Nov. 1896): 2; quoted in Ramos (2002a, 137). Lacalzada de Mateo provides a full account of Sárraga's association with freemasonry (2006, 155–7). Sárraga's affiliation with various lodges contradicts Mario López Martínez and Juan Ortiz Villalba's contention that there is no reliable evidence to substantiate this association (1990, 462n14).

14 Regarding these two points, see Ramos (2005a, 77–8, and 2002a, 137 respectively).

15 Ortiz Albear also refers to Sárraga's work being read at a meeting of the Hijas de la Regeneración lodge on 31 August 1895, while at the meeting of 20 October 1896 Amalia Carvia writes of Sárraga's imprisonment in Barcelona and proposes that the lodge buy several copies of a special issue of *La Conciencia Libre* explicitly published to raise funds for Sárraga's release (2005, 228, 231). Regarding Amalia Carvia, see Álvarez Lázaro (1985, 197–201).

16 Sanfeliu calculates that the first issue of *La Conciencia Libre* appeared in June 1896 (2005, 97n15). The choice of name for the periodical may also have been motivated by a Madrid society of the same name. Affiliated with the Federal Republican Centre, its purpose was to "promote freethinking ideas and civil acts, establish ties of fraternity and solidarity among those who proclaim freedom of conscience, and, in short, wage a constant, lively, and energetic battle against fanaticism and intolerance" (see *Las Dominicales del Libre Pensamiento* 569, Year XI [4 Aug. 1893]: 3).

17 Indeed, between April and August 1897 there were sixteen court cases against *La Conciencia Libre* because of its criticism of the Jesuit order (Mateo Avilés 1986, 167).

18 With regard to this point, María Ángeles García-Maroto gives Sárraga's name as Segarra, and adds that she was a member of the Sociedad Libertaria de Amigos del Progreso (Libertarian Society of Friends of Progress) and helped found the Federación Madrileña Obrerista (Madrid Workers' Federation) (1996, 240).

19 The imminent reappearance of *La Conciencia Libre* was announced in López de Ayala's *El Gladiador: Órgano de la "Sociedad Progresiva Femenina"* 11, Year II (23 Feb. 1907): 13.

20 These issues of *La Conciencia Libre* are held as follows: no. 108 (14 July 1898) at the Hemeroteca Municipal, Madrid, bound with *La Antorcha Valenciana*; nos 240, 250, 252–4, 256–9, 262–3, 266–8, 271–3, all from 1902, at the Seville Hemeroteca; and

no. 59 from 1907 at the Arxiu Històric de la Ciutat in Barcelona. Sanfeliu refers to thirteen extant issues, eleven of which are in addition to those that I have found: one issue from 5 Feb. 1898, four issues from 1901 dated 7, 13, 21 Sept. and 12 Oct., four issues from 1905, dated 9, 16, 28 and 29 Dec., and two issues from 1907, dated 16 March and 4 May (Sanfeliu 2005, 97n14).

21 See *La Conciencia Libre* 59, Second Epoch, Year II (16 Mar. 1907).

22 That this kind of coverage was common in *La Conciencia Libre* is suggested by an earlier lengthy article, "Crímenes de un fraile," this time in relation to occurrences in Barcelona, which featured in no. 254, Year VII (19 July 1902): 1–2.

23 *Las Dominicales del Libre Pensamiento* 766, Year XV (5 Mar. 1897): 3.

24 See *La Conciencia Libre* 267, Year VII (8 Nov. 1902): 4.

25 For an article on *La Conciencia Libre* and rare photographs of its principal contributors – Sárraga, López de Ayala, Amalia Pérez, Álvarez Pool, Pilar Cañamaque, and Soledad Areales, see *El País* 6,701, Year XIX (10 Dec. 1905): 1.

26 Regarding these legal obstacles, see Sanfeliu (2005, 105–7).

27 "La mujer española despierta," *Las Dominicales del Libre Pensamiento* 785, Year XV (15 July 1897): 4.

28 On the Asociación General Femenina in Valencia, see Sanfeliu (2005, 102–3, 107–10). Later, in Málaga, Sárraga also opened a secular school for children of both sexes (Ramos 2002a, 141).

29 According to Sanfeliu, Sárraga did not leave Valencia for Málaga until 1900, citing two Republican events at which she spoke in Valencia in February that year (2005, 110–11). However, Mateo Avilés reproduces an article from the Málaga periodical *La Unión Mercantil,* which states on 21 April 1898 that Sárraga had arrived there a year earlier (1986, 265).

30 Regarding the Federation and Sárraga, see Mateo Avilés (1986, 165–82). On the societies of resistance, see Carr (1982, 449).

31 On Sárraga's involvement with federal republicanism in Málaga, see also Ramos (1986).

32 For an excellent overview of the relationships between bourgeois revolution, republicanism, and anarchism in the Andalusian context, see Temma Kaplan (1977, 61–91).

33 Quoted in Ramos (1986, 68); original: *La Unión Mercantil,* 14 Nov. 1933, n.p.

34 See *La Conciencia Libre* 258, Year VII (16 Aug. 1902): 2.

35 See *La Conciencia Libre* 271, Year VII (13 Dec. 1902): 3.

36 *La Conciencia Libre* 272, Year VII (20 Dec. 1902): 1.

37 For instances of Sárraga's activity as orator in Valencia, see Sanfeliu (2005, 101–4).

38 See "En el casino republicano progresista," *La Conciencia Libre* 273, Year VII (27 Dec. 1902): 3.

39 For a summary of federal Republican objectives, see Ramos (2002a, 133).

40 For a more detailed account of Sárraga's writings in *El Liberal* and her travels in Uruguay, see Vitale and Antivilo Peña (2000, 36–46).

41 Ramos states that Sárraga toured Latin America on four occasions: 1912–13, 1915, 1918, and 1930, and that she collaborated with the Uruguayan president, José Batlle y Ordóñez, the governor of Yucatán, Felipe Carrillo Puerto, and the Mexican presidents Francisco Madero, Álvaro Obregón, and Plutarco Elías Calles (Ramos 2005a, 77–8).

42 According to Vitale and Antivilo Peña, Sárraga also gave a lecture tour in Mexico in 1914 (2000, 145).

43 For details regarding Sárraga's visits to Cuba, see Ramos (2000, 226–7).

44 Five of these six addresses were subsequently published in Sárraga's 1913 *Conferencias*: "La mujer como entidad social" (Eighth Lecture), "La moral" (Fourth Lecture), "La familia" (Third Lecture), "Los pueblos y las congregaciones religiosas" (Fifth Lecture), and "El jesuitismo y el porvenir de América" (Seventh Lecture).

45 The above details regarding Sárraga's stay in northern Chile are from Pedro Bravo-Elizondo. He states that Sárraga was also in Chile in 1914, 1930, and 1947 (1989, 35n4). Sárraga's 1913 tour of northern Chile also encompassed Coquimbo, Taltal, Copiapó, and La Serena; for a full account, see Vitale and Antivilo Peña (2000, 90–102).

46 For additional details on Sárraga's travels and activities in Latin America, see Antivilo Peña (2011, 413–18).

47 Details on Sárraga's activities 1931–8 are available on digitalized press at Spain's National Library, Madrid.

48 Ramos maintains that Sárraga's adoption of Zárraga was in recognition of her Basque roots (2005a, 76). Variations in Sárraga's surname in scholarly studies also make tracking biographical details difficult; she is given by her maiden name as Sárraga Hernández by both Tavera (2000, 681–5) and Ortiz Albear (2005, 243). According to Javier Rubio, the *Flandre* was the first of the four major ships destined for Mexico with Spanish exiles. It set sail from Saint Nazaire on 4 April 1939, arriving at Veracruz on 21 April (Rubio 1977, 174). The passages of those on board the *Flandre* were paid for by the Servicio de Evacuación de Refugiados Españoles (SERE) (Llorens 1976, 126). For details regarding the SERE, set up by Juan Negrín, the last prime minister of the Second Spanish Republic, see Rubio (1977, 130–9). On the Spanish exiles in Mexico, see also María de la Soledad Alonso (1980).

49 Quoted in Pilar Domínguez Prats (2009, 200); original: AMAE M-192 (Archivo del Ministerio de Asuntos Exteriores, Madrid).

50 The JARE was established by Indalecio Prieto, the Spanish socialist leader and former minister of defence ousted by Negrín, to succeed Negrín's SERE. It was financed with the substantial treasure taken to Mexico on board the yacht *Vita* (see Rubio 1977, 130–49).

51 Before Antivilo Peña's research (2011), there had been confusion over when Sárraga died.

52 Regarding the censorship of Odón de Buen's works, see Domingo Soler, "Días de lucha," *La Luz* 26, Year XVII (7 Nov. 1895): 213–14.

53 *La Luz* 26, Year XVII (7 Nov. 1895): 216–21. Indeed, in that same issue López de Ayala's manifesto for the meeting, also entitled "¡Ciudadanos! ¡Ciudadanas!," had called to the meeting liberals, Republicans of all persuasions, freemasons, spiritists, and all those who supported advanced ideas (214).

54 "Belén Sárraga en Orán," *Las Dominicales del Libre Pensamiento* 884, Year XVII (8 June 1899): 2.

55 See "El Libre Pensamiento en Orán," *Las Dominicales del Libre Pensamiento* 887, Year XVII (30 June 1899): 1.

56 See "Virtud del Libre Pensamiento," *Las Dominicales del Libre Pensamiento* 882, Year XVII (25 May 1899): 4.

57 "Viajes de propaganda," *Las Dominicales del Libre Pensamiento* 900, Year XVII (28 Sept. 1899): 4.

58 "Revolución en las conciencias," *Las Dominicales del Libre Pensamiento* 907, Year XVII (16 Nov. 1899): 1.

59 "Propaganda librepensadora," *Las Dominicales del Libre Pensamiento* 908, Year XVII (23 Nov. 1899): 4. Regarding Málaga's homage to Sárraga on 19 October 1899, see Mateo Avilés (1986, 168–9).

60 Regarding the Germinal group and its importance for the so-called 1898 Generation, see Rafael Pérez de la Dehesa (1970).

61 See *La Conciencia Libre* 250, Year VII (14 June 1902): 1–3.

62 See "Viaje de propaganda," *La Conciencia Libre* 259, Year VII (30 Aug. 1902): 2.

63 See "Ovaciones a Belén Sárraga," *Las Dominicales* 213, Year IV (24 Mar. 1905): 2.

64 See "Belén Sárraga en Villa del Río," *Las Dominicales* 218, Year IV (28 Apr. 1905): 2.

65 "Congreso del Libre Pensamiento en Roma," *Las Dominicales* 150, Year IV (3 Jan. 1904): 1.

66 Conferences prior to 1900 were those in London (1882), Amsterdam (1883), Anvers (1885), London (1887), Paris (1889), Madrid (1892), and Brussels (1895) (*Las Dominicales* 150, Year IV [3 Jan. 1904]: 1). Domingo Soler celebrates the Brussels conference in her poem "El Congreso de Librepensadores de Bruselas" (*La Luz* 9, Year XVII [11 July 1895]: 86–8). For an excellent overview of the conferences in Geneva, Rome, and Buenos Aires, see Álvarez Lázaro (1985, 17–29, 219–27, 242–6).

67 See "Congreso de Ginebra," *La Conciencia Libre* 253, Year VII (12 July 1902): 3.

68 See "Rosario de Acuña," *Las Dominicales* 84, Year II (3 Oct. 1902): 2.

69 See *La Conciencia Libre* 263, Year VII (11 Oct. 1902): 1–2.

70 *La Conciencia Libre* 266, Year VII (1 Nov. 1902): 2. Ramos notes that Sárraga already had connections with Swiss feminism through her association with the *Revue de Morale Sociale*, founded in Geneva in 1899 (1999b, 80).

71 The announcement of the forthcoming publication was given in "El Congreso de Ginebra," *La Conciencia Libre* 266, Year VII (1 Nov. 1902): 4. Ramos gives its publication details as *Congreso de Librepensadores en Ginebra*, Málaga, 1903 (1995, 120n3).

72 For details regarding this committee, see "Comité Nacional Librepensador," *Las Dominicales* 89, Year II (7 Nov. 1902): 1.
73 See *Las Dominicales* 150, Year IV (3 Jan. 1904): 1–2.
74 See *Las Dominicales* 191, Year IV (21 Oct. 1904): 2, and *Las Dominicales* 189, Year IV (7 Oct. 1904): 4, respectively.
75 See *Las Dominicales* 190, Year IV (14 Oct. 1904): 1.
76 "Para Roma. A las mujeres," *Las Dominicales* 180, Year IV (5 Aug. 1904): 2.
77 See "La delegación española en Roma," *Las Dominicales* 189, Year IV (7 Oct. 1904): 1. This same article also alludes to a second female orator from Spain – perhaps López de Ayala – and states that the ovations given to her and Sárraga constituted "the glorious triumph of the Spanish delegation."
78 "Las sesiones del Congreso de Roma," *Las Dominicales* 193, Year IV (4 Nov.1904): 1.
79 *Las Dominicales* 200, Year IV (22 Dec. 1904): 4.
80 See "En desgravio de Belén Sárraga" and "Por Belén Sárraga," *Las Dominicales* 192, Year IV (28 Oct.1904): 2.
81 See "La delegación española en Roma," *Las Dominicales* 189, Year IV (7 Oct. 1904): 1.
82 See *Las Dominicales* 224, Year VI (9 June 1905): 1. Sárraga did not attend the 1905 Paris conference, possibly because of the death of her daughter that same year.
83 Kaplan indicates that opposition to a national standing army was a central tenet for federal Republican Francesc Pi y Margall (1977, 70).
84 See "Avance. El Congreso del Librepensamiento. Crónica de las sesiones," *Las Dominicales* 296, Year VII (26 Oct. 1906): 1.
85 "Congreso internacional del Librepensamiento," *Las Dominicales* 297, Year VII (2 Nov. 1906): 1. This same column refers to Sárraga's "brilliant performance" at the conference.
86 See "El Congreso Internacional Librepensador de Buenos Aires," *Las Dominicales* 303, Year VII (14 Dec. 1906): 1–2. The Buenos Aires conference and Sárraga's protagonist role there was given extensive coverage in López de Ayala's *El Gladiador* 8, Year I (24 Nov. 1906): 6–9.
87 See "Congreso Republicano Español," *Las Dominicales* 297, Year VII (2 Nov. 1906): 1.
88 "Belén Sárraga," *Las Dominicales* 302, Year VII (7 Dec. 1906): 2.
89 In a review from 28 February 1902, *Minucias* was described as "various poems expressing love for humanity, inspired by noble and lofty ideals" (*Las Dominicales* 53 [Year II]: 4). As readers are informed in the issue of *Las Dominicales* on 6 March 1902, the volume could be ordered from Sárraga herself, the "director of *La Conciencia Libre*, Málaga" (3). *La Conciencia Libre* also advertises *Minucias* as "poems for the people," costing one peseta (no. 261, Year VII [20 Sept. 1902]: 3).
90 Likewise, in "Libertad" Sárraga refers to the "león ibero" (Iberian lion), while in "De ayer a hoy" the Spanish people is described as "el pueblo de raza Ibera" (the people of Iberian race) (1901, 82, 106).

91 The republic as symbolic of a people's self-redemption is evident in the following statement to commemorate the anniversary of the founding of the First Republic on 11 February: "The holy day of Christmas will pass, which celebrates the legend of the birth of a saviour who has not redeemed anybody, and taking its place will be the celebration of 11 February, which commemorates the day when the Spanish people told the world: – I am sovereign and determined to redeem myelf" ("El 11 de febrero," *Las Dominicales* 364, Year IX [14 Feb. 1908]: 3).

92 *Las Dominicales del Libre Pensamiento* 641, Year XII (23 Nov. 1894): 4.

93 "A la República," *Las Dominicales del Libre Pensamiento* 649, Year XIII (18 Jan. 1895): 3.

94 *Las Dominicales del Libre Pensamiento* 715, Year XIV (24 Apr. 1896): 2.

95 *Las Dominicales del Libre Pensamiento* 716, Year XIV (1 May 1896): 3–4.

96 *Las Dominicales del Libre Pensamiento* 658, Year XIII (22 Mar. 1895): 2.

97 Similarly, López de Ayala describes the Catholic Church as "esa plaga original / que por gozar en el suelo, / vende pedazos de cielo / cual si Dios fuese industrial" (that original plague / that, for enjoyment on earth, / sells pieces of heaven / as if God were an industrialist) ("En la coronación de Chíes," *Las Dominicales del Libre Pensamiento* 587, Year XI [24 Nov. 1893]: 1).

98 Regarding these attacks, see María Amàlia Pradas Baena (2006, 50).

99 The symbolic import of Bastille Day for Spanish freethinking and federal republicanism is evident in the special commemorative edition of *La Conciencia Libre* on 14 July 1898.

100 The incompatibility of the church with women's aspirations to equality is palpable in the tenor of articles published in *La Conciencia Libre* on 16 March 1907, where no fewer than three columns in the twelve-page publication take up this issue within a transnational arena.

101 The concept of the domestic sphere as a temple for the advancement of civilization and progress is commonplace among female freemasons, with Mercedes Vargas de Chambó affirming in 1883: "La mujer masona debe hacer de su casa un templo donde se rinda ferviente culto a la virtud y a la razón" (quoted in Lacalzada de Mateo 1999, 249n22; The female Mason must make her house a temple for the fervent worship of virtue and reason).

102 One of Sárraga's contemporaries, Mañé (Soledad Gustavo), remarks in "La monja" that the nun is "un cuerpo sin cerebro, una voluntad sin acción" (a body without a brain, a will without action), whose existence is criminal in an age that works so hard for the emancipation of women (*Las Dominicales del Libre Pensamiento* 647, Year XIII [4 Jan. 1895]: 3).

103 *Las Dominicales* 293, Year VII (5 Oct. 1906): 3.

104 Such discourse was common among Sárraga's female contemporaries as borne out by Mañé (Gustavo), who describes the freethinking woman as a "nueva palanca"

(new lever) that “mueve los mundos del sentimiento; esa diosa de la familia donde todos acatan su voluntad” (moves the worlds of feeling; that goddess of the family whose wishes are respected by all) (“Reparación sublime,” *Las Dominicales del Libre Pensamiento* 653, Year XIII [14 Feb. 1895]: 2).

105 However, as women were integrated into the public sphere, a social citizenship based on maternal identity foundered, with maternity seen as an obstacle to political action. It was not until the 1980s that maternal identity would be reclaimed as a vital component of the ethics of care that should underpin all political activity and civic virtues (Ramos 2005b, 45–6).

106 “Most nineteenth- and early twentieth-century feminists,” Susan Moller Okin remarks, “did not question or challenge women’s special role within the family. Indeed, they often argued for women’s rights and opportunities … on the grounds that these would either make them better wives and mothers or enable them to bring their special moral sensibilities, developed in the domestic sphere, to bear on the world of politics” (1998, 123).

107 “Reparación sublime,” *Las Dominicales del Libre Pensamiento* 653, Year XIII (14 Feb. 1895): 2.

108 *La Luz* 10, Year XVII (18 July 1895): 77–86.

109 López de Ayala’s poem, “Himno a la igualdad,” also from 1895, adopts an identical rhetoric on arguing for women’s equality: “La mujer es la base sagrada / del gran templo de la redención; / es del hombre la madre y la esposa, / es emblema del más santo amor. / … / ¡Dadle, dadle instrucción y cultura, / ya que ansiosa reclama este bien[!]” (*La Luz* 9, Year XVII [11 July 1895]: 72; Woman is the sacred foundation / of the great temple of redemption; / she is man’s mother and wife, / the symbol of the most holy love. / … / Give her, give her education and culture, / because she eagerly demands this moral right!)

110 Jagoe notes that in 1877 an amendment in the Spanish parliament proposed limited female suffrage, while in 1883 feminist conferences took place in Palma de Mallorca and Barcelona (1994, 122–3).

111 Domingo Soler refers to Sárraga’s reading of “¡Abajo la caridad!” at a spiritist gathering in 1896: “Una de las poesías de nuestra hermana Belén, por su título y por su lenguaje enérgico, separado de la rutina y de la costumbre de proclamar a la caridad como el consuelo de los consuelos, produjo en el auditorio diversas impresiones … Belén, al decir ¡abajo la caridad!, … quiere que los pobres no sufran los horrores de la miseria, quiere que los ricos no atesoren ni gasten en superfluidades, cuando mueren de hambre centenares de desamparados … quiere hombres libres que tengan conciencia de la grandeza de su origen; esto pide Belén en su poesía con palabras duras y amargas, porque dura y amarga es la situación del pobre en las postrimerías del siglo del vapor.” (One of the poems of our sister, Belén, because of its title and forceful language, rejecting the routine and custom of proclaiming charity as the greatest of

all consolations, produced various impressions among the audience ... Belén, when she says, "Down with charity!," … does not want the poor to suffer the horrors of destitution, or the rich to hoard and spend on what is unnecessary, when hundreds of homeless are dying of hunger … she wants free men who know the greatness of their origin; this is what Belén demands in her poetry with hard-hitting, bitter words, because the situation of the poor at the close of the century of the steam engine is hard and bitter.) ("A mi hermano en creencias Luis Curbelo [Carta abierta]," *La Luz* 37, Year XVII [16 Jan. 1896]: 310).

112 "¡Cuidado!" was first published in *La Luz* 41, Year XVII (13 Feb. 1896): 345–7. Segments of the version reproduced in *Minucias* in 1901 have been rewritten. As Sárraga's footnote from *Minucias* indicates, the poem was inspired by real-life occurrences (Sárraga 1901, 161n1).

113 José de Espronceda's work opens: "Era más de media noche, / antiguas historias cuentan, / cuando en sueño y en silencio / lóbrego envuelta la tierra, / los vivos muertos parecen / … / Era la hora … / … / En que tal vez la campana / de alguna arruinada iglesia / da misteriosos sonidos / de maldición y anatema" (1978, vv. 1–18; It was past midnight, / so ancient stories tell, / when in sleep and gloomy silence / the world enveloped, / the living appear dead / … / It was the hour … / … / in which perhaps the bell / of some church in ruins / rings out mysteriously / warning of damnation and curses).

114 Espronceda's Doña Elvira is described as follows: "Bella y más segura que el azul del cielo / con dulces ojos lánguidos y hermosos, / donde acaso el amor brilló entre el velo / del pudor que los cubre candorosos" (1978, vv. 140–3; Beautiful and truer than the blue of heaven / with sweet, languid, beautiful eyes, / where perhaps love shone from behind the veil / of modesty that covers their innocence).

115 Espronceda's verses are as follows: "Cruzan tristes calles, / plazas solitarias" (1978, vv. 943–4; They cross dismal streets, / solitary squares).

116 Espronceda's verses read: "Sombras de horror girando aterradoras, / que allá aparecen en medrosa huida; / … / Y en él enclavan los hundidos ojos / … / mil vueltas dando, a los abismos rueda [Montemar]: / … / ya oyendo gritos, voces y palmadas, / y aplausos y brutales carcajadas" (1978, vv. 1231–7, 1324–32; Horrific shadows spin terrifyingly, / appearing there in fearful flight; / … / And pierce him with their sunken eyes / … / turning round and round, down to the depths he tumbles: / … / hearing screams, shouts and claps, / and applause and loud, vulgar laughter).

117 Rivera states that, despite numerous court cases against her, Sárraga was never once convicted. The most notorious court case arose from her condemning in 1904, at a Málaga demonstration organized by her, General Polavieja's execution of José Rizal, a leader in the Philippines uprising (Rivera 1913, 169). Regarding Republican attitudes to Spain's colonies, see López-Cordón (1975, 301–5).

118 Compulsory drafting had proven a thorny issue for Republicans. Their promise to abolish it was a crucial factor in garnering popular support for the 1868 Glorious Revolution. Various factors, however, made it impossible for them to deliver on that pledge: the Cuban uprising and the continuation of the inequitable social system on which drafting was based, whereby the better-off bought themselves out of military service. Once the First Republic came into being, it was beset by wars on three fronts – from its colonies, the Carlists in northern Spain, and the self-proclaimed federal cantons in eastern Spain and Andalusia – which meant that the army was indispensable (López-Cordón 1975, 416–24).

119 A similar critique of the inadequate recompense given to working-class soldiers who return maimed from war is effected by Sárraga in "Los dos entorchados," which contrasts the aristocratic general, promoted for his military service, with the crippled beggar, Valentín, who states, "Mi madre me dio sus besos / y su silencio la patria" (Sárraga 1901, 136; My mother gave me her kisses / and the fatherland, silence).

120 *Las Dominicales del Libre Pensamiento* 715, Year XIV (15 Apr. 1896): 4. Another of López de Ayala's anti-war poems is "Librada" from 1895, which condemns war from a young girl's perspective: "¡¡¡Oh!!! qué costumbres tan brutas / son mamá, las de la guerra!!!" (*La Luz* 20, Year XVII [26 Sept. 1895]: 171; Oh! What brutal customs, / mother, those of war are!)

121 *La Concienca Libre* 108, Year III (14 July 1898): 2.

Final Reflections

1 *La Luz* 28, Year XVII (14 Nov. 1895): 240.

2 Donald Shaw, among others, recognizes the influence of Romanticism on the "1898 Generation" (1989, 22).

3 Regarding Don Juan and the "1898 Generation," see also José Luis Abellán (1973, 40-41).

4 *Las Dominicales del Libre Pensamiento* 696, Year XIII (13 Dec. 1895): 1–2.

5 *Las Dominicales del Libre Pensamiento* 698, Year XIII (27 Dec. 1895): 3.

Works Cited

Abellán, José Luis. 1973. *Sociología del 98*. Barcelona: Península.

Ackelsberg, Martha. 1991. *Free Women of Spain: Anarchism and the Struggle for the Emancipation of Women*. Bloomington: Indiana University Press.

Aldaraca, Bridget. 1982. "*El ángel del hogar*: The Cult of Domesticity in Nineteenth-Century Spain." In *Theory and Practice of Feminist Literary Criticism*, edited by Gabriela Mora and Karen S. Van Hooft, 62–87. Ypsilanti, MI: Bilingual.

Alonso, María de la Soledad. 1980. *Contribución a la historia de los refugiados españoles en México*. Vol. 1 of *Palabras del exilio*, edited by Eugenia Meyer and Alicia Olivera. 4 vols. Mexico: Instituto Nacional de Antropología e Historia, Secretaría de Educación Pública.

Álvarez Junco, José. 1983. *Periodismo y política en el Madrid de fin de siglo: El primer lerrouxismo*. Madrid: Ayuntamiento de Madrid, Delegación de Cultura / Instituto de Estudios Madrileños del Consejo Superior de Investigaciones Científicas.

– 1987. "Magia y ética en la retórica política." In *Populismo, caudillaje y discurso demagógico*, edited by José Álvarez Junco, 219–70. Madrid: Centro de Investigaciones Sociológicas / Siglo XXI.

– 1990. *El Emperador del Paralelo: Lerroux y la demagogia populista*. Madrid: Alianza.

– 1994. "Los 'amantes de la libertad': La cultura republicana española a principios del siglo XX." In Townson 1994, 265–92.

– (2001) 2004. *Mater Dolorosa: La idea de España en el siglo XIX*. Madrid: Taurus.

Álvarez Lázaro, Pedro. 1985. *Masonería y librepensamiento en la España de la Restauración (Aproximación histórica)*. Madrid: Publicaciones de la Universidad Pontificia Comillas.

Álvarez Rey, Leandro. 1990. "La Masonería en Sevilla: Entre el compromiso y la militancia política (1900–1936)." In Ferrer Benimeli 1990, 1:227–62.

Antivilo Peña, Julia. 2008. "Belén de Sárraga y la influencia de su praxis política en la consolidación del movimiento de mujeres y feminista chileno." In *Mujeres chilenas:*

Fragmentos de una historia, edited by Sonia Montecino Aguirre, 99–104. Santiago de Chile: Catalonia.

– 2011. "Crónica de un Torbellino Libertario en América Latina: Belén de Sárraga (1906–1950)." In *Viajeras entre dos mundos*, edited by Sara Beatriz Guardia, prologue by Losandro Antonio Tedeschi, 407–22. Peru: CEMHAL.

Arias, Arturo, ed. 2001. *The Rigoberta Menchú Controversy*. Response by David Stoll. Minneapolis: University of Minnesota Press.

Arkinstall, Christine. 2009. *Histories, Cultures, and National Identities: Women Writing Spain, 1877–1984*. Lewisburg: Bucknell University Press.

Astell, Mary. 1996. "Reflections upon Marriage." In *Astell: Political Writings*, edited by Patricia Springborg, 1–80. Cambridge: Cambridge University Press. http://dx.doi.org/10.1017/CBO9780511802164.005.

Bahamonde Magro, Ángel, and J. Toro Mérida. 1978. *Burguesía, especulación y cuestión social en el Madrid del siglo XIX*. Madrid: Siglo XXI.

Ballarín, Pilar. 1993. "La construcción de un modelo educativo de 'utilidad doméstica.'" In Duby and Perrot 1993, 598–611.

Bernal Muñoz, José Luis. 1996. *¿Invento o realidad?: La generación española de 1898*, prologue by Pío Caro Baroja. Valencia: Pre-Textos.

Beverley, John. 1992. "Introducción." In *La voz del otro: Testimonio, subalternidad y verdad narrativa*, edited by John Beverley and Hugo Achugar, 7–18. Lima: Latinoamericana.

– 2004. *Testimonio: On the Politics of Truth*. Minneapolis: University of Minnesota Press.

Bhabha, Homi K. 1994. *The Location of Culture*. London: Routledge.

Bieder, Maryellen. 1992. "Woman and the Twentieth-Century Spanish Literary Canon: The Lady Vanishes." *Anales de la Literatura Española Contemporánea* 17:301–24.

Blanco, Alda. 1989. "Introducción." In *Una mujer por caminos de España* by María Martínez Sierra, edited by Blanco, 7–40. Madrid: Castalia.

Bloom, Harold. 1973. *The Anxiety of Influence: A Theory of Poetry*. London: Oxford University Press.

Bock, Gisela. 2002. "*Querelle des femmes*: A European Gender Dispute." In *Women in European History*, translated by Allison Brown, 1–31. Oxford: Blackwell.

Bolado, José, ed. 2007–9. *Rosario de Acuña y Villanueva: Obras reunidas*. 5 vols. Oviedo: KRK.

– 2009. *Cuentos, cartas y teatro*, Vol. 4 of *Rosario de Acuña y Villanueva: Obras reunidas*, edited by Bolado. Oviedo: KRK.

Bookchin, Murray. 1977. *The Spanish Anarchists: The Heroic Years, 1868–1936*. New York: Free Life.

Boon, Vivienne, and Gerard Delanty. 2007. "Cosmopolitanism and Europe: Historical Considerations and Contemporary Applications." In *Cosmopolitanism and Europe*, edited by Chris Rumford, 19–38. Liverpool, UK: Liverpool University Press.

Botrel, Jean-François. 1974. "La novela por entregas: Unidad de creación y consumo." In *Creación y público en la literatura española*, edited by Botrel and Serge Salaün, prologue by Francisco Ynduráin, 111–55. Madrid: Castalia.

– 1993. *Libros, prensa y lectura en la España del siglo XIX*, translated by David Torra Ferrer. Madrid: Fundación Germán Sánchez Ruipérez.

– 2003. "La construcción de una nueva cultura del libro y del impreso en el siglo XIX." In *Orígenes culturales de la sociedad liberal (España siglo XIX)*, edited by Jesús A Martínez Martín, 19–36. Madrid: Biblioteca Nueva.

Bravo-Elizondo, Pedro. 1989. "Belén de Sárraga y su influencia en la mujer del Norte Grande." In *Canción de Marcela: Mujer y cultura en el mundo hispánico*, edited by David Valjalo, 31–9. Madrid: Orígenes.

Brennan, Teresa, and Carole Pateman. 1998. "'Mere Auxiliaries to the Commonwealth': Women and the Origins of Liberalism." In Phillips 1998, 93–115.

Bretz, Mary Lee. 2001. *Encounters across Borders: The Changing Vision of Spanish Modernism, 1890–1930*. Lewisburg: Bucknell University Press.

Brooks, Linda Marie. 2005. "*Testimonio*'s Poetics of Performance." *Comparative Literature Studies* 42 (2): 181–222. http://dx.doi.org/10.1353/cls.2005.0028.

de Buen, Odón. 2003. *Mis memorias (Zuera, 1863–Toulouse, 1939)*, transcribed by María del Carmen de Buen de López de Heredia. Zaragoza: Institución "Fernando el Católico" / Excma. Diputación de Zaragoza.

Campbell, Joseph. 1973. *The Hero with a Thousand Faces*. 1949. 1st ed. Princeton: Princeton University Press.

Campbell, Julie. 2006. *Literary Circles and Gender in Early Modern Europe: A Cross-Cultural Approach*. Aldershot, UK: Ashgate.

Capmany, Maria Aurèlia. 1973. *El Feminisme a Catalunya*. Barcelona: Nova Terra.

Carmona González, Ángeles. 1999. *Escritoras andaluzas en la prensa de Andalucía del siglo XIX*. Cádiz: Publicaciones Universidad de Cádiz / Instituto Andaluz de la Mujer.

Caro Baroja, Julio. 1980. *Introducción a una historia contemporánea del anticlericalismo español*. Madrid: Istmo.

Carr, Raymond. 1982. *Spain, 1808–1975*. 2nd ed. Oxford: Clarendon.

Castro Alfín, Demetrio. 1987. "Jacobinos y populistas: El republicanismo español a mediados del siglo XIX." In *Populismo, caudillaje y discurso demagógico*, edited by José Álvarez Junco, 181–217. Madrid: Centro de Investigaciones Sociológicas / Siglo XXI.

Charnon-Deutsch, Lou. 1994. "New Women." In *Narratives of Desire: Nineteenth-Century Spanish Fiction by Women*, by Charnon-Deutsch, 141–85. University Park: Pennsylvania State University Press.

– 2001. "Concepción Arenal and the Nineteenth-Century Spanish Debates about Women's Sphere and Education." In *Recovering Spain's Feminist Tradition*, edited by Lisa Vollendorf, 198–216. New York: Modern Language Association of America.

– 2003. "Gender and Beyond: Nineteenth-Century Spanish Women Writers." In *The Cambridge Companion to the Spanish Novel from 1600 to the Present*, edited by Harriet Turner and Adelaida López de Martínez, 122–37. Cambridge, UK: Cambridge University Press. http://dx.doi.org/10.1017/CCOL0521771277.008.

– 2008. *Hold That Pose: Visual Culture in the Late Nineteenth-Century Spanish Periodical*. University Park: Pennsylvania State University Press.

Correa Ramón, Amelina. 2002. "Amalia Domingo Soler, una escritora 'en la sombra.'" In *Cuentos espiritistas*, by Domingo Soler. Selection, prologue, and edition by Correa Ramón. Illustrations by Marina Arespacochaga, 7–50. Madrid: Clan.

Crespo Gutiérrez, María Victoria. "Consuelo Álvarez Pool (1867–1957)." 30 June 2013. http://www.telegrafistas.es/telegrafistas-ilustres/biografias-historicas/272-1-consuelo-alvarez-pool-1867-1957.

Criado y Domínguez, D. Juan P. 1889. *Literatas españolas del siglo XIX: Apuntes bibliográficos*. Madrid: Imprenta de Antonio Pérez Dubrull.

Cuenca, Francisco. 1921. *Biblioteca de autores andaluces modernos y contemporáneos*. Havana: "Tipografía Moderna" de Alfredo Dorrbecker.

Culla i Clarà, Joan B. 1986. *El Republicanisme lerrouxista á Catalunya (1901–1923)*. Barcelona: Curial.

Culla, Joan B., and Àngel Duarte. 1990. *La Premsa republicana*. Barcelona: Diputació de Barcelona / Col·legí de Periodistes de Catalunya.

Delgado, Buenaventura. 1979. *La escuela moderna de Ferrer i Guardia*. Barcelona: Ceac.

Dietz, Mary G. 1985. "Citizenship with a Feminist Face: The Problem with Maternal Thinking." *Political Theory* 13 (1): 19–37. http://dx.doi.org/10.1177/0090591785013001003.

– 1998. "Context Is All: Feminism and Theories of Citizenship." In Phillips 1998, 378–400.

Dijkstra, Bram. 1986. *Idols of Perversity: Fantasies of Feminine Evil in Fin-de-Siècle Culture*. New York: Oxford University Press.

Domingo Soler, Amalia. 1880. *El espiritismo refutando los errores del catolicismo romano: Colección de artículos escritos*. San Martín de Provensals, Barcelona: J. Torrens.

– (1900) 1985a. *Memorias del Padre Germán*. San Martín de Provensals, Barcelona: J. Torrens y Corral. Reprint, Barcelona: Teorema.

– (1903) 1985b. *Ramos de violetas: Colección de poesías y artículos espiritistas*. Barcelona: Carbonell y Esteva. Reprint, Barcelona: Teorema.

– 1903a. *Consejos de ultratumba: Historia de dos almas*. Barcelona: Maucci.

– 1903b. *Sus más hermosos escritos*. Barcelona: Maucci.

– (1904) 1991. *¡Te perdono!: Memorias de un espíritu*. Barcelona: Maucci. Reprint, Barcelona: Humanitas.

– 1909. *Flores del alma*. Barcelona: Carbonell y Esteva.

– (1912) 1990. *Memorias de una mujer*, prologue by Cristóbal Fernández. Barcelona: Amelia Boudet.

– (1926) 1989. *Cuentos espiritistas*, prologue by Juan José Fernández. Barcelona: Amelia Boudet.

Domínguez Prats, Pilar. 2009. *De ciudadanas a exiliadas: Un estudio sobre las republicanas españolas en México*, prologue by Dolores Plá Brugat. Madrid: Cinca.

Duarte, Ángel. 1987. *El republicanisme català a la fi del segle XIX*. Vic: Eumo.

Duby, Georges, and Michelle Perrot, eds. 1993. *El siglo XIX*. Vol. 4 of *Historia de las mujeres en Occidente*, translated by Marco Aurelio Galmarini. 5 vols. Madrid: Taurus.

Elorza, Antonio. 1996. "Utopía y revolución en el movimiento anarquista español." In *Sindicalismo y vida obrera en España*, 51–72. Madrid: Universidad Complutense de Madrid.

Enríquez de Salamanca, Cristina. 1998. "La mujer en el discurso legal del liberalismo español." In *La mujer en los discursos de género*, edited by Catherine Jagoe, Alda Blanco, and Enríquez de Salamanca, 219–52. Barcelona: Icaria.

Espigado Tocino, Gloria. 2002. "La mujer en la utopía de Charles Fourier." In Ramos and Vera 2002, 321–72.

de Espronceda, José. (1837–40) 1978. *El estudiante de Salamanca*. 4th ed. Edited by Benito Varela Jácome. Madrid: Cátedra.

Fagoaga, Concha. 1985. *La voz y el voto de las mujeres: El sufragismo en España, 1877–1931*. Barcelona: Icaria.

Favret, Mary A. 1993. *Romantic Correspondence: Women, Politics and the Fiction of Letters*. Cambridge, UK: Cambridge University Press.

Fay, Elizabeth A. 1998. *A Feminist Introduction to Romanticism*. Oxford: Blackwell.

Ferman, Claudia. 2001. "Textual Truth, Historical Truth, and Media Truth: Everybody Speaks about the Menchús." In Arias 2001, 156–70.

Ferrer Benimeli, J.A., ed. 1990. *Masonería, revolución y reacción*. IV Symposium Internacional de la Historia de la Masonería Española. Alicante, 27–30 September 1989. 2 vols. Alicante: Instituto de Cultura "Juan Gil-Albert" (Diputación de Alicante) / Caja de Ahorros Provincial de Alicante / Generalitat Valenciana.

Ferreras, Juan Ignacio. 1972. *La novela por entregas: 1840–1900 (Concentración obrera y economía editorial)*. Madrid: Taurus.

Fine, Robert. 2007. *Cosmopolitanism*. London: Routledge.

Gabriel, Pere. 1994. "Insurrección y política: El republicanismo ochocentista en Cataluña." In Townson 1994, 341–71.

García-Maroto, María Ángeles. 1996. *La mujer en la prensa anarquista: España, 1900–1936*, prologue by Consuelo Zabala. Madrid: Fundación de Estudios Libertarios Anselmo Lorenzo.

Gutiérrez Lloret, Rosa Ana. 1990. "Republicanismo y masonería en el Alicante de la Restauración." In Ferrer Benimeli 1990, 2:619–31.

Heywood, Paul. 1990. *Marxism and the Failure of Organised Socialism in Spain, 1879–1936*. Cambridge, UK: Cambridge University Press. http://dx.doi.org/10.1017/CBO9780511523656.

Hooper, Kirsty. 2008. *A Stranger in My Own Land: Sofía Casanova, a Spanish Writer in the European Fin de Siècle*. Nashville: Vanderbilt University Press.

Horta, Gerard. 2001. *De la mística a les barricades: Introducció a l'espiritisme català del XIX dins el context ocultista europeu*. Barcelona: Proa.

– 2004. *Cos i revolució: L'espiritisme català o les paradoxes de la modernitat*. Barcelona: Edicions de 84.

Hurtado, Amparo. 1998. "Biografía de una generación: Las escritoras del noventa y ocho." In *Breve historia feminista de la literatura española (en lengua castellana)*, edited by Iris M. Zavala, 139–54. Vol. 5 of *La literatura escrita por mujer: Desde el siglo XIX hasta la actualidad*. Barcelona: Anthropos.

Irigaray, Luce. 1993. "The Bodily Encounter with the Mother." In *The Irigaray Reader*, edited and introduction by Margaret Whitford, translation by David Macey, 34–46. Oxford: Blackwell.

Jacob, Margaret C. 2006. *Strangers Nowhere in the World: The Rise of Cosmopolitanism in Early Modern Europe*. Philadelphia: University of Pennsylvania Press.

Jagoe, Catherine. 1994. *Ambiguous Angels: Gender in the Novels of Galdós*. Berkeley: University of California Press.

Johnson, Roberta. 1993. *Crossfire: Philosophy and the Novel in Spain, 1900–1934*. Lexington: University Press of Kentucky.

– 1998. "The Domestication of Don Juan in Women Novelists of Modernist Spain." In *Intertextual Pursuits. Literary Mediations in Modern Spanish Narrative*, edited by Jeanne P. Brownlow and John W. Kronik, 222–38. Lewisburg: Bucknell University Press.

– 2003. *Gender and Nation in the Spanish Modernist Novel*. Nashville: Vanderbilt University Press.

Johnson, Roberta, and Maite Zubiaurre, eds. 2012. *Antología del pensamiento feminista español (1726–2011)*. Madrid: Cátedra.

Kaplan, Temma. 1977. *Anarchists of Andalusia, 1868–1903*. Princeton: Princeton University Press.

Kirkpatrick, Susan. 1991. *Las Románticas: Escritoras y subjetividad en España, 1835–1850*. Madrid: Cátedra.

– 1999. "Gender and Modernist Discourse: Emilia Pardo Bazán's *Dulce Dueño*." In *Modernism and Its Margins: Reinscribing Cultural Modernity from Spain and Latin America*, edited by Anthony L. Geist and José B. Monleón, 117–39. New York: Garland.

Labanyi, Jo. 1995. "Liberal Individualism and the Fear of the Feminine in Spanish Romantic Drama." In *Gender and Culture in Nineteenth-Century Spain*, edited by Lou Charnon-Deutsch and Jo Labanyi, 8–26. Oxford: Clarendon.

– 2000. "History and Hauntology; or, What Does One Do with the Ghosts of the Past? Reflections on Spanish Film and Fiction of the Post-Franco Period." In *Disremembering the Dictatorship: The Politics of Memory in the Spanish Transition to Democracy*, edited by Joan Ramon Resina, 65–82. Amsterdam: Rodopi.

Lacalzada de Mateo, María José. 1990. "Masonería y Revolución liberal: La vía de la emancipación humana (1834–1902)." In Ferrer Benimeli 1990, 1:91–104.

– 1999. "La intervención de la masonería en los inicios de la ciudadanía femenina." In *Género y ciudadanía: Revisiones desde el ámbito privado*, 243–57. Madrid: Instituto Universitario de Estudios de la Mujer / Universidad Autónoma de Madrid.

– 2006. *Mujeres en masonería: Antecedentes históricos entre las luces y las sombras (1868–1938)*. Barcelona: Clavell Cultura.

Landes, Joan B. 1988. *Women and the Public Sphere in the Age of the French Revolution*. Ithaca: Cornell University Press.

Larra, Mariano José de. 1982. *Artículos*, edited by Enrique Rubio, 376–91. 2nd ed. Madrid: Cátedra.

Lecuyer, Marie Claude, and Maryse Villapadierna. 1995. "Génesis y desarrollo del folletín en la prensa española." In *Hacia una literatura del pueblo, del folletín a la novela: El ejemplo de Timoteo Orbe*, edited by Brigitte Magnien, 15–45. Barcelona: Anthropos.

Llorens, Vicente. 1976. *La emigración republicana*. Vol. 1 of *El exilio español de 1939*, edited by J.L. Abellán. 6 vols. Madrid: Taurus.

Lokke, Kari E. 2004. *Tracing Women's Romanticism: Gender, History, and Transcendence*. London: Routledge.

López-Cordón, María Victoria. 1975. *El pensamiento político-internacional del federalismo español (1868–1874)*. Barcelona: Planeta.

López de Ayala, Ángeles. 1888. *Cuentos y cantares para los niños*. Madrid: José Matarredona.

– 1889. *De tal siembra, tal cosecha*. Barcelona: Maucci.

– (1896) 1907. *El abismo: Novela original*. Barcelona: Imprenta de la Vda. de José Miguel.

– 1906–7. *Primitivo: Novela recreativa y moral*. In *El Gladiador: Órgano de la "Sociedad Progresiva Femenina,"* 23 June 1906–30 November 1907.

López Martínez, Mario N., and Juan Ortiz Villalba. 1990. "La propaganda de Belén Sárraga en Andalucía." In *La mujer en Andalucía: Primer Encuentro Interdisciplinario de Estudios de la Mujer*, edited by Pilar Ballarín and Teresa Ortiz 1:459–69. Granada: Universidad de Granada.

de Maeztu, Ramiro. (1925) 1972. "Don Juan o el poder." In *Don Quijote, Don Juan y la Celestina: Ensayos de simpatía*, 71–106. Madrid: Espasa Calpe.

Magnien, Brigitte. 1995. "Introducción." In *Hacia una literatura del pueblo, del folletín a la novela: El ejemplo de Timoteo Orbe*, edited by Magnien, 7–12. Barcelona: Anthropos.

Maier, Linda S. 2004. "Introduction." In *Woman as Witness: Essays on Testimonial Literature by Latin American Women*, edited by Maier and Isabel Dulfano, 1–17. New York: Peter Lang.

Mandrell, James. 1992. *Don Juan and the Point of Honor: Seduction, Patriarchal Society, and Literary Tradition.* University Park: Pennsylvania State University Press.

de Marañón, Gregorio. (1924) 1968. "Notas para la biología de Don Juan." In *Obras completas*, edited by Alfredo Juderías, 4:75–93. 10 vols. Madrid: Espasa Calpe.

Martínez Martín, Jesús A. 2003. "Las transformaciones editoriales y la circulación de libros." In *Orígenes culturales de la sociedad liberal (España siglo XIX)*, edited by Martínez Martín, 37–63. Madrid: Biblioteca Nueva.

Mason, Laura, and Tracey Rizzo, eds. 1999. *The French Revolution: A Document Collection.* Boston: Houghton Mifflin.

de Mateo Avilés, Elías. 1986. *Masonería, protestantismo, librepensamiento y otras heterodoxias en la Málaga del siglo XIX.* Málaga: Diputación Provincial.

McKenna, Susan M. 2009. *Crafting the Female Subject: Narrative Innovation in the Short Fiction of Emilia Pardo Bazán.* Washington: Catholic University of America Press.

Mellor, Anne K. 1993. *Romanticism and Gender.* New York: Routledge.

Méndez Bejarano, Mario D. 1922. "López de Ayala y Molero (Ángeles)." In *Diccionario de escritores, maestros y oradores naturales de Sevilla y su actual provincia* 1:388–9. Seville: Tipografía Gironès.

de Molina, Tirso. (ca. 1630) 1990. *El burlador de Sevilla y convidado de piedra*, edited by Alfredo Rodríguez López-Vázquez. Madrid: Cátedra.

Monroe, John Warne. 2008. *Laboratories of Faith: Mesmerism, Spiritism, and Occultism in Modern France.* Ithaca: Cornell University Press.

Montero Barrado, Jesús María. 2003. *Mujeres Libres: Anarcofeminismo en España; La revista* Mujeres Libres *antes de la Guerra Civil.* Madrid: Fundación de Estudios Libertarios Anselmo Lorenzo.

Moreiras, Alberto. 1996. "The Aura of Testimonio." In *The Real Thing: Testimonial Discourse and Latin America*, edited by Georg M. Gugelberger, 192–224. Durham: Duke University Press.

Moreno Seco, Mónica. 2005. "Republicanas y república en la guerra civil: Encuentros y desencuentros." *Ayer: Revista de Historia Contemporánea* 60:165–95.

Nash, Mary. 1993. "Identidad cultural de género, discurso de la domesticidad y la definición del trabajo de las mujeres en la España del siglo XIX." In Duby and Perrot 1993, 585–99.

– 1994. "Experiencia y aprendizaje: La formación histórica de los feminismos en España." *Historia y Sociedad* (Rio Piedras, San Juan, P.R.) 20:151–72.

– 1999. *Rojas: Las mujeres republicanas en la Guerra Civil*, translated by Irene Cifuentes. Madrid: Taurus.

– 2000. *Gènere, identitat urbana i participació ciutadana.* Barcelona: Institut de Cultura de Barcelona.

Okin, Susan Moller. 1998. "Gender, the Public, and the Private." In Phillips 1998, 116–41.

Ortega, Marie-Linda. 2008. "Amalia Domingo Soler: La escritura *plus ultra*, entre deseo y comunicación." In *La mujer de letras o la letraherida: Discursos y representaciones sobre la mujer escritora en el siglo XIX*, edited by Pura Fernandez and Ortega, 221–41. Madrid: Consejo Superior de Investigaciones Científicas.

Ortega y Gasset, José. (1923) 1988. *El tema de nuestro tiempo*. Introduction by Manuel Granell. Madrid: Espasa Calpe.

Ortiz Albear, Natividad. 2005. *Las mujeres en la masonería*. Málaga: Universidad de Málaga.

Paraíso, Isabel. 1998. "La mirada de un biólogo reformista: Marañón ante Don Juan." In Pérez-Bustamante 1998, 313–37.

Pardo Bazán, Emilia. 1976. *La mujer española y otros artículos feministas*, edited and introduction by Leda Schiavo. Madrid: Nacional.

Pateman, Carole. 1985. *The Problem of Political Obligation: A Critique of Liberal Theory*. Cambridge, UK: Polity.

– 1988. *The Sexual Contract*. Stanford: Stanford University Press.

– 1989. *The Disorder of Women*. Stanford: Stanford University Press.

Pérez-Bustamante, Ana Sofía, ed. 1998. *Don Juan Tenorio en la España del siglo XX: Literatura y cine*. Madrid: Cátedra.

Pérez de la Dehesa, Rafael. 1970. *El grupo "Germinal": Una clave del 98*. Madrid: Taurus.

Perinat, Adolfo, and María Isabel Marrades. 1980. *Mujer, prensa y sociedad en España, 1800–1939*. Madrid: Centro de Investigaciones Sociológicas.

Phillips, Anne. 1991. *Engendering Democracy*. Cambridge, UK: Polity.

– 1993. *Democracy and Difference*. University Park: Pennsylvania State University Press.

– ed. 1998. *Feminism and Politics*. Oxford: Oxford University Press.

Pradas Baena, María Amàlia. 2006. *Teresa Claramunt: La "virgen roja" barcelonesa; Biografía y escritos*. Barcelona: Virus.

Pulido Tirado, Genara. 1998. "El Don Juan de Ramiro de Maeztu: Una teoría nacionalista y nietzscheana del mito." In Pérez-Bustamante 1998, 339–59.

Ramírez Gómez, Carmen. 2000. *Mujeres escritoras en la prensa andaluza del siglo XX (1900–1950)*. Seville: Universidad de Sevilla, Secretariado de Publicaciones.

Ramos, María Dolores. 1986. "Belén Sárraga y la pervivencia de la idea federal en Málaga (1898–1933)." *Jabega* 53:63–70.

– 1995. "Belén Sárraga de Ferrero: Congreso Internacional de librepensadores en Ginebra (1902)." *Arenal* 2 (1): 119–34.

– 1999a. "La construcción de la ciudadanía femenina: Las librepensadoras (1898–1909)." In *1898–1998: Un siglo avanzando hacia la igualdad de las mujeres*, 91–116. Madrid: Dirección General de la Mujer / Consejería de Sanidad y Servicios Sociales / Comunidad de Madrid.

– 1999b. "Mujer, asociacionismo y sociabilidad en la coyuntura de 1898: Las afinidades con el fin de siglo europeo." In *Sociabilidad fin de siglo: Espacios asociativos en torno a 1898*, edited by Isidro Sánchez Sánchez and Rafael Villena Espinosa, 73–99. Cuenca: Ediciones de la Universidad de Castilla–La Mancha.

– 2000. "Belén Sárraga o la República como emblema de la fraternidad universal." In *El siglo XX: Balance y perspectivas; V Congreso de la Asociación de Historia Contemporánea*, 219–27. Valencia: Fundación Cañada Blanch.

– 2002a. "Federalismo, laicismo, obrerismo, feminismo: Cuatro claves para interpretar la biografía de Belén Sárraga." In Ramos and Vera 2002, 125–64.

– 2002b. "La cultura societaria del feminismo librepensador (1895–1918)." In *Les Espagnoles dans l'histoire: Une sociabilité démocratique (XIXe–XXe siècles)*, edited by Danièle Bussy Genevois, 103–24. Saint-Denis: Presses Universitaires de Vincennes.

– 2005a. "Heterodoxias religiosas, familias espiritistas y apóstolas laicas a finales del s. XIX: Amalia Domingo Soler y Belén Sárraga Hernández." *Historia y Sociedad* (Rio Piedras, San Juan, P.R.) 53:65–83.

– 2005b. "Pautas socializadoras de la nueva ciudadanía: Una aproximación histórica desde el género." In *Mujeres: Ciudadanas; La identidad de género en la construcción de la nueva ciudadanía*, 29–57. Córdoba: Instituto de Estudios Transnacionales.

– 2006. "Belén de Sãrraga: Una 'obrera' del laicismo, el feminismo y el panamericanismo en el mundo ibérico." In *Baetica: Estudios de Arte, Geografía e Historia* 28:689–708.

– 2010. "Las primeras modernas: Secularización, activismo político y feminismo en la prensa republicana: *Los Gladiadores*(1906–1919)." In *Historia Social* 67:93–112.

Ramos, María Dolores, and María Teresa Vera, eds. 2002. *Discursos, realidades, utopías: La construcción del sujeto femenino en los siglos XIX y XX.* Barcelona: Anthropos.

de los Ríos, Blanca. *Las hijas de Don Juan.* (1907) 1989. In *Novelas breves de escritoras españolas (1900-1936)*, edited by Ángela Ena Bordonada, 67–125. Madrid: Castalia.

Rivera, Carlos. 1913. "Belén de Sárraga: Noticas de su vida." In Sárraga 1913, 165–73.

Robles Egea, Antonio. 1994. "Republicanismo y horizonte europeo." In Townson 1994, 293–312.

Romero Tobar, Leonardo. 1976. *La novela popular española del siglo XIX.* Barcelona: Ariel.

Ross, Marlon B. 1988. "Troping Masculine Power in the Crisis of Poetic Identity." In *Romanticism and Feminism*, edited by Anne Mellor, 26–51. Bloomington: Indiana University Press.

Rousseau, Jean-Jacques. (1762) 1997. *The Social Contract and Other Political Writings.* Edited and introduction by Victor Gourevitch. Cambridge, UK: Cambridge University Press.

Rubio, Javier. 1977. *La emigración de la guerra civil de 1936–1939: Historia del éxodo que se produce con el fin de la II República española*, vol. 3. 3 vols. Madrid: San Martín.

Rumford, Chris. 2007. "Introduction: Cosmopolitanism and Europe." In *Cosmopolitanism and Europe*, edited by Rumford, 1–15. Liverpool, UK: Liverpool University Press.

Salaün, Serge, and Carlos Serrano, eds. 1991. *1900 en España*. Madrid: Espasa-Calpe.
Salomón Chéliz, María Pilar. 2005. "Las mujeres en la cultura política republicana: Religión y anticlericalismo." *Historia y Sociedad* (Rio Piedras, San Juan, P.R.) 53:103–18.
Sànchez i Ferré, Pere. 1990. *La Maçoneria a Catalunya (1868–1936)*, prologue by José A. Ferrer Benimeli. Barcelona: Edicions 62.
– 1998. "Els orígens del feminisme a Catalunya: 1870-1926 (2)." *L'Avenç* 223 (March): 6-11.
Sánchez Sánchez, Isidro. 2001. "Propaganda de ideas en la España del siglo XIX." In *Movimientos sociales y estado en la España contemporánea*, edited by Manuel Ortiz Heras, David Ruíz González, and Isidro Sánchez Sánchez, 153–202. Cuenca: Universidad de Castilla–La Mancha.
Sanfeliu, Luz. 2005. *Republicanas: Identidades de género en el blasquismo (1895–1910)*. Valencia: Universitat de València.
Sárraga, Belén. 1901. *Minucias (Poesías)*. Málaga: Imprenta Popular.
– 1913. *Conferencias Sociológicas y de Crítica Religiosas, dadas en Santiago de Chile en Enero y Febrero de 1913 seguidas de sus Críticas, por Federico R. Tonda*, edited by *La Razón*. Santiago de Chile: Imprenta "Victoria."
– 1914. *El Clericalismo en América: A través de un continente*. Lisbon: Lux. Accessed http://archive.org/details/MN5009ucmf_4, 22 July 2013.
Scanlon, Geraldine M. 1986. *La polémica feminista en la España contemporánea (1868–1974)*, translated by Rafael Mazarrasa. Madrid: Akal.
Scrivener, Michael. 2007. *The Cosmopolitan Ideal in the Age of Revolution and Reaction, 1776–1832*. London: Pickering & Chatto.
Segura, Isabel, and Marta Selva. 1984. *Revistes de Dones, 1846–1935*. Barcelona: Edhasa.
Segura Soriano, Isabel. 2006. "Memory: A Form of Architecture." In *Urbanism & Gender*, 27–30.
Seoane, María Cruz. 1996a. *El siglo XIX*. Vol. 2 of *Historia del periodismo en España*. 3 vols. 1st ed. 1983. Madrid: Alianza.
– 1996b. *El siglo XX: 1898–1936*. Vol. 3 of *Historia del periodismo en España*. 3 vols. 1st ed. 1983. Madrid: Alianza.
Sharp, Lynn L. 2006. *Secular Spirituality: Reincarnation and Spiritism in Nineteenth-Century France*. Lanham, MD: Lexington.
Shaw, Donald. 1989. *La generación del 98*, translated by Carmen Hierro. Madrid: Cátedra.
Showalter, Elaine. 1990. *Sexual Anarchy: Gender and Culture at the Fin de Siècle*. New York: Penguin.
Simón Palmer, María del Carmen. 1991. *Escritoras españolas del siglo XIX: Manual bio-bibliográfico*. Madrid: Castalia.
– 1993. "Amalia Domingo Soler, escritora espiritista (1835–1909)." In *Homenaje al Profesor José Fradejas Lebrero*, vol. 2, edited by José Romera Castillo, Ana Freire López, and Antonio Lorente Medina, 731–44. Madrid: Universidad Nacional de Educación a Distancia.

Sklodowska, Elzbieta. 2001. "The Poetics of Remembering, the Politics of Forgetting: Rereading *I, Rigoberta Menchú*." In *Arias* 2001, 251–69.

Spain, Daphne. 2006. "The Importance of Urban Gendered Spaces for the Public Realm." In *Urbanism & Gender*, 31–9.

Stallybrass, Peter. 1986. "Patriarchal Territories: The Body Enclosed." In *Rewriting the Renaissance*, edited by Margaret Ferguson, Maureen Quilligan, and Nancy J. Vickers, 123–42. Chicago: University of Chicago Press.

Stoll, David. 1999. *Rigoberta Menchú and the Story of All Poor Guatemalans*. Boulder, CO: Westview.

Suárez Cortina, Manuel. 1994. "La quiebra del republicanismo histórico, 1898–1931." In Townson 1994, 139–63.

Tavera, Susana, ed. 2000. *Mujeres en la historia de España: Enciclopedia biográfica*. Barcelona: Planeta.

Townson, Nigel, ed. 1994. *El republicanismo en España (1830–1977)*. Madrid: Alianza.

Tsuchiya, Akiko. 2011. *Marginal Subjects: Gender and Deviance in Fin-de-siècle Spain*. Toronto: University of Toronto Press.

Turner, Victor. 1991. "Dramatic Ritual / Ritual Drama: Performative and Reflexive Anthropology." In *Interculturalism and Performance: Writings from PAJ*, edited by Bonnie Marranca and Gautam Dasgupta, 99–112. New York: PAJ.

Ugarte, Michael. 1994. "The Generational Fallacy and Spanish Women Writing in Madrid at the Turn of the Century." *Siglo XX / 20th Century* 12:261–76.

Urbanism & Gender: A Necessary Vision for All. 2006. Forewords by Celestino Corbacho, Josep Bargalló, and Soledad Murillo. Barcelona: Diputació de Barcelona.

Valis, Noël. 1991. *Carolina Coronado: Poesías*. Edited, introduction, and notes by Valis. Madrid: Castalia / Instituto de la Mujer.

Villanueva, Laura Vicente. 2006. *Teresa Claramunt (1862–1931): Pionera del feminismo obrerista anarquista*. Madrid: Fundación de Estudios Libertarios Anselmo Lorenzo.

Vitale, Luis, and Julia Antivilo Peña. 2000. *Belén de Sárraga: Precursora del feminismo hispanoamericano*, prologue by Virginia Vidal. Santiago: Cesoc.

White, Sarah L. 1999. "Liberty, Honor, Order: Gender and Political Discourse in Nineteenth-Century Spain." In *Constructing Spanish Womanhood: Female Identity in Modern Spain*, edited by Victoria Lorée Enders and Pamela Beth Radcliff, 233–57. Albany: State University of New York Press.

Zavala, Iris M. 1971. *Ideología y política en la novela española del siglo XIX*. Salamanca: Anaya.

Zorrilla, José. 2002. *Don Juan Tenorio*, edited by Juan Francisco Peña, prologue by Francisco Nieva. Madrid: Espasa Calpe.

Index

TORONTO IBERIC

1 Anthony J. Cascardi, *Cervantes, Literature, and the Discourse of Politics*
2 Jessica A. Boon, *The Mystical Science of the Soul: Medieval Cognition in Bernardino de Laredo's Recollection Method*
3 Susan Byrne, *Law and History in Cervantes' Don Quixote*
4 Mary E. Barnard and Frederick A. de Armas (eds), *Objects of Culture in the Literature of Imperial Spain*
5 Nil Santiáñez, *Topographies of Fascism: Habitus, Space, and Writing in Twentieth-Century Spain*
6 Nelson Orringer, *Lorca in Tune with Falla: Literary and Musical Interludes*
7 Ana M. Gómez-Bravo, *Textual Agency: Writing Culture and Social Networks in Fifteenth-Century Spain*
8 Javier Irigoyen-García, *The Spanish Arcadia: Sheep Herding, Pastoral Discourse, and Ethnicity in Early Modern Spain*
9 Stephanie Sieburth, *Survival Songs: Conchita Piquer's* Coplas *and Franco's Regime of Terror*
10 Christine Arkinstall, *Spanish Female Writers and the Freethinking Press, 1879–1926*

www.ingramcontent.com/pod-product-compliance
Lightning Source LLC
LaVergne TN
LVHW090156080826
844660LV00013B/834/J

9781442647657